When Women Ask the Questions

When Women Ask the Questions
Creating Women's Studies in America

Marilyn Jacoby Boxer

Foreword by Catharine R. Stimpson

The Johns Hopkins University Press   Baltimore and London

© 1998 The Johns Hopkins University Press
All rights reserved. Published 1998
Printed in the United States of America on acid-free paper
9 8 7 6 5 4 3 2 1

The Johns Hopkins University Press
2715 North Charles Street
Baltimore, Maryland 21218-4319
The Johns Hopkins Press Ltd., London
www.press.jhu.edu

Library of Congress Cataloging-in-Publication Data
will be found at the end of this book.
A catalog record for this book is available from the British Library.

ISBN 0-8018-5834-8

For my children

Claire Jacoby, Lawrence Robert, and Brian David Boxer

and

For my granddaughter

Jenny Amelia Boxer

We are not 'the woman question' asked by somebody else; we are the women who ask the questions.

—Adrienne Rich, *Blood, Bread, and Poetry* (1986)

Tradition in itself is a fine thing if it satisfies the soul, but the perturbed soul prefers research.

—Judah Halevi (1140)

Contents

In 1872, Frances E. W. Harper, an African American writer, published "Learning to Read," a poem about Aunt Chloe, an elderly ex-slave in the American South whom the Civil War has freed. Defying hostile sneers and friendly skepticism, Aunt Chloe decides that she will become literate in order to read "the hymns and Testament." She does so. Her rewards are literary competence and the compelling sense of dignity and freedom that accompanies it. The last words of the poem are:

> *Then I got a little cabin*
> *A place to call my own—*
> *And I felt as independent*
> *As a queen upon her throne.*

Aunt Chloe symbolizes the struggle for literacy and education of African American men and women, and of women of all races—indeed, of anyone who must surmount obstacles in order to satisfy the thirst to read and write. The history of this struggle is a tribute to its participants and to the appeal and power of language and learning.

A great intellectual and educational movement, women's studies is a vital part of this history. The promise and premise of women's studies are that all women are capable of becoming richly, fully educated. If they choose, they can become educators. As women become public knowers, they change what is known about them. Our pictures of reality possess new clarity, greater depth, more visions and voices. So do our imaginings. Moreover, the impact of the transformation in the relations between women and knowledge is not limited to women—immense though this will prove to be. Life for all of us, as well as the life of the mind, will be renewed, reclaimed, refreshed.

When Women Ask the Questions, as the first comprehensive account of women's studies in the United States, is tremendously valuable. This new scholarly world has vital antecedents in the work of individuals in such areas as anthropology, history, literature, and sociology. Various groups have also labored at different times to explore and remember women's lives.

However, as a world that is still in process, as a self-conscious and dynamic force, women's studies has its origins in the 1960s and that decade's confluence of demographic, educational, social, and political movements, including feminism.

Marilyn Jacoby Boxer maps these origins as part of her overall plan of showing the intellectual, pedagogical, and institutional development of women's studies. Moving on parallel tracks, women's studies has worked both to reform existing institutions and to form its own. Although Boxer states accurately that women's studies is now burgeoning internationally, her focus is on the United States, where the movement's first roots spread most rapidly and widely. Her book perceptively analyzes the connections among ideas, classroom practices, and institutions. Doing so, it demonstrates the significance of such "academic" issues as whether women's studies is a department, an interdisciplinary program, or a discipline.

Quantitatively, the growth of women's studies has been extraordinary. If there were a handful of courses in 1970, there were over six hundred programs a quarter of a century later. Another example: in 1978, *Dissertation Abstracts International* began to use "Women's Studies" as an indexing category. By 1995, Boxer found, the cumulative total of doctoral degrees under that rubric was 10,786. Qualitatively, the growth has been even more extraordinary. For women's studies has not only exposed errors in our thinking about women and gender that now seem appallingly obvious. It has also generated a vast amount of information, major ideas, and striking theories. In the past, I have organized this scholarship under the rubric of differences—that is, it has dealt with the invidious, destructive differences between men and women; the differences that women have made; and the differences among women.

Inevitably, people within women's studies have argued with each other. One of Boxer's strengths is that she shows how continually they have done so. Today, one dispute, at once epistemological and political, is about the value of postmodern theory. Another is about whether the proper subject of women's studies is women—in all their diversity—or gender. Still another, far more tentative in tone, is how to think through the connections among women now that the differences among them have been explored—at least partially. Women's studies has also stimulated opposition. A second of Boxer's strengths is her willingness to discuss these external critiques and call for greater dialogue between women's studies and its opponents.

Given such fertility, given such controversies, Boxer is right to repudiate a "simple evolutionary or linear model of development" in favor of presenting "a mosaic of individuals and programs." Her approach is especially
convincing because of her pioneering relation to women's studies. Her story
is not atypical of the field's first generation. In the 1950s, she was a young,
divorced mother. While keeping body, soul, and children together—on her
own for years—she managed to get her education, including, much later, a
Ph.D. in European history. In 1974, she took a job at San Diego State University as a faculty member and chair of the women's studies program,
which, founded in 1969–70, was the first in the United States. She now
writes as a seasoned participant-observer who has also occupied high-level
administrative positions in California institutions of higher education. As
a participant, she wants to speak "with and to" rather than "for" others in
women's studies. As an observer, she respects the demands of scholarship.
She reads widely, documents her sources, and acknowledges difficulties and
complexities. Carefully measuring the bonds between the women's movement and women's studies, she writes, "Women's studies need not indoctrinate. It is sufficient that it empower students with the passion to learn
and to utilize their learning in living."

Boxer's own history and her position as a professional historian help
to prevent a delusory, dreamy romanticizing of any world, including that of
women's studies. Yet to partake of women's studies is to dwell in an in-
cubator of optimism—despite the field's obduracies, penuries, blindnesses,
fallacies, and disputes. As I do, Boxer belongs to the party of hope. As I do,
she believes deeply in the ability of women's studies to improve teaching,
learning, and human society. To her, it is nothing less than a feminist enlightenment, "the realization of a new capacity for vision that illuminates
the dark and enlarges the landscape."

Crucially, women's studies does even more. It also reimagines and
reinvigorates education as a moral inquiry. It asks education to add "care,
concern, and connection" to the curriculum (a phrase Boxer adapts from the
philosopher of education Jane Roland Martin) without subtracting reason
and inquiry. Women's studies practitioners should then serve as "civic humanists" who will translate academic expertise into public knowledge. If
women's studies were to exercise the influence Boxer argues that it deserves,
"higher education would connect what scholars and students study with
the lives they lead, and would offer inspiration to all who seek more than

instrumental knowledge. Liberal education might truly liberate people from the narrow constraints of their lives." In brief, higher education would succor a bountiful freedom and dignity.

Like Boxer, I have been a part of women's studies since "the old days." I taught my first women's studies class, on images of women in literature, in 1969, and vividly remember the ferocious quarrels about the proper women's studies interpretation of Virginia Woolf's To the Lighthouse—if indeed one existed. Throughout her book, Boxer generously acknowledges my activities. I am grateful to her for this and for her scrupulous, wide-ranging, and indefatigable work. In the last words of When Women Ask the Questions, Boxer confesses that "it takes a lot of energy to practice women's studies," but, she continues, "as it satisfies the longing for meaning of questing minds and helps to integrate divided lives, it gives back in full measure. I hope that this study returns to readers some of what women's studies has given to me." I share these feelings and trust that everyone who genuinely cares about the nature and place of higher education will use this book as a guide to wiser, stronger deliberations and decisions.

Catharine R. Stimpson
New York University

Perspective

My purpose in writing this book is to share with readers my perspective on women's studies as a field that questions conventional knowledge, dissolves boundaries, and facilitates the quest to integrate one's intellectual, professional, and personal experiences. Women's studies as a part of American higher education began three decades ago. Very little has been published about women's studies as an academic field, although several studies are now under way. Its institutional history remains to be written after many partial, local studies, often inspired by twentieth, twenty-fifth, and later anniversaries, become available. This work will review the field's origins and development, survey important issues in its theory and practice, and set it in the context of higher education in the United States.

As readers will note, this book offers a reflection on experience of many aspects of women's studies, as interpreted then and now by one participant in its development. I came into women's studies inadvertently, as I imagine is true of many of its practitioners; and for more than a quarter of a century I have been both participant and observer. I spent a decade as a full-time wife and mother, assumed administrative roles soon after my re-entry into academia, and lived most of the time in California. Trained as a historian of modern Europe, I taught women's history at five institutions of higher education.

I first discovered women's studies through my academic and professional interests and aspirations. In the spring of 1971, as a single mother of three putting myself through a Ph.D. program, I needed a way to increase my income beyond that provided by my university teaching assistantship and the one evening class in American history that I was teaching at a local community college. Recalling how the department chairman there had one day thrust a copy of William O'Neill's newly published history of the American woman suffrage movement into my hands and suggested that I, as a woman, should be doing that kind of work, it occurred to me to propose to him that I teach a second course, one that would focus on the history of women. About the same time that he said yes, I chanced to hear from my older son, then a beginning student at San Diego State University (SDSU), about the newly formed women's studies program there, and I made my way to that campus to visit him and to seek information that might help in planning my new course. Having just begun doctoral studies with grave doubts that my financial resources would see me and my family through to a degree, I could not have imagined the series of events that brought me back to SDSU in 1974 to serve as a faculty member and chair of the women's studies program for a transformative six-year period, under circumstances that impelled me to do my first research on the history of women's studies. I also could not have foreseen that those experiences would provide the base from which I would some day write this book. But I had taken the first steps toward a career that would interweave the scholarly inquiry to which I had aspired since I first heard the word *scholar*, and the feminist advocacy that reflected my life's experience—for I had already lived many of the roles of girls and women in the mid-twentieth-century United States.

The second, more typically "personal" source of this work is my history as a passionate learner who was sidetracked from her goal by a head full of romance and the absence of timely useful advice. By age twenty-one I was a divorced mother of two babies and was completely on my own. (If welfare existed in those days, I did not know of it.) While I would not universalize my experience as a single, undereducated mother of the early 1950s, let alone transfer it to the 1990s, my children and I suffered enough from isolation, dependency, and deprivation to provide me with an unextinguishable belief in the necessity of changing the social and gender arrangements of our society. Thanks to some good people who at critical times offered food, clothing, child care, money, and moral support, we survived. Years later, with my children—now numbering three—present at my graduation, I attained a bachelor's degree, to be followed, after another decade of both part-time and full-time study and teaching at various levels, by a doctorate. I later spent twelve years as a dean and academic vice-president at two large urban comprehensive universities in California.

Probably not many pregnant teenagers of the 1950s had by the 1990s become university vice-presidents. Everyone's perspective, of course, is unique. Mine draws on the opportunities I have had to view the academy from many angles: as a dropout from an elite college and as a member of the president's cabinet in a state university; as a part-time lecturer and as an academic budget chief; as a working mother and as a department chair. Having also taught at every level save elementary school, and having attended countless meetings as a parent and with parents, I have sat among and worked with many of education's constituencies. I was invited to write this book as a result of another study I did, a review essay tracing the early history of women's studies which was published, originally, in *Signs* in 1982. It, in turn, had been solicited after the editor chanced to read a brief history of the San Diego State program that I, as chair, had prepared for the department's first external academic review. Treating many difficult and complex issues, I tried there and have tried again here to offer a comprehensive and balanced account. I will be critical, acknowledge problems, and own up to the kernels of truth that often lie within negative charges. I will even admit to having censored myself at times from speaking thoughts that counter prevailing orthodoxy.

But as I read prior to writing, I became ever more convinced of the value and validity of women's studies. I believe that it constitutes one of the great intellectual movements of our century, one in which I am privileged to have taken part. My intention is to write *for* as well as *about* women's studies. Knowing well the dangers of dealing with controversial subjects, I expect that I will be addressing a wide range of readers—not only the administrators and leaders in higher education who are the target audience of the Johns Hopkins University Press's higher-education list, but also many practitioners, scholars, and students of women's studies, all of whom are likely to find this account lacking in some ways. I hope to offer something useful to all. I have tried to stretch my mind around a complex and ever-expanding subject. In 1981, when I wrote the essay on the origins and development of women's studies in the United States, it seemed possible to obtain access to virtually everything that had been published about academic feminism. The result of my reading and reflection was a thirty-five-page essay that had, in its initial draft, almost two hundred footnotes. Today I cannot aspire to such comprehensiveness. Reflecting the explosive growth of the field, the volume of literature has, I suspect, expanded beyond one individual's capacity to encompass. It is hardly possible even to keep up with the daily exchange on the Internet. Unlike other academic studies I have done, this one did not sit still under inspection. While writing, material coming to hand has constantly provoked me to review, rethink, and sometimes to rewrite earlier portions.

This study will perforce be limited to an idiosyncratic perspective. In the process of writing it, I delved deeply enough into philosophy, theory, literary criticism, and other fields to recognize how difficult it is to grasp the full content and context of many of the issues under discussion. The range of reading required, from Jean Bethke Elshtain on women and war through Judith Butler on "gender trouble," is mind-boggling. This does not, of course, prevent many people with limited knowledge from making pronouncements about women's studies. The subject of each chapter could sustain a volume, or many, of its own (and several have). Every reader will know of exceptions and point to examples of different practices. I invite correction of detail and dialogue on meaning. I wish also to acknowledge the inadequacy of my usage of certain terms. Writing of *women's studies*, I use the term that largely took over the field at its inception and that exists in the vast majority of places today. I speak of *feminism*—academic or otherwise—in the singular, despite the voluminous literature witnessing its many varieties, because the plural form is awkward; the multiplicity of feminisms, however, is discussed in several places and is to be understood everywhere. Similarly, as will be apparent, *woman* and *women* are often used conventionally; and *First Wave* and *Second Wave*, which cannot withstand comparative or close historical analysis as metaphors for feminist history, are employed only because of common usage.

While drawing on the work of countless persons who have been my colleagues or have provided intellectual inspiration and leadership through their publications, the book reflects most of all the experience of my twenty-seven years as an academic feminist, scholar, teacher, and administrator in institutions of higher education in California. The strong institutional support that both women's studies and I have had in the California State University no doubt affects my optimistic view. I hope that my work encourages others to provide similar support. I hope as well that it adds to the accumulated knowledge about women's studies as an academic field and inspires readers to learn more about women's lives and women's perspectives, to bring currency to courses and curricula where it is still lacking, and to advance the spread of serious research and teaching about women in higher education and beyond.

But it is only a beginning. Perhaps, I would like to think, this is just as well. If the time has come to assess "where have we been, where are we going?" in women's studies—the title of a twenty-fifth-anniversary conference at San Diego State in 1995—the enterprise must be shared. I know of several programs now engaged in preparing the individual histories that, along with memoirs, will eventually provide source material for more complete studies. As women of my generation prepare to pass the mantle of leadership to our academic daughters, we need to talk more than we have done about our successes and our failures and to examine our impact on the world of higher education. We must answer the questions of our critics, but it is more important that we also ask of ourselves the questions that we think are most likely to help open the way to the future to which we aspire. That future will surely be a world where no young girl will accept allegations of the inferiority of the female mind because of its "field dependence" (a "fact" that I was taught in an undergraduate class) or will need, as I did, to discover Simone de Beauvoir's *Second Sex* to learn that a woman can produce major works of history and philosophy. It is in this spirit, and in recognition of the importance of women's studies to our children and grandchildren, and of the value of its contributions to higher education, that I offer this work.

After many years in women's studies, it is impossible for me to acknowledge individually all the scholars and students, friends and colleagues, whose ideas and work have gone into the formation of my own. I want here to thank all for what I have absorbed from them through reading and conversation—and to ask pardon if, despite every effort to cite the contributions of others, I fail to give proper credit. The creation of women's studies has truly been a collective effort made possible through the generosity of the many who have shared their work in order to provide opportunities for others.

Let me mention two specific instances that must stand for many of the gifts I have received. In 1971, when I set out to write a rationale to offer to the curriculum committee whose approval I sought for the course I proposed to teach in women's history, I was able to draw on the work made available in *Female Studies II* by its editor, Florence Howe, and its publisher, KNOW, Inc. The course was approved. Looking back at that publication many years later, I found that it was Maurine Greenwald whose work, borrowed for my own, had been so effective. I thank her, and Florence Howe, now. Three years later, when I was seeking my first university teaching job, I received another boost in the form of a postcard notice from the American Historical Association about an opening in women's history of which I had been ignorant; the notice was sent to me because they had included my name, as an advanced graduate student, in their first directory of women historians. I got the job; and I thank whoever compiled the list, doubtless at the behest of the women's caucus, and mailed me the notice. I have tried, over the years, to pass along these gifts, and I hope that, in the process, they have multiplied.

I also want to thank my former colleagues in women's studies at San Diego State University, who taught me about their fields, the value of interdisciplinary perspectives, and the importance of collegiality; and the many students who for thirty years have encouraged me by their enthusiastic responses.

In acknowledging those who contributed directly to this book, I must begin with George Keller, a leader in higher education whom I have never met but who had the perspicacity to see the need for a book like this and suggested that I write it. I am deeply grateful to all those who gave so generously of their time to read parts or all of the manuscript. Nupur Chaudhuri, Kathy Jones, Betty Schmitz, and Anita Silvers each read a portion and offered helpful comments. Three people who read the entire manuscript deserve special recognition. Barely having renewed an old acquaintance, Gloria Bowles generously offered to read along as I completed each chapter. Karen Offen, my colleague in women's history and a friend since a chance meeting at the Bibliothèque Marguerite Durand in Paris in 1972, added to a long list of gifts her counsel on this work. Joanne Ferraro, sister historian, hiking companion, and friend, offered a thoughtful appraisal of the manuscript as a work in women's history, as well as encouragement throughout my struggle to keep my scholarship alive despite the demands of academic administration. All three provided a cheering section, along with thoughtful conversation and constructive suggestions that have greatly enhanced the results. Jean Fox O'Barr likewise reviewed the entire manuscript and provided encouragement as well as excellent suggestions. The work required as well countless instances of help in procuring materials, maneuvering information through machines, and producing the manuscript. Staff at the National Women's Studies Association office always responded to requests promptly and cheerfully. Inez Bomar, Mary Ann Irwin, and Mary McFadden stand out among the many San Francisco State University staff who assisted; the late Joyce Stansfield, longtime secretary to vice-presidents at San Francisco State University, encouraged me at the outset by her example of grace under pressure. Jacqueline Wehmueller, executive editor at the Johns Hopkins University Press, provided enthusiastic support at every step in the process from idea to reality. My copyeditor at the press, Miriam Kleiger, added many improvements, and Janet Hamann, of San Diego State University, helped me again by preparing the index.

Finally, I want to mention the academic feminist whose national leadership and personal interest provided the inspiration, knowledge, and opportunity that ultimately led to this book: Catharine Stimpson. In 1979, when I was serving as chair of women's studies at SDSU, we were scheduled for the program's first external academic review. Wanting to impress the administration, we decided to invite the most outstanding exemplars of academic feminism we knew, or knew of. As a result, the visiting team consisted of Judith Stiehm, Catharine Stimpson, and Myra Strober, all of whom donated three days to our program. Those who are familiar with the field will appreciate our good fortune.

That event, in addition to assuring the continued prosperity of women's studies at SDSU, resulted in my writing a review essay on women's studies for *Signs,* which ultimately provided the stimulus for this book. Once again, despite the many demands on her time, Catharine Stimpson, in preparing a foreword for the book, has exemplified the unflagging support that has enabled women's studies to flourish.

I am grateful for friends who have witnessed with compassion my struggle to be mother, scholar, administrator, and breadwinner; faculty members who did not reduce me to my role in the bureaucracy but became friends; and family who have loved and supported me steadfastly. I hope that the result is worthy of the contributions of so many.

When Women Ask the Questions

At the January 1994 meeting of the American Historical Association in San Francisco, a young professor who had just presented an illustrated lecture on reformers "acting out spectacles of poverty" in late-nineteenth-century America was asked how he had moved from traditional approaches to the social history of the welfare state to the use of literary tropes and representations. After a moment's hesitation, he answered, "I think it all started with women's studies."[1]

What is "women's studies" and how did it come to influence this young scholar? What are the origins of this academic enterprise that started with one program in 1970 and now numbers more than six hundred—plus thousands of practitioners and tens of thousands of courses? What are its goals? Who are its students and its teachers? What constitutes its courses, curricula, and degree programs? How does it define its field, and what basic assumptions and interpretations, methods of research and teaching, are characteristic of women's studies? How much truth is there in the claims of its advocates—and in the charges of its critics? Who speaks for women's studies? Should we talk about it in the singular, as though it were a discipline like history or sociology? How should academics—faculty and, especially, administrators—respond to it? What has been its impact on higher education in the United States? How important is women's studies to the future course of American higher education?

This book aims to answer these and many other questions about women's studies as it has developed and currently exists across the academic landscape in the United States. It surveys the history and the philosophical and political goals of women's studies practitioners; examines the field's present status in various types of institutions of higher education around the country, assessing its strengths and weaknesses; and traces the impact of almost three decades of feminist scholarship, teaching, and academic advocacy since the founding of the first integrated program under the women's studies rubric at San Diego State University in 1969–70.

Even more important, perhaps, this book looks at women's studies as a part of American higher education and of women's efforts to gain equality in that domain. Studies about women go back a long way, and a prototype for women's studies even existed in Paris at the turn of this century.

This volume suggests that women's studies as we know it, though not the first new, interdisciplinary field of studies—far from it—reflects the emergence of a special kind of educational program within the academy. Such programs draw their energy from social and political action and bring to the American academy new intellectual perspectives, along with people whose backgrounds and life experiences are unlike those of the generations of traditional scholars and academicians who led higher education in the United States in earlier decades and centuries. They are also part of larger movements that result in the constitution of new fields of knowledge and new approaches to pedagogy and research. This book argues that, in addition to providing new faces, alternative perspectives, and innovative approaches to scholarship as well as teaching, women's studies has (re)introduced to higher education a type of moral inquiry long absent from most secular institutions. It attempts to show women's studies as a powerful agent for transformation in colleges and universities of all types in all parts of the country, precisely because it incorporates important recent trends and current concerns about teaching, research, education, and contemporary life.

Women's studies has changed many institutions and many individuals' lives. Although it was common in the 1970s for college and university administrators to assume that women's studies was an academic fad, sure to disappear along with the current wave of feminism, it remains today on a growth path. In the early years, strong student interest, which helped to counter a concurrent and massive decline in enrollments in other social science and humanities fields, probably convinced more administrators to provide resources for the new courses than did scholarly presentations or earnest pleas by the graduate students or younger faculty who developed and taught many of the first women's studies courses. By the second decade—the 1980s—women's studies had become a field of choice for women (and some men) writing dissertations and obtaining faculty positions in many, if not most, humanities and social science fields. Using "the master's tools,"[2] these scholars—including many who were new to academia and marginal, and some who were tenured veterans—created a new field of scholarship and teaching. Their newly liberated passion for learning produced the academic world of women's studies.

The rapid, indeed explosive, growth of women's studies also reflects demographic shifts that accompanied the huge increase in the numbers and size of academic institutions which began in the 1960s. By the 1980s, women outnumbered men in student bodies and occupied a significantly larger fraction of teaching posts in many colleges and universities, especially in the liberal arts fields. Whatever their academic specializations or professional goals, many of these women wanted to learn new ways of thinking about themselves, and they filled classrooms and libraries seeking new knowledge and fresh perspectives on the old. They created the "first concerted effort by women to question and change definitions of sex and gender."[3] The concurrent "ratcheting up" of research expectations, which helped to fuel the multiplication of scholarly journals and professional associations in this period, also provided opportunities for growth in the new field of women's studies, and university presses and trade publishers stood ready to aid in the distribution of the new scholarship. By the 1990s, a review of the American academy could easily show with minimal exaggeration that women's studies was everywhere. And as it developed, women's studies set in process another multiplier effect: by liberating women from intellectual constraints that had previously repressed knowledge about "the sex," it stimulated new awareness of the potentialities opened to women by opportunities for higher education in concert with changing demographic patterns of longevity, fertility, labor force participation, marriage, divorce, and parenthood.

The term *women's studies* is used to cover a wide range of activities, from scholarship and teaching that are traditional in all but their focus on women to innovative attempts to revise methods of inquiry, develop new categories of analysis, reconceptualize pedagogies, and restructure institutional relationships. Women's studies' origin in the political and intellectual ferment of the mid to late 1960s and early 1970s, and the continuing efforts of many of its leaders to maintain an activist stance as a vital part of an academic movement, have elicited much well-publicized criticism. Several best-sellers of the early 1990s targeted women's studies as a major antagonist in the "culture wars." Sometimes attacks on women's studies served as a proxy for attacks on feminism in society. Accusations by critics from within the academy, such as Camille Paglia, Daphne Patai and Noretta Koertge, and Christina Hoff Sommers, have received more media attention than has been given to informed analysis; the popular press headlined their work but not the rebuttals. Much scholarly work has been written within the field of women's studies, as contributions to the disciplines, and numerous volumes are available on selected topics. But very little has appeared about women's studies as a broad field of academic endeavor that now boasts more than twenty-five years of institutionalization in American higher education. This book undertakes that task.

In 1970, in her introduction to the first published compilation of syllabi for women's studies courses, which she then expected to be called "female studies," Sheila Tobias, then assistant to the vice-president at Cornell University, laid out a series of issues for discussion that, interestingly, could hardly be improved upon as an outline of the important and controversial matters to be examined in this book.[4] Should "female studies" be institutionalized as a department or interdisciplinary program; should its focus be on teaching, on what Tobias called "pure" research, or, alternatively, on "intervention" research; should it be offered as a minor for the Ph.D. (to make research on women readily available to doctoral students in traditional fields); how should academic feminists relate to women's liberation groups in the community; what, if any, should be its role in advancing the status of women faculty; "how innovative in educational techniques" could women's studies "afford to be"; should it focus on "sex-differentiation"? These questions remain at the heart of the matter today. They continue to stimulate controversy across a multifaceted field. Every answer bears the mark of the speaker, and each speaker is subject to interrogation. "Who can speak for women's studies?" has become itself one of the critical questions.

Feminist theorists now debate such matters as whether one speaks "*as . . . for . . .* [or] *in the place of*" a woman (or women);[5] who or "what speaks now that the subject is dead";[6] and from what "location" the speaker speaks.[7] Whatever their positions regarding feminist theory, however, most scholars in women's studies agree that knowledge is always based in theoretical assumptions and want to get on with telling their story. In this spirit, this book sets out to tell a part of a larger, longer, and far from complete— in fact, barely started—story of a major intellectual movement. Speaking sometimes in the first person and sometimes in the third person, I attempt below to show many aspects of the collective enterprise of women's studies—speaking, I hope, "with and to" rather than "for" any others.[8] While in the face of immense diversity and great complexity it is impossible not to oversimplify and to err, a greater fault, given the prevalence of criticism by anecdote and sound-bite, may be to be silent.

Fortunately, thanks to the work of thousands and to the prolific literature available, it is now possible to begin to assess the implications of the many questions about women's studies as a field, and about the impact, real or potential, of various possible approaches to the answers. The first chapter provides an overview of the main themes of the study. After examining the origins of women's studies in feminist advocacy, it traces academic feminism's transformation, through scholarly inquiry, from a movement with relatively limited curricular goals but far-reaching aspirations for reconstructing academic institutions, to a new quasi-discipline challenging existing interpretations, methodologies, and epistemologies. It seeks to demonstrate how the privileging of women's experience has provided a strong and broad base on which to build and paradoxically has led to internal challenges to both theory and practice which may even threaten women's studies' existence. While recognizing some historical dimensions, the chapters below offer no simple evolutionary or linear model of development but show a mosaic of individuals and programs at various places and positions in the process of creating a new academic field. Separate chapters are devoted to the constitution of this field, which only a quarter century after its inception was offered at over two-thirds of universities, about half of four-year colleges, and more than 40 percent of all institutions of higher education;[9] to its engagement with curriculum and with classroom; and to its involvement in theory and practice with other major issues affecting the contemporary academy. They will review recent criticism by academics, both within women's studies and outside it, as well as criticism by feminist and non- or antifeminist observers outside the academy. Serious studies as well as media attacks will be considered.

An issue that stimulates vital support for, as well as vehement attacks against, women's studies is its commitment to feminist politics. Echoing the early twentieth-century sociologist Robert Lynd's famous question "Knowledge for what?" I address the purposes of feminist education and its role within the academic establishment. Much attention has been paid to the changing functions of higher education in society, which have made university attendance desirable, indeed essential, to large populations of "nontraditional" students. Huge financial programs drawing on both private and public funds have been made available to encourage that attendance. A new focus on what is learned as well as what is presumed to be taught has led to major conferences on student achievement, new tools for assessing learning outcomes, a rethinking of faculty roles, new measures of accountability, and so forth. For those invested in student-centered education, these can be very positive developments. But something is still missing. Aside from an occasional lament that contemporary students seem to be more interested in employment and less interested in literature than earlier generations, little attention has been paid to how changing cohorts in the classroom might affect the content of the curriculum. In contrast to the Allan Blooms who denigrate the interests of these new students, I will point to evidence that they—especially the students who flock to women's studies classes and create what Page Smith called "an internal armed feminist camp in the midst of a more or less traditional university"—are seeking what only a liberal education can offer: the way toward a "better, more humane society."[10] And they are finding it in women's studies.

In the last chapter, the place of women's studies in the evolution of American higher education and its impact on a changing institution will be explored and evaluated. Drawing on the work of intellectual historians and philosophers, I suggest that women's studies presents a challenge to the purposes of the secular university as it has existed for much of the last century, by bringing back into it a moral purpose. That purpose requires reconstituting academic curricula and institutional structures to incorporate both traditional concerns of women for caring, concern, and connection,[11] and the new scholarship about women that broadens and deepens its scope, while shifting its perspective. Finally, I venture some conjectures regarding the future of women's studies in the academy—a future that most certainly includes the increasing feminization of higher education.

With the successful institutionalization of women's studies, the danger that the work of this academic feminist generation will suffer the fate of its predecessors is virtually gone. No researcher need ever again declare, like "Henriette, artiste," a nineteenth-century Frenchwoman recently discovered by an American historian, "What! Such things have happened and no women were taught about them."[12] The danger that this feminism will be defined out of existence or subsumed under, assimilated into, or eclipsed by other concerns with greater purchase on the public attention, as has happened to other feminisms in history, is greatly diminished by the existence of academic programs in women's studies. In the past, it has been too easy to convince people, including some feminists, that women's claims are less weighty than those of others, that they have been met, or that they admit of no solution. Thanks to women's studies, the long historical project for the equality of the sexes will remain a vital part of the education that is transmitted from generation to generation. The vision for learning and living that it has to offer to all is the subject of the pages that follow.

Feminist Advocacy,
Scholarly Inquiry,
and the
Experience of Women

1

The Origins of Women's Studies

Women's studies in higher education grew out of advocacy for and inquiry about women, and the experiences of the women who collectively built a new academic field. It began spontaneously in many places and continues today—for, about, and of women around the world. The women of San Diego, California, played a special role, and it is fitting to begin this study there, with the founding, over a quarter century ago, of the first integrated women's studies program. On November 3, 1970, Dean Warren Carrier at San Diego State College (now San Diego State University) wrote the following letter to a student journalist:

> *Miss Cathy Clark*
> *Editor*
> *Daily Aztec*
> *San Diego State*
>
> *Dear Miss Clark:*
> *I am writing belatedly to correct an item which appeared in the* Daily
> Aztec *last week with respect to Women's Studies. The article said that*
> *Women's Studies had received 15 positions. A decimal point was omit-*
> *ted in the figure. It should have read one point five. The figure 15 has*
> *caused some consternation amongst some competing departments and*

programs. One and a half positions is an extremely modest allotment to a program that is ranked across the nation not unfairly low as our football team at 14th but accurately as No. 1.

That autumn, the eyes of the nation were directed westward to observe what *Newsweek* magazine in its October 26 issue highlighted as "one of the hottest new wrinkles in higher education." *Newsweek* noted the overflowing enrollment in Professor Lois Kessler's women's studies class at San Diego State and quoted the prediction of Betty Friedan, a recent guest lecturer at Sacramento State, that "women's studies will one day fill libraries and create whole new courses in psychology, sociology, and history."[1] San Diego State soon fell from the top ranks of Division I-A football teams, but the academic venture it launched that fall has continued to maintain visibility among the leaders in a burgeoning field.

The ten-course curriculum formally launched with Dean Carrier's "modest allotment" appeared in *Female Studies I,* an anthology of syllabi of women's studies courses taught or proposed during 1969–70, collected and published by Sheila Tobias. The same set of courses was still in place in August 1974 when I arrived at San Diego State, fresh from the University of California, Riverside, and still lacking the doctoral dissertation, and was appointed as a lecturer to teach and coordinate the program.[2] In the intervening years, a series of other faculty had come and gone, teaching courses, working sometimes together and often in conflict against others—faculty as well as students, staff, and community women—to build something radically new under the academic umbrella, a center for women's studies and women's services. Along with other founders of women's studies, they shared a passion for women's history, a need for a "female heritage," and a conviction that it was possible to construct a "successful female revolution"—all of which (according to *Saturday Review* in 1971) were fueling the new feminism on campus.[3]

For its founders, women's studies was more than a search for a useable heritage to justify their feminism. It was, I believe, a passion for justice that moved them then and that now helps to explain the continued vitality of women's studies. Few would have expected it to last twenty-eight years. More typical was the opinion of the history department chair at the research university in California where I took my Ph.D. degree. Having heard in 1972 that I had chosen a topic in women's history for my dissertation, he urged me to reconsider—or at least to hurry up, since women's history must certainly be a passing fad and if I didn't have a book out and a job by 1974, I'd be passé. Similarly, an academic administrator asked me in 1976, in an interview for a newly established tenure line in the women's studies program at San Diego State, whether the field wasn't "just a fad," to be forgotten in a few years when its work of adding women to the curriculum was done. In those days, no one could imagine the extent of the forthcoming "knowledge explosion."

Since then, women's studies courses have been developed and women's studies programs founded at institutions across the country from Alabama to Washington, and from Arizona to Vermont. By my count, California alone houses sixty-nine, while New York State is home to sixty-five. The central states of Ohio and Minnesota house twenty-nine and twenty-one, respectively, while Michigan and Wisconsin each support nineteen. Two southern states, Georgia and North Carolina, each have listed eleven.[4] In many of these colleges and universities, women's studies has become an integral part of the academic base. It has spread into general education, where it may be offered or even required as part of every student's baccalaureate program; and into professional programs, from which students go forth to preach and to practice what they have learned in their classes. In 1994, more than six hundred women's studies programs (including a very small minority at community colleges) were said to be operating in the United States. The fastest-growing frontier is abroad, as women's studies programs are founded and flourish on every continent. This study, however, focuses on women's studies in four-year institutions of higher education in the United States.

Women's studies began at San Diego State University with the vision of a group of about twenty women—students, staff, faculty, and community feminists—active in the women's liberation movement in San Diego, who in 1969 constituted themselves as a "Women's Studies Committee" and "struggled for months . . . to become part of the College of Arts and Letters." The broad-based women's center they planned would include not only academic women's studies but six other components labeled research, publication, child care, storefront, cultural center, and recruitment and tutorial. Representatives of the community, the center staff, and San Diego State College Women's Liberation, along with the coordinator, constituted the center's coordinating committee. They would be advocates *for* women across-the-board.[5]

Women's studies began with their advocacy. Women's studies came out of the women's liberation movement. Women's studies began as part of a self-help movement that also brought women's health clinics and the claim for reproductive rights and has changed the way the medical profession and medical research treat women. It brought legal reform and new employment opportunities. And it brought advocacy for women to higher education, to both the academic structure and the curriculum. Like the journal *Feminist Studies*, which was also conceived in 1969 (though first published only in 1972) and began with strong links to the feminist community, women's studies "grew out of the women's movement at its early, spontaneous and energetic phase, bringing together political commitment and scholarship. Then merely to assert that women should be studied was a radical act."[6]

The second integrated program of women's studies also appeared in the 1970–71 academic year, at Cornell University, and was soon followed by many others. At public and private, four-year and two-year, church-affiliated, polytechnic, research, comprehensive, and liberal arts colleges and universities, at institutions of virtually all kinds in regions that spanned the United States, women's studies courses and programs proliferated. The 150 programs counted in 1975 had doubled by 1980, reached 450 at mid-decade, and exceeded 600 by the early 1990s. Women's studies courses, as noted above, then existed at a majority of four-year institutions of higher education. Often all it took was a faculty member willing to teach and an administrator willing to sanction the new venture—at times, not even money was required, for volunteers stepped forward to teach, to coordinate, to work through academic committee structures, in the interests of bringing new questions, research, and teaching to the academy.

The expansion of women's studies was fueled by a pervasive need for a usable past and validation for change in the present. The rapidity of its growth was explained as early as 1971 by Elaine Showalter, who wrote, "When the ideas could be spoken, the teachers were there, for unlike blacks, Puerto Ricans, Chicanos, or American Indians, women are already represented in the academic world in substantial numbers."[7] By 1971, fourteen regional conferences had been held, in locations ranging from the University of Pennsylvania to Portland State, in Oregon. The early growth was encouraged as well by the flow of pamphlets, manifestos, and newsletters from feminist communities to campuses, and the circulation of course outlines and reading lists from instructor to instructor. In this period—before answering machines and e-mail, without a national organization or other formal networks of communication—information was obtained by each practitioner somewhat randomly. A graduate student in the University of California system might send off for the *Female Studies* series originally housed in Pittsburgh but might know only vaguely if at all about what was happening at San Diego State. The Feminist Press, whose *Women's Studies Quarterly* began as a newsletter dedicated to spreading knowledge about the new field across the country, played an enormous formative role in the early years. Linking academic feminists on campuses and in communities, its pathbreaking publications facilitated the exchange of ideas and materials for instruction across class, racial, and geographic borders.[8]

Despite the scattered beginnings of women's studies, key themes and similar titles appear repeatedly in the course outlines compiled by Tobias in *Female Studies I.* Featured prominently in those syllabi are authors who present woman as "other" (Simone de Beauvoir), as victim (Betty Friedan), and as minority (Helen Hacker), as well as rediscovered feminist voices from history (those of Mary Wollstonecraft, John Stuart Mill, Henrik Ibsen, Charlotte Perkins Gilman) that provided positive reinforcement for the anger elicited by others whose work had reinforced women's subordination. Among the other voices from history especially prominent in these early courses was that of Freud, whose negative influence in the psychologizing culture of the 1950s and 1960s made his limited (if not misogynistic) vision a ready and common target. Eleanor Flexner's *Century of Struggle* led the historical works; Margaret Mead, Alice Rossi, Caroline Bird, and Eleanor Maccoby were featured in the fields of anthropology, sociology, economics, and contemporary psychology, respectively. Recognition that the study of women required a multidisciplinary approach is also reflected in these early courses. Notable features also include the frequent appearance of Leo Kanowitz's study of women and law and the appearance of courses offered in schools of business and social work.

While seeking role models for rebellion, these early women's studies instructors set out to analyze the sources of women's oppression and to present ways to overcome it. The transition from consciousness raising in the community to feminism in the academy is captured in a statement by Kay Boals in her syllabus for a "student-initiated" course entitled "The Politics of Male-Female Relations," which she offered in the spring of 1970 in the Department of Politics at Princeton University. Noting that she would raise questions that were "historical-anthropological, ideological, and psychological, as well as socio-economic," Boals argued that this broad prospective was "inevitable—and indeed essential—if we are to come to grips realistically with the problem of transforming women's consciousness so that they may go on to transform society."[9]

Like numerous others, Boals's course included readings about women of many ages and places—Algeria and parts of Asia as well as the contemporary United States; and the final week's topic was "Parallels with Other 'Minority' Groups—Blacks, Students, Colonized." Among the seventeen syllabi in *Female Studies I* are a 1969 course proposal on women and race, and Carl Degler's "Race and Sex in America," offered at Stanford University in the spring of 1970. Of the seventeen, seven include some readings about women of color; many deal with class. Several of these courses were taught by men.

The importance of feminist advocacy in the women's liberation movement as a foundation for women's studies is reflected in the readings included in these first courses as well as in the larger number compiled in *Female Studies II* and subsequent issues in that series. Often free or inexpensive, mimeographed copies of feminist statements could be picked up from literature tables at meetings of all types, from national meetings of the National Organization for Women (NOW) to small, local gatherings of groups who met to explore the status of women in their communities. Eagerly picked up, read, and recirculated—and sometimes used in classes— some of these works were destined to become famous, including Margaret Benston's "The Political Economy of Women's Liberation," Pat Mainardi's "The Politics of Housework," Judy Syfers's "My God, Who Wouldn't Want a Wife?," Del Martin and Phyllis Lyons's "The Realities of Lesbianism," and especially, the Boston Women's Health Collective's *Our Bodies, Ourselves*, which cost this author eighty cents (marked up already from fifty-five cents) and taught its readers, including young students and their mothers, a lot about their own reproductive systems.

Circulated through feminist hands as well as by the "underground press" and newly established women's bookstores, the writings of feminist activists provided the basic questions that spurred the development of women's studies. These early statements are responsible for the fact that women's studies was more than academic work about and (largely) by women but also was for women—intended to further women's access to equality in society as well as academia. According to the political theorist Judith Grant, the "core concepts" developed in the pamphlets and manifestoes written by radical feminists of this foundational period account for "much of the richness of feminist theory as well as a good portion of its problems." Three core concepts that constitute dominant concerns of a radical feminism deeply influenced by the Left—"'woman,' experience, personal politics"—laid the basis for women's studies and would be elucidated by it.[10] New Left influence also accounts for the primacy given to grassroots politics, class relations, and revolutionary movements. The heavy and long-lasting emphasis on women's work (which during the decade of the 1980s captured more scholarly attention by women's historians than any other single topic) reflects not only the struggle of many women to integrate economically productive and familial activities in their own lives but also the Marxist background of many founding mothers of women's studies.[11] From the beginning, the goal of women's studies was not merely to study women's position in the world but to change it.

The word *feminist* itself, however, appeared rarely in early women's studies course titles. More typical were "women in . . ." and ". . . of women." The first collections of course syllabi and reading lists bore the titles *Female Studies I* and *Female Studies II.* Although Feminist Press founder Florence Howe spoke of the new field in *Female Studies II* as "feminist" studies, the first two programs differed in their choice of name, Cornell University using the term *female* and San Diego State choosing *women.* It was the latter title, "women's studies," with the apostrophe that blurs the difference between studies by, about, and belonging to women, that caught on. That women's studies was also for women, intended to promote the advancement of women, went without saying. That work in the new field would be done largely by women remained for future determination. If the originators of women's studies recognized any perils in naming, they were likely to have been concerned about accusations of a lack of objectivity or bias against men. "Where are the men's studies?" was a more likely challenge in those days than "Who do you mean by 'women'?" The recuperation of *feminist* was slow and difficult; even use of the word *woman* or *women* in the title of a proposed course might suffice to doom a new initiative. Criticism of *woman* and *women* as "hegemonic" terms implying "homogenizing norms," and as reifying the sexual differences that feminism purported to overcome, lay a decade or more away.[12]

In the 1990s, when it is not unusual to find feminists fretting over alleged dangers posed by the success of women's studies in institutionalizing itself, it is worth remembering how radical it once seemed to study women. "Is there enough material for a whole course?" was another common query. The term *women's studies* was preferred, not least because it sounded more "objective" and more comprehensive than *feminist studies*. From the beginning, however, most women's studies practitioners shared the concerns identified by the theorist Kirstie McClure in her analysis of foundational feminist "frameworks": "a normative commitment to women's emancipation, a scientific commitment to the explanation of women's oppression, and a practical commitment to social transformation."[13]

Forms of Advocacy

The complex relationship between advocacy and academic concerns in women's studies is evident throughout the field's history, its structures, and its courses and curricula. This subject will be discussed more fully in chapter 7, but here I want to suggest some of its most important expressions. The dual purpose is manifested clearly in the major institutions that support women's studies. The National Women's Studies Association (NWSA) pledges in its statement of purpose to be guided by "a vision of a world free not only from sexism but also from racism, class-bias, ageism, heterosexual bias—from all the ideologies and institutions that have consciously or unconsciously oppressed and exploited some for the advantage of others."[14] In its definition of its constituency, in its organizational structure, and in its deliberative processes, the NWSA embodies the continuing commitment of women's studies to advocacy—that is, to political action in the interest of women. Its leadership and membership hold themselves accountable to a feminist community (or communities) to a much greater extent than do other academic professional organizations, for the NWSA takes as its mission feminist education at all levels and in all settings.

This sense of purpose is reflected in the NWSA's experiments in democracy. It seeks, as the sociologist Robin Leidner points out, to combine structures of liberal democracy (one person, one vote) with structures typical of corporatist democracy (votes by regions and caucuses) and to maintain a decentralized structure and a flat administrative hierarchy. Drawing on feminist ideals, it attempts to provide women not only equal opportunity but also equal power, equal outcomes, and equal satisfaction.[15] Not all women's studies practitioners are comfortable with either the forms or the goals of the national organization. In fact, the NWSA has tended to alienate some feminist scholars and has teetered on the brink of destruction several times. But it persists; and perceptions of its annual meeting in Oklahoma in 1995 and the response of its 1996 president to a recent challenge by "Grrls [sic] against Professionalism" suggest that it is gaining strength as an academic association while maintaining its core commitments to feminist values. The more assertive role taken recently by program administrators and the increasingly scholarly style of the NWSA Journal, the national organization's publication, suggest greater success in balancing the claims of its academic and activist missions. A former editor of that journal asserts that "scholarship can be social action."[16]

For this reason, the policies and practices of feminist academic journals offer another useful case study of the role of advocacy in building women's studies. In her prize-winning 1994 book Politics and Scholarship: Feminist Academic Journals and the Production of Knowledge, Patrice McDermott traces the history of three leading interdisciplinary women's studies publications: Feminist Studies, Frontiers, and Signs: A Journal of Women in Culture and Society. While their histories and sense of purpose vary significantly, all three have struggled successfully with issues of combining feminist advocacy and academic authority. Each of the three today enjoys substantial support from a prestigious university or university press. Like women's studies programs on campus, feminist academic publications owe their origins to the community, and they reflect the oppositional stance of the underground press of the late 1960s. They also aspire to play a major role in the production of new knowledge about women.

In the view of its founding editor, Catharine R. Stimpson, the University of Chicago Press publication Signs "set out to beat the academics at their own game." It has enjoyed from its inception a reputation as the leading interdisciplinary scholarly journal in the field. At some universities, it has been the only feminist journal credited by conservative scholars. It has handled the question of its political perspective cautiously. In the first issue, Stimpson very carefully acknowledged the new journal's ties with both its trio of highly respected supporting institutions—the University of Chicago Press, Barnard College, and the Ford Foundation—and the "great social movements, particularly the New Feminism," to which it owed its appearance. In defining "the new scholarship on women" to which it would devote its pages, Stimpson focused not on feminism but on new conceptual tools and techniques and on patterns of interdisciplinarity that it would foster. Five years later, when Signs made its first regularly scheduled move to another institution, Stimpson's successor, Stanford's Barbara Gelpi, announced in her first editorial that the journal would maintain its "feminist commitment" and a "participatory commitment in the process whereby ideas become action." Succeeding editors and editorial groups have followed this policy.[17]

A feminist purpose has been evident in *Signs* from the beginning. It is expressed in the feminist content of the journal's articles and the topics of its special issues. The list of pathbreaking articles published by *Signs* began with Carroll Smith-Rosenberg's "The Female World of Love and Ritual," in volume 1, no. 1 (1975), which reconceptualized women's relations with other women in the nineteenth century. *Feminist Studies*, which is generally considered more open to diverse types of scholarship than *Signs*, offered in its first volume (1972–73) Judith Walkowitz's "Prostitution and the Poor in Plymouth and Southampton under the Contagious Diseases Acts," which opened many minds to new perspectives on an eternally maligned profession. *Frontiers*, which was founded and was edited until recently at the University of Colorado and is now at Washington State University, turned the attention of feminist scholars to women of rural America, Chicana women, and indigenous American women, as well as women of other cultures and nations. All have featured scholarship on topics such as abortion, job discrimination, sex roles, and sexuality. They (and other feminist academic journals) have reinforced the first essential message of women's studies, a message saturated with political concern: women and women's issues are important. They are important enough to constitute the subject of serious scholarly study, of research, and of the inquiry that forms the basis for courses, curricula, and degree programs.

While a diverse group of women's studies journals have helped to define the field, they have also underlined in theory and practice that women's studies does not seek to be "objective" about women. Rather, it makes a statement about women's subordinate status in society, and it seeks change. As McDermott says of the feminist academic journals she has studied, women's studies

—*takes gender as its "primary category of analysis";*
—*"emphasizes the relations of power between women and men";*
—*foregrounds "women's experience in a way that does not objectify, victimize, romanticize, or overgeneralize"; and*
—*seeks to effect "social change."*

It also recognizes the importance of race, class, and sexual identity.[18] These perspectives have been infused into the production of new knowledge through feminist inquiry. Even as women's studies programs and journals addressed subject matter that some considered primarily political, women's studies leaders asserted that scholarly research, not politics as conventionally defined, formed the basis for its inclusion in the academy.

In the academically strongest programs, including San Diego State's after 1974, feminist faculty attempted to make it clear that this movement was about scholarship and that people could not dismiss it as merely political. Observers needed to recall that *politics* is derived from *polis*, from community. Academic feminism was no oxymoron but an effort by scholars pursuing questions that arose out of the concerns of women as citizens and members of communities. Feminist inquiry would be no less valid than the research of anthropologists convinced of the value of other cultures or sociologists sympathetic to the needs of working-class populations that they studied. Feminist scholars argued that the new scholarship on women, carried out largely (although not exclusively) by women with Ph.D. degrees from the leading research universities, met the usual academic standards. Thesis advisors and colleagues posed hard questions and generally received satisfactory answers. In discipline after discipline, the leading scholars opened the doors of their universities and departments to their former students, now become the new women's studies faculty. Advisory boards soon began to welcome their scholarship to the pages of leading academic journals. Women's studies scholarship was different because it drew its questions from feminism and applied its answers to feminist ends. It was nonetheless sound scholarship.

The Nature of Feminist Scholarship

Inquiry in women's studies has come in many forms, and exists throughout the disciplines. The initial compensatory search for forgotten feminists, an attempt to provide a politically and psychologically useful heritage by recovering and discovering women's biography and history, continues today, as feminist scholars continue to ask and to answer the question "Where were the women and what were they doing?" Having found many more fascinating foremothers than anyone could have dreamed of, women's studies scholars also reexamined traditional interpretations and conventional wisdom, asking if the old truths were true when reassessed including the women or when re-viewed from a female perspective. And if not, if some of those truths were demonstrably false, if women did not have a Renaissance—to cite an influential article from the 1970s—then how did scholars and sages arrive at such flawed conclusions? How do we know what we know, they asked, challenging their thesis advisors as well as the exemplars, past and present, of their fields.

By this path, many feminist scholars began—on their own, before they had ever heard of Foucault and Derrida and poststructuralism—to challenge the dominance of methodologies of research, categories of analysis, and ways of interpreting evidence that distorted or blocked understanding of women and gender. They learned that knowledge depends on point of view, and that nothing in human experience is exclusively "natural," least of all "femininity." So they set out to ask more questions and to question prevailing answers. And they created—to use the most common of terms—"a knowledge explosion." That is what this generation of daughters—the daughters of educated men as well as uneducated or undereducated mothers and fathers—have done. They have not simply followed Virginia Woolf's imaginary academic procession.[19] They have created what is arguably the most expansive new field of knowledge in higher education of our era. It is impossible to mention here the names of all the scholars who have produced this vast outpouring of work. Only with the aid of reference librarians using the most up-to-date online databases could one even list all the books *about* the books on women. Guides to surfing the Internet so as to find the maps through all this feminist scholarship are distributed regularly via several Internet mailing lists ("listservs"). Women's studies flourishes on campuses and in cyberspace.[20]

What has been learned from all this feminist inquiry? First, feminist scholars argue, they have learned that deploying gender as a category of analysis opens people's minds to new ways of thinking. In 1974, in their preface to *Clio's Consciousness Raised*, a collection of essays from the first Berkshire Conference in Women's History, Mary Hartman and Lois Banner pointed out that the new work showed the "value of raising questions as provocative as their conclusions." In the first outpouring of the new feminist scholarship, Gerda Lerner and Joan Kelly challenged accepted ways of periodizing history. Carroll Smith-Rosenberg and Lillian Faderman questioned commonplace interpretations of female sexuality and women's relationships with women. Michelle Rosaldo, Gayle Rubin, and Sherry Ortner rethought androcentric and ethnocentric views of the effects of biology on what were then called "sex roles." Sandra Bem, Phyllis Chesler, and Naomi Weisstein reconsidered common psychological definitions of femininity, and the sociologist Pauline Bart demonstrated what those definitions could do to women who accepted them. Heidi Hartmann and Arlie Russell Hochschild explained why women worked so hard and earned so little, and Ester Boserup discussed why international development could cause regression for women in economic matters. Jessie Bernard showed why marriage failed to keep its promises to many women; and Joyce Ladner showed why growing up black necessitated other dreams for women's lives. Tish Sommers explained why aging hurt so much despite PMZ—postmenopausal zest. Jo Freeman brought new understanding to women's roles in liberation politics. Barrie Thorne, Robin Lakoff, and Suzette Haden Elgin urged women to hear themselves as they spoke a language that kept them in a restricted place. Dolores Hayden explored gendered configurations of physical space. Annette Kolodny, Barbara Smith, Adrienne Rich, and Alice Walker offered new insight into imagery and metaphor in poetry and prose, seeing anew what it said about and did to women's thinking and women's being.[21]

In the flowering of the second decade, thanks to research and insight by scholars whose names are so many as to defy any attempt to sketch for the 1980s the outline just compressed for the 1970s, women's studies scholars continued to look within and across the disciplines. They created new interpretive frameworks for understanding women's lives, past and present. They recognized women not only as victims of subordination but as agents of transformation and artists of life. And in new and challenging—if controversial—ways, they set out to put it all together with theories of their own. Progressively, from feminist thought to feminist theory to feminist epistemology, using gender as a category of analysis has led to the rethinking of the foundations of all knowledge, including women's studies' own foundational paradigms: the social construction of femininity as well as the biological underpinnings of the word *woman*.

What is worthy of note here is the vast quantity as well as the remarkable quality of feminist scholarship. Many of the finest minds of a generation of female scholars, freely admitted to full membership in the academy only in the last few decades, have produced, in women's studies, major works in language, literature, biography, history, sociology, anthropology, philosophy, political theory, and many other domains of late-twentieth-century knowledge. Women's studies practitioners can now boast of a scholarly field of their own, a field grounded in the humanistic and social science disciplines and richly threaded through them, but woven further into artful and interesting interdisciplinary tapestries in which women can see themselves and the world anew. In many of the liberal arts disciplines, courses and curricula that lack women's studies content can no longer meet the test of scholarly currency. Lying outside the dominant pre-poststructuralist ethos of the academy, women's studies recognizes all knowledge as the product of contests for the power to name, to paint, to weave. Feminist scholarship claims and has helped to advance the idea that there are many truths. It incorporates female experience in all its diversity as the basis for a feminist epistemology. Feminist inquiry builds on female experiences—while also posing a formidable challenge to our understanding of their complexity.

Scholarship Grounded in Women's Lived Experiences

The privileged place given to women's experiences began early in the building process, for the consciousness raising of the 1960s and early 1970s was a means for women to share experience and, through sharing, to come better to understand its meaning for their lives. This sharing of experience gave rise to the proposition that "the personal is political" and taught women to question conventional, categorical thinking and to blur boundaries. Like consciousness raising, women's studies offers new and powerful intellectual and emotional insights into experience.[22]

Women's studies has learned and taught many lessons in better understanding and reevaluating women in all their diversity. From the beginning, feminists spoke in many voices. The tables of contents of Robin Morgan's *Sisterhood Is Powerful* (1970) and other early anthologies belie the criticism that the founders of the midcentury "Second Wave" of feminism represented *only* a monocultural, middle-class women's movement.[23] But it took many years of conflict within feminism, and what Susan Stanford Friedman terms "scripts of denial, accusation, and confession," before women's studies practitioners could conceptualize the multicultural, multiethnic "relational positionality" that now offers a way to "move beyond the essentialism of fundamentalist identity politics without denying the material realities of identity." Academic feminists learned—from Gloria Hull, Barbara Smith, Gloria Anzaldúa, Paula Gunn Allen, Audre Lorde, and many others whom they wished to call "sister"—about their own "process[es] of othering" women of color. Borrowing a felicitous line from Henry Louis Gates Jr., Friedman urges feminists to take up a new "challenge to move from a politics of identity to a politics of identification."[24] Clearly, differences still divide women's studies and sometimes splinter efforts to build together. From diversity of experience has come both the weakness and the strength of academic as well as political feminism. But, as a button seen at the 1985 NWSA conference put it, "Sisterhood Is Trying."[25] No other academic professional organization, no other group of academic practitioners, has staked so much on living up to its best humanistic principles. This effort is explored in chapter 5.

The attempt to validate every woman's experience, whatever her identity, has infused every aspect of women's studies: teaching and scholarship, theory and practice. Drawing on the ground rules of consciousness raising, which prescribed equal opportunity for self-expression and validation of each woman's experience and proscribed interrupting and criticizing, many women's studies instructors deliberately structured "the construction of knowledge in the classroom."[26] They adopted circular seating and rules for classroom participation like those used in consciousness raising, downplaying their authority and encouraging students to acknowledge their own and each other's experientially won expertise. Bringing the tools of intellectual inquiry to bear on women's own, or similar, experiences, they introduced into classroom discussion dynamics unlike those found in traditional lecture or lecture-discussion courses. As Margo Culley and Catherine Portuges declare, "Once experience becomes an appropriate subject of intellectual inquiry, the classroom is forever changed."[27] The more diverse the students' experience, the headier the charge.

In the 1980s, Carol Gilligan's widely influential study of moral development, purporting to show that women spoke "in a different voice," one based in an "ethic of responsibility and care," stimulated further work on women's "styles of learning." It inspired a prize-winning and influential study of female cognitive development, *Women's Ways of Knowing.*[28] Suggesting that women come to knowledge differently than had previously been assumed, pedagogical experts have studied how women's studies students and faculty respond to differences of ethnicity and to race and racism in feminist classrooms, while also transforming their perceptions of self and other.[29] The assertion that "women know differently," which posits special "women's ways of knowing" stemming from their ways of living in the world, reflects the feminist attempt to build on and validate women's own interpretations of experience. Whether or not women "know" differently from men, after centuries of woman as "problem" and woman as "other," most feminist scholars would agree on the need to include in the construction of knowledge the experience both of woman as knower and of women, in all their differences, as knowers. These concerns have given rise to the feminist pedagogy that is the subject of chapter 4.

While in classrooms, in scholarship, and in professional associations women's studies practitioners continue to struggle with different experiences, seeking through theory and practice to overcome divisions of ethnicity, race, sexual preference, and class, feminist theory, under the influence of poststructuralism as well, now problematizes the building block "woman" itself. *Am I That Name?* asks the title of an important work in feminist theory.[30] For some, *experience* has become a buzzword or "scare word" that, as it authenticates the individual, serves also to separate and intimidate. For others, it masks an assumption of innocence, of self-evident awareness of reality. While the latter agree that experience deserves attention and respect, they would nevertheless agree with the historian Dominick LaCapra, that experience in and of itself neither authenticates nor invalidates an argument or point of view.[31] At the extreme, privilege bestowed upon individual identity invalidates all other bases for expertise— the discipline of history, for example, dissolves if one cannot understand and teach what one has not personally experienced. Most historians, and many others, would argue that the human spirit *can* transcend time, distance, and difference. The personal can also lead to solipsism. According to some critics, this is an ever-present threat in women's studies.

There is also danger to women's studies in the formulation "I feel, therefore I am," which is the feminist philosopher Judith Grant's term of challenge to a feminist critique of reason that invites, in her view, a return to the concept of a stereotypically female intuition. Against Mary Daly and other ecofeminists, Grant objects to stressing gender connections to nature; against Hélène Cixous and some other theorists, she objects to privileging female embodiment. "It is not obvious," says Grant, "precisely what it is about the female reproductive system that would make women think differently than men."[32] Problems abound in privileging and generalizing from categories that mask differences; but the danger of turning to the specificity of individual experience, suggests the philosopher of education Jane Roland Martin, is that it may "stultify intellectual inquiry."[33] The historian Joan

Scott, analyzing the uses of experience as evidence for the production of knowledge, problematizes it further:

> When experience is taken as the origin of knowledge, the vision of the individual subject (the person who had the experience or the historian who recounts it) becomes the bedrock of evidence on which explanation is built. Questions about the constructed nature of experience, about how subjects are constituted as different in the first place . . . are left aside. The evidence of experience then becomes evidence for the fact of difference.[34]

Seeing, Scott reminds her readers, is an active verb. Experience incorporates interpretation—and itself needs to be interpreted through a "dialogic reading." By giving deference to every individual's experience, by bowing to privilege based on difference, women's studies threatens to divide women into ever more narrowly drawn, personalized statements of identity politics; or, by acid-tests of theory, to dissolve its own base into faceless, disembodied elements of discourse. Experience is a tricky subject.

Challenged from within and without the academic world, women's studies scholars ask many provocative questions, and they express multiple points of view in their answers. In many ways, women's studies seems to have become an academic field like others: with courses and curricula; assignments and exams; studies in history, literature, anthropology, and sociology; and monographs and textbooks—all the accoutrements of traditional academia. Feminists of the Second Wave have built women's studies into the academy as a legacy for the Third Wavers who are now beginning to take their places, far better prepared than their predecessors, with women's studies degrees in hand and bibliographies at hand, to pursue scholarly inquiry on women. Feminist scholars of both generations, however, bring to the academy a different sense of institutional purpose, a commitment to service beyond the disciplinary devotion of many of their colleagues. Along with intellectual and professional advancement, they also pursue a *moral* goal, envisioning a new kind of society that includes women as fully empowered people. Women's studies, by insisting on integrating advocacy for, inquiry about, and the experiences of women, says that it is not enough to study and to teach but that academicians must "take the big step from thought to action, from moral analysis to fulfilled commitment." They are not alone; it was Robert Coles who pointed this out in a recent article entitled "The Disparity between Intellect and Character."[35] Women's studies seeks to integrate moral reasoning and action. It strives to bring moral inquiry back to our universities and to make moral claims on peoples' lives.[36] Women's studies challenges higher education, for it looks beyond enrollments accumulated, degrees granted, books published, grants and prizes awarded, to knowledge reconstituted and lives reinvented. It is a discipline in pursuit of a new integrity of the life of the mind and the whole of life.

2

Thinking Anew about the World and Women

Tom Wolfe has vividly described how Ken Kesey's Merry Pranksters in California and Timothy Leary's League for Spiritual Discovery in New York considered themselves "two extraordinary arcane societies, and the only ones in the world, engaged in the most fantastic experiment in human consciousness ever devised. The thing was totally new."[1] To appreciate the aspirations of women's studies, it is helpful to recall its origins in the 1960s, before the disillusionment that now darkens memories of that era, a youthful and hopeful time. American prosperity had encouraged dreams in which education—higher education—was central; and among the dreamers many were women. America began to send its daughters to college in larger numbers than ever, and in greater proportion to its sons than at any time since the 1920s. Away from home, some of the "coeds" joined the cheerleading squad but many others sought alongside their brothers and boyfriends to play a role in the vital issues of the day—civil rights, the New Left, Free Speech and student power, and the "New University" movement. Ultimately, women's experience in these causes led to the renaissance of an American feminism that had been absent from the public eye for close to half a century.

As women students played a central role in many of the political battles of the 1960s, some noticed their second-class status in movement groups as well as in the larger society and began to ask why.[2] By 1965 and 1966, organized classes about women were taught in Seattle, New Orleans,

Chicago, and New York City. They were taught in "free universities" and in prestigious colleges. What they shared in addition to their central subject matter was a conviction that women's studies was an "educational strategy" that might bring about a "breakthrough in consciousness and knowledge" that could transform individuals, institutions, relationships, and societies.[3] Knowledge was power, and women, newly empowered, could remedy the faults of the (man-made) world. "Coeds" no longer, they would claim an education on equal grounds. It was still an era of hope.

If the idealism of the 1960s was one parent of women's studies, its other parent was activism, which began about 1969 to bring change to many academic professional associations. In anthropology, economics, history, literature, political science, psychology, and dozens of other fields, including the sciences and engineering, women began to form caucuses and placed the professional interests of their sex on the agendas at national as well as local and regional meetings.[4] At the annual meeting of the American Historical Association (AHA) in 1970 one panel, unlikely to have appeared on the AHA program in earlier years, was entitled "Up from the Genitals: Sexism in the Historical Profession."[5] A small stream quickly became a tide of oceanic proportions; evidence of a sea change can be seen in the slate of officers for 1996 elected by the AHA's membership: nine of thirteen were women, as was the president-elect chosen to succeed the then-current, also female, president. In this venerable institution's 112-year history, only once, in the war year 1943, did a woman hold this position until Natalie Zemon Davis, a historian of France and of women, took the helm in 1987. With the service of Louise A. Tilly as president in 1993, Caroline Walker Bynum in 1996, and Joyce O. Appleby in 1997, four women, all selected by the membership in a national ballot, were accorded this high honor in the decade from 1987 to 1997. Other disciplines have also experienced changes in leadership. As the professional caucuses have promoted the appointment and advancement of women, they have also indirectly helped to nurture the growth of women's studies, since so many female scholars have turned their research and teaching skills to the study of women.

While women become increasingly visible as leaders at the national level, back at the grassroots, on campuses across the country, women's studies also shows no signs of slackening. Programs burgeon, courses proliferate, and students enroll in increasing numbers in women's studies classes. A U.S. Department of Education report based on national longitudinal studies shows that in 1993 more than 12 percent of students earned credit in women's studies classes, up from 6 percent in 1972, and more than in any other interdisciplinary field.[6] The report lists women's studies along with business, computer science and related engineering fields, mass communications, and hospitality and recreation studies as the growth fields of this period. Given that women's studies largely comprises coursework in history, literature, philosophy, psychology, sociology, other social sciences, and the arts, these data suggest the importance of academic feminism to the current state of the liberal arts on American campuses.

What is it that women's studies students are studying? It is beyond the scope of this study to review the content of the many courses whose titles refer to "women in" a particular discipline, or to "women and" a discipline, which are generally offered by the departments as part of their regular curricula. Numerous published studies are available criticizing the traditional curriculum and demonstrating the impact of feminist scholarship on research and teaching in the disciplines.[7] However, with more than two hundred institutions now reporting that they offer the baccalaureate in women's studies, and more than four hundred degrees awarded in the field in 1992–93, it may be useful to look at the content of a typical undergraduate degree program. A 1991 study by the National Women's Studies Association, co-published with the Association of American Colleges (the AAC; now called the Association of American Colleges and Universities, or AACU), reports that a women's studies major typically requires thirty-five semester hours, including an introductory course (most often called "Introduction to Women's Studies"); a number of elective courses offered both by the program itself and by traditional departments (the two parts about equally represented in the major); and a capstone course that may take the form of a senior seminar, an internship, or independent study. Nearly 40 percent of the majors mandate study of feminist theory, with almost as many requiring a course that incorporates perspectives on gender and ethnic, racial, and cultural differences. Reflecting the fervent desire of academic feminists to be (and to be recognized as) inclusive of women of color and sensitive to issues of cultural diversity, 95 percent of the programs surveyed in the NWSA-AAC study offer coursework on cultural diversity. It is notable that a large majority (72%) of the programs covered in another survey require coursework outside of women's studies. In a typical program, about half of the work falls under the rubric of social science and half under that of the humanities.[8]

Women's studies is no different than many other academic fields in the humanities and social sciences in the variety of approaches taken by instructors, and it would be foolhardy to suggest a common content for its introductory course. Many instructors continue to assign course readers of their own making, reflecting their disciplinary training, scholarly interests, and political perceptions, as well as local expectations governing curricular approaches and academic requirements. Nevertheless, a review of three of the most popular texts offers insight into the type of material likely to be covered.

The genesis of women's studies in the radical student movement of the 1960s, and its persisting influence, is demonstrated in a tale of the first major introductory textbook, published in 1975 and issued in its fifth edition in 1995. Jo Freeman, editor of *Women: A Feminist Perspective*, was a first-year student at the University of Chicago in 1968 when she was moved to investigate the background to a sit-in there over the dismissal of a female professor. Having discovered in her research for a paper on the history of women at the university a turn-of-the-century proto–women's studies class offered by Sophonisba Preston Breckinridge on the legal and economic condition of women, she later taught, at student request, a noncredit "Breckinridge memorial" course on the same topic. Her text grew out of that class. "It too was a response to the sit-in," she recalls.[9]

Turned down by several eastern publishers whom she first approached, Freeman found her publisher on the West Coast, where women's studies was growing rapidly. The first two editions of *Women: A Feminist Perspective* (1975, 1979) each sold some fifty thousand copies; with three subsequent editions, the latest in 1995, the total sales come to about two hundred thousand, making this probably the most widely used introductory women's studies text. It has changed extensively over the years; even the first edition included only two of the selections included in Freeman's original course readings, others having been solicited in broad calls distributed through feminist media. Its point of view reflected the stance of the liberation movement: "It is a social control perspective," wrote Freeman in the introduction to the first edition. "It rejects the idea that there is any meaningful choice for members of either sex as long as there are socially prescribed sex roles and social penalties for those who deviate from them." Freeman challenged the "national ideology about living in a 'free society.'" She conceived of the book as a series of concentric circles affecting women's lives, beginning with the body, the family, and sex-role socialization, moving to the arenas of work, images, and social institutions, and ending with historical and contemporary feminist movements. In the context of a women's movement accused of neglecting women's traditional concerns, it is interesting to remark how contemporary some of the selections appear. "Who Shall Care for Our Children? The History and Development of Day Care in the United States" opens with a statement about the "shocking extent of childhood poverty" and its neglect among current social concerns.[10]

Freeman's third edition was essentially a new book, with only four (primarily historical) selections reappearing. By 1984 she could draw on the increasing wealth of feminist-inspired inquiry. Keeping essentially the same framework, she also added several articles reflecting a wider range of female identities. The most striking contrast she noted between the materials submitted for the first edition and those submitted for the third was the "lessening of personal involvement by the authors with their topics" and its replacement with data. "For the first edition I edited out a lot of rhetoric and unsubstantiated speculation. The articles for the third edition were occasionally so dry I wished I could put some rhetoric in."[11]

Not unexpectedly, the fourth edition, appearing in 1989, was heavy with theory. Much of the feminist theory discussed here in chapter 6 dates from that decade. In editing the fourth edition and the fifth, published in 1995, Freeman encountered an interesting problem: the wealth of scholarship now available made it hard, she observed, for the authors to find their own voices. "The nemesis of the fifth edition was literature reviews." On the positive side, diversity also makes its mark here. While Freeman's goal remains to analyze the situation of women, to offer data about women's lives and interpret them from "a feminist perspective," she now finds "less consistently" the unifying point of view of earlier editions. Properly speaking, the subtitle of the latest, largest edition might be "feminist perspectives."[12]

Multiplicity of perspectives is a fundamental feature of another frequently adopted text, *Women's Realities, Women's Choices: An Introduction to Women's Studies.* Published in 1983 as a basic textbook written expressly for introductory women's studies courses, it is the collective work of a group of faculty at Hunter College (in New York City) who express the hope that "its use will encourage and regularize the teaching of women's studies introductory courses." Prepared with support from the National Endowment for the Humanities, it was greeted by Hunter's then-president, Donna E. Shalala, in her foreword to the volume, as cause for "a celebration . . . [a book that] deserves fireworks."[13]

Also adopting the concentric-circle framework, with three parts that widen from individual women to family circles to society, the authors contrast generally androcentric social and cultural structures with the realities of women's lives and suggest possible women-oriented alternatives to "help bridge that gap." Because they assumed that women's studies is, like the writing of their book, a collective learning endeavor and that the teaching of women's studies comprises "cooperative ventures between teachers and students," the authors struggled to decide how to use pronoun forms. Should they refer to women, the subjects of their work, as though objects, as "they" or "them"; or should they, identifying with all women, speak of "we" and "us"? Writing and rewriting as they considered the problems with each approach, which seemed variously to be "awkward," "artificial," "disrespectful," or "silly," they finally opted for the first person, "trying to speak, however haltingly, for all women." They hoped that this choice would encourage readers "to see the world from the point of view of *women*, from the points of view of all of *us*, from *our* diverse perspectives," to recognize women as subjects rather than as "passive objects."[14]

Before "defining women" (in the first section), the authors offer an introduction to the field of study: "Women's studies is not simply the study of women. It is the study of women which places women's own experiences in the center of the process. It examines the world and the human beings who inhabit it with questions, analyses, and theories built directly on women's experiences." Women, therefore, appear here not only in the images, symbols, and philosophical and scientific theories of men's devising. Each section of "Defining Women" offers creative work by women or female-centered interpretations of issues and information, in art, literature, philosophy, and science. The breadth of coverage—from the Song of Solomon to Judy Chicago, from the stages of labor in giving birth to the patterns of women's political participation around the world—as well as the masses of information compressed within the pages of this text are impressive. Also offering many full-page illustrations of women and of women's work, the volume does seem to merit Shalala's accolade. It is not surprising that it has sold more than thirty-five thousand copies.[15]

Especially in light of the justifiable criticism that some women's studies practitioners carry "political correctness" and political ambitions to an absurd length—pledging to fight enemies such as "ablebodyism," "adultism," "looksism," and "sizeism"—it is worth remarking that the Hunter collective eschews such strained neologisms and states its goals in temperate terms. They acknowledge existing controversies within the field and recognize its condition as a work in progress. "The field of women's studies is still so new," the authors point out, that "it has no traditional subgrouping, no standard way of presenting materials, not even a general agreement about its definition." Especially noteworthy is their recognition that women's studies offers a basis for "criticism in both *moral* and practical terms" (emphasis added). The ethical dimensions of women's claims are insufficiently recognized in many discussions of feminism.[16]

A third approach to introducing women's studies to beginning students is reflected in another popular and recently reissued text, Sheila Ruth's *Issues in Feminism*. First published in 1980, this volume combines the author's commentaries on the sexually asymmetrical, "patriarchal" images, beliefs, and social institutions affecting women's lives with dozens of selections from authors both traditional and famous, recent and revisionist. Students may read Aristotle, Aquinas, Rousseau, and Freud along with Wollstonecraft and Beauvoir; Lionel Tiger and Friedrich Engels as well as Susan Brownmiller and Elizabeth Janeway. A 1977 excerpt from an article by Ruth Bader Ginsburg which appeared in the American Bar Association's journal was included in the first edition, more than a decade before Ginsburg's appointment to the United States Supreme Court.

As its title suggests, this volume focuses on women's subordination and their efforts toward gaining equality. It, too, is packed with information and introduces women's work and words. Drawing her material broadly from many disciplines, Ruth takes her lead conceptually from philosophy. She hopes to engage students through a "shock of the [re]appraisal" of their experiences, in a Socratic process of questioning, assessing multiple responses, and pressing further into ambiguities and unknowns. The book ends with a chronology of women's history in America, from the birth of Virginia Dare in 1587 and the Constitution of the Iroquois Confederation (which gave women important powers) to President Carter's creation in 1977 of a National Commission on International Women's Year, and the related National Women's Conference held that year in Houston. A third edition, published in 1995, continues the chronology through 1993, when Ruth Bader Ginsburg became the second female justice of the U.S. Supreme Court. Sheila Ruth also adopts the first person plural in her commentary, but in the latest edition she indicates a new awareness of her "own particularity."[17]

In teaching women's studies, at all levels (as chapter 4 will explore) but especially at the introductory level, pedagogical principles and classroom dynamics are often considered to be of equal importance with the text. At the NWSA's National Conference in 1995, a session entitled "Strategies for Teaching Introduction to Women's Studies" attracted fifty participants to explore a series of basic questions. They sought to locate women's studies in relation to the history of knowledge and its various disciplinary domains; to issues of class and race; to student concerns based on stereotypes of feminism (especially as lesbian and antimale); and to concerns about academic standards. Like the leading texts in the field, the speakers agreed that the introductory course should begin by defining women's studies and feminism and their relationship. It should then review individual and social behavior, examine the female life cycle through socialization, family, marriage and other relationships, and aging; and include issues of education, language, media, religion, law, violence against women, work, and feminist efforts toward change. The importance of recognizing "multiple voices speaking on every issue" was underscored by the discussion leaders. Possibly defying a common assumption, an underlying thread of agreement in this discussion was the recognition that the tens of thousands of students flocking to women's studies courses are there not to hear their political beliefs confirmed but to seek and engage new perspectives. Few are self-proclaimed feminists.[18]

Introductory courses may be structured around women's studies' scholarship across the disciplines or may be framed to focus on feminist issues. But is there a standard body of material to be taught, a canon, a "knowledge base"? The answer at this stage in the development of the field is mostly negative. "No, let there not be!" said a majority at one large, public university in the Southeast, to the question of a canon. The same group, however, agreed that a knowledge base does exist. Following the responses to their survey of instructors in women's studies and crosslisted courses, this group identified five concepts that they deemed essential:

—*the systematic, interlocking oppression of women;*
—*women's varied relations to patriarchy;*
—*the social construction of gender;*
—*the social construction of knowledge; and*
—*the redefining and reconceptualizing of women's power and empowerment.*[19]

From an examination of its courses and curricula, women's studies emerges as a project in critical thinking. "What I found in women's studies was a body of knowledge that taught me to question not only the answers, but also the questions," reported a women's studies graduate at one of the larger urban public institutions, this one also on the East Coast.[20] At this stage, it can be fairly said that women's studies queries every notion impinging on women's experience and, at the present, houses under its rubric far more good questions than definitive answers.

It was this critical, problem-centered approach that led Florence Howe, one of the founders of the women's studies movement as well as the founder (in 1972) and still the publisher of the *Women's Studies Quarterly*, to advocate women's studies as a particularly appropriate way to advance the goals of liberal education.[21] Similarly, the AAC's 1988 report, *A New Vitality in General Education*, credits women's studies' pervasive questioning of conventional wisdom with having "motivated an emphasis on accurate development, analysis, synthesis, and theory building."[22] The extensive inclusion of women's studies courses in general education programs seems to confirm these views. The administrators of women's studies programs at two comprehensive universities on the West Coast recently described their programs as the "workhorses of general education."[23]

Defining Parameters

Women's studies, however, is more than a useful way to enrich liberal education. It adopts a particular approach to the study of women. Within women's studies it is generally understood and accepted that not every course about women belongs in women's studies. Women's studies, it is said, is for women as well as about them. Its relationship to feminism is usually stated explicitly. The popular, and even the academic, media may use the term *women's studies* loosely to encompass any woman's deed or product of a female hand: the *Chronicle of Higher Education* recently, in its weekly survey of new academic books, reported publications on "pregnancy in a high tech age" and *The Autobiography of an Aspiring Saint* under the women's studies rubric, and the *San Francisco Examiner* termed a portrait of female baby-boomers by Susan Cheever a "mere footnote to the growing shelf of women's studies."[24] With such a range of material, and so much of the women's studies curriculum based in traditional departments over which women's studies instructors exercise little control, the question frequently arises as to which courses may be designated as women's studies and may be taken by students to fulfill requirements in women's studies degree programs.

The question of what makes a course "women's studies" is not simple. What content distinguishes women's studies as a field of study? Can the new scholarship be integrated into a "mainstream" without changing the latter's direction—that is, revising the discipline? Can anybody teach it? Would the new scholarship still be women's studies if taught by just any instructor, possibly a nonfeminist one? Must pedagogy as well as content reflect feminist principles? Does women's studies depend on distinctive research methodology? When should courses that are in the disciplines but have titles that indicate that they are about women be crosslisted in women's studies curricula? Does everything about *all* women belong in women's studies? These questions appear and reappear in many contexts—in discussions of curriculum and pedagogy, of staffing and structure, and of theory and practice. They will surface again in several chapters below.

The answers reveal more openness to diversity of approach than critics sometimes assume. They reflect a challenge that, along with some of its other most vexing issues, women's studies shares with many other multidisciplinary fields. Defining women's studies is similar to defining American studies, environmental studies, and religious studies. Lacking a full-time faculty of their own, interdisciplinary programs as a rule find curricular planning, class scheduling, and quality control to be sources of frustration. For women's studies, however, controversy tends to center around feminist perspectives as well as course content—and to a lesser extent, around pedagogical practices as well. To the degree that women's studies is expected to incorporate a critical perspective, exploit new sources, adopt inclusive vocabulary, stress diversity, and employ classroom techniques designed to empower students, then not just any class on women will do. However feminism is defined, at least a minimal awareness of the ethical dimensions of feminist claims is expected, and efforts to teach about women, gender, and feminist theory from a nonfeminist perspective are rare. In one notable case that attracted national attention, Elizabeth Fox-Genovese, a former director of the women's studies program at Emory University, in Atlanta, attempted to maintain this stance. According to Fox-Genovese, "women and gender are not necessarily feminist in outlook." To some critics, the implicit if not always explicit feminist commitment of women's studies betrays an ideological bias that fits poorly with their view of the academy. For them, terms such as *feminist theory, feminist methodology,* and *feminist research* undermine women's studies' claim to an equal place in the academy.[25]

The problem of establishing parameters for women's studies has received considerable attention in recent years. Drawing on work originally done by Jean O'Barr, women's studies director at Duke University, the Project on the Status and Education of Women (PSEW) of the AAC in 1988 published a questionnaire, "Evaluating Courses for Inclusion of New Scholarship on Women." Its purpose, according to the authors, was not to develop grounds for the exclusion of courses from a curriculum. Rather, working from the assumption that the liberal arts "remained relatively untouched by women's studies" and that most students, therefore, continued to be educated without any awareness of the new scholarship on women, PSEW proposed that the publication of guidelines for an evaluation of course content and class format geared to the new work would encourage its acceptance and diffusion. The questions covered many matters, including the extent to which women appeared as subjects and as authors in various components of the course and the way in which they were depicted, individually as well as according to differences of sex, ethnicity, power, and perspective.[26]

Between 1992 and 1996, the topic of policies for crosslisting courses appeared several times as a thread on the e-mail list WMST-L. It began with a query (under the subject line "We are new at this!") by an assistant professor of sociology at a public university in Kentucky, then attempting to establish a minor program in women's studies. "Some members of the committee," she wrote, "advocate including any course which currently has 'woman' in the title. Others are more concerned about content"; the latter wanted to establish criteria according to which syllabi would be submitted for committee review and approval. The discussions engaged participants from Maryland to California, and from Maine to Virginia. The responses included several sets of criteria for "core" and "affiliated" courses, with "stricter standards" suggested for the former. Most of the criteria mentioned the extent to which the courses dealt with women, prepared students to identify and analyze stereotyped assumptions and biases about women, incorporated the new feminist scholarship, and employed pedagogy that encouraged "active learning." Several of the responses included an open-ended inquiry about why a proposed syllabus constituted a "women's studies course rather than just a course about women or gender," or about whether courses would be taught from a "feminist or nonsexist" point of view. Others looked for awareness of the diversity of women's experiences.[27]

Joan Korenman, director of women's studies at the University of Maryland, Baltimore County (UMBC), and manager of the list, shared her program's position. "We do not ask or even desire that faculty toe a narrow ideological line; we do ask that courses designated WMST be informed by contemporary Women's Studies scholarship and provide students with an understanding of feminist perspectives." The women's studies committee at UMBC asks for a course description or syllabus, including the list of readings and a summary of teaching methods—all of which are questions typically asked by curriculum committees about any new course—and poses three further questions:

1. *Is the central focus of the course gender roles, women's issues, and/or the status of or portrayal of women in history, the arts, or the sciences? Please explain.*
2. *How does the course material reflect knowledge of contemporary feminist scholarship about women?*
3. *Why do you think that this is a Women's Studies course rather than just a course about women or gender?*[28]

None of the respondents in this discussion proposed a strongly directive stance. However, other scholars have suggested a feminist teaching model that starts with the assumption that the women's studies classroom is a "laboratory of feminist principles." Their table of thirteen guiding assumptions includes the preference that a women's studies course "deal with women only and treat women as the norm"; in addition, "if at all possible, the primary coordinators of the course should be women." This more directive approach would also extend to the use of female-gendered language in a generic sense as "an effective teaching-learning tool" and create opportunities for women and men to separate for part of the class time. Mostly, however, these guidelines emphasize that teaching and learning in women's studies should reflect the goals of "connected learning," as discussed in chapter 4.[29]

The only mention of having used such criteria to reject a course came from a private Midwestern research university, whose faculty were reported to be "quite comfortable" with not crosslisting a course about women taught by a professor who described herself as nonfeminist. This program had consciously adopted the name "women's studies" rather than "women studies" on the grounds that it emphasized a feminist stance.[30] For every attempt to exclude, however, one finds in women's studies countless calls for inclusion. It is worth noting both that self-selection among faculty, more than deliberate exclusion of women or men, probably accounts for the overwhelming predominance of female feminist instructors in women's studies, and that many women's studies programs do include courses taught by men.

The Discipline and Department Question

The issue of crosslisting is critical for women's studies because so few of its courses are controlled by faculty whose primary tenure location is in a women's studies program or department. Questions of institutional structure and control, therefore, take on a highly consequential role in determining what is offered—who teaches and what is taught—and often, what is seen as defining women's studies. Institutional arrangements may also carry ideological freight. From the early days—witness Sheila Tobias's questions in *Female Studies I*—it was clear that how the new field of study was organized was of major importance. Since the early leaders saw the goals as transformation of not only curriculum and university but also the lives of women, as well as culture and society, they assumed that the standard departmental structure would not do. Drawing on her background in the "free university" movement of the 1960s, Florence Howe feared that women might "rest content with their piece of turf rather than turn their energetic movements into strategies for changing the university as a whole." Another important early voice, that of the historian Gerda Lerner (later president of the Organization of American Historians), declared that women's studies' "all-encompassing challenge cannot be approached by a narrow disciplinary focus." At San Francisco State, the women's studies board initially chose "to *not* work towards a separate 'Women's Studies' department since our major purpose is the recognition of women's important 'place' at every level in all disciplines rather than its 'special' character."[31] Allusions to the potential dire effects of women's studies becoming a "ghetto" were common. The influential poet Adrienne Rich wrote in 1977 that "the universities and the intellectual establishment intend to keep women's experience as far as possible invisible, and women's studies a barely subsidized, condescendingly tolerated ghetto."[32] The linkages among institutional organization, the allocation of resources, and the achievement of academic influence have led to the rethinking of such assumptions. As the novelist Marge Piercy stated recently, "I wrote an essay in 1969 arguing against the creation of women's studies departments, because I thought it would further marginalize women and prevent us from changing existing disciplines. I was wrong."[33]

In the late 1970s there was in the United States probably only one full-fledged department of women's studies, the one at San Diego State University. However, the absence of departments was probably more the result of timing than of the early warnings against ghettoization, or of any theoretical argument against separatism. Women's studies emerged in higher education precisely as a long-sustained period of growth ended; and, equally telling, as humanities and social science departments were beginning to experience massive losses of enrollment to business-related and other vocationally oriented fields. In many cases it was primarily the appeal of courses on women to large numbers of students that accounted for the willingness of skeptical administrators to invest in it even marginally. Taught to a considerable extent by temporary and junior faculty, if not graduate students, the courses came cheap. At a time when cost effectiveness loomed increasingly large as a factor in academic planning, women's studies courses, taught by lower-paid faculty to burgeoning classes, attracted positive administrative attention. Growth followed enrollment patterns, and by default women's studies on most campuses took the shape of loosely coordinated interdisciplinary programs. As chair of the department at San Diego State from 1974 to 1980, I watched closely as very occasionally, but with increasing frequency, authors of articles in women's studies in journal publications and elsewhere identified themselves as members of *departments* of women's studies.[34]

There were good reasons, practical as well as theoretical, for the trend, which has continued. In most universities, resources, rewards, and recognition follow departmental lines. Advocates of departmentalization stress its normative aspects—"funding agencies understand 'department'"—and the decision-making power it confers. After a transition from program status to department, one women's studies chair declared, "The survivalist days are over." The director of another long-standing program with recently elevated status said that her department could now look beyond "the quilting years."[35] For faculty, the best argument for departmentalization is probably the need for a community of scholars with shared intellectual interests who can stimulate, criticize, and support each other's work. For students, it is the need for focus and validation, for a figurative as well as literal place within the large, bureaucratic institutions where most of them today study, a place that helps them to feel at home in the academy. Without women's studies programs (or departments), the sources of scholarship for transformation might not dry up—its springs seeming to arise virtually everywhere—but much of the wealth it produces might be marginalized, for it does not, by definition, fit the old categories into which knowledge has long been compartmentalized.

Today women's studies at San Francisco State, in response to its explicit request in 1990, is a department, but the network model still predominates elsewhere. According to a listing posted on WMST-L in 1995, and my own findings, there may be only twenty programs with formal departmental status. However, the number of departments increases regularly, as practitioners discover the facts of university life: resources (especially faculty lines) and rewards (including tenure, promotion, and important committee assignments) tend to follow departmental lines. Departmentalization is now acknowledged as a strategy suited to the long haul. It may offer a measure of security against budget cuts in tough times. It reduces the danger of trivialization: "a day [of] now we do women," as an online communicator argued recently. It recognizes that the task of transformation will require decades, and likely generations, of research, teaching, and the slow change in consciousness that follows the diffusion of new knowledge.[36]

If departments remain scarce, tenure lines dedicated exclusively to women's studies are also rare. This is a fact with major consequences for women's studies. Most coursework in women's studies continues to be offered by faculty trained in the traditional disciplines, appointed to traditional departments, and hired, reviewed, and evaluated according to the usual departmental criteria. Few campuses allocate more than a handful of positions fully to women's studies programs or departments. Because of variation in the ways that instructional, research, and administrative positions are defined at different institutions, comparisons among them are apt to be misleading. However, it appears that eight lines, with tenure home attached, are controlled solely by women's studies at Arizona State University; the University of Maryland, College Park; San Diego State University; and the University of South Florida. The University of Arizona (where women's studies recently became a department) has ten, the University of Minnesota anticipates having an equal number soon, and the University of Washington has nine, but in each of these three instances, several positions are shared with other departments. A number of programs have four to seven, but many have fewer lines established solely in women's studies. According to a recent survey, the majority of women's studies programs and departments still house no full-time faculty positions.[37] Joint appointments and/or split assignments appear to be the most common way of staffing women's studies programs; the average program has eighteen affiliated faculty who teach crosslisted courses. Institutional structure affects virtually every academic, political, and professional issue in women's studies.

The trend toward departmentalization probably reflects both a backing away from emphasis on the more radically transformative goals of changing university structures, and women's studies' striking success in institutionalizing itself. In addition, it is likely that until recently, few if any women's studies faculty had a choice. Women's studies programs developed along the lines of least resistance; and in almost all cases this meant that courses that included subject matter dealing with women were established here and there across the disciplines. With minimal if any independent fiscal resources, the best way to put together a program was to collect the scattering of courses developed in various departments, to label them women's studies through crosslisting (if possible), to establish a committee of faculty (often also students and staff and sometimes community representatives as well), and to seek recognition as an interdisciplinary program.

But institutional structure is more than a matter of politics, resources, and institutional power. It also carries important intellectual and professional connotations. Jill Ker Conway, a former president of Smith College, reflecting on the beginnings of academic feminism at the University of Toronto, recalls that she opposed establishment of a separate curriculum in women's studies because

> *I thought it a basic error in strategy to allow those, almost exclusively women, who wanted to study women's experience to be driven out of the core disciplines of the humanities and social sciences, segregated in a separate underfunded department without sponsors in the expense allocation process of the university, and so swamped with students that their research output could often not be competitive with more traditional faculty. This led to what I thought of as specious ideologies about*

"feminist" or excessively nurturant teaching styles as a justification for less real research. Overly nurturant teaching, from which all overt criticism has been removed, seemed to me to run the same danger for the young as permissive child rearing.[38]

While Conway points to a real problem, namely the heavy expectations for service to students or to the institution that pioneering faculty (minorities as well as women) sometimes face, she does not touch on the more important issues surrounding the debate over "autonomy or integration." The question of diffusion of the new scholarship has two dimensions. At one level, it requires a decision on whether to integrate the material throughout the curriculum, infusing women's studies into all courses, or to create separate courses, including (as appropriate) surveys, topical studies, and research seminars. At the next level, a choice lies between coursework bearing the rubrics of traditional departments and a separately constituted administrative unit for women's studies. This latter argument is often couched in terms not of "department" but of "discipline." The high stakes of disciplinary status as well as the intriguing intellectual debate over the definition of disciplines have elicited extensive discussion of this issue.

"Is Women's Studies an Academic Discipline?" was the title of a session at the first annual meeting of the NWSA in 1979. This question helped to frame discussion throughout the decade of the 1980s and remains an important issue in the 1990s. (See chapter 3 for a corollary debate over whether women's studies should aim to be "mainstreamed.") According to one view, separate women's studies programs represent a ghetto that could hinder achievement of the long-term goal of transforming higher education. Women's studies might become a discipline housed in a department of its own and might devolve into a kind of latter-day home economics (a field that, a century earlier, had also begun with a feminist impulse). Women's studies should instead aim to serve as a stage in the transformation of all knowledge. The historian Nancy Cott argued that "in the long term, women's studies will not be necessary from a separate perspective because the perspective that it suggests will become the normal one, that is, a perspective in which women are as much recognized as men are." Cott defined "long term" as "fifty years or so."[39]

Others pointed out that, without scholars devoted full-time to research and teaching in the field, women's studies would never develop sufficiently to attain that new normality. The historian Sandra Coyner felt that it would profit the new scholarship more to discard the concept of interdisciplinarity altogether and take on the identity of an academic discipline like all others—others that, she pointed out, were no more "pure" than women's studies in any epistemological or methodological sense. Let's just call ourselves a discipline, she told her audience. "Just use the words. When people ask your discipline, say 'Women's Studies.' Refer to everybody else as the 'other' disciplines." The appropriate administrative unit for a discipline was, of course, a department. Coyner hoped to see older disciplinary boundaries crossed to the extent that a faculty member might teach courses on "Women in American History, Psychology of Women, The Family, and a Women's Studies survey or seminar." Preparation for faculty would include the Ph.D. degree in women's studies.[40]

The importance of interdisciplinary perspectives to women's studies is evident in the titles of undergraduate courses offered as electives by most programs. A sampling would include courses such as the core offered at San Francisco State University, all of which are expected to include perspectives drawn from multiple disciplines:

WOMS 200 *Women: The Basic Questions*
WOMS 301 *Women in Groups*
WOMS 302 *Translating Women's Experience*
WOMS 303 *Woman as Creative Agent*
WOMS 400 *Critical Analysis and Feminist Research*

Other multidisciplinary courses in this program include

WOMS 552 *Lesbian Lives and Thought*
WOMS 591 *Aging: The Older Woman*
WOMS 611 *Female Sexuality: Social and Theoretical Perspectives*
WOMS 630 *Matriarchy/Patriarchy*
WOMS 750 *Issues of Gender, Race, Class, Sexuality*

and a number of courses dealing with women of various ethnicities. In discussing such courses, the term *interdisciplinary* is employed where *multidisciplinary* might be more descriptive. These terms coexist with statements calling women's studies itself a discipline.

After discussing the ways in which women's studies is both like and unlike other "disciplines," Jean Fox O'Barr concluded that it is *both* a discipline and an interdisciplinary field."[41] On closer examination, this seemingly oxymoronic statement can be seen to reflect the pervasive confusion between departments and disciplines which exists within higher education, as well as the evolutionary process through which subjects such as economics, political science, and psychology came to be considered disciplines. Many fields typically described as disciplines address multiple subject matters and use a variety of research methods. This is true, for example, of anthropology, biology, and classics. For women's studies, the problem of structure is both practical and intellectual. According to Claire Moses of the University of Maryland, College Park, women's studies on that campus maintains a dual status as both a department and a program. It gains thereby the perquisites of a department while enjoying the opportunities for collaboration afforded by the interdisciplinary program model.[42] In chapter 3, I will discuss some of the implications of structure for the movement to change the traditional curriculum.

Graduate Education and Research Centers

Graduate work in women's studies began early and is now well established. In 1970 the Union Institute, a university centered in Cincinnati which offers doctoral study through a widely dispersed faculty and seminars presented across the country, added an "emphasis" in women's studies to its interdisciplinary program. Sarah Lawrence College launched its master's program in women's history in 1972, the same year that George Washington University first offered its M.A. degree in women's studies. Clark Atlanta University (then called Atlanta University) initiated a doctor of arts degree in Africana women's studies in 1982. By 1994, according to a NWSA report, graduate programs existed in thirty-eight states and the District of Columbia, with the master's degree offered in women's studies at about fourteen institutions and jointly, as an emphasis or concentration, with other programs at more than fifty institutions. Three universities indicated that they offered interdisciplinary doctoral degrees in "women's studies," and an additional twenty-plus indicated that they offered a minor or concentration at the doctoral level in one or more disciplinary fields.[43] In May 1995, an international conference on graduate education in women's studies was held at York University in Ontario, where freestanding master's and Ph.D. degrees were launched in 1992. Clark University in Massachusetts, Emory University in Atlanta, and York, the three universities in North America where the interdisciplinary Ph.D. could be taken as of 1996, were joined recently by the University of Iowa and the University of Minnesota, where Ph.D. proposals were approved the following year. A doctorate of education (Ed.D.) in women's studies is offered at Northern Colorado University.

Discussions about graduate education commanded major attention at a conference of women's studies program administrators held at Arizona State University (ASU) in February 1997. Representatives of a number of major research universities in the Midwest and the East indicated that Ph.D. proposals were underway on their campuses, affirming a 1997 survey of the field whose author declared that "doctoral work in women's studies is, gloriously, in an expansionist mode." This report, by Ann Shteir of York University, added the University of Michigan and the University of Toronto to the list of universities where Ph.D. programs are available in particular disciplines, and referred to interdisciplinary doctorates in the final stages of development at Iowa and the University of Washington. The University of Maryland has announced similar plans.[44] Numerous other programs now offer Ph.D. minors, doctoral certificates, and coursework from which doctoral degrees are likely to emerge. As more and more students graduate with women's studies undergraduate or master's level degrees, and a very considerable proportion (a majority, according to one study) continue on for further education, the demand for doctoral programs may be expected to increase.

In developing doctoral-level degree programs, university faculty address challenging intellectual, political, and economic issues. Depending on their perspectives about discipline-based education and their definition of interdisciplinarity, they may envision a freestanding program or one that involves collaboration among departments. They may require grounding, and even preliminary degrees and/or a Ph.D. concentration, in a traditional discipline, as at Emory University; or, as at Clark University, they may mandate seminars and coursework in one or more broad multidisciplinary areas such as geography, environment, and development; language, literature, and the arts; and history, psychology, and society.

Fundamental questions about the role of disciplinary methodology and interdisciplinary contributions to the production of knowledge play a

part in determining the kinds of doctoral degrees proposed and the requirements established. So also do questions about marketability. "Will we ourselves hire candidates with interdisciplinary degrees as faculty colleagues?"
asked an administrator at the ASU conference. A survey undertaken as part
of the Ph.D. proposal process at the University of Iowa found that over a
three-year period, an average of fifty positions for faculty with specialization in women's studies appeared in the *Chronicle of Higher Education*
and/or the *Women's Review of Books*. Iowa planned a broadly conceived
and strenuous program requiring no fewer than seventy-two semester hours
in graduate-level coursework, including seven core courses, a number of
electives, and a disciplinary concentration of at least eighteen semester
hours. As instructors the program could draw on six "appointed faculty,"
four "associated faculty," and forty-eight "affiliated faculty" in the College
of Liberal Arts, plus seven others housed in other schools and colleges. The
university could, the proposers pointed out with good reason, "realistically
aspire to educate some of the first and finest Ph.D.'s in the field."[45]

Through doctoral programs in women's studies, further progress will
likely be made in defining the field and determining answers to questions
of (inter)disciplinarity. Similarly, relationships among traditional and innovative teaching and learning methods, new research and pedagogical approaches, uses of internships and service learning, and strategies for dealing
with issues of governance and structure will all be highlighted for creative
attention through women's studies. Like other developing (and mature) academic fields, women's studies may be expected to struggle over issues of criteria and standards. The extent to which it will follow conventional paths
cannot be predicted, of course; but the statement, made by an administrator at the ASU conference, that women's studies programs should be ranked
nationally in the customary manner of research-oriented departments suggests new ambitions on the part of some academic leaders in the field.

What do these developments mean for higher education? Many historians have pointed out that research on women is not new. As the sociologist Jessie Bernard noted, "Courses about, by, and for women have a long
academic history." She cited especially two "traditions," home economics
and social service—noting, however, that they differed in respect to feminist orientation. Even feminist women's studies as an integrated course of
study offering multidisciplinary instruction about women had a predecessor in a course on "feminology" offered by Mme. Souley-Darqué at the
Collège libre des sciences sociales in Paris in about 1902.[46] What is unprece-

dented, however, in addition to the thousands of courses in which the new knowledge about women is taught, is surely the scope of the enterprise devoted to conducting women's studies research, to discussing it at academic conferences, to publishing it in established, mainstream journals as well as newer reviews, and to preserving it in libraries and diffusing it through media both traditional and innovative. Degrees in women's studies, topped by the doctorate, signal the point where these quantitative changes require a new map of the educational landscape.

The rapid growth of women's studies programs across the country has helped to spur the development of an extensive institutional base. Among the organizations overseeing its growth is the National Council for Research on Women (NCRW). Founded in 1981, the council describes itself as "the central source for information that can change the lives of women and girls." The NCRW counts as members seventy-five research centers, councils, and projects in twenty-four states, plus fourteen organizations in the District of Columbia. All but a handful were founded after 1970. Most are affiliated with institutions of higher education, and according to a survey conducted in the early 1980s, they supported or sponsored a combined research and operating staff of more than one thousand and commanded a median budget of $350,000.[47]

One of the NCRW's oldest members, the Mary Ingraham Bunting Institute at Radcliffe College, which dates from 1960, owes its foundation to concern over the struggles of women to gain higher education in the 1950s. The high dropout rate of female doctoral candidates attracted attention during the studies of "scientific manpower" that followed the Soviet launching of *Sputnik* in 1957, and helped Bunting, a Ph.D. bacteriologist who was appointed as Radcliffe's president in 1960, to raise substantial funds in support of a new institute designed to facilitate independent research studies by (not about) women. The Bunting Institute has supported numerous scholars-in-residence doing research on American women based on the collections of Radcliffe's Arthur and Elizabeth Schlesinger Library on the History of Women in America, which dates from 1943.[48] The neighboring Center for Research on Women at Wellesley College, founded in 1974, draws on that institution's tradition of faculty and student activism and emphasizes applied social science and policy studies. Many of its published working papers and conferences have focused on issues of employment, labor force segregation, women's roles in economic development, and the like. Its list of authors and project directors includes many who have served in important governmental posts. This is also true of the Center for the American Woman and Politics at Rutgers University's Eagleton Institute of Politics, which dates from 1971; and the Center for Women Policy Studies, in Washington, D.C., founded in 1972.[49]

Across the country, Stanford University's Institute for Research on Women and Gender (IRWG), founded in 1974 (as the Center for Research on Women), provided a model research center with a broad-based interdisciplinary women's studies focus. Instituted with support from the Ford Foundation, Stanford's was the first of a dozen centers that received Ford funding as part of a program to build a solid institutional base for women's studies. Centered in a house on campus, the IRWG provides institutional support and a home base for Stanford faculty as well as a small core of "affiliated" scholars and a rotating series of visiting scholars, altogether now numbering about two hundred, who comprise an important international network. Their work is featured in seminars, lectures, and conferences offered by the IRWG to academic and community audiences. Along with more tangible help (library access and clerical and research assistance), these scholars enjoy what the NCRW's founding president Mariam Chamberlain deems most critical, a supportive academic community. "Mutual support was particularly essential," she states, "in the early days of the research centers when the academic community was hostile to women's studies."[50]

The IRWG's roster today reflects a changed academic world. It includes a Guggenheim fellow, scholars who hold prestigious endowed chairs, authors of prize-winning books, and at least one university president. The institute is supported in part by Stanford University and in part by donations from corporations, foundations, and individuals, including dozens of leaders representing virtually every area of business, education, and industry. Numerous articles, books, and special issues of scholarly journals have appeared under the auspices of the IRWG. The institute's national advisory board and its "associates" groups in New York and Los Angeles serve to enhance its outreach and bring the work of its scholars to a public audience (see chapter 9).

Another beneficiary of the Ford Foundation, the Southwest Institute for Research on Women (SIROW), located at the University of Arizona, was founded in 1979 as a regional center. Now linked with thirty campuses in six states as well as two institutions in northern Mexico, SIROW has led efforts to broaden the scope of research to include rural women, Chicanas, and Native American women, as well as other women of the Southwest and border regions. It has attracted numerous federal and foundation grants that have enabled it to sponsor a wide range of research, events, and publications.[51] The first women's studies research center at a historically black institution, the Spelman College Women's Center, received initial support from both the Ford Foundation and the Charles Stewart Mott Foundation. In 1988, the Ford Foundation established a competitive grant program to support the institutionalization of minority women's studies.

In 1992, the NCRW's Chamberlain, who had also served as a program officer at the Ford Foundation and chair of the Russell Sage Foundation Task Force on Women in Higher Education, and Alison Bernstein, then at Princeton University but long affiliated with major private and public funding agencies and recently appointed as vice-president at the Ford Foundation, published an important article tracing the impact of philanthropy on the emergence of women's studies. They credit the Ford Foundation, along with others concerned to advance civil rights and promote education, with providing through their grant-making activities both recognition and material sustenance that helped defy the prophecy that women's studies would be a passing fad. Having supported curricular change since the 1950s and 1960s, the Ford Foundation had been an early promoter of both foreign area studies and black studies. It had shown concern for women's opportunities since the 1940s and began affirmative action in its own ranks in 1970. In 1972 it established a national program in support of faculty and dissertation research on topics related to women. Beyond providing financial support for innovative work, this program helped at a critical time to legitimize women's studies as a field of scholarly endeavor. Other foundations, including the Carnegie, Rockefeller, and Russell Sage Foundations, as well as the National Endowment for the Humanities, soon followed suit. But it was the Ford Foundation, which had, according to Bernstein and Chamberlain, provided $22 million of the $36 million in private funds spent to that date on women's studies, that deserves the most credit for its contributions to the new field.

Support from the Ford Foundation also helped to sustain the Feminist Press, whose publications furnished teaching ideas, course materials, and communication channels for women's studies practitioners, and provided a planning grant to the organizers of the NWSA. Rounding out the range of its assistance to constituent parts of the new field, the Ford Foundation helped as well to launch *Signs*, published by the University of Chicago Press and the foremost scholarly interdisciplinary journal in women's studies. No doubt this record of strong foundation support encouraged government agencies, including the Department of Education's Fund for the Improvement of Postsecondary Education (FIPSE) and the Women's Educational Equity Act program, to look favorably upon grant proposals in women's studies.[52]

By the mid 1980s, when Catharine R. Stimpson, founding editor of *Signs*, announced in a report to the Ford Foundation that "women's studies has changed the intellectual landscape of many traditional disciplines," the new field was strong enough to survive Reagan-era cutbacks in federal support and the attacks mounted by conservative critics such as William Bennett and Allan Bloom. Stimpson, who left Barnard College to become a professor and graduate dean at Rutgers University and went on to serve as director for the MacArthur Foundation's fellowship program, is now dean of the graduate school of arts and sciences at New York University. The Ford Foundation recently awarded the first grants in a new program designed to incorporate women's studies into global area studies. According to its program officer, the new initiative "provides an international lens on women's studies and a gender lens on the area programs." Recipients include Spelman College in Atlanta, the State University of New York at Albany, the University of Arizona, the University of Maryland, the University of Wisconsin, and the "Five Colleges" group in western Massachusetts (Amherst, Hampshire, Mt. Holyoke, Smith, and the University of Massachusetts), all institutions housing women's studies research centers.[53] Venerable and prestigious philanthropic organizations, along with private donors who respond to university development efforts, continue to help women's studies transform higher education.

From radical beginnings in the free classes of an antiestablishment political movement, women's studies has developed into an integral part of American higher education and of the network of private and public institutions that support it. Like no other educational movement in recent history, it has begun to change human consciousness—not in the ways that the experimenters who sought to expand mental awareness in the 1960s might have envisioned, but in more profound—and likely to be permanent—ways. Women's studies is developing everywhere.

In the more than twenty-five years since I taught my first class in women's history, I have watched women's studies grow from a few isolated courses to an international movement. While it is beyond the scope of this study to survey and assess the state of women's studies around the world, it is impossible, if one attends conferences and reads literature in the field, not to recognize that the fastest growth area today is abroad. An "international handbook" published in 1993 lists 108 countries as sites of women's studies courses, research centers, training programs, or publications. In Britain, women's studies courses date from the late 1960s; by 1992, the Women's Studies Network in the United Kingdom listed sixty-six institutions "offering several qualifying courses." A 1991 report showed fourteen university women's studies centers in Germany, ten in France, nine in Sweden, and five in Norway. Other Western European countries provide a "state budget" for women's studies or house libraries and journals. Feminist scholars in Eastern European countries moved quickly after 1989 to develop women's studies courses, which by 1996 were reported to exist in Belgrade, Budapest, Lodz, Moscow, Prague, St. Petersburg, Vilnius, Warsaw, Zagreb, and elsewhere in the former Communist countries, as well as in Ankara, Istanbul, and other cities in Turkey. Women's studies is well developed in Australia, Canada, New Zealand, and other English-speaking nations. Women's studies courses and/or centers, some dating from the late 1970s or early 1980s, exist in African and Asian countries including China, India, Japan, Kenya, Thailand, Uganda, and Vietnam. They appear in Argentina, Brazil, Costa Rica, Mexico, and a number of other Latin American countries. Specialized training courses for women and research focused on women are reported from several island nations as well. In 1995 Beverly Guy-Sheftall reported to the Ford Foundation on successful efforts to institutionalize women's studies in African, Arab, and Caribbean settings, often under Ford Foundation or United Nations auspices.[54]

The expansion of women's studies abroad both reflects and contributes to an increase in educational opportunities for girls and women. As it spreads around the globe, feminist-inspired education will necessarily take on different institutional forms and develop different types of curricula. Because many universities abroad do not offer undergraduate liberal education, women's studies has to a considerable extent developed at the graduate level or in research centers apart from institutions of higher education. It may well pursue other goals than it does in the United States, for feminisms express differing cultural values and relationships to modernization and nationalist movements. Academic feminism nevertheless will likely play a transformative role in women's, and men's, lives. Women's studies is a dynamic force that neither its proponents or its opponents can easily capture.

3

Questioning the Content of Higher Education

Florence Howe has characterized the women's studies movement as the third stage in a long encounter of American women with higher education. In the eighteenth century no institution for higher learning in the United States admitted women to its student body. In the early national period, following what the historian Linda Kerber labels "the great debate over the capacities of women's minds," women sought to gain admittance to seminaries and colleges where they were likely to be offered a separate course of study for "ladies." In the late nineteenth century, they demanded access to the "men's curriculum," a claim that was posed with special intensity at newly founded women's colleges and was followed by an extended period of putative "co-education" in the many institutions that increasingly accepted students of both sexes. Several generations of women both took and taught the men's curriculum, believing all the while in what Howe terms the "myths of coeducation." Quoting the late historian Joan Kelly, Howe notes the phenomenon of a "new double vision" (with one eye seeing men, and the other seeing women) that in the late 1960s and 1970s led a more radical generation to challenge the content of what they now discerned to be "men's studies." In this third period, they demanded fundamental change in the courses and curricula that reinforced stereotypes about, and supported continuing discrimination against, women by perpetuating misinformation about and ignorance of women's history, lives, and perspectives. To remedy the flaws and fill the gaps, they created women's studies.[1]

In retrospect, the initial strategy of demanding terminology, topics, and even whole courses inclusive of women seems more modest than militant. As Annette Kolodny points out with reference to literary criticism, feminists were simply seeking "an honored berth on that ongoing intellectual journey." However, as the new converts peered into car after car, they found what they saw disturbing. Confirming Kelly's findings, they observed that sometimes women were missing altogether, sometimes women appeared only in images that reflected men's perspectives, and sometimes women's activities and everything considered feminine were devalued. But soon, traveling beyond rediscovered foremothers and asking what women had done in the male-defined world, they began to formulate new questions. As Elisabeth Young-Bruehl points out, they "made a revolution by adding to the query, What do women want? the question, How and by whom have women's wants been determined? It is one thing, for example, when a psychological study is conducted to try to assess differences between women and men, and quite another when the assumptions—the perceptual and conceptual biases—that shape such a study are themselves the object of study." In essence, the new women thinkers asked, Who's driving this train, where is it going, and why? Almost half a century after Virginia Woolf's famous query about the destination of the "procession of educated men," scholars in women's studies began to question whether they wanted only to join the parade or also to change its route and objective.[2] They questioned virtually everything about higher education.

The development of women's studies demonstrates the truth in the observation that "questions are instruments of perception." The process of challenging the "men's curriculum" began with new questions, which led to a search for new sources, new methods, new definitions, and new interpretations. In discipline after discipline, feminist scholars, mostly but not exclusively women, have applied the tools provided by the "masters" who trained them to examining the contents and structure of "the master's house." While Audre Lorde argued that "the master's tools will never dismantle the master's house," feminist scholars have wielded the instruments with sufficient skill to make a major impact on the academy. Though hardly a dismantling, refurnishing if not remodeling is well under way. Thousands of articles have been published in both disciplinary and interdisciplinary journals and in anthologies issued by numerous university and trade publishers. Large numbers of books have appeared, and virtually every scholarly press now promotes a women's (and gender) studies list. The sheer volume of publications suggests the impressive dimensions of the academic feminist enterprise and, to quote the subtitle of one volume, "the difference it makes."[3]

In that volume's lead essay on that "difference," Patricia Meyer Spacks discusses how Jane Austen was portrayed and the way in which Austen's work was assessed before and after the emergence of feminist criticism. She begins with a 1961 essay, "Jane Austen: A Depreciation," whose author observed Austen's neglect of the great events of history and pronounced her ideals to be "irredeemably humdrum" and her "ethical standards . . . monotonously subdued," presumably to match her "so narrowly and so contentedly confined" experience. Not quite two decades later, critics were pointing to Austen's "revolutionary" contribution, citing the "less obvious, nastier, more resilient and energetic female characters who enact her rebellious dissent from her culture." Spacks comments that it would be "difficult for men writing about that woman ever to sound quite the same again. . . . Feminist criticism, in other words, has provoked new debates: arguably the most important contribution any critical mode can make." "Never before in history," she observes, "have so many people declared so loudly that women *matter*." With that new consciousness, Spacks describes how she herself has begun to read Austen differently, now noticing—and not taking for granted—the "tiny stories of sexual betrayal embedded" in her work.[4]

This re-visioning process, through which Spacks, now a professor of English at the University of Virginia, became a feminist critic, is exemplary. A decade later, twenty well-published literary scholars, most of whom held tenured faculty positions at major research universities, described similar experiences in an anthology appropriately entitled *Changing Subjects.* From the interaction of their changing personal and professional lives emerged new subjects, new subjectivities, and a new field of academic endeavor. These scholars came of age with the rebirth of feminism, which, they reflected, "transformed our lives and our scholarship. We saw it as a growing point that enabled us to connect our deepest passions and energies with our work, to think more deeply and originally." These feminist scholars have renewed the meaning of the term *intellectuel engagé,* refusing what Yeats called the choice between "perfection of the life, or of the work" and fashioning in the intersection a new and distinctive field of literary criticism.[5]

By 1980 the immense scope of the women's studies project and the possibilities it provided were becoming clear. Nannerl O. Keohane—then a professor of political science at Stanford, later the president of Wellesley

College, and now the president of Duke University—commented, in an essay on the difference that women's studies might make in her field, that it was likely that "more would be learned about women and politics in the 1970s than in all previous decades of the history of the discipline combined." After identifying aspects of political science (such as the dominance of men in the public sphere that constituted its primary subject matter) that had contributed to the field's silence about women, she wondered why so little attention had been paid to the exceptions (why there was no *"eminence rose"* to parallel the *eminence grise*) or to the variety of ways in which basic categories such as authority might be exercised and experienced. The inclusion of women would serve to broaden the field to include material dealing with the participation of women in political life, the treatment of women by political theorists, the legal and moral issues related to women's concerns, the importance of language related to sex differences, and the structures of social and institutional power. There was plenty of "work cut out for us," she told her readers.[6]

The disciplines subject to feminist criticism are probably co-extensive with the intellectual concerns of the contemporary professoriate. Surveying just a few recent volumes on the impact of feminist research, one finds articles on anthropology, archaeology, art, biology, classics, economics, education, English, French, Spanish, ethnic studies, history, literary criticism, philosophy, political science, psychiatry, religious studies, sociology, theater, and more—especially if one includes subdisciplines and interdisciplinary fields. At least two publishers, Oxford University Press and Twayne Publishers, have established series devoted to the impact of feminism on disciplines in the arts and sciences. Twayne plans to publish

> volumes on anthropology, art history, bioethics, biology, classics, education, economics, film, history, law, literature, music, philosophy, political science, psychology, religion, sociology, and theater. . . . [The press] anticipate[s] that each one will combine the virtues of accessibility with original interpretations of central issues of gender, genre, methodology, and historical perspective. These are the questions that feminism has explicitly and implicitly unsettled in every field of knowledge, forcing us all to reconsider how we learn, how we choose what we learn, and how we change what and how we learn.[7]

Across the disciplines, scholars in women's studies have adopted strategies that can for the most part be categorized under a few rubrics that are often used to frame the inquiry. One typical anthology uses as section headings "The Articulation of Gender as an Analytical Category"; "Methodological Moves from Margin to Center"; "The Sticking Power of Stereotypes"; and "Paradigmatic Implications." Women's studies, often itself accused of bias, uses these means to assert a "lack of objectivity in science that has permitted an all-too-ready acceptance of what are essentially unproved explanations of unproved gender differences." Another collection of essays begins its table of contents with "Outsiders Within: Challenging the Disciplines," followed by "The Difference That Gender Makes" and "Feminism and the Politics of Intellectual Inquiry"; in the last section, "Dialogues: Feminist Scholarship and/in the Disciplines," the first section's challenge has turned to dialogue. From a mid-1990s perspective, the editors of this volume identify anthropology, literature, and history as fields "deeply transformed" by feminist scholarship; economics, political science, psychology, and sociology as less so; and, within language studies, French more than Italian or Spanish. They call attention as well to a "paradigm shift" within women's studies itself, due to recognition of the "particularity" of the "'woman' in women's studies." The profundity of the impact on the disciplines varies, they suggest, according to the degree to which the field itself is self-reflective. This may be one reason that women's studies has moved more slowly in the natural sciences. By the 1990s, however, Sue V. Rosser felt that feminism had stimulated new approaches to biological research and had "begun to play a substantial role in policies, funding, and technological development and application in areas of women's health, reproductive technologies, and the environment."[8]

The range of fields influenced by women's studies is likely to increase further as a result of efforts such as a new three-year project on "women and scientific literacy," sponsored by the Association of American Colleges and Universities with funding from the National Science Foundation. Its purpose is to "make science more attractive to women by integrating it into women's-studies courses and incorporating new scholarship on gender studies into the teaching of science and mathematics." Ten institutions, all with "strong" women's studies programs, were selected from among seventy-six applicants to participate.[9]

Women's studies has become increasingly visible in academic journals. In addition to examining feminist critiques of methodologies, interpretations, and "invisible paradigms," one multidisciplinary group assessed the impact of women's studies scholarship by analyzing patterns of publication of articles on women between 1966 and 1980 by the major journals in anthropology, education, history, literature, and philosophy. Their study of ten publications in each discipline provides suggestive data on feminist influence. Granting problems of definition, especially in anthropology, education, and literature, where dominant traditions encompassed the study of topics that might be assumed to have included woman-oriented analyses (e.g., kinship studies and mythology) but in fact most often did not, they counted publication rates by discipline as well as change at five-year intervals over the fifteen-year period. In the aggregate, the publication of articles on women increased dramatically. Between 1966–70 and 1971–75, the number almost doubled (from 32.6 articles per year to 63.2), rising to 84.6 by 1976–80 (constituting, however, just 5.31% at the highest). Among the five fields, the most pronounced change occurred in history, where the percentage of articles on women grew from 1.1 percent of all research published to 6.45 percent; and expanded in presence from four to all ten journals. In philosophy, the increase in number was much smaller—but began from a base of zero.[10] In view of the exponential growth of women's studies, a replication of this study today might well show dramatic change. Chapter 9 presents data on the increasing prevalence of Ph.D. dissertations (from which many publications ensue) in women's studies.

Academic feminism's encounters with the disciplines reflected its ambiguous stance and the often ambivalent position of its practitioners—located both within and in opposition to the traditional fields. For some the goal was simply to conduct research, to add knowledge about women to the canon, and to "mainstream" feminist scholarship, in order to gain legitimacy for women's studies. For others the new approach spanned disciplinary borders and engaged the foundations of all fields of knowledge. Using feminist criticism as the vehicle through which to assert radical attacks on the epistemological presuppositions, bodies of knowledge, and methodologies of the fields in which they were trained, some feminist scholars, influenced by European thinkers, participated in criticism of what they considered "master narratives" or "totalizing theories" that they associated with the Enlightenment. Others sought to recuperate the Enlightenment for feminism, pointing out the ways in which feminism itself depended on concepts and values derived from that intellectual source (see chapter 6).

Critics of the academy have attributed great influence to women's studies because of its challenge to the curriculum. The late Page Smith, a traditional if idiosyncratic historian concerned with the dangers of "presentism," specialization, relativism, and the decline of spiritual and universalistic values in the academy, saw women's studies as both symptom and cause. Commenting on the argument that female scholars should not study women because they lacked objectivity, Smith said, "What was laughable [in the traditional academicians' resistance to feminist criticism] was that it never occurred to white males to question *their* objectivity." Despite grave misgivings about its rapid growth and "imperialistic form" on his campus, Smith perceived women's studies as advancing his agenda: "It is difficult to overestimate the importance of women in undermining the academy's notion of 'objectivity.' . . . By accelerating the process of fragmentation, already far along, Women's Studies may force a re-evaluation of the whole of higher education." Smith also grudgingly credited academic feminists with being "the last utopians." For Claire Goldberg Moses, women's historian and long-time editor of *Feminist Studies,* and for the postmodernist literary scholar Leslie Wahl Rabine, academic feminism had major responsibility for what they term the "contemporary crisis of the disciplines, abetted and in large measure instigated by women's studies."[11]

Page Smith hoped that by "breaking the disciplines," women's studies would hasten the end of a century of increasing specialization. Using that provocative term as her title, Florence Howe has drawn an interesting parallel between the "transformation of the curriculum" by the newly emerging sciences in the late nineteenth century and the transformation sought by feminist scholars today. Only after the late-nineteenth-century battle did the disciplines now deemed "traditional" emerge to supplant an earlier, holistic, religious, and morally focused "discipline" that constituted higher learning (for an elite intended for leadership in the ministry, law, and society). The new "galaxy" of specialized disciplines, rapidly organized into departments, became today's powerful mainstream with which feminist scholars contend.[12]

Whether challenging or defending the traditional academic disciplines, partisans on both sides of the curricular debates tend to forget that "school subjects are constructions too." Jane Roland Martin, a philosopher of education, has examined what she terms "the dogma of god-given subjects," pointing out that people tend to recognize as a subject suitable for study "only those things which in the past have been considered suitable candidates for a general and a liberal education. There is a much greater range to choose from than we realize."

> *Neither Chairs, Hamburgers nor Humphrey Bogart has the ring of a bona fide subject to most of us. Yet if we shed our narrow frame of reference we realize not only that these can be subjects, but that they undoubtedly are—Chairs a subject in a curriculum for furniture makers, Hamburgers a subject in a curriculum for McDonald trainees, Humphrey Bogart a subject in a curriculum for film enthusiasts. Even a brief glance at the wide variety of curricula there are should convince us that anything can be a subject; that French, Mathematics and Physics can give way to Identity, Community and the Reality of Material Objects or to the Rights of Animals, Mary Queen of Scots and Dying.*
>
> *Anything can be a subject because subjects are made, not found. They are not "out there" waiting for us, but are human constructions.*

Martin goes on to discuss the judgments of "importance" that determine what "subject-entities" become subjects of study, and the ways in which teaching goals determine their usage. In another essay she traces the process through which a double standard may be applied in decisions concerning which subject-entities are chosen and which are seen to constitute a worthy "field of knowledge."[13]

Comparing politics and education, for example, Martin argues that while both exist as important social activities and institutions, only the former, taught as political science or government, has become accepted as a basic field of knowledge suitable for general or liberal education.

> *Why have curriculum makers favored politics as a subject-entity over education? Politics' advantage is that, considering it one of society's "productive" processes, North American culture has situated it in the public world and placed it in men's care. Education's problem is that even though school has moved it out of the private home and into the public world, it is seen as a "reproductive" societal process whose "natural" practitioners are still assumed to be women.*

In Martin's view, the exclusion or trivialization of women-dominated activities as subjects of study constitutes a kind of "hidden curriculum in the validation of one gender, its associated tasks, traits, and functions, and the denigration of the other." She would revise the definition of subjects of study and fields of knowledge to include not only women's studies but the "3 C's of caring, concern, and connection." "Compassion 101a need no more be listed in a school's course offerings than Objectivity 101a is now." But the definition of an educated person would be expanded, in the spirit of John Dewey, turning education into what Martin would call "a journey of integration, not alienation," which, in her opinion, it now is.[14]

Institutional Transformation Projects and Phase Theory

The use of radical rhetoric such as "breaking the disciplines" and the suggestion of fanciful ideas such as "Compassion 101a" are consistent with the far-reaching aspirations of women's studies' initial call for transformation not just of courses and curricula but also of institutions and societies. Women's studies advocates made Charlotte Bunch's comment that it was not enough to "add women and stir" into a feminist cliché.[15] They elaborated on it by repeating the geographer Janice Monk's observation that one could not "integrat[e] the concept of a round earth into a course that assumes a flat earth."[16] Adding the new scholarship on women to existing stores of knowledge would necessarily require fundamental change in the assumptions, interpretations, and structures that shape intellectual domains. New questions would have to be asked; new sources identified; new categories of analysis and methods of conducting research and interpreting evidence devised. No simple additive process would do. As early as 1976, when Princeton University faculty conducted a study of several hundred course outlines from 172 departments in several institutions and found minimal curricular impact by the new scholarship on women, it was clear that change would not come quickly or easily.[17]

An immense effort toward that end soon began. Described variously as mainstreaming, integrating, transforming, or gender-balancing the curriculum, it was underwritten by government agencies and private foundations as well as universities. In 1981, the Southwest Institute for Research on Women (SIROW) at the University of Arizona, with funding from the National Endowment for the Humanities (NEH) and the Rockefeller Family Fund, organized an invitational workshop entitled "Integrating Women's Studies into the Curriculum." That same year, the Ford, Lilly, and Johnson Foundations provided support for a second invitational conference for this purpose. Soon, across the country, other conferences were convened, institutes held, reports issued, and proceedings published, all testifying to the vitality of the "transformation" movement. Increasing responsiveness to the diversity among women (as discussed in chapter 5) and collaboration between ethnic studies and women's studies programs encouraged inclusion of a rapidly growing body of research on women of color. Projects at Memphis State University and at Spelman College, in association with other institutions of higher education in Atlanta, provided exemplary models for transforming curricula, both within women's studies and across the broader reaches of academia.[18] Drawing on several published reports in the early to mid-1980s, Mariam Chamberlain, director of a three-year study of the status and prospects of women in higher education that was sponsored jointly by the Ford, Carnegie, and Russell Sage Foundations, could report that "feminist scholarship has indeed begun to alter the state of knowledge of the disciplines." "But," she declared, "women's studies has yet to have any substantial influence on the traditional curriculum." From a longer perspective, in 1991 Ellen Messer-Davidow concluded more optimistically that feminist inquiry, while it had "not transformed" the disciplines, had "altered" them. For Messer-Davidow, more fundamental change would require greater "know-how" about the ways in which human agents can affect social systems.[19] The intellectual tools for further change are now readily available.

By 1992 almost two hundred curriculum transformation projects had been reported. In 1993, a National Center for Curriculum Transformation Resources on Women (NCCTRW), partially supported by the Ford Foundation and the Department of Education's Fund for the Improvement of Postsecondary Education, was established at Towson State University, in Maryland, to provide continuing leadership. A recent NCCTRW catalog includes a list of curriculum consultants in many disciplines, representing major research universities and leading liberal arts colleges across the country; bibliographic resources; Internet resources; suggestions for obtaining funds for transformation projects; designs for evaluating curricula; "discipline analysis" essays in sixteen fields; panels of experts in seven areas; and essays on diverse interdisciplinary and international perspectives. While research that explores the results of such efforts remains relatively scarce, several "before and after" studies of course syllabi suggest that faculty participation in transformation projects does make a difference. According to one recent review, "It is rare that a faculty member participates in one of these projects without making changes: Some add one or more new texts or concepts; some integrate material throughout the course; some completely change the structure and topics of the course to make the study of gender and cultural diversity central."[20]

Among the national leaders in transformation efforts whose names appear on the NCCTRW's list of consultants and are frequently cited in the literature are Elizabeth Kamarck Minnich and Peggy McIntosh. The philosopher Minnich (once a graduate assistant to Hannah Arendt) has published a book explaining that she set as her task thinking through the "*root problem* underlying the dominant meaning system that informs our curricula." It was Minnich who in 1979 had grasped the revolutionary potential of replacing an androcentric, or male-centered, perspective with a woman-centered view of the world. In a memorable phrase, she compared the epistemological impact of replacing androcentric with gynocentric scholarship to "Copernicus shattering our geo-centricity, Darwin shattering our species-centricity. We are shattering andro-centricity, and the change is as fundamental, as dangerous, as exciting." Now her search produced "really only a few basic realizations." Stubbornly and pervasively embedded in common knowledge, the root problem, she argued,

> reappears in different guises in all fields and throughout the dominant tradition. It is, simply, that while the majority of humankind was excluded from education and the making of what has been called knowledge, the dominant few not only defined themselves as the inclusive kind of human but also as the norm and the ideal.
>
> Faulty generalization, *even universalization, is compounded by . . . privileging central singular terms, notably "man" and "mankind," which lead directly to such singular abstract notions—and ideals—as "the citizen," "the philosopher," "the poet." Such singularity makes thinking of plurality, let alone diversity, very difficult indeed. . . . Whole systems of knowledge built around such concepts come to appear to have neither contexts nor consequences that should be considered central (rather than peripheral) to their truths and meaning. The result is* partial knowledge *masquerading as general, even universal.*

Given these systemic errors, only fundamental reconception of "false universals" could open the dominant curriculum to the new scholarship. It would then be necessary to revisit basic questions about human existence.[21]

While Minnich justified the necessity of transformation, analysis of the process of change was provided by the historian Peggy McIntosh, director of a faculty development program at the Wellesley College Center for Research on Women. Under McIntosh's leadership, for several years the center offered fellowship awards for residence at Wellesley to scholars working to integrate materials on women into the traditional curriculum. It gave faculty resident in New England stipends for attendance at regional seminars on the implications of the new scholarship and gave matching funds to institutions around the country that invited consultants on integration to work with their faculties. Drawing on the field of history for her model, McIntosh built on the pioneering work of Gerda Lerner, who called in 1969 for a new conceptual framework in women's history, to lay out a progressive transformation process. Lerner projected five phases for the transition: recognizing that women have a history (which differs by class); then seeking women's contributions to "male-defined society"; conceptualizing women as a group "defined in their own terms"; posing new questions about history based on knowledge of women, including rethinking traditional periodization from women's perspective; and reconceptualizing the discipline to create a total human history. McIntosh outlined the five phases as:

Phase 1: *Womanless History*

Phase 2: *Women in History*

Phase 3: *Women as a Problem, Anomaly, or Absence in History*

Phase 4: *Women as History*

Phase 5: *History Reconstructed, Redefined, and Transformed to Include Us All*[22]

Writing in the foreword to a guidebook, published by Betty Schmitz in 1985, that includes designs for overall project management, examples of campus projects, and resources for revision, McIntosh characterizes the transformation process as a dynamic faculty development project to enhance the teaching and learning of a new curriculum. "Phase theory" may also be used for content analysis of an existing program, to assess the extent of "gendered knowledge" present in a given course or curriculum. McIntosh's five phases, expanded slightly, generalized, and interwoven with the developmental schemes of several other analysts, reappear in the six "stages of curriculum change" developed by Marilyn R. Schuster and Susan R. Van Dyne, professors, and former deans, at Smith College, which appeared in both the *Harvard Educational Review* and an anthology of essays on transformation that they edited and published with support from McIntosh and the Wellesley College Center for Research on Women (see table 1). The contributors to this volume included leaders of transformation projects spanning the country, at public and private, large and small institutions, major research universities along with liberal arts colleges. This work also highlights the first partnership project to link black studies and women's studies in transformation efforts.[23]

Reviewing more than fifty projects, Schuster and Van Dyne found three predominant models for institution-wide change: "top-down," "piggy-back," and "bottom-up," each with varying strengths and risks. They recognized the importance of respecting local conditions but warned against "mere assimilation of what's most affordable or readily acceptable," and they emphasized the necessity of offering an "inclusive vision . . . not merely white women's studies . . . [and including also] our own often-silenced minorities, such as lesbians."[24]

The results of the many curriculum transformation projects remain uncertain, and like many other educational processes, these projects may bear fruit only after years of maturation. What is all too clear is that these efforts may encounter serious resistance. Reporting on one of the largest curriculum integration projects, a four-year effort at the University of Arizona, begun in 1981 with sponsorship by the NEH, a multidisciplinary team called attention to the many ways in which their efforts had proved frustrating. Involving forty-five participants from thirteen departments, who were mostly typical of tenured men at universities everywhere, the project provided the volunteer participants either stipends or released time, and required that they attend seminars and revise at least one course to include materials about women.

While the project evaluators reported that many did make "measurable alterations in the perspective and content of their courses," they also felt as directors that they had "seriously underestimated the magnitude and intractability of the resistance [they] would confront." They found reading and hearing on the part of many participants to be "cursory" and "selective," their agreement "polite" but "limited," and the changes induced

Table 1. Stages of Change in the Curriculum and the Classroom

Stages	Questions	Incentives	Means	Outcomes	Classroom Practice
1. Invisibility	Who are the truly great thinkers/actors in history?	Maintaining standards of excellence	Back to basics	Pre-1960s, exclusionary core curriculum; fixed products, universal values	Students as passive vessels
2. Search for missing women, absent "minorities"	Who are the great women? Where is the female Shakespeare?	Affirmative action/compensatory	Add data within existing paradigms	"Exceptional" women added to the curriculum; role models sought for women and "minority" students	Notice the presence of female and minority students
3. Minorities understood as oppressed; women as subordinate in male-dominated society	Why has history of "minorities" been ignored? distorted? Why is women's work considered marginal?	Anger/social justice	Protest existing paradigms, but within perspective of dominant group	"Images of women" courses, African-American studies begins	Student engages more in debate; may resist identification with gender or ethnic group
4. Women studied on own terms, oppressed cultures studied from insider's perspective	What was/is women's experience? What are differences among women? (attention to race, class, sexuality, cultural differences, different meanings of gender)	Intellectual	Outside existing paradigms; develop competing paradigms	Links among ethnic studies, cross-cultural studies, and women's studies; interdisciplinary courses	Student values own experience, gathers data from more familiar sources

Table 1. *(Continued)*

Stages	Questions	Incentives	Means	Outcomes	Classroom Practice
5. New scholarship challenges the disciplines	Question adequacy of current definitions of historical periods, norms for behavior? How must questions change to account for gender, ethnicity, class and sexuality in context? Shift from stable subject to shifting subject positions.	Epistemology	Testing the paradigms; gender, race, class and sexuality as categories of analysis	Beginnings of transformation; theory courses	Teacher as coach, student as collaborator
6. Visibility; transformed curriculum	How are gender, race, class, sexuality, imbricated? How can we account more fully for diversity of human experience?	Inclusive vision founded on attention to differences and diversity rather than sameness and generalization	Transform the paradigms	Reconceptualized, inclusive core; dynamic process, transformed introductory courses	Empowered student, knowledge defined as much by skills, abilities, as by content

Source: Elaine Hedges, *Getting Started: Planning Curriculum Transformation* (Towson, Md.: National Center for Curriculum Transformation Resources on Women, 1997), 92. Prepared by Susan R. Van Dyne and Marilyn R. Schuster, Smith College, Northampton, Mass., 1983; updated 1996. Reprinted by permission of Susan R. Van Dyne and Marilyn R. Schuster, and the National Center for Curriculum Transformation Resources on Women.

superficial and minimal. The cross-disciplinary team was accused of "territorial invasion"; their work was contested as "ideologically motivated," while their critics left the "ideological grounding of their own epistemologies unexplored." The team, comprising younger female experts facing senior male colleagues, experienced in their leadership roles an "inverted gender dynamics" in which they were perceived either as a "police force" or as a "group of schoolteachers." They concluded that "the tools of rationality alone are inadequate to the task of intellectual change when the investments in ideas regarding gender are deep-seated and self-interested for all parties." The fundamental proposition guiding women's studies, the social construction of gender, was contested with sociobiological interpretations, leading the team to introduce the following year readings on biology and to recommend that biological issues should be highlighted early in curriculum integration projects. The "authority of the *texts*" was not enough to change men's minds. The Arizona team, tempered by its trial, provided a wealth of suggestions for future efforts.[25]

Transformation projects may also run aground for other reasons. As noted in chapter 2, the absence of tenure lines that permit faculty to concentrate all of their academic work in women's studies may mean that curriculum transformation becomes "something they [do] on the side." If left to others who are less knowledgeable, it may lose its critical edge and be diluted. At one rural research university, "diversity" came to equal "variety," and a major effort at changing the curriculum to encompass the new scholarship on both race and gender failed. Evaluations of that attempt suggest that ignorance is at least as great an obstacle as hostility. Success requires education in the fundamental perspectives of women's studies, especially its epistemological claims about the positionality of knowledge.[26]

The most extensive of all transformation endeavors is the New Jersey Project on Inclusive Scholarship, Curriculum, and Teaching, funded by the state of New Jersey and William Paterson College. Established in 1986 with a line item of $100,000 in the state's higher education budget, an additional $25,000 to $50,000 from the state department of education's New Jersey Humanities Grant program, and various in-kind contributions from the college, the project survived the elimination of the New Jersey Department of Education as well as attacks from the National Association of Scholars and others. More than a decade later it was still publishing *Transformations*, a semiannual, nationally distributed journal, and sponsoring numerous conferences, networks, exhibits, and special events. Journal issues generally include experiential studies of curriculum revision in various disciplines, suggestions for integrating material on nondominant groups of women (and men), discussions of pedagogy, model course outlines, bibliographies, and reviews of books and other instructional media. Beyond answering "why" and advising "how-to," the project (especially through its journal) also "protects change-minded professors from isolation on their campuses," according to one women's studies coordinator for whom it seems to have made "all the difference."[27]

The challenge to tradition from women's studies elicited criticism from former NEH director Lynne Cheney, who objected to a comment in *Transformations* that "a truly transformed curriculum wouldn't contain a Western Civilization course" (ignoring the movement within the field of history itself to replace Western Civilization with World History as a foundational course). Cheney also mocked the use of Minnich's audacious comparison of the impact of re-visioning in women's studies—the replacement of androcentricity with women-centered learning—with the Copernican revolution by citing an erroneous statement about the astronomer's discovery as indicative of "low levels of scientific literacy in women's studies departments." Cheney reserved her strongest criticism for the work of "the ubiquitous Peggy McIntosh" and the taxpayer-supported New Jersey project, which she sees, along with numerous other contemporary intellectual projects, as putting "scholarship and teaching into the service of politics" (see chapter 8).[28]

Curriculum change projects have encountered criticism on other grounds as well. Margaret Andersen spoke for many who found the terminology problematic: "mainstreaming" implies the existence of one stream when there are many; "balancing" suggests that all claims to truth are equal; "integrating" suggests the possible loss of feminist goals through assimilation. Furthermore, transformation requires personal change, not just new knowledge.[29] Sandra Coyner expressed the fears of others for whom externally funded transformation projects threatened the movement toward the establishment of women's studies programs, potentially diverting resources and weakening the rationale for developing the "discipline" itself. If material on women were diffused throughout the curriculum, would a need for separate courses and autonomous centers of feminist scholarship still be perceived? Was women's studies' goal to accomplish a finite mission, reach a final stage in the transformation of knowledge, and then make a graceful exit? Coyner thought not. Some of these questions reappear in contemporary debates on naming (*women's studies* versus *gender studies*) as well.

Speaking at a 1989 panel discussion entitled "Transforming the Knowledge Base," Coyner expressed the opinion that the authors of "stage theories" had confused a "developmental stage" and a "historical stage." They had likely experienced the various types of change successively as they participated in the creation of women's studies knowledge; for them it was useful to think in terms of stages. But what of the new generation? Would women's studies preserve its feminist thrust if transformed into "the highest form of knowledge?" Coyner wrote, "I came to women's studies through the women's movement and such ideas as 'the personal is political,' there is sexism, there is patriarchy, and there is women's solidarity. Now I meet students coming to women's studies through deconstruction. They start in a very different world." It was crucial, felt Coyner, to maintain a separate "space" for women's studies. This was a reiteration of her call, initially put forward at the first annual meeting of the National Women's Studies Association in 1979, for the establishment of women's studies as a separate discipline.[30]

Women's Studies as a New Discipline

Coyner spoke initially at a time when "mainstreaming" across the disciplines was promoted as women's studies' ultimate strategy, but, in her view, this approach encountered more resistance than receptivity. Appearing everywhere, women's studies had a home nowhere. Survival for the long haul, she argued, required that "Women's Studies should abandon our fierce adherence to 'interdisciplinarity' and become more like an academic discipline." "Interdisciplinarity" was a fact of life in women's studies, indicative perhaps more of its multiple locations and marginality than of any intellectual coherence or collaborative joining of work by people trained in different fields. Most research continued to emerge from the disciplines; traditional departments held the keys to faculty status and survival. Coyner focused also on the disadvantages to faculty of split assignments and dual loyalties.[31]

Despite such problems as what Catharine Stimpson, in her capacity as founding editor of the interdisciplinary journal *Signs*, termed the "fallacy of misplaced originality" (the discovery, by a scholar trained in one field, of something that is familiar in another), there were also intellectual arguments favoring Coyner's resolution that women's studies should be declared a discipline. Drawing on intellectual history and philosophical debates over the structure of knowledge, she anticipated a number of rebuttals, including the allegation that women's studies, unlike other fields, was not "objective" or "apolitical." Coyner found her most convincing argument by borrowing Thomas Kuhn's theory of scientific revolutions. Point by point she elucidated parallels between the stages of development of women's studies and the processes that, in Kuhn's scheme, led to the establishment and then replacement of "normative science." In Kuhnian terms, women's studies was at a "pre-paradigm" stage and feminist scholars were ready for "disciplining ourselves." Coyner saw women's studies as challenging established paradigms, identifying useful methods and concepts, creating new professional structures, and generally fomenting an intellectual revolution that would, ultimately, lead to a new normative science. It was time to abandon other disciplinary identities and "to think like a women's studies person." Women's studies required a separate location as a department, where practitioners could control their own curriculum, schedule their own classes, and hire their own faculty, who would be evaluated specifically for their teaching and research on women. Eventually, with the development of the Ph.D. degree in women's studies, graduates trained in several traditional disciplines would be prepared to bring true interdisciplinarity to the new field. Meanwhile, women's studies practitioners "could now pay more attention to each other and correspondingly less to our colleagues in the traditional disciplines." The community of scholars, professional associations, and "shared language" that served other sciences already existed in women's studies. Typically, the shared concepts that were emerging did not fit established paradigms; the Kuhnian period of anomaly and crisis leading to a scientific revolution was well under way in women's studies. New paradigms were emerging in and across the disciplines.[32]

The application of a Kuhnian model outside the natural sciences has been faulted on various grounds. Reflecting on the decades of feminist scholarship and her experience of curriculum transformation at the University of Arizona, Myra Dinnerstein questioned the usefulness of the "paradigm shift" concept. She drew on the work of the anthropologist Marilyn Strathern to suggest that the Kuhnian analysis may be inappropriate for disciplines with multiple perspectives, where competing points of view frequently coexist. Furthermore, she noted, women's studies must reinterpret the meaning of calls for curriculum transformation in the light of the postmodernist challenge to truth claims (further discussed in chapter 6).[33]

Apart from considerations of disciplinary definitions, the appeal of departmentalization has continued. In Coyner's 1979 vision, women's studies would, after the revolution, become an autonomous discipline for which, she noted, the appropriate structure was a department. Evelyn Torton Beck, then chair of women's studies at the University of Maryland, College Park, cited Coyner as she reiterated this position a decade later. Declaring that proponents of women's studies should not "acquiesce in our own marginality," she argued that it was "time to insist that women's studies be recognized as a newly established discipline which can be properly taught only within an autonomous department by faculty whose 'tenure home' is women's studies." For women's studies, with its ambition to cross academic borders and transform entire domains of knowledge, the implications of structure loom larger than perhaps they do in other fields. As women's studies develops, its multidisciplinarity will stimulate thought across intellectual and institutional boundaries. But to overcome the potential problem of partial knowledge and incomplete perspective, it must develop new models to facilitate the labor-intensive and costly work essential to good interdisciplinary research and teaching. Bonnie Zimmerman, former chair of the women's studies department at San Diego State University, anticipates that women's studies will create "complex learning communities" to push the cutting edge in intellectual work.[34]

By maintaining a stance that recognizes the need to institutionalize women's studies as if it were a discipline as well as to transform the curriculum of many other disciplines, women's studies can perhaps help to create a new model for a larger academic world increasingly expanding beyond long-established forms. The debate over structure is complicated by the existence of an extensive discussion about the uniqueness of "women's ways of knowing" and our ways of doing scholarly work. If women's studies is a "discipline," what are its defining characteristics? Is there a specifically feminist methodology?

The search for particular feminist approaches to method and methodology grows out of the recognition that traditional ways of creating knowledge have led to false views of women. The philosophers of science Sandra Harding and Evelyn Fox Keller are two leading voices among the many who have raised the question of feminist method. Asking, "Is there a feminist method?" Harding responds by distinguishing between "methods of inquiry," or ways of collecting information and documenting experience, and "methodology," which she defines as theory plus analysis; she answers yes on method and no on methodology. In her view, what is new in feminist work is its grounding in women's experiences, its purpose of seeking research intended to serve women, and its placing of researcher and subject in "the same critical plane." Keller argues, against conventional understanding and scientists' claims, that "method and theory may constitute a natural continuum." Referring to the work of Barbara McClintock, she links paradigm with methodological style.[35]

The feminist challenge is more profound than the simple question of a unique feminist method. Feminist analysts often answer such inquiry by broadening the context. Women's studies they see as part of the larger postpositivist movement that goes back a hundred years and more, to a much older tradition that denies the existence of absolute knowledge. Joyce McCarl Nielsen, for example, associates the feminist approach to research with other philosophical perspectives that challenge positivistic scientific method: namely, hermeneutics and critical theory. With the former it shares a belief in the importance attached to social interaction and the meanings attached to human behavior by the subjects themselves. Like the latter, it rejects the claim that any position can be neutral or disinterested, and it adopts a commitment to liberating people from constricting ideologies. In these schools of thought, as in feminism, knowledge is seen as socially constructed and interpreted.

Nielsen also points to two events within the natural sciences in the twentieth century which advanced the "demythologizing" of science as "pure truth in an ultimate sense": the development of quantum physics and Thomas Kuhn's reinterpretation of scientific progress as a historical process of paradigm transitions. Following the path sketched by Sandra Coyner in 1979, Nielsen notes the ways in which Kuhn's work can serve to explain the emergence of women's—feminist—studies. First she points to the "presence and awareness of anomalies. . . . What is important is not only that they exist . . . but that scientists take note of them and define them as counterinstances that challenge the truth or accuracy of the dominant paradigm, rather than defining them as irrelevant, bothersome, and unimportant minor deviations." This describes closely, in feminist perspective, the treatment of women in the construction of knowledge. Kuhn's second necessary condition for a paradigm shift, or scientific revolution, is "the presence of an alternative paradigm"—and what else is women's studies? In Nielsen's words, "to consciously adopt a woman's perspective means to see things one did not see before and also to see the familiar rather differently." As examples of feminist inquiry that brought anomalies to the fore and led to alternative explanations, Nielsen offers two famous instances: Joan Kelly's 1977 essay "Did Women Have a Renaissance?" and Carol Gilligan's 1982 book *In a Different Voice*. These studies led, respectively, to questioning the grounds of periodization in history and to alternative views of human moral development. In other disciplines, similar cases abound.[36]

The revision, if not revolution, in perspective that was provoked by feminist criticism has created a new framework within which reforms and new, revised, and more nuanced interpretations will continue to emerge. Throughout the humanities, women's studies and other antipositivistic schools of thought have stimulated increased self-reflexivity and methodological self-consciousness. For all the talk of "feminist methods," no one approach is unique to women's studies. On the contrary, feminist researchers employ many methods. Coyner, for one, finds nothing wrong with using any or all of "the master's tools." Associating herself with Sandra Harding's views, she takes a pragmatic approach: "We should look at methodologies that have worked for us, find out what characterizes them, and call that feminist methodology instead of letting the prescriptive writings of people who say 'this is what you have to do for your work to be feminist' define what is feminist." Harding also warns against making a fetish of method. Method, she explains, arose with the institutionalization of science, as a way of enforcing "norms of inquiry" that operated as a sort of "invisible administrator" to enforce rules. Seen as emancipatory in an earlier age that was breaking away from the authority of church and state, "rule by method" no longer serves that purpose. In particular, principles calling for value-free, uninvolved approaches to research should be replaced with "conscious partiality" and active participation.[37]

However, feminist scholars assert that feminist researchers should share guiding principles. The sociologists Judith A. Cook and Mary Margaret Fonow suggest the following five: (1) "attending to the significance of gender and gender asymmetry"; (2) recognizing the "centrality of consciousness-raising" as a key to interpretation; (3) "challeng[ing] the norm of objectivity that assumes that the subject and object of research can be separated"; (4) considering the "ethical implications" of treating persons as research objects; and (5) employing research as a means toward the "empowerment of women and transformation of patriarchal social institutions." Cook and Fonow also turn from prescription to description and identify four common themes in much contemporary feminist scholarship: "the role of reflexivity"; "an action orientation"; "attention to the affective component of the research act"; and "use of the situation at hand."[38]

The way in which adopting such principles affects scholarship is captured in the sociologist Judith Stacey's "trajectory in the borderlands," her account of an "accidental ethnology" of white families who lived and worked in the Silicon Valley of northern California. Originally intended as a comparative study of "working-class gender relationships under postindustrial conditions" among white and Latino families, Stacey's "formal research design . . . unraveled rapidly." She describes how her initial two interviews challenged her preconceptions by revealing a putative feminist to be a convert to evangelical Christianity and a long-abused wife to be a feminist. Lured by the unexpected into an ethnology reported in a "reflexive, first-person, and occasionally dialogic narrative style," Stacey offers her work as an example of "un-disciplined" research. Both postmodernist and humanist, it is feminist as well. Not only does Stacey transgress what she considers "arbitrary and increasingly atavistic disciplinary divisions of knowledge" but she declares that she has now "adopted that surprising new feminist fashion here of studying men."[39]

If women's studies does not have any singular method, it does have a pervasive attitude. Implicit when not explicit in its affinity with hermeneutics, critical theory, and various standpoint perspectives is a firm rejection of the positivist stance toward objectivity which has served to define many social science disciplines as well as scientific method. Often seen as a core value of the academy, fundamental to the search for truth, the notion of objectivity is rejected by many feminists, who see it instead as a mask for bias. Critics of women's studies frequently use the concept of objectivity as a handy tool for attack. But feminist scholars who challenge the dominant tradition and its creators for their slanted views of women build on a long heritage. In the early fifteenth century, Christine de Pizan lamented that the ills men attributed to women existed in their own minds, not in female nature; "the books that so sayeth, women made them not."[40]

Half a millennium later, feminist critics reiterate this point. According to the historian Christie Farnham, "It is the lack of objectivity in science," which "has permitted an all-too-ready acceptance of what are essentially unproven explanations of unproven gender differences," that has spurred feminist research. The literary critic Leslie W. Rabine notes that "men used a rhetoric of objectivity as a kind of armored vehicle for projecting masculine subjectivity." The sociologist Margaret Andersen declares that "women's labor makes the male mode of operation—detached and rational—possible."[41]

Male objectivity/female subjectivity appears in the feminist lexicon as one more false and uneven dichotomy. Carol P. Christ, writing from the perspective of religious studies, calls on feminist scholars to "deconstruct and disavow the *ethos of objectivity*." However, she also warns of the difficulty of that task, which is due not only to an "androcentric veil" that shields judgments of value and power structures in the university but also to the dualism that posits irrationality and chaos as objectivity's opposite. For the defenders of objectivity, Christ argues, "ways of thinking not firmly rooted in so-called rational principles lead directly back to the chaos monster, to Nazi Germany." For objectivity's feminist critics, it merely hides the perspective from which a speaker speaks, offering disembodied speech and a god's-eye "view from nowhere." It may also disregard the influence of language differences that affect perception. Norma Alarcón has criticized native English-speaking Americans for inventing theory that ignores the "linguistic status" of subjects, failing to acknowledge that "we are culturally constituted in and through language in complex ways and not just engendered in a homogeneous situation."[42]

The importance of the debate over objectivity in the feminist challenge to the traditional curriculum justifies taking a closer look at the uses of objectivity in the academy. The ideal of objectivity did not achieve its place on the university heights without struggle. In recent studies that buttress the feminist argument, intellectual historians have traced its role in the professionalization of the social sciences in the United States. Peter Novick, a historian of science, portrays objectivity as the "noble dream" of founders of the American historical profession. In "Objectivity Enthroned," the first part of his 1988 book, Novick demonstrates objectivity's importance and utility, amid a crisis of authority in American intellectual life, in separating amateurs from professional keepers of the past. By redefining their audiences, standardizing their technique, privileging academic over activist goals, and separating fact from value, historians created a myth of the reality of the past. They portrayed historical truth as correspondence to that reality, to be uncovered progressively by the application of a Baconian scientific method and reported in monographic literature in which, following the style of Flaubert, the "direct appearance of the author was anathema." Presented objectively, interpreted impartially, this recovered fact constituted the ideal to which the professional historians aspired, and on which they built their "discipline."[43]

In a subsequent section of the book entitled "Objectivity Besieged," Novick follows the collapse of consensus in the 1920s and 1930s. War guilt, revisionist challenges to dominant interpretations of the Civil War and Reconstruction, and postwar developments in physics, music, painting, linguistics, psychology, anthropology, and law all challenged the founding myth. Objectivity was reinterpreted following World War II, Novick asserts, and a Whiggish Western civilization dominated general education until collapse began again in the mid-1960s, this time instigated by leftist historians and abetted a bit later by minority groups and women. Today, Novick found, objectivity was "in crisis"; this finding was developed in a chapter entitled "Every Group Its Own Historian"—a title borrowed from the presidential address of Carl Becker to the American Historical Association in 1931. There would have been, of course, few female, or feminist, historians in Becker's audience to applaud.

In this historical perspective, contemporary feminist (and postmodernist) challenges to objectivity seem less radical than they are sometimes said to be. Objectivity historicized is objectivity dethroned. For feminists, explains the anthropologist Donna Haraway, a frequent participant in the "objectivity debates," "objectivity means quite simply *situated knowledges*." This is not, she explains, an invitation to relativism—a bogey often employed in objectivity's defense. Instead it offers an alternative: "partial, locatable, critical knowledges sustaining the possibility of webs of connections called solidarity in politics and shared conversations in epistemology."[44]

It may not be easy to distinguish Haraway's position from the classic *ad hominem* argument that dismisses a point of view because of its origin. If truth exists, it should be possible to state it—but who can do so, and in what language? In an article in which he sets out to explain what is at stake in contemporary curriculum debates, the philosopher John Searle acknowledges that "objectivity only functions relative to a shared 'background' of cognitive capacities and hence is, in a sense, a form of intersubjectivity." Searle asserts that "a public language presupposes a public world." Some feminist scholars would say that this is exactly so: knowledge is produced through conversation. The question is, who gets to participate and who defines the terms? Often unspoken in the debate is the distribution of power to decide outcomes. Who gets the last word—the right to name what will be known as reality? Who tells the truth(s) about women?[45]

Critics such as Searle complain of the "Nietzscheanized Left" (borrowing Allan Bloom's term) and chastise women's studies for departing from the norms of what Searle calls the "Western Rationalistic Tradition" in their efforts to destabilize concepts and rename accepted versions of reality. As women lead the search to find and tell new truths about women, and feminist scholarship grows apace, they join a long line of critics of objectivity. Nevertheless, they are often singled out as a force especially destructive of traditional wisdom and values. As Joyce Appleby, Margaret Jacob, and Lynn Hunt point out in *Telling the Truth about History*, "a great transformation has recently occurred in Western Thinking about knowledge. . . . As the twentieth century closes, it becomes obvious that new definitions of truth and objectivity are needed in every field of knowledge. . . . The chief cause of the present crisis of knowledge is the collapse on all fronts of intellectual and political absolutism." As befits intellectual leaders in a democratic society, the authors conclude their work with the statement "Telling the truth takes a collective effort."[46]

Transformation projects in women's studies represent academic feminists' collective effort to add women's voices to the conversations through which knowledge is created and transmitted. Often that has meant attacking the disciplines. After hundreds of organized projects and thousands of individual efforts in women's studies, and challenges by many other interdisciplinary programs as well, the disciplines nevertheless retain their structure, their courses, and their curriculum largely intact. Sometimes women are added and not stirred. Despite the success of academic feminists in gaining legitimacy for their work, tenure and many excellent positions for themselves, and institutional acceptance for their courses, curricula, and programs, women's studies often remains marginalized, which fuels continuing debates about its structure, future, and especially in the last decade, even its name. Grounded in and shaped by the disciplines, where most of its research continues to take place, women's studies thrives both as an interdisciplinary community and, probably even more, as a vital presence within communities based on discipline. Existing both inside and outside traditional academic structures, feminist scholars now ponder "how to be or not to be marginal at one and the same time." Ellen Messer-Davidow, in a thoughtful article assessing the impact of women's studies' success in institutionalizing academic feminism, finds that the "disciplinary grid . . . disempowers women."[47]

Messer-Davidow's concern is primarily with the loss of impetus toward the use of academic change to leverage social change. Exploring the extent to which women's studies programs teach courses that are explicitly about social change, Messer-Davidow surveyed the curricula of two dozen "large, radical, community-oriented and/or prestigious programs" and found that only four emphasized change or taught practice. One of the questions initially raised in the debates over "mainstreaming women's studies" and "transforming the curriculum" was whether success would kill women's studies. Many of the founders transferred their energies from the women's liberation movement to the women's studies movement and have not, Messer-Davidow points out, engaged in community-based social action since the early 1970s. However, beyond suggesting that investigators become involved with their subjects in social science research and adding curricular coursework and internships in "social change" (which, interestingly, resonates with a national movement toward institutionalizing "service learning"), Messer-Davidow has little to offer about the "how" side of her article's title, "Know-How."[48]

The relationship between women's studies and the (other) disciplines invokes questions of institutional structure as well as intellectual boundaries, and the controversy over "autonomy versus integration" of the early 1980s reappears in another guise in the 1990s, as a debate over naming. Not only the structural separation of women's studies but also the use of the term *women* to define and label the field was seen by some as perpetuating a dichotomy in which woman is subordinate to man, and as reinforcing ahistorical, essentialist views of sexual differences. *Gender-balancing* and *gender studies,* advocated sometimes as less threatening terms for the academic feminist project because they include men, can also be construed as the more radical approach, for they imply dissolving concepts, categories, and institutions that maintain a dichotomous inequality. For those who recognize gender as a social system that pervades all institutions (family, sexuality, economy, politics, law, marriage, and education) and permeates the intellectual foundations of knowledge, *gender feminism*—a term used pejoratively by the critic Christina Hoff Sommers—is the way to achieve transformation in the university as well as in society (see chapter 6).[49]

For others, however, fundamental change through women's studies requires not only revision of organizational structures in the academy and changes in curricula but also alternative ways of delivering instruction. Many hold the view that how to teach is as important as what to teach. Classroom organization and environment matters as much as the syllabus. Transformation necessitates not only revising course content, sources, and interpretations and "breaking the disciplines" by blurring the genres and also the genders, but also bridging the separation between cognitive and affective modes of learning. In this view it is essential to connect the content of courses with the character of students' lives. Effective instruction— teaching that would "take"—must link inquiry with experience in the lives of both faculty and students. Much of this could be lost in projects focused primarily on transforming the curriculum. Like the authors of the 1969 book *Teaching as a Subversive Activity*,[50] some feminist educators believe that in education as well as in media, "the medium is the message," and they seek to alter virtually every aspect of the teaching-learning experience.

Experiments in creating totally alternative educational environments have been relatively few, largely in the form of summer "institutes" or "communities" where feminists struggled over problems of content, structure, and funding. While they provided spaces in which women could think and be together "free of the constrictions of male-dominated institutions," these efforts never served as a viable alternative to women's studies in mainstream higher education in the United States.[51] Instead, efforts to open the academy to feminist education meant adding to the challenge to the curriculum efforts to change the learning environment through what came to be called "feminist pedagogy."

4

The Importance of Pedagogy

In January 1996, the American Council on Education (ACE) held its fifth conference on "faculty roles and rewards," to explore further ways of enhancing the practice of teaching in higher education. Similarly, a second leading national organization, the American Association for Higher Education (AAHE), continued to expand the work of its Assessment Forum, a decade-long effort to improve methods of enhancing as well as assessing the quality of instruction in postsecondary institutions. These efforts assume that one reason for a perceived lack of emphasis on teaching in many colleges and universities has been the difficulty of evaluating faculty performance in the classroom. Both of these major professional associations have been responding to concerns that date back at least to the mid-1980s, when the National Institute of Education and the Association of American Colleges published reports dealing with "involvement" and "integrity" in college teaching.[1] Interest in pedagogy had been spreading far beyond teachers colleges.

These studies reflected an educational climate of fear in the United States resulting from worries that our dominant position in the global economy and political power were threatened because American students were reported to perform more poorly than their counterparts in other leading industrial nations. The question of why this generation of students seemed less competent than its predecessors led not only to discussion of demographic change among students but also to heightened debates about curricular content and pedagogical strategies. The issue was amplified by William Bennett's media successes during his term as secretary of education and helped to boost the sales of Allan Bloom's surprise best-seller of 1987, *The Closing of the American Mind.* By the 1990s much of higher education had revised its sense of mission to highlight teaching, and many pledged allegiance to pedagogical principles that put student learning in the center. For women's studies, whose founders aimed to effect transformation in individual and social consciousness, the classroom had been in the center from the beginning. Feminist teachers were there to help students "claim" the education that the poet Adrienne Rich had told them was their due. Feminist faculty had put "students in the center"; and student enrollments had ensured women's studies' place in the curriculum.[2]

Reflecting women's studies' beginnings in the student power and "new university" movements, the "how" was initially as important to the field's practitioners as the "what." From Paulo Freire's "pedagogy of the oppressed" (though he did not mention gender in his analysis) and Jerry Farber's provocative (and also highly gendered) essay of 1967, "The Student as Nigger," came theory justifying radical revision in teaching methods; from experience with consciousness-raising groups came ideas on practice. Women's studies entered the academy along with a widespread challenge to the traditional teacher-centered, hierarchically structured classroom. Linking learning to both the personal and the political, raising ethical issues, rethinking the relationship of reason and affect, questioning the role of teachers in the creation and transmission of dominant cultures as well as differences, academic feminists developed a new form of "critical pedagogy." While practitioners of feminist pedagogy share no singular method of teaching, they do often focus on such themes as the role of the teacher as nurturer, the problem of exercising authority, and the importance of classroom dynamics, all reflecting the experience of consciousness raising, all germane to student "empowerment."[3]

Historians of education and scholars of pedagogy will recognize in this agenda the influence of important educators who, from John Dewey to Henry Giroux, have offered similar prescriptions as means to achieve educational goals in a democratic society. What is different about women's studies is how seriously many of its practitioners take the responsibility to pay attention to pedagogy as well as to content. The level of interest they show in teaching techniques, their degree of concern with course structures, required assignments, textbooks, classroom dynamics, and the resulting student responses, is uncommon. It is unlikely that annual meetings in many fields other than women's studies, excepting professional education, include in their schedules as many sessions devoted to teaching, or that as many professors of any other subject spend as many hours in discussion about what happens in the classroom. At the National Women's Studies Association's national meeting in June 1995, 30 of 207 sessions, or 14 percent, were devoted to pedagogy. By way of contrast, the program of the American Historical Association's January 1996 meeting included 10 out of 140, or 7 percent. A session at the NWSA on teaching the introductory course drew an audience of fifty, while one on teaching research methods all but overflowed its room capacity of about thirty-five. For many academic feminists, pedagogy is not only about ways of conveying knowledge. It is also a means to practice feminist principles.

The national attention currently devoted to pedagogy—which, according to a recent issue of AAHE's *Change* magazine focusing on "collaborative learning," is "the central issue of higher education today"[4]—suggests that the larger community may be moving to adopt elements of what has come to be called "feminist pedagogy." While definitions of this term vary, all emphasize the importance of engaging students as active learners and encouraging them to make connections between the materials being studied, their own lives, and those of others (faculty as well as students) with whom they interact, beginning in the classroom. Active learning requires students to think critically, to ask questions and question answers—to re-think everything, including the meaning of their own experiences. One art student expressed her experience in a women's studies literature class by creating a small print of herself "crouching totally naked except for a large pair of spectacles, with the knuckles of one hand pressed hard into her mouth and a fiercely contemplative glare on her face. The print was entitled THINK!"[5] Another, a women's studies graduating senior who was challenged to explain how she would use her major after she left the university, answered, "I'm going to think!"[6]

By emphasizing student involvement in learning, practitioners of feminist pedagogy intend to encourage students' individual and collective empowerment—a central goal of women's studies being to develop connections between academic work and the world beyond (see chapter 7). It is in this sense that the political scientist Carolyn M. Shrewsbury declares that feminist pedagogy begins with "a vision of the classroom as a liberatory environment."[7] The emphasis on liberation harkens back to the women's liberation movement (the middle word is sometimes forgotten in references to the feminism of the 1960s and 1970s), and to the origins of women's studies. Feminist pedagogy seeks to enact a democratic process that, like the early consciousness-raising groups, decenters authority and shares leadership among participants. This is a process that may be more preached than practiced and that tended to be slighted, at least in the women's studies literature (except for the *Women's Studies Newsletter*—later, the *Women's Studies Quarterly*), during the field's period of most rapid development, between the early 1970s and the mid-1980s. It remains today controversial, even "radical."[8]

For some, feminist process evokes an image of students sitting in a circle, even on the floor, talking about personal experiences in the manner of consciousness raising, where each in succession speaks out on an issue and no one interrupts, criticizes, or talks twice before every person has a turn, including the convenor, who participates on an equal basis with other group members. One goal of such process was said to be "breaking the artificial separation between theory and practice, learning and being. If what we are teaching really means, All women are sisters, then we must teach it in a classroom environment where competition is minimized and cooperation is stressed and rewarded." The means included assignments designed to encourage cooperative learning, and attempts by faculty members to dissolve "the artificial hierarchies and vertical slots of the usual academic structure."[9]

The "centrifugal classroom" of feminist ideology aims to replace the "audience-like arrangement of student chairs, the lectern or podium reminiscent of a pulpit, the gaze of student spectators focusing on that central point, the instructor": as a result, the instructor will be "uncrown[ed]."[10] Women's studies faculty, in this scheme, remove their own crowns. However, like Barbara Omolade, teaching an evening course to black women in New York City, they may face a conflict between their desire to empower students, acting out their own egalitarian values, and the students' hunger for knowledge embodied in the instructor.[11] Students themselves, like those of Susan Stanford Friedman at the University of Wisconsin, may not share the feminist problem with authority and may resist feminist efforts at democratization, looking for "more direction, structure and lecture."[12] Despite their increasing diversity in age as well as class and ethnicity, most of today's students are a generation removed from the young man in my 1970 American history class who, at the initial meeting, stood up in the back the entire time to make the point that students should not be expected to be sitting at the feet of a standing instructor. Teaching my first women's history class the following year, I sat in a circle with my students.

For many women faculty, the antiauthority inheritance from the 1960s is problematic. Strongly attracted by criticism of the exercise of powers from which most women had historically been excluded, they adopted a position developed largely by men attacking other men. As Friedman points out, they ignored the "lens of gender" and their own "socializ[ation] to believe (frequently at a non-conscious level) that any kind of authority is incompatible with the feminine." Men's denial of authority to women placed female faculty in a double bind: "To be 'woman,' she has no authority to think; to think, she has made herself 'masculine' at the cost of her womanhood." Women faculty were caught between pressures to reject authoritarian behavior and pressures to express their own intellectual command. Yet it was important, Friedman asserts, for feminist faculty not to join in the "patriarchal denial of the mind to women."[13]

Caught between dissonant claims to share authority with men and to reject it altogether as corrupt, feminists might resolve this problem with authority by reconstructing the basic concept. The political theorist Kathleen B. Jones proposes envisioning a new "compassionate authority" to replace the common interpretation of authority as "sovereign imperative control."[14] An alternative, and easier, answer to the dilemma of dealing with the reality as well as the symbols of authority inherent in the teaching role is to back away and accept conventional arrangements and relationships. (In recent years, classrooms designed to employ information technology sometimes make rearranging physical facilities impossible, anyway.) Still another solution is to make feminist process itself a part of the curriculum, as proposed by Nancy Schniedewind, a professor of education and a frequent contributor to the literature of feminist pedagogy. She believes that students need to learn how to take on a new role, how to accept some of the power and responsibility for the class. Sharing leadership in planning assignments, assigning exercises designed to teach students to "differentiate between their thoughts and feelings," practicing conflict resolution skills, and working in groups on term projects are some of the means she suggests.[15]

For faculty as well as students, departing from conventional pedagogical strategies requires taking risks. It is likely that in many or most classes, especially the discipline-based courses that comprise the bulk of women's studies, conventional practices continue to predominate, as is suggested in a national assessment study discussed below. Advocates of student-centered and feminist learning see this as a mistake. The new scholarship cannot be incorporated into a traditional format, for "process and content are inextricably linked, . . . [for] how we teach is inevitably linked to what students learn." Evaluating student experiences in women's studies classrooms, women's studies director Jean O'Barr and Mary Wyer note, however, "There is no accepted orthodoxy in the use of traditional authority structures in women's studies classrooms. . . . [and] individual pedagogical experiments are episodic."[16]

How Do Women Learn?

Contemporary discussion about pedagogy in women's studies draws not only on Dewey, Freire, and an ideology that was inherited from the 1960s and favors challenging hierarchical structures, but also on recent studies in cognitive development. In October 1994, Blythe Clinchy, a professor of psychology who holds an endowed chair in ethics at Wellesley College, reported, in her keynote address to the ninth annual conference of the Midwest College Learning Center Association, on college students' "ways of knowing," about the longitudinal studies that led to her (co-authored) 1986 prize-winning book, *Women's Ways of Knowing* (hereafter abbreviated as *WWK*). Inspired by Carol Gilligan's famous and influential study of psychological and moral development and women's "different voice," Clinchy, along with Mary Belenky, Nancy Goldberger, and Jill Tarule, set out to see if there was something about the ways in which women learn—their "modes of learning, knowing, and valuing"—that was important to understanding their development and to furthering their education.[17] In a multiyear, FIPSE-supported study for the Education for Women's Development Project, Clinchy and her co-workers examined how women engage in these processes and reported their findings in their co-authored book. This volume's tenth anniversary is celebrated in a recent volume of essays assessing its extensive influence in a large and broad range of fields.[18]

Drawing on in-depth interviews with 135 women, 90 of whom were students at six institutions of secondary or higher education and 45 of whom were clients in family service agencies, the four authors identified five "different perspectives from which women view reality and draw conclusions about truth, knowledge, and authority." They found "women's self-concepts and ways of knowing" to be deeply intertwined, determining together how far they could travel as learners. Some women remained silent, powerless to develop or express thought, isolated, obedient to authority, and accepting of stereotypes about "woman's place." A second group were more open to learning, but only by absorbing the views of others; defined as "received knowers," they had little sense of their own potential capacities for questioning truth and therefore might "feel confused and incapable when the teacher requires that they do original work." A third group could progress to recognition of a multiplicity of possible opinions but would understand them as grounded only in subjective experience, not as validated by principle or evidence. Such "subjectivist women" would have little regard for expertise or rational analysis. These would become the students whom "faculty often perceive . . . as arbitrary, emotional, overly personal, concrete, and unmanageable." A fourth group, labeled "procedural knowers," were more attuned to the outer world and replaced subjective with "objective" knowledge, and intuition with reason, in their approach to learning. Procedural knowers (men as well as women) approach learning in a manner opposite to that of the subjective knowers: doubting, questioning evidence, looking for contradictions, and using "impersonal procedures for establishing truth." This group manifested two forms of procedural knowing labeled "separate" and "connected."[19]

The two groups of procedural knowers behave similarly to Carol Gilligan's famous two groups: those (analogous to "separate" knowers) who ground morality in justice, and those (analogous to "connected" knowers) who ground it in an ethic of care. The first, stereotypically male, are given to impersonal reasoning; the second, like stereotypical females, add empathy to this learning style. They care about the objects or persons they seek to understand. While separate knowers only "yearn for a voice that is more integrated, individual, and original—a voice of their own," connected knowers use personal knowledge to create one. It is "connected knowing" that allows women to achieve the fullest development postulated by the authors, understanding that all knowledge is constructed and integrating themselves as part of that which is known. These "constructivist" knowers face a formidable task. They must integrate knowledge gained from all sources and contextualize and analyze everything, questions as well as answers, "weaving together the strands of rational and emotive thought and of integrating objective and subjective knowing." Those who achieve this level of development are the women who exhibit a passion for learning. But also, accord-

ing to this scheme, they "aspire to work that contributes to the empowerment and improvement in the quality of life of others. More than any other
group of women in this study, the constructivists feel a part of the effort to
address with others the burning issues of the day and to contribute as best
they can." They stand at the pole opposite the voiceless, obedient women
resigned to stereotypical female roles, unable to question, disconnected,
closed to creative learning.[20]

The results of the much-discussed work of Gilligan and the *WWK*
team have reinforced the idea—even among those not convinced that women
learn differently than men or progress through separate stages of cognitive
development—that successful teaching must begin where the student is (a
notion traced by historians of education back at least to Rousseau and
Pestalozzi). Attention to the role of the learner, and the interactive nature
of knowledge acquisition, points to experience as a critical factor in pedagogy as well as in feminist theory. It also is consistent with the postmodernist critique that stresses the blurring of borders, the problematizing of
experience, and examination of the role of power relations in the construction of knowledge. From one perspective, however, works such as *Women's
Ways of Knowing* pose the danger of reinforcing a traditional, binary opposition between two sexes. The practice of a feminist pedagogy that privileges experience may also err in adopting static, essentialist views of women
(and men) as well as of sexuality, class, race, and other attributes assumed
by feminists to be largely socially constructed.[21] The sociologist Susan Johnston, who teaches a course on "sex and identity," declares: "If we want our
pedagogical practices to resist heterosexism, then we must avoid rearticu-
lating the logic that underlies it."[22] The same logic applies to other forms
of personal identity.

Many interpretations of *WWK* are discussed in the tenth-anniversary
volume, where Goldberger in her introduction elaborates the origins of the
study and answers criticism—for example, denying the charge of "essentialism" as a misreading. If the team studied only women, she indicates,
it was to correct psychologists' previous neglect of women's cognitive development. Furthermore, they "did not claim the five perspectives were dis-
tinctively female," although they were salient aspects of women's experience. Goldberger characterizes as misinterpretation the idea that connected
knowing is opposed to reason; instead, it represents in her view an "instance of rationality." She also refutes criticism that the five "ways" constitute a series of progressive stages in which a traditionally "feminine"

mode is denigrated. What is important for feminist pedagogy, in Gold-berger's view, is that *WWK* takes women seriously as thinkers and as know-ers. It also stresses developmental possibilities for learners, Ann Stanton points out, when teaching is appreciated as a form of inquiry and acknowl-edged as a "moral enterprise."[23]

The anniversary volume includes an essay by Frances A. Maher and Mary Kay Thompson Tetreault on *WWK*'s influence in women's studies. They note that the book was cited by a third of the authors in a special jour-nal issue devoted to feminist pedagogies in 1987, as well as in much of the recent literature on teaching in women's studies.[24] Maher and Tetreault speak from experience, having drawn heavily on *WWK* in their own work. The strengths as well as the weaknesses of feminist pedagogy in practice can be seen in *The Feminist Classroom*, Maher and Tetreault's study of the teaching behavior of seventeen feminist professors at six colleges and uni-versities. For these authors, feminist pedagogy differs from other "libera-tory" methods of teaching in its focus on the "needs of women students and its grounding in feminist theory as the basis for its multidimensional and positional view of the construction of classroom knowledge." Maher and Tetreault use the *WWK* scheme to interpret their interviews and to inform their observations of feminist classrooms. They document the prevalence, in some women's studies classes, of "reliance on the authority of personal intuition and each person's individual experience, as grounds for assessing the validity of knowledge or truth claims," and they point out that such reliance is characteristic of "subjective knowing." It fails to recognize, they agree (citing the historian Joan Scott's work on the problematic use of expe-rience as evidence), that "experiences, as well as identities, have no real meaning prior to their interpretations." Whether identity is expressed in terms of sex or in terms of race, it may lead to a solipsistic and divisive dead end. Some feminist teacher-scholars, they find, move beyond subjectivist interpretations and take a multidimensional, interactivist, "constructivist" approach to interpreting meaning through a "positionality" in which all knowledge is grounded in a multifaceted context. This is the stance that the authors set out to apply in their own interactions with their seventeen fac-ulty interviewees and that the faculty sought to develop in their students.[25]

Maher and Tetreault observed "both men and women demonstrating stereotypic female and male behaviors." They suggest that "arguments based on abstractions and universals perhaps reflect a cognitive style indicative of privilege—academic training, not maleness." But the emphasis on "giving voice" to students, "positioning students as academic authorities," and integrating cognitive with affective learning which they document suggests the strong possibility that some feminist teachers may deny their own intellectual authority and fail to problematize "experience" in practice to the degree that they have done in theory.[26] To test this conjecture, it may be useful to look more closely at some strategies and assignments utilized in women's studies classrooms and to listen to students' own perceptions of their experiences.

Academic feminism asserts that the personal is intertwined with the political and that active, effective learning requires integrating personal experience with political analysis. Like instructors in English composition, faculty in women's studies often rely on required writing in journals as one way to encourage the self-reflection conducive to such integration.[27] Carol Mattingly, a professor of English, believes that "expressivist writing" has been "valued by feminists because women have been silenced in the past. [Instructors felt that] women needed to give voice to their experience in order to reclaim it, to validate it, and to construct their own reality and identity apart from that categorized for them by men." The journal is considered a safe place for students to address difficult personal issues; and women's studies practitioners often aim to extend the boundaries of safety to the feminist classroom. It takes "courage to question," as Caryn McTighe Musil, a former director of the NWSA, points out in the introduction to her book of that title; women's studies seeks to help students develop that courage. In addition to journal writing, assignments encouraging personal revelation include autobiographical essays, oral histories, visual presentations using film, videotape or slides, and role playing.[28]

Critics have long attacked women's studies for overpersonalizing instruction and even for harming students by invading their privacy. Some women's studies practitioners have also expressed reservations, on diverse grounds. Belenky recognizes the "danger in a narrow focus . . . [that might keep] a person lodged in the subjectivist mode."[29] Others fear that too much of the personal encourages narcissism and separates experience from its social and historical contexts. It presents dangers for the classroom as well. "In acknowledging difference and calling forth the voices of all students, [feminist] pedagogies raise to the surface the tensions and angers of an unequal society. Thus conflicts that are hidden in more authoritarian classrooms are called forth and then must be addressed by feminist teachers. The feminist classroom is not the 'safe haven' imagined by early feminists influenced by women's consciousness raising groups."[30] Students who expose themselves may become susceptible to manipulation and control. Others may simply be silenced by the very tactics intended to draw them out. The vulnerabilities of black students in this regard were pointed out by bell hooks.[31] From another perspective, Victoria Steinitz and Sandra Kanter argue in favor of conflict in the classroom, as a means of preparing women "to advocate for themselves in the competitive, conflict-laden society where, unfortunately, we continue to live."[32]

One might argue, however, that women's studies now is less oriented to the personal than it was in its beginnings and understands the self as a more complex construct than is implied by the early assertion "The personal is political." Today, with a more fully defined subject matter produced through prodigious feminist scholarship, practitioners must struggle in order to accommodate the new academic riches they have accumulated. Even for the best instructors, combining the personal with the academic requires much effort and experience. Good pedagogy must be learned. Teaching the academic in conventional ways is easier. If an emphasis on the personal seems to persist, it is because personalized learning is effective. Women's studies faculty do not want just to teach; they want students to find meaning, to make connections, to link with their own lives what they learn about women and the world as seen from women's points of view.

In feminist pedagogy, the "giving of voice" to students is a metaphor for fostering in students a sense of themselves that is essential to their full personal development. The women's studies students who speak out clearly express this sense of seeking to integrate their intellectual understanding into their personal lives, in some cases even consciously applying to themselves a developmental framework based on "women's ways of knowing." "Students [who] speak up and speak out"—as the subtitle of a collection of journal entries written between 1986 and 1990 by sixty undergraduate and graduate students at Duke University puts it—reveal how the subject matter of women's studies leads them to intense scrutiny of their own beliefs and relationships, as they seek to apply new information to what they have already learned. Students were asked to record in their journals their reactions to course readings, classroom discussions, and related material. According to the collection's editors, Jean O'Barr and Mary Wyer, they were not asked, or expected, to record personal experiences. Some did so, but the editors report being "struck with how rarely students wrote about themselves in the process of learning." What comes through in these student voices is their search for meanings. They are clearly critical thinkers, critical of feminism and women's studies as well as of institutional arrangements, social attitudes toward women, sexuality and race, and themselves—especially of their relationships with others in and out of class. As one (male) student, seeking to sort out the connections between emotion and action, wrote: "The personal is problematic." These students applied to texts and to their lives the methods of critical analysis they learned in women's studies classes.[33]

While it may be accurate to state that the Duke University students did not focus on personal experiences, their individual voices are present and insistent on expressing personal opinion. As they rethink what they formerly took for granted, these students often challenge authority, including the women's studies faculty, who may also find themselves in new and risky relationships. O'Barr and Wyer state that

> feminist pedagogical practices sparked by the new scholarship on women . . . challenge nothing less than the structuring assumptions of teacher/student relations in American higher education. When teachers assume that competition, isolation, and self-doubt are productive motivators (or teach as if they assume this), they subordinate their students' skills and talents to the idea that rewardable achievements preclude collaboration, cooperation and trust. Such assumptions were honed by white male faculty on white male students; they do not helpfully address the more diverse interests and learning practices of peoples of color, women, or (for that matter) white men.[34]

Even though most of these student writings at Duke University were drawn from advanced courses in women's studies, it is clear from their opinions that many of the writers did not define themselves as feminist. In this regard they are typical of the students who enroll in women's studies classes. Many faculty have long noted that women's studies students hold reservations about feminism. On the basis of her experience teaching women's studies at the University of Oklahoma, Barbara Hillyer Davis proposes that feminist teachers respond to their "mixed" classes, with their traditional majority and feminist minority, by avoiding typical female roles. They should avoid playing the superwoman, wife, or mother who tries to accommodate all needs, and should think of themselves as "translators," helping members of each group to learn the language of the other. "The feminist student is then asked to appreciate the skills involved in balancing the emotional needs of husband and children, while the traditional student comes to understand how the institution of motherhood limits people." Estelle Freedman, professor of history at Stanford University, observes that "students who signed up for FS 101 arrived in a state of extreme fear of feminism." By the end of the semester, she reports, the majority "had shifted from discomfort with feminism to enthusiastic embrace of the term and its complexity." Some students report experiencing a feminist "click," or conversion, parallel to the spiritual conversions described by such "First Wave" feminists as the British suffrage leaders Annie Kenney and Lady Constance Lytton. Jean O'Barr says, "The new ideas [students] obtain in the classroom turn on lights in their heads."[35]

Assessing Student Learning

The differences among students are reflected in their responses to the women's studies learning experience. This phenomenon is not, of course, restricted to women's studies courses; a wide range of opinion expressed by students in evaluations of their classes is normal. Nevertheless, because of the many attacks on women's studies during the 1980s (some highly publicized and others local and lower-key), when the director of the NWSA, Caryn McTighe Musil, was invited in 1989 to join in the national movement to assess student learning in the academy, she had to resist an inclination to decline (which grew stronger, she says, as "the muscles in my neck tightened"). She was fearful of the very idea of exposing a field already under attack to open investigation. But she did agree to the proposal, the result of which is a very interesting NWSA-AAC report on a three-year, FIPSE-funded study of seven women's studies programs by a national team of experts on assessment of student learning.[36]

Unlike many studies, the NWSA-AAC assessment does not rely only on self-reporting, and in some instances it offers comparison with non–women's studies classes. The participating institutions included both research universities and liberal arts colleges—public and private; large and small; East Coast, West Coast, and Midwestern; urban, rural, and suburban; single-sex and coeducational. The report is entitled *The Courage to Question* to highlight the statements of students who said that women's studies "gave me courage" and that it "opens with questions . . . that's really the biggest difference . . . you question all the time, all the time."[37]

The assessment team carefully designed a plan that, while similar to others, also reflected feminist values and assumptions: for example, that, as the AAHE's evaluator Pat Hutchings put it, "what students learn in class will affect their lives outside of the class because gender is not contained by the walls of the classroom."[38] Knowledge, in short, is "connected." Therefore, multiple-choice tests—increasingly abandoned elsewhere as well—would not do. What *was* deemed indispensable was student involvement, both in accordance with feminist values and in hopes of motivating student participation. It was also assumed that the voice of each institution should be heard in the questions posed; and therefore one full year of the three-year study was spent by each campus team in developing a research design that reflected its particular program goals in four areas: "knowledge base, learning skills, feminist pedagogy, and personal growth." In each instance, participants developed a set of "passionate questions" that generated a group of eight "key" background questions that all campuses could (but were not mandated to) use.[39]

A major theme that emerged as characteristic of women's studies classes was "personalized learning," which was distinguished from "active learning" to emphasize that it "allows the student to use the intellectual to explain the personal—a 'compelling connection'" that may help to explain both the attraction of women's studies classes and why students report working so hard in them. "When content links with lives, the transformation in students is palpable and lasting," argues Musil. She also supports her assertion by citing an AAC study entitled "Liberal Learning and the Arts and Science Major," which showed women's studies as better than the ten other majors surveyed in "connecting different kinds of knowledge, . . . connecting course materials and assignments to personally significant questions, . . . identifying and exploring problems in the field in relation to significant questions of society, . . . exploring values and ethics important to the major, . . . and helping students develop an overview of the field's intellectual history."[40]

While it is impossible here even to summarize the reports from these seven assessment projects, a few salient points regarding each may be illustrative. At the University of Colorado, one women's studies course was compared with two non–women's studies courses (in English and American Studies), all upper division. The women's studies students sat in traditional formation while the others formed circles; and participation rates were higher in the latter. But only in the women's studies class did students make connections between the material and their lives. The pedagogical practices associated with women's studies were employed more extensively in the non–women's studies classes and perhaps account for the greater participation in discussion. Nevertheless, the "connections" were made in women's studies and not elsewhere, leading the assessment leaders to conclude that "content was more important to fostering personalized learning than pedagogy alone." Testing this conclusion in five other classes (of which two were in women's studies), they found a similar pattern. Interestingly, despite an emphasis on teaching methods, at several schools, including Colorado, Old Dominion University (in Virginia), and Wellesley, it was found to be course content rather than pedagogy that was the most influential factor.[41]

The theme that emerges most emphatically from several campus studies is that of making connections. At Lewis and Clark College in Oregon, which offers a curriculum in "gender studies," the assessment focused on the program's impact on the institution and on students' personal growth. Here the results, based on responses to questionnaires completed by students, faculty, and graduates, emphasized connections between academic and personal experience, between men and women students, and between gender studies and other areas of knowledge. The majority of respondents perceived the gender studies program as an important force on campus, fostering integration of the curriculum and the college community. At Old Dominion University, evaluators sought to learn why women's studies students become "connected knowers." How did students gain the analytic skills—"skills that come hard to a majority of our students"—to move beyond the stage of "subjective knower"? Exit interviews suggested that they succeeded with about 25 percent of these students. One student explained that she had been asked to consider connections between an author's life and work. "In other courses, ideas are posed to us as 'this is the way it is,' but in women's studies courses an idea would be given to us to evaluate. I learned to question things I read for the first time. . . . You gave your opinion, but you were also asked for evidence." Women's studies classes also fostered friendship, with students of both sexes finding that they gained more close (female) friends than in other classes. Likewise, faculty made connections among themselves by talking about the FIPSE project, showing "just how starved we were for discussion about teaching."[42]

Wellesley College, which had initially rejected a proposal to institute women's studies (in 1971), was the only women's college to participate. Already focused on teaching and on giving "voice" to women, Wellesley evaluators wanted to learn whether women's studies affected students differently than other programs did and whether "students feel pressure to give 'politically correct' answers and to identify only with 'feminist' ideas, as women's studies often is charged with in the media and by conservatives." A questionnaire submitted to students in selected women's studies classes and a matched sample of other social science courses (only 4% of either group being women's studies majors) showed "little difference" in student perceptions of the impact of the course on their "intellectual lives and political beliefs." The personal effects, however, differed. More women's studies students felt pressured to conform, by other students—30 percent compared to 14 percent; but perhaps, conjectured the team, this reflected the emotionally charged content of some of the material discussed. They also reported greater intellectual involvement. Students in women's studies classes felt that the course had made them "more critical learners and participants in social change." Alluding to Allan Bloom's charge against women's studies, the Wellesley team found that "rather than 'closing' the American mind, women's studies courses seem to have 'opened up' our students to critical and different ways of thinking and valuing knowledge." They found the personal changes reported by women's studies students to be "clearly rooted in intellectual considerations, demonstrating William Blake's dictum, 'for a tear is an intellectual thing.'" Once more, the theme of connection emerges. "The self becomes rooted in an intellectual agenda," the team observed. In the courses taken by members of the control group, students found their skills enhanced, but more narrowly, "helping them read the newspaper better . . . or direct[ing] their job searches." In contrast, the women's studies students came to see "their lives as connected to others in a globally linked way." Like the researchers at Colorado and Old Dominion, the Wellesley group found that subject matter made the difference.[43]

At Hunter College, which saw enrollment in its women's studies program increase by 81 percent between 1985 and 1990, the assessment project measured achievement in the areas of multiculturalism, critical thinking, and the integration of knowledge. Its team examined the curriculum, faculty appointments, and faculty development for inclusion of diversity; queried students and reviewed syllabi regarding assignments that required critical thinking; and surveyed students about connections made between women's studies courses and other aspects of their lives. Echoing women's studies students across the nation, a Hunter student said, "First of all, you have to think." She also found women's studies, contrary to some students' expectations, "probably the hardest courses." Students at Oberlin College agreed that they were "very challenged" by women's studies. Three-quarters of the women's studies majors and minors in a student survey project found women's studies the "most intellectually stimulating courses they had taken at Oberlin." "I've not learned as much in any other class at Oberlin in the past three and one half years," said a senior art major. If, as is commonly assumed, knowledge is power, then students seem to be achieving the number one goal they identified: "self-empowerment." The same term appears conspicuously in a discussion of women's studies student learning at the University of Missouri–Columbia; they reported that "Women's Studies transformed their lives." The core courses, described as "feminist" and "radical," characterized by "more discussion and more collaborative learning," were considered the most effective. Crosslisted courses, where students schooled in feminism mixed with majors better prepared in the discipline, seemed to offer less opportunity to employ a distinctive pedagogy.[44]

The theme of connecting learning to life appears often in the first comprehensive national study of women's studies graduates, published in 1995. Based on a questionnaire completed by 89 individuals who graduated from 43 women's studies programs, the study included 88 women and 1 man, who ranged in age from twenty-one to seventy-three and represented twenty-four states across the nation and many cultural backgrounds; 5 of the participants were women of color. The participants were slightly older than a traditional group of recent alumnae (almost half were aged thirty or older), and all but a few defined themselves as feminists. Almost half (45%) had completed women's studies along with a second major, almost half (19) of those in psychology and English, and others in fields ranging from art to economics. One of the most striking facts is their tendency to pursue further education: more than half (52%) had continued studying for master's (26 earned; 9 in progress), doctoral, or professional degrees. They were Protestant (33), Catholic (16), Jewish (11), Quaker (3), and Mormon (2), and one each represented the Buddhist, Greek Orthodox, and other religions. About one-third (29) identified themselves as lesbian or bisexual; an almost equal number of heterosexual women were married, engaged, or "partnered" (32). Twenty-two had children, ranging in age from three months to forty-four years. One noticeable feature of the demographic information collected about the graduates is their diversity.

Nevertheless, they offered similar responses to the three questions put to them: "Why did you major in women's studies?" "How has your women's studies major affected you professionally since your graduation?" and "How has your women's studies major affected you personally since your graduation?" The answer to the first question often led back to enrollment in an introductory course that challenged students to rethink old ideas and past experiences. In the authors' words: "They had 'aha!' experiences." One (a communications consultant) said that she had majored in women's studies because she had "followed [her] heart"; another (an artist), that women's studies provided a "philosophy of life and learning not unlike radical Christianity"; a third (a union organizer), that she had chosen her major because "it appealed to my passion for social justice"; a fourth (a yacht broker), that her motive had been "curiosity . . . and then it became the greatest intellectual challenge of my life"; and a fifth (an airline pilot), that she had chosen women's studies because it "challenged me to think in a new way." The effects? The answers tend toward a mode: a sense of empowerment and self-confidence; learning to think critically and to appreciate differences; becoming part of a community within a larger, impersonal academic world.[45]

The widely reported work of Alexander Astin, director of the Graduate School of Education Information Studies and the Institute for Higher Education Research at the University of California, Los Angeles, whose annual surveys have tracked the attitudes of first-year college students for thirty years, shows dramatic differences over time in students' motivations for seeking higher education. Whereas in 1967, 82.9 percent ranked the search for "a philosophy of life" as an important goal, by 1986 only 40.6 percent did so.[46] In the stories that women's studies graduates tell, what strikes the reader is how many found in their major something that helped them to integrate learning and life, that is, to develop a "philosophy of life." They entered with—or were challenged by—questions about themselves, their values, and their goals. One can open this book almost at random and hear the voice of a women's studies graduate saying, along with a seventy-year-old grandmother who had enrolled in women's studies at age fifty-eight, "Women's studies gave me a fuller life." It is a more fully examined life. One 1985 graduate who is now in her mid-thirties and is coordinator of women's services at a university praises women's studies for "enhanc[ing her] self-esteem, critical/analytical skills, and political savvy" but adds, "The only negative aspect is that Women's Studies majors know too much.

Professional decisions then become ethical and moral decisions." Evaluators at the University of Colorado also noted this ethical dimension. Students there sought to use their women's studies learning to guide their
moral actions.[47]

While self-selection inevitably affects self-reported information, supportive behavioral evidence can also be found in the study of women's studies graduates. If the proof is in the pudding, or if (in more contemporary
terms) the measure of student success lies in "learning outcomes," these
students' "life after women's studies" should reassure the field's proponents. They have achieved an impressive initial degree of success within a
few years. Having selected a nontraditional major, these students might
have been expected to follow uncommon paths after graduation, but it is
still noteworthy to discover the degree to which members of this group
have exercised ingenuity in their post–women's studies lives.

As liberal arts majors, they were often challenged about what they
intended to do with their education. One responded: "You live your life.
You use your education to enhance the quality of your existence." Over and
over, these students defend the value of a liberal arts education in words
that might please even defenders of the most classical education. "You are
not limited to a single discipline, and you can develop critical analysis and
writing skills that will prove most valuable when you enter the work world.
Women's studies is a liberal arts education in its truest sense," reported a
graduate now seeking a master's degree in politics. A health clinic medical
assistant agreed, saying, "the major allows/prepares one to do anything any
other liberal arts major does."[48]

These women exude self-confidence. The authors could have no doubt
of a negative answer when, responding to a critic, they asked the reader,
"After reading the profiles, would you conclude that majoring in women's
studies promotes a victim identity?" Faculty role models and mentors, and
friendships begun in class, contribute to a sense of belonging that, especially
on larger commuter campuses, strengthens both individuals and programs.
Feelings of exclusion on grounds of differences are occasionally mentioned,
and the women's studies classroom is not without stress, sometimes due to
faculty efforts to incorporate diverse voices. Maher and Tetreault also record
the struggles required for faculty and students to accommodate difference
in discussions of identity, voice, and theory.[49]

What women's studies faculty seek is to foster student engagement in
learning. Contrary to the numerous reports of faculty indifference to teach-

ing and to students that led one AAC report to speak of "two cultures in
academia," in which the students and the faculty are said to be living virtually separate existences, the NWSA-AAC study points to women's studies as a place that fosters a connection between students and faculty. In
Courage to Question, students offer praise for faculty: "We have wonderful
teachers who care about us, are telling us something real and tangible. They
validate our existence as women, and they are great role models, something
women don't have much of."[50]

The importance placed on making connections with students, however, goes beyond women's studies' origins in an antiauthoritarian ideology
and theories about "women's ways of knowing" to another important factor: sex-role socialization. Feminist pedagogy also reflects female styles of
relationship. A recent study of sex differences in teaching behavior, drawing on role theory, suggests that women may experience "role conflict"
when functioning in an occupation traditionally defined by male modes
of behavior. Seeking to resolve "status inconsistency," women professors
used teaching techniques that "simultaneously legitimated their authority
and reduced the appearance of authority." More than the men who were
studied, women professors encouraged student participation. Striving to
"nurture independent thinkers," they were observed to "focus more on the
student as the locus of learning . . . [to place] more emphasis on students'
participation . . . [and to form] personal, individual relationships with their
students." Interestingly, women full professors were found to be "less invested in their teaching; they resembled the men full professors more
closely than they resembled the women assistant or associate professors."
(But the study observed few women at that rank, reflecting the concentration of women at the lower ranks.) There was little difference, incidentally,
in the ways in which men and women structured their classrooms or presented material. Ultimately, the authors of this study conclude that "feminist pedagogy itself is based directly on the experience of being female in
this society."[51]

Advocates might suggest that academic administrators consider the
success of women's studies as a measure of good teaching; they might propose that, like Uri Treisman's highly lauded work on enhancing the performance of ethnic minority students in advanced mathematics through the
use of small study groups, feminist pedagogy offers lessons of value for other
subjects and other populations. "Student-centered, relationship-focused

teaching styles" may also be effective in promoting the collaborative learning that is increasingly fashionable today.[52]

For feminist educators, however, collaborative teaching and learning continue to encounter the divisive forces of "difference." On grounds of class, race, and ethnicity, some critics within women's studies dissent from the "midwife-teacher" model and the "maternal thinking" implied in feminist pedagogy.[53] In women's studies, teaching and learning are expected to incorporate an understanding of the situational basis of knowledge ("positionality") that precludes creating boundaries that marginalize individuals on any categorical basis (even that of male gender). In practice, however, the importance of personal experience and personal relationships—and the emergence of "identity politics"—has made it difficult to mediate differences among women. While recognizing that women's studies no longer belongs to its founders, feminist teacher-scholars still wrestle with the tendency of the majority to speak as if for all women. Feminist efforts to embrace diversity remain the source of struggle in the theory and the practice of women's studies.

5

Recognizing Differences

Virtually all of the students who filed into my "women in history" class-room in the fall of 1971, many of whom were making an antifashion state-ment—wearing their hair long and straight, with their feet bare—carried as a kind of badge of their feminism (for it was not on the reading list) a copy of Robin Morgan's *Sisterhood Is Powerful.* All women, the book implied, were united as sisters. Women's studies was founded on the assumption of common interests among women, whatever their individual characteristics. Yet today, the women of women's studies are divided, both by differences that mark individuals and groups in distinctive ways and by the concept of difference itself. "Twenty years ago," as the philosopher Jane Roland Mar-tin observes wryly, "no one would have guessed that difference would emerge as the privileged perspective in feminist theory and research and that any attempt to find commonalities among women would be condemned out of hand."[1]

This chapter examines the evolution of academic feminists' varying responses to the recognition of differences in the experiences and perspec-tives of women. It cites examples of angry conflict as well as mutual support and relates many efforts to deal constructively in personal relationships, organizational structures, and scholarly work with a subject that all of higher education, and indeed all of contemporary society, now finds urgent and difficult. The importance of "diversity" in women's studies reflects the commitment of feminism to serve the interests of all women. The recognition of differences between and among women affects every aspect of women's studies, from curriculum and pedagogy to theory and practice, and especially the complex relationships among them. Grounded in advocacy for women as a group, and inquiry about their experiences, women's studies grew, as we have seen, out of a movement that underscored the importance of individual perceptions to its political analysis. As the field has grown, its scholarship has become ever more sophisticated in defining its terms. Reflections about individual experience have elicited new attempts to define identity, to question claims of authenticity, and to examine relationships with regard to the many differences that characterize women. These issues have led to intense exchanges about the meanings of feminism and to confrontations based on the politics of identity. Efforts to deal with diversity as a concept within feminist theory will be discussed in chapter 6. The struggle of academic feminists to integrate multiplicity into the broader field of women's studies is discussed here.

The founders of women's studies were largely white women. For reasons related to the history of higher education and to socioeconomic conditions and race relations in the United States, relatively fewer women of color appeared on either side of the podium (or amid the circles of chairs) than in feminist marches down Fifth Avenue or in picket lines protesting discrimination on grounds of sex. Despite the presence of many homosexual women as both students and teachers, "lesbian invisibility" persisted through the early years. The presence of women who differed on the basis of what was then called sexual preference sometimes first became apparent in "gay/straight splits," while heterosexual feminists struggled to recognize their own homophobia and deal with their fears that the visible participation of lesbians undercut their charges against what they called "male chauvinism." Other forms of diversity later acknowledged but also underrepresented in—if not missing altogether from—most courses and curricula included differences in class, religion, language, age, physical condition, and appearance.

It is not true, however, as sometimes charged or assumed, that differences were discovered only in the 1980s, or even in the late 1970s. In her introduction to *Sisterhood Is Powerful*, Robin Morgan discussed the participation of "black sisters" in women's liberation and cautioned against taking "a simplistic view of *any* group of women, including ourselves."[2] As early as 1970, Alice Echols points out, "the rhetoric of universal sisterhood had given way to wrenching discussions of women's difference, as lesbians and working-class women challenged the assumption that there was a uniformity to women's experiences and interests. From 1970 onward, excoriations of the movement as racist, classist, and heterosexist became routine if not obligatory at feminist gatherings." Recollections differ, of course, for experiences of difference varied greatly among feminists. Gloria Bowles recalls, "Women's studies was an open tent. All were welcomed."[3]

Most (white) readers of Frances Beale's 1969 essay "Double Jeopardy: To Be Black and Female" or the several other articles on women in the black liberation movement and on Mexican American and Chinese "colonized women" in Morgan's book would have been shocked by the accusation embedded in the term *racist feminism,* used by the poet Audre Lorde in her 1979 presentation at a thirtieth-anniversary celebration of Simone de Beauvoir's *Second Sex,*[4] for they would likely have understood racism in terms of acts of commission of which they felt innocent. Nor would they have anticipated their own experience of what Sylvia Yanagisako, drawing on her Hawaiian origins, terms "becoming haole." By this she refers to the development by majority feminists in the United States of a white race consciousness and their recognition that they themselves are shaped by a specific culture that is also marked by its differences from others. Believing in "sisterhood," they could not have foreseen the many separate caucuses that would be formed in professional organizations, including their own national association, on the basis of personal identity, or Sokari Ekine's 1996 invitation to followers of a women's studies e-mail list to subscribe to an electronic communications link labeled "Black Systers."[5]

The "feminism" that fueled the founding of women's studies has now given way to a spectrum of feminisms. In the 1970s, feminists were divided into a number of groups, often labeled "liberal feminists," "socialist feminists," and "radical feminists," on the basis of their differing theories about the origins of women's subordination and concomitant strategies for liberation (see chapter 6). Today, differences are marked by national origin, race, ethnicity, religion, sexual orientation, and other attributes of personal identity. Along with black feminism (sometimes called "womanism"), Latina feminism, lesbian feminism, and many others, stands "middle-class" or "mainstream" feminism, now also sometimes termed "hegemonic" or "white" feminism. As one analyst put it in a recent work on feminism and theory, "Things change. . . . It would seem that dealing with the fact of differences is *the* project of women's studies today. . . . It is impossible to exaggerate the importance of the critique of feminism's (*white* feminism's) exclusions."[6]

It is difficult as well to deny the seriousness with which feminist leaders and practitioners of women's studies have addressed questions of diversity among women. Recognition of difference is not only divisive. It also encourages the embracing of diversity. An emphasis on difference pervades the language, theory, textbooks, courses and curricula, conference programs, and professional organizations of academic feminism. When a regional women's studies conference announced the title of its 1996 annual meeting as "Celebrating Difference/Exploring Commonality: Women's Studies in the '90s," it captured the essence of the current debate on diversity. Similarly, the triennial Berkshire Conference in Women's History, generally recognized as the premier forum for presentation of scholarship on women in history, labeled its 1996 meeting "Complicating Categories: Women, Gender, and Difference." Questions of difference permeate curricula and classrooms as well as relations among feminist faculty and students in women's studies. "Dilemmas of difference" confront theorists and practitioners alike.[7]

The problem was there in the beginning. Many just did not see it; or, seeing it, did not understand its import. Yet it has frequently been pointed out that women's studies, like the midcentury rebirth of feminism that engendered it, grew out of and drew on the black liberation movement and its academic offspring, black studies (while generally eschewing its militance). Feminist historians have acknowledged the importance of the black liberation movement in revitalizing a dormant women's movement and have pointed to the contributions of black women active in that struggle as exemplars for white activists. "For the first time," said one Southern white woman of the 1960s, "I had role models I could really respect."[8] Black women marched alongside white women on August 26, 1970, in the famous parade down Fifth Avenue to celebrate the fiftieth anniversary of women's suffrage. Two of the six "generative works of contemporary feminism" of that year which the pioneer feminist historian Berenice Carroll mentions in a 1994 retrospective prepared for the twenty-fifth anniversary of the Coordinating Committee on Women in the Historical Profession were written by black women.[9] Frances Beale's much cited and often reprinted 1969 essay appeared in one of these—Toni Cade's *Black Woman*, which itself appeared on many early women's studies reading lists along with *Sisterhood Is Powerful* (both published in 1970).

Language evocative of the civil rights era was featured prominently in popular readings of the first women's studies classes, including Helen Hacker's 1951 "Women as a Minority Group," Vivian Gornick's "The Next Great Moment in History Is Ours," and Naomi Weisstein's "Woman as Nigger," the latter two published in 1969.[10] The likening of women's oppression to racism and slavery gave feminists a powerful tool. It had been prominent before, in the rhetoric of English and French feminists of the seventeenth and eighteenth centuries. "If all Men are born Free, how is it that all Women are born Slaves?" asked Mary Astell three centuries ago. The comparison now became commonplace, repeating—probably unwittingly, given the neglect of women's history in that era—a practice employed a century earlier by leaders of the American women's rights movement. Like Susan B. Anthony and Elizabeth Cady Stanton, however, the feminists of the 1970s did not truly analyze and develop strategies for overcoming the "double jeopardy" of black women which they acknowledged.[11] The use of the racism analogy was "more often an attempt to prove the existence of sexism than to analyze the conditions of minority women's experience."[12] Thinking from an inclusive perspective, however, is another matter; and, as has been pointed out, the last sentence of Joreen's essay in *Sisterhood Is Powerful*, "The 51 Percent Minority Group," which declares that "women are tired of working for everyone's liberation except their own," cannot be understood to be speaking for women of color.[13]

Although in the early 1970s the evidence of difference was there, few of the founders of women's studies were prepared to appreciate its meaning. Each spoke first of what she knew personally, and learned only by observation to broaden her view. My own first women's history class included an African American student (making her own antifashion statement by wearing an "Afro" hairstyle) who, to my surprise, not only did not share my fondness for Mary Wollstonecraft's attack on the privileges accorded English ladies but objected to the portrayal of the small courtesies offered women by men as condescension. When I cited one of my favorite passages in Wollstonecraft's *Vindication*—"I scarcely am able to govern my muscles, when I see a man start with eager, and serious solicitude, to lift a handkerchief, or shut a door, when the *lady* could have done it herself, had she only moved a pace or two"—this student informed me and the class that she enjoyed small favors from men.[14] I later learned that she had only recently returned to school after a twenty-one-year absence. At age thirty-four, she was the mother of a twenty-one year-old daughter whose birth had caused her to drop out of junior high school. The priorities that brought her to the classroom differed from those of Betty Friedan's more educated and privileged but unhappy housewives, who were also beginning to return to the classroom in the late 1960s and early 1970s.

Women of color questioned the relevance of many feminist findings and often interpreted them differently. In her introduction to *The Black Woman*, Toni Cade asked, "Are women after all simply women? . . . In the whole bibliography of feminist literature, literature immediately and directly relevant to us wouldn't fill a page." According to the founders of black women's studies, slightly less than 1 percent of the 4,658 women's studies courses listed in a 1974 journal focused on black women. Chicanas and numerous other women of color likewise expressed anger at "incidents of intolerance, prejudice and denial of differences" within feminism and women's studies. Lesbians charged women's studies itself with sexism, coining a new term of accusation: *heterosexism*.[15] But change was already under way. By 1976, when Florence Howe reviewed fifteen women's studies programs for a report to the National Advisory Council on Women's Educational Programs, she found that "on all the campuses . . . the issues of race and class were critical." The fifteen curricula presented in her appendix show only one lacking a course that specifically referred to women of color in its title; ten of the fifteen offered two or more. (San Francisco State listed six.) In contrast, only San Francisco State and the University of Washington listed courses with *lesbian* or *homosexuality* in the title.[16]

New Concepts and New Choices

It was in materials prepared for the classroom that the multiple perspectives of women of color began to have their first major impact on women's studies. Leadership in producing materials inclusive of greater diversity for the women's studies classroom must be credited to the Feminist Press. From its inception, the press undertook to publish works that other publishing houses neglected. Florence Howe has described how the Feminist Press "searched deliberately for lost literature by white working-class women to begin with, and then, before the mid-seventies, by black women." One of the first documentary collections on women of color available for classroom adoption, *Black Women in White America*, was compiled by Gerda Lerner in 1972. *Sturdy Black Bridges*, an anthology celebrating the "analytical," "conversational," and "creative vision" of dozens of black writers (all but a few of whom were women), appeared in 1979. It was the first of several books in which women of color used the word *bridge* both as a metaphor for strength and also to connote linkages and coalition. As first employed, it refers to the last stanza of a poem by Carolyn Rodgers that is the final selection in the book. Rodgers writes:

> My mother, religious-negro, proud of
> having waded through a storm, is very obviously,
> a sturdy Black bridge that I
> crossed over, on.[17]

In 1981, Cherríe Moraga and Gloria Anzaldúa published *This Bridge Called My Back*, an anthology, said Toni Cade Bambara, of "cables, esoesses, conjurations and fusile missiles" written by "radical women of color." Moraga and Anzaldúa stated, provocatively, that they hoped to see the book become a "*required* text in most women's studies courses. And we don't mean just 'special' courses on Third World Women or Racism." They intended it to be a "revolutionary tool" for Third World women everywhere. Anzaldúa declared that feminists were "notorious for 'adopting' women of color as their 'cause' while still expecting us to adapt to *their* expectations and *their* language." This book threw out a challenge.[18]

Originally compiled as a set of class readings, the two editions of *This Bridge* (1981 and 1984) and a less widely adopted successor volume, *Making Face, Making Soul: Haciendo Caras* (1990), have exerted a major influence in women's studies. As Norma Alarcón reflected in the later work, "There is little doubt . . . that *Bridge* . . . has problematized many a version of Anglo-American feminism, and has helped open the way for alternate feminist discourses and theories."[19] Still, she argued, the impact was largely "cosmetic." She agreed with the philosopher Jane Flax and others that the "modal person" of feminist discourse remained a "self-sufficient individual adult" modeled on the white male, who does not reflect the cultures of women who fit the categories "native female" or "woman of color." This led Alarcón, in postmodernist prose, to question the category of "woman."[20]

Reacting similarly to their relative invisibility in women's studies, lesbians also challenged generalizations about women. Despite the seven thousand entries that had already appeared in one bibliography on lesbians in literature, Bonnie Zimmerman found in a survey of introductory women's studies texts in the early 1980s that material on lesbians was so lacking that she declared, "Heterosexism is alive and well in the women's studies textbook market." In another study, Kathy Hickok found that of several dozen anthologies taught in women's literature classes, only a handful presented lesbian writers effectively.[21] At least partially to satisfy the classroom problem, two books soon appeared that addressed issues of diversity from the perspectives of black women and lesbians, respectively, both including sample course outlines and bibliographies as well as theoretical analyses. Both also spoke to multiple differences of ethnicity and sexuality. They encouraged faculty and students in women's studies programs to address questions of difference through books, if not by personal experience.

In 1982, the black feminist scholars Gloria T. Hull, Patricia Bell Scott, and Barbara Smith published their groundbreaking and provocatively entitled book *All the Women Are White, All the Blacks Are Men, but Some of Us Are Brave*. Its subtitle, "Black Women's Studies," Hull and Smith announced in their introduction, was intended to name a new discipline. This represented "a stance that is in direct opposition to most of what passes for culture and thought on the North American continent. To use the term and act on it in a white-male world is an act of political courage."[22] Henceforth, black women would define themselves and adopt their own politics, struggling against multiple forms of oppression based on race, sex, class, and sexuality. In addition to making a political statement about the need for black women's studies, this book offered source materials to assist in the building project. It included scholarly essays reviewing disciplines and social institutions from the perspective of African American women, bibliographic essays, and syllabi for twenty courses taught across the country between 1972 and 1980, the earliest being those of Alice Walker (at the University of Massachusetts at Boston, and Wellesley College in 1972) and Barbara Smith (at Emerson College, in Massachusetts, in 1973). The book foreshadowed the founding in 1983 of *Sage*, a scholarly journal devoted to studies of black women, by Patricia Bell Scott and Beverly Guy-Sheftall.

Several years later, in 1988, Deborah King articulated the concept of "multiple jeopardy" to express a black feminist consciousness. Pointing to the history of the race-sex analogy, King reminded readers that it was not invented by white women in the 1960s but had been used by Anna Julia Cooper and Mary Church Terrell in the late nineteenth and early twentieth centuries. Concerned about its effects, King cited studies that showed how "the assumption of parallelism led to research that masked the differences [in oppressions] for different groups." She also demonstrated why "monistic" liberation politics, focused on single, separate forms of dominance, failed black women. Like bell hooks, King asserts that "no other group in America has so had their identity socialized out of existence as have black women." In her view, black feminism and black women's studies empower black women to define themselves and to maintain the "multiple consciousness essential for our liberation, of which feminist consciousness is an integral part." The more complex perspective can also reveal more clearly the strengths of black women as "powerful, independent subjects."[23]

Theorists building on these works have developed an increasingly sophisticated critique. "The theme of double jeopardy marks the starting point for all literature on black women," remarks the historian Evelyn Brooks Higginbotham. Patricia Hill Collins, in her influential essay "Learning from the Outsider Within," draws on the experience of black women and on her discipline of sociology to suggest a valuable potential heuristic model. Testing facts, observations, and "worldviews" against the reality of black women's lives, she argues, challenges conventional paradigms and stimulates new insights. "A variety of individuals can learn from Black women's experiences as outsiders within." She cites as examples "Black men, working-class individuals, white women, other people of color, religious and sexual minorities."[24] Echoing Collins, bell hooks proposes that scholars study black women to understand "women in general."[25]

Appearing the same year as *But Some of Us Are Brave,* Margaret Cruikshank's *Lesbian Studies* (1982) provided an anthology of sample syllabi for courses on lesbians and a thirty-five-page bibliography of books and periodicals, fiction and nonfiction, and biography and criticism, as well as essays about the personal and political experiences of lesbians in academia. Cruikshank intended her book to "add a new political dimension to women's studies by implicitly demanding that lesbian-feminist issues be taken more seriously." She also recognized the good news, the "euphoria . . . due partly to emergence from the closet and recognition of our sheer numbers . . . [and to experiencing] for the first time a passionate connection between our lives and our work."[26] That this connection was much more difficult for lesbians of color to forge was noted explicitly in one selection, the transcript of a 1981 dialogue between Cherríe Moraga and Barbara Smith, who wondered aloud how exceptional their presence in the book would be. Smith reflected that "there are virtually no women of color who are out as

Lesbians who are in a position to teach courses in universities." She was "angry about straight white women's studies teachers . . . [because] they can never see where women of color and Lesbians would logically fit into their subject matter." Moraga pointed out that white women, who had long taught "white-boyism," should be able also to teach "Third World women's literature." Women's studies courses, they agreed, "should reflect the experiences of *all* women." Women's studies instructors should stop assuming that "white people are *normal*."[27] In a similar vein, Adrienne Rich's now-famous essay of 1980, "Compulsory Heterosexuality and Lesbian Existence," made the point that, in her view, heterosexual women's sexual preference "may not be a 'preference' at all but something that has had to be imposed, managed, organized, propagandized, and maintained by force." Heterosexuality was an "institution" that required analysis in the women's studies classroom.[28]

That same year, participants in the National Women's Studies Association meeting heard Marilyn Frye protest the assumption "that widespread heterosexuality and the dominance of heterosexual conceptions have always been and will always be The Way It Is for humans on this planet." Frye dared heterosexual academic feminists to question their own sexual preference. "I wish," she declared, "you would notice that you are heterosexual. I wish you would grow to the understanding that you *choose* to be heterosexual—that you are and choose to be a member of a privileged and dominant class, one of your privileges being not to notice."[29]

Another major effort to broaden the scope of women's studies has come from a group of "Third World" women—including women born in the West with roots in Africa, Asia, and Latin America, indigenous North American women, and recent immigrants—who associate themselves with postcolonialism. While some of their work falls within the poststructuralist critique of anthropology and engages feminism in a highly theoretical mode, it has exercised considerable influence in women's studies. Their presence was made strikingly visible at an international conference entitled "Common Differences: Third World Women and Feminist Perspectives," held at the University of Illinois in 1983. The conference attracted two thousand participants.

Defining "Third World" broadly, this meeting brought to women's studies new international contexts and postcolonial critiques. It also led to a volume of essays that furthered dialogue about the varying effects of "systems of domination" and "relations of rule" on race, class, sexuality, and the experiences of colonialism. It emphatically made the point that "Western women" should cease ignoring, objectifying, and generalizing about other women, and it provided a text useful for that purpose.[30]

One measure of the impact of these internal criticisms has been the increasing proportion of space allotted to women of color and to lesbians in popular texts. The authors of early introductory women's studies textbooks have made major changes in their choices of focus and in the selections included in subsequent editions. In the first edition of Jo Freeman's *Women: A Feminist Perspective*, published in 1975, lesbians were indeed invisible; there were no listings, no articles on the topic. The third edition, published in 1984, included five index citations for "lesbians/lesbianism," in addition to seven for "gay" or "homosexual," and one article discussing lesbianism. The fifth edition, published in 1995, included eleven listings and two substantial articles under the three rubrics. The first edition of Sheila Ruth's *Issues in Feminism* (1978) includes in its index four listings on lesbianism and homosexuality, with only one article. The third edition (1995) offers seven listings, with numerous "mentions" and five substantive articles or discussions. The Hunter College Women's Studies Collective's text *Women's Realities, Women's Choices* offered in the index of its first edition in 1983 six references to lesbians; the second edition in 1995 includes twenty-four subtopics referring to many pages.[31] Because of these books' differing structures—there are only thirty-some substantial readings in the Freeman collection, a more typical textbook discussion of more than eighty topics in the Hunter volume, and fifty-some topics accompanied by numerous very short readings in the Ruth text—it is inappropriate to compare these numbers across the books. What is significant is to observe these textbooks' evolution over time in the treatment of diversity.

Another case in point is Laurel Richardson and Verta Taylor's *Feminist Frontiers*. It first appeared in 1983, with four selections of ninety-three devoted to racial diversity and homosexuality; in 1993 its third edition included twenty-nine selections on these topics among its seventy-four selections and "inserts." Beyond numbers is the revision of conceptual frameworks: where the earlier volume opened with a section on socialization entitled "Learning the Culture," the latter one begins with a section on "Diversity and Difference." This widely adopted text is notable for its inclusion of many selections representing the experience of women of color, lesbians, and working-class and older women. The articles are intended "to underscore the pervasive cultural, racial, ethnic, and other differences that interact with gender." Amy Kesselman, Lily D. McNair, and Nancy Schniedewind's 1995 anthology *Women: Images and Realities*, which is designed as an introductory women's studies text, defines women's studies and feminism in terms of their meanings for multiple groups of women. Its first selection is an excerpt from bell hooks's *Talking Back,* and the book includes the testimony of women of color of diverse ethnicities telling "what women's studies has meant to me."[32]

The newer works are possible because women of color themselves have addressed the paucity of classroom materials. Those preparing materials for the women's studies market are also aware of differences in sexuality. Lesbian and gay studies is said today to constitute a "minor growth industry." Thanks to the work of lesbian scholars, it is "no longer possible," according to Toni A. H. McNaron and Bonnie Zimmerman, "to produce an exhaustive bibliography."[33] Nevertheless, in some instances, lesbians may remain or may again become invisible. For example, in a recent anthology of work drawn from a Ford Foundation–funded project on "mainstreaming minority women's studies,"[34] lesbians of color are not even mentioned. While "lesbianness" as a "position" from which many speak is still underdeveloped, it may be subsumed into "lesbian and gay studies" or the newer "queer studies." In their 1996 anthology *The New Lesbian Studies,* McNaron and Zimmerman point out that lesbians have achieved a new presence in the academy. However—ironically, at least partially as a result of the expansion and sophistication of lesbian studies—they find in the emergence of queer studies a new threat. "Now, with the growth of gay studies and queer theory, lesbians once again find ourselves in danger of becoming invisible. In place of the gendered terms 'lesbian' or 'dyke,' we are invited to place ourselves under the sign of 'queer.'" While of course responses to this possibility differ, McNaron and Zimmerman express their concern about the potential loss of a woman-centered perspective if the rubric "lesbian" were to be subsumed within a larger concept and category.[35] These issues are also explored in an anthology, edited by two lesbians, that expands Adrienne Rich's 1980 formulation on heterosexuality and seeks by examining "heterocentricity" to clarify sexual identities for all women.[36]

Generalizing from any position taken to be normative now draws criticism in women's studies, perhaps with special intensity due to women's long-endured exclusion from discussion of human experience that was based on a unisexual male model. Anita Silvers, a philosopher and a pioneer in the field of disability studies, has suggested that the very conceptual framing of attempts to provide equal treatment to relatively deprived individuals or groups draws on an assumption of normality. In Silvers's view, both the historical record of feminism and feminist theory have distanced women with disabilities "by imposing a 'tyranny of the normal'" based on unexamined concepts of embodiment that exclude many women. "To be equalized by being normalized," she argues, "is only to be neutralized, which proves to be no effective route to equality."[37] It creates, she believes, only a facade of diversity.

Confronting Diversity in Practice

For many white, heterosexual feminists, the criticism directed at them by other feminists required a shift of focus from recognizing and expressing their anger at exclusion and subordination by men to facing anger directed at themselves. At the very time they were braving personal and institutional hostility to bring forth new women's studies programs or to bring those programs through their early formative stages, they found themselves dealing with attacks from within. Quickly, however, they recognized that their ignorance was no claim to innocence but rather a proof of privilege. They acted to remedy it. Nevertheless, as women's studies mushroomed in the 1970s and the importance of differences among women became increasingly evident, relationships among academic feminists were strained, especially about issues of sexuality and, even more, about race. Studies in women's history which brought into view racist statements by feminist heroes of the nineteenth-century suffrage movement revealed the inadequacy of—and even perhaps the racism embedded in—race-sex analogies. At the founding conference of the NWSA in 1977, a Third World women's caucus was formed and special representation was demanded for women of color on the coordinating council. It was proposed to give veto power to the Third World caucus. In 1980 the second annual meeting was disrupted by conflict over issues of race, class, and sexual identity. Challenged from the start because of its overwhelmingly white membership, the NWSA devoted its third annual meeting, at the University of Connecticut, Storrs, in 1981, to the theme of women's responses to racism. Daily consciousness-raising sessions in which participants could confront their own experiences with race were built into the program but did not eliminate conflict.

The importance, even dominance, of racial and ethnic identity issues in the national organization was responsible for an unusual resolution adopted at the NWSA's 1982 meeting. When it was proposed to add anti-Semitism to sexism, racism, and other "isms" among the organization's targets for elimination, an amendment was proposed and passed to specify "anti-Semitism directed against Arabs" as well as Jews. That year saw the publication of Evelyn Torton Beck's *Nice Jewish Girls: A Lesbian Anthology*, which challenged the Jewish community to acknowledge the existence of its female sexual minority. It also highlighted the omission of Jewish women as the subject of writings in feminist texts (although not as authors) and as representatives of a nondominant and persecuted culture in feminist events dealing with minorities and multiculturalism. By defining ethnicity in terms that excluded Jews, women's studies had allowed a "'benign' anti-Semitism of indifference and insensitivity . . . to flourish unchecked."[38] Many Jewish women who had long been active in both the feminist movement and women's studies would begin to represent themselves consciously as Jews.

The following year, a plenary session on racism and anti-Semitism was held at the NWSA's annual meeting and led to a joint publication by three lesbian feminists who describe themselves, respectively, as "white Christian-raised Southern, Afro-American, [and] Ashkenazi Jew." In three individual essays, Minnie Bruce Pratt, Barbara Smith, and Elly Bulkin explore their personal experiences and express their political views on how to work together constructively against racism and anti-Semitism. Using autobiographical as well as historical materials, they examine black and white, and black and Jewish, relations, interrogating themselves, their group, and the other, talking openly about their negative as well as positive experiences. Both Bulkin and Smith quote Cherríe Moraga's pessimistic conclusion about the "impact on individuals of suffering oppression": "Oppression does not make for hearts as big as all outdoors. Oppression makes us big and small. Expressive and silenced. Deep and dead."[39] Smith added, "We are certainly damaged people. The question is, finally, do we use that damage, that first-hand knowledge of oppression, to recognize each other, to do what work we can together? Or do we use it to destroy?"[40] Bulkin also challenged Mary Daly and other radical feminists who portrayed women as "Jews in a Nazi world," used the Holocaust metaphorically, and defined "men's violence against women [as] the ultimate in violence." She questioned the feminist hostility to men that included among its targets progressive men on the Left, hostility that had even silenced her.[41]

Despite such efforts at dialogue, the greater visibility of women of color among women's studies students and faculty, and the increasing representation of women's diversity in texts, courses, and curricula, conflict based on racial difference has continued to trouble women's studies and the national organization. A decade after the confrontation at Storrs, the 1990 NWSA conference at Akron, Ohio, collapsed in a race-based controversy about personnel practices in the organization's own central office. The question that brought the NWSA as close as it has ever come to dissolution involved the dismissal of an African American staff worker from the NWSA's national office. Aggressive and defensive postures were taken, as the NWSA was charged with racist behavior as well as insensitivity to the personal needs of a co-worker. The caucus of women of color, demanding that the national coordinator be fired, walked out, withdrawing from the NWSA and pledging to establish a separate feminist organization. Amid invective and vituperation, deliberative processes failed. Regular conference proceedings were overwhelmed by special forums and meetings called to discuss "racism and feminism." The Coordinating Council voted against the proposed dismissal but decided to substitute a retreat on governance issues for its annual meeting in 1991.

While the facts of the case remained in dispute, the difficulty of fulfilling the expectations of its diverse constituencies and of "managing inclusivity" in a complex organization founded on the ideology of sisterhood overwhelmed the NWSA's intentions. The NWSA found itself in "disarray. Its legitimacy was undermined . . . membership declined precipitously, and within months the entire national staff resigned." The national director, Caryn McTighe Musil, reflected that "we set ourselves up for failure by trying to be all things to all people."[42] Anger and guilt surely played pivotal roles as well.

Skipping its national meeting in 1991, the NWSA instead sponsored a relatively small meeting of program administrators. It began to rebuild with a small conference held at the University of Texas in Austin in 1992, where action was taken to revise its organizational structure and reduce the formerly preponderant role of the caucuses and regions in electing the governing council. Lamenting the de-emphasis of scholarship at this meeting, some members, while agreeing on the centrality of the struggle against racism to the NWSA's mission, began to call for greater focus on academic issues. (The debate over the relationship between women's studies activist and academic goals is explored further in chapter 7.)

By the fall of 1994, the national organization had begun to recover. In October, the chair of its membership committee, Bethania Maria, herself a member of the caucus of women of color, wrote to former members, soliciting renewal by reassuring them of the organization's progress in repairing the racial rift. The June 1994 conference, she noted, had featured among its plenary speakers African American, British, Bulgarian, Canadian, Chinese American, Egyptian, European American, Indian, Jewish American, Mexican American, Native American, and Nigerian feminists. She urged lapsed members to rejoin the effort to "find a common ground . . . and a common language," and she signed the letter, "In Sisterhood." The coordinator of the 1994 conference, Kris Anderson, later announced her readiness to plead guilty to a "charge of 'harmoniousness'" concerning that summer's meeting.[43] The 1995 conference, which she also chaired, featured several women of color in its plenaries and, like its predecessor, managed to avoid acrimony. The new challenge, it was said, was for all to understand not only that "they" are different from "us," but that "we" are different from "them."[44]

White academic feminists had clearly learned by the 1990s to acknowledge their earlier error of purporting to speak for all women. Just as men had falsely universalized as human many characteristics of their sex, so they— white women—had ignored differences among their own. Within women's studies, awareness developed that race affects everyone. Increasing attention to people of color elicited recognition that whiteness and Euro-Americanness also represent racial and ethnic identities; racial identity is not just an attribute of an "other." White women began to explore, as bell hooks proposed, the meaning of "whiteness" in their lives. They had, as Sylvia Yanagisako suggests, "become haole."[45]

Beyond Identity Politics

In the context of continuing divisions, however, it now appeared important to find ways to move beyond identity politics, to declare that there had been enough of what Susan Stanford Friedman labels "narratives of denial, accusation, and confession." One way to transcend differences and build upon commonalities might be to place one's work within what feminist theorists term a "narrative of relational positionality." Offering a way out of the "difference impasse," this concept allows for a more complex understanding of relationships, one that lies "beyond white and other." By creating "a multiplicity of fluid identities defined and acting situationally," this approach, Friedman hopes, can "permeate boundaries between races and ethnicities."[46]

Implicit and sometimes explicit in this approach is criticism of the reliance of identity politics on an "essentialist" view of differences as inherent, irreducible, natural qualities of individuals or groups. For Friedman, positionality, unlike poststructuralist deconstruction, acknowledges "the material realities of identity" while also avoiding what the philosopher Jane Roland Martin terms the "trap" of essentialism. Challenged to avoid an essentialist view of women by both women of color and poststructuralist critics, the editors of the first volume of a new journal of feminist cultural studies, appropriately labeled *differences: A Journal of Feminist Cultural Studies*, chose as its theme "The Essential Difference: Another Look at Essentialism." Blaming Western culture's imputed long history of deriving justifications for women's subordination from notions of an ahistorical, immutable female essence, feminist scholars had rightly rejected essentialism for the uses to which it had been put, as well as for the denial of differences among women implicit in its definition. Instead of discussing "woman," feminist scholars would now speak about "women" of specific histories, cultures, characteristics, and experiences. New dangers have arisen, however, for in privileging differences, commonalities are obscured. Martin, for one, warns against difference itself becoming a "privileged perspective."[47]

Several scholars have expressed concern about the negative consequences of the emphasis on differences. Like Martin, Susan Bordo cautions against the "dogma that the only 'correct' perspective on race, class, and gender is the affirmation of difference." Christine Crosby notes that differences may appear to be "self-evident, concrete, *there*," rather than historically situated. By emphasizing diversity but denying differences within and across categories, these ideas tend to reconstitute the self/other dichotomies that feminism seeks to transcend. The privilege afforded to difference tends to inhibit any search for commonalities and may serve as well to promote self-censorship and limit inquiry about how knowledge is produced. Dealing with difference can also become a substitute for challenging political structures and professional practices that buttress traditional exclusionary tendencies in academic culture.[48]

Inderpal Grewal and Caren Kaplan bring an analogous perspective to their discussion of postcolonial feminism. Reminding readers that "all peoples of the world are not solely constructed by the trinity of race-sex-class;

... other categories also enter into the issues of subject formation both within and outside the borders of the United States," they draw on postmodernist thought to argue for a "transnational feminism" that rejects all "economic and cultural hegemonies," including some forms of feminism. "For those termed minorities," Grewal and Kaplan argue, it is not "resolution of identity" that is essential to feminist politics but "oppositional mobilization and coalitional, transnational feminist practices." Other new studies of women in former colonial nations also recognize that feminisms must be studied in relation to conflicting values and forces of nationalism. These works reflect an apparent trend away from an "iron triangle of race/class/gender" wherein identity politics serves to locate each person, toward a more open, fluid, complex, accessible, and pragmatic approach that acknowledges both the importance of differences and their limitations.[49]

How to approach the subject of difference in practice poses a dilemma for women's studies. While feminist theorists, whose work is discussed more fully in chapter 6, debate such questions as whether identity is a "stable" category, whether privileging difference tends to reinforce stereotyping and separation, and whether identity and difference are in fact mutually exclusive concepts, many faculty, students, and practitioners of all types act out dramas based on categorical characteristics. As individuals they may struggle with impossible choices: the African American literary scholar Barbara Christian finds that the oft-asked question "But who do you really belong to—black studies or women's studies?" elicits anger and frustration, directed at both academic theorists and institutional structures. As teachers or bibliographers they may face perplexing problems in classifying course topics and materials. For bibliographers of "the pluralistic classroom," "the act of naming categories—Native American, African American, and so forth—maintains the structure of margin and center and the resulting gender/racial biases the articles seek to redress. These categories are also fictitious in that they emphasize that the needs of, for example, all Latinos or lesbians can be lumped together. Paradoxically, then, the desire to recognize difference among groups simultaneously maintains boundaries of sameness within each group." There is no category labeled "European American" or "middle class"; these titles are placed under headings marked "general" or "overview."[50]

Intellectual frameworks built around race or class or sexuality alone cannot survive these challenges. A more complex formulation is required. Recognizing the interdependence of constituent categories, some scholars now speak of "racialized gender." Others, including the historian Gerda Lerner in an essay reflecting on the category of class, demonstrate how gender and ethnicity together serve to create the experience of class, which Lerner defines as a "set of relations [controlling] access to resources and privileges . . . [and] dependent on other power relations among people." The class status of brother and sister, she points out, sometimes differs on account of sex. Similarly, the historian Tessie Liu finds female sexuality and reproduction implicated in the formation of lineage-based European societies that were stratified in terms constituent of race—conceptualized as blood and soil—even before colonization. Rose Brewer points out that the simultaneity of determining forces, which black feminists have articulated to explain the multilayered oppression of black women, is a key concept for understanding the ways in which many people all over the world experience their lives. The literary critic Bonnie Zimmerman suggests an image that lends concreteness to this abstraction: Zimmerman likes to think of the multiple perspectives that constitute personal experience as if they were the systems of the human body as she saw them displayed in an encyclopedia she recalls from her childhood, each portrayed on one of several overlapping transparencies, each traceable separately but also visible as part of a whole.[51]

Despite feminists' acknowledgment of the complexity of multiple systems of subordination, and their general adherence to social constructionism to explain traditional femininity, identity politics remains in practice an important factor in women's studies. Outside the realm of feminist theorizing, the differences that divide women continue to be validated on the grounds of experience—one of the founding blocks of women's studies. While the concept of a socially and historically constituted and variable positionality allows in theory for a more complex presentation of self than an essentialized and fixed identity, many students as well as professors still introduce themselves by stringing together a list of their personal attributes. Women's studies takes theory personally and politically. In feminist classrooms, as Maher and Tetreault show, students (and faculty) may position themselves and read texts in terms of their race, gender, class, and/or sexual identity. This offers both strength and weakness. While ideally it might serve only to "locate" an individual's starting point and lead to increased knowledge and understanding, Maher and Tetreault found that it also tends to foster "fixed and absolute categories, which are at least as resistant to positional understandings as the silences about social class and homosexuality. The process of claiming group identities becomes rigid and confining."[52]

The politics of identity politics is played out in many women's studies venues. Facing such consciousness of self and others, the well-intentioned feminist may, before offering her opinion on an issue, feel impelled to recite a long inventory of personal identity markers: "deconstructing yourself" is de rigueur. A white woman may introduce herself as "European American." Hypersensitivity to personal attributes may be stretched to extremes. Opening her report to the membership at the NWSA's sixteenth annual meeting in 1995, the president chided the speaker at a previous session for having stated, "We all look to the Greeks for our sacred words." In her defense, another officer interpreted the comment as a sarcastic reference to "those fat Greek guys," whereupon a member of the audience challenged the latter comment as "sizeist." It also carries a considerable cost. As the outgoing president, Sandra Coyner, lamented in one small group discussion at that meeting, identity politics has led the NWSA toward a "tyranny of inclusiveness," multiplying its number of plenary sessions and featured speakers at great expense.[53]

Numerous academic feminists have addressed the implications of diversity for feminist politics. In order to encompass diversity without inciting division, some feminist scholars have sought to distinguish between "deploying" or "activating" essentialist attitudes and "falling into" or "lapsing into" them. "In a political climate which has elevated the achievement of identity to the very status of liberation," the philosopher Diana Fuss believes that identity politics can be useful, but dangerous. She writes:

> While I do believe that living as a gay or lesbian person in a post-industrial heterosexist society has certain political effects (whether I wish my sexuality to be so politically invested or not), I also believe that simply being gay or lesbian is not sufficient to constitute political activism. A severe reduction of the political to the personal leads to a telescoping of goals, a limiting of revolutionary activity to the project of self-discovery and personal transformation. "The personal is political" re-privatizes social experience.

She calls for "re-assessing and *re-politicizing* 'identity politics,'" using the difference dilemma to teach students the political process through which ideology is produced.⁵⁴

Fuss is joined in her criticism of the uses of essentialism by Jenny Bourne, who complains that "oppression" has replaced "exploitation," and "political culture" has ceded to "cultural politics." "What is to be done has been replaced by who am I." Focusing on Jewish feminist politics, Bourne recalls the important roles played by "feminists who just happened to be Jews" in the civil rights and antiwar movements of the 1960s and 1970s and in the antiracism and antifascism groups of other periods. Lamenting the loss of "liberatory socialist principles" among feminists, Bourne finds that "the organic relationship we tried to forge between the personal and the political has been so degraded that now the only area of politics deemed to be legitimate *is* the personal. . . . We are no longer politically active feminists who happen to be Jews, but Jewish feminists whose main purpose is to seek out our identity." Applying her analysis to issues of anti-Semitism and racism, she chides Elly Bulkin for equating the oppression of Jews and blacks and criticizes Bulkin's and Barbara Smith's entire approach to racism for failure to deal with the material origins of racial exploitation. "Nowhere in all the discussion of anti-Semitism amongst black feminists and anti-black racism among Jewish feminists . . . is there any appreciation of how ideas, however bigoted, are shaped by material experience. . . . In a true coalition the black feminist would tell the Jewish feminist that she would attend to her own anti-Semitism, but in return would expect the Jewish feminist to look at racism as it affects *all* black people." Bourne then joins her discussion to questions about Israel and anti-Zionism.⁵⁵

The overpersonalization and narrowing of feminist politics in the interest of accommodating differences of identity are also of concern to bell hooks. Carefully avoiding an "either/or" stance on questions of identity politics, she challenges essentialist formulations that imply a homogeneous group identity and experience, while recognizing their usefulness. Like Fuss, she quotes with approval a passage from Edward Saïd criticizing exclusions based on the view that "only women can understand feminine experience, only Jews can understand Jewish suffering, only formerly colonial subjects can understand colonial experience." However, she finds disturbing a tendency she perceives in Fuss's work to attribute the "misuse" of "essence, identity, and experience" in the classroom primarily to "marginalized groups." Fuss also fails to appreciate "how systems of domination already at work in the academy and the classroom silence the voices of individuals from marginalized groups and give space only when on the basis of experience it is demanded." There is a difference, hooks points out, between using the authority of experience to "dead-end discussion" and employing it strategically, to connect abstract concepts to reality. She is "concerned that critiques of identity politics not serve as a new, chic, way to silence students from marginal groups." Offering a lesson in pedagogy, hooks recommends this approach: encourage all students to speak, validate each, privilege none, but challenge all—faculty included—to learn from the "passion of remembrance" that is transmitted through personal testimony; then engage the experience critically. Elsewhere, hooks advises black students inclined to reject (white) feminism out of hand to maintain a similar openness: "The notion that black folks have nothing to learn from scholarship that may reflect racial or racist biases is dangerous." Racial separation, she argues, "erases the reality of common female experience ... [and] constructs a framework in which differences cannot be examined comparatively." It may deny to each group an awareness of the other's history, and of important experience they share, as women's studies student Tiya Miles learned through the breakup of her multiracial "young feminist collective."[56]

A growing group of women of color now recognize that, in considerable part due to their own work, feminist thought has undergone fundamental change in understanding the significance of differences. While hooks sometimes challenges other black scholars who present work on gender as though it were politically neutral, she also points out to all that "we [black scholars] have an incredible work built around the issue of gender-enhancing feminist scholarship without explicitly naming itself as feminist."[57] Lauri Umansky has stressed the importance of black women, through their defense of "matriarchy," in eliciting an "enduring feminist reassessment of motherhood." Following the defense by Frances Beale and Toni Cade Bambara against pronatalism in the Black Power movement, Angela Davis's now-classic 1971 article on the role of black women under slavery initiated a feminist position on motherhood. African American women such as Patricia Robinson and Alice Walker also stressed female roles and relationships as powers of creativity and strength. "White feminists in search of black allies noted clearly the strong and positive emphasis that black feminists themselves, having come through the fire of the matriarchy debates, placed on motherhood."[58] Not only did white feminists learn to rethink the rhetoric of reproductive rights to include the concerns of women whose goal was to have and support children as well as gain access to abortion, they also became more sensitive to the material needs of women in poverty and to the diversity of interests among women and sought to reach women of color on the basis of specific common interests.

Lisa Albrecht and Rose M. Brewer, in an anthology of works by women of color, portray coalitions of women as "bridges of power." At least partly in response to a growing "climate of intolerance" in the United States in the 1980s, they called for alliances to fight against racist, anti-gay, anti-Semitic, and sexual violence.[59] While "scripts of accusation" continued to appear in this collection, many of the authors, such as Gloria Anzaldúa, also recognized that "alliances are made between people who are different."[60] They accept alliances as a necessity, while also maintaining a critical posture. "Does this whitewoman [sic] or woman-of-color or man-of-color want to be our ally in order to atone for racial guilt or personal guilt?" Anzaldúa asks. Citing Lacan, Anzaldúa suggests that the other's motive for reaching out may be only a "desire for self-recognition." What Anzaldúa wants is that "whitewomen go out on limbs and fight for women-of-color in workplaces, schools, and universities." All women and (men) should work for the liberation of all women.[61]

Some critics remain skeptical about the depth of commitment by academic feminists to diversity in practice.[62] Change is evident, however, throughout the academic enterprise. The convergence of efforts to incorporate diversity in women's studies can be seen in course syllabi, in projects on curricular revision, in texts, program structures, professional associations, group interaction—virtually everywhere across the academy. Women's studies faculty routinely include in their syllabi literature by and about women of color.[63] Latter-day consciousness-raising groups join women of diverse ethnicity and sexuality for the sharing of culture-defining experiences.[64] Instructors utilize the concept of "relative positionality" in feminist classrooms to "counter a rigid conception of identity politics."[65] Textbook authors seek alternative frameworks in which to integrate material about women of diverse cultures.[66] Universities establish joint faculty appointments in and joint departments of ethnic and women's studies, as well as women's studies departments or programs that focus on the "interconnectedness" of "multicultural, nonsexist education"; these departments and programs include those at San Francisco State University, at Spelman College, in Atlanta, and at the University of Massachusetts at Amherst.[67] At San Francisco State, the objective became a program in which an emphasis on women of color would predominate, a goal at least partially achieved by 1989, when 50 percent of classes were taught by women of color to a student body more than half nonwhite. In other instances, faculty may opt for a separate program in "minority women's studies" or may develop projects, such as those coordinated by the National Council for Research on Women under a Ford Foundation grant, to "incorporate" or "infuse" material on women of color, and work with faculty of all types to "balance" liberal arts' curricula. To avoid the hazard of reinforcing separation by emphasizing difference, these projects may adopt a thematic approach, attempting to place the formerly marginal in the center, while redefining concepts of the "normative, classical, canonical." The question to be asked in "teaching the differences," suggests the historian Tessie Liu, is "who is the feminist self and . . . 'who is the feminist other?'" The goal is to blur the line between margin and core, to show difference as a relationship.[68]

Much work in women's studies seeks to transcend dichotomies between center and margin, as well as between academic concerns and advocacy, theory and practice, essentialism and constructionism, by insisting on the relational nature of the supposedly separate and opposing parts. Experience is no longer a sufficient basis for assertion of authority when personal histories are deconstructed and ideological components in identity formation are exposed. But can recognition of one's identity as an "active construction and a discursively mediated political interpretation of one's history" (in Teresa de Lauretis's postmodernist terms) help to resolve feminist dilemmas of difference? Can feminism—and women's studies—survive identity politics by applying a line-blurring approach here as well? Is identity a natural, political, historical, psychological, or linguistic construct? What implications does the deconstruction of identity have for those who rely on an identity politics?[69] These are critical questions for women's studies.

For individuals struggling with a multiplicity of identities, for professional associations seeking harmony among members, or for instructors moderating classroom discussion, the political challenge is formidable. "Too often," complains the Chinese American literary critic Leslie Bow, "women of color are only visible within feminist conferences when they critique some aspect of white feminism. The role that garners most attention and validation is that of a watchdog who keeps white feminists honest about their own theories." But critics such as Teresa de Lauretis are also correct in pointing out that most criticism by women of color has been directed at white feminists, not at "patriarchal power structures, men of color, or even white women in general."[70]

Escaping from the dilemma of difference, removing the cloak of identity politics, which may serve as strait jacket as well as ceremonial robe, is not easy. Neither avoidance nor a facile pretense of equality, such as the "United Colors of Benetton" advertisements that illustrate the commodification of racial identity, can satisfy women's studies' pledge to work toward a world free of racism as well as sexism. Is there a way, beyond the scripts of accusation, denials, confession, and fractured personal identities? Will the "feminist voices [that] are powerfully influencing the direction of the diversity curriculum transformation movement" succeed in building a "house of difference where there is a home for every woman," as a national report from the campuses optimistically anticipates?[71] Can women's studies truly encompass the diversity it seeks to embrace?

Two feminist writers, one a theorist, the other a leader in ethnic studies and higher education, both drawing on years of feminist work, propose to solve the problem by transforming the very way in which we conceptualize ourselves and the world. For Jodi Dean, "feminism after identity politics" requires moving beyond the "me" (and the "me" decade of the 1980s), to conceive of a "we" for the 1990s. But unlike the "we" of diverse ethnic, sexual, political, tribal, national, and other exclusionary identity groups, this would be a "'we' without labels." Between the poles of identity and universality, she would posit and position "reflective solidarity." The new "we" would "be interpreted not as given but as 'in process,' as the discursive achievement of individuated 'I's." According to Dean,

> *Solidarity can be modeled as an interaction involving at least three persons: I ask you to stand by me over and against a third. But rather than presuming the exclusion and opposition of the third, the ideal of reflective solidarity thematizes the voice of the third to reconstruct solidarity as an inclusionary ideal for contemporary politics and societies. On the one hand, the third is always situated and particular, signifying the other who is excluded and marking the space of identity. On the other, including the third, seeing from her perspective, remains the precondition for any claim to universality and any appeal to solidarity.*[72]

Dean omits, unfortunately, to deal adequately with problems of ego and power. Her solution seems theoretically sophisticated, pragmatically naive.

Johnnella Butler puts it more simply. In her view, the Western conception of the world as a collection of individuals must yield to the recognition of human interdependence. Understanding the individual as part of larger entities, of family and community, grows out of women's traditional experiences. It resonates harmoniously with the West African proverb, "I am because we are. We are because I am." In this context, Butler advocates close analysis of the connections among the long list of "isms" and oppositions that have separated peoples, and she calls for replacing individualism with a "sense of communality and interdependence."[73] As Patricia Hill Collins's "outsiders-within," perhaps women's studies faculty can mediate between the false universalisms that have denied individuality to many white women and persons of color, and the separatist particularism that flourishes today, in the academy as well as elsewhere. Like many persons of color, these feminists emphasize the roles of women in communities. Their critiques resonate with the long tradition of "relational feminism" identified by the historian Karen Offen.[74]

Challenged by women of color "not [to] stop at adding and celebrating diversity . . . [but to] do something,"[75] the advocates of women's studies have clearly responded. Perhaps more than any other academic constituency, they have taken the challenge of diversity seriously, in theory as well as practice. Despite some critics' allegations that they have substituted theory for action and accepted tenure while relinquishing transformative goals, academic feminists have not abandoned feminist advocacy. Nowhere is the dual purpose of women's studies more apparent than in its long, difficult, and ongoing engagement to overcome differences. The question remains, however, whether women's studies can, along with its critical and salutary accommodation to differences, maintain its grounding in the experiences that many continue to believe are shared by women as women. This will depend on how a new and more diverse generation of academic feminists, schooled in women's studies in the classroom and growing up in an era of feminist entitlement, will utilize the new knowledge about themselves and others made available by their predecessors.

6

From the "Big Three" to New Models

The search for feminist theory began for me in the need to provide an intellectually compelling answer to the "so what?" question posed by one of my professors in the early 1970s about the new research on women. By that time I already knew that the study of women was important, for it had occasioned the "click" of enlightenment in my consciousness. As a graduate student embarking on the exhilarating labor of research in women's history, I felt the urgency of discovering new meanings and not just counting new data, as it seemed that many of my fellow students in the "new social history" were then doing. That I was writing in late-nineteenth- and early-twentieth-century European history, steeped in socialism, fascism, positivism, phenomenology, and theories of evolution and revolution, made it even more important to find some great explanatory power that would prove the work of pioneers in women's studies to be serious—that is, worthy of the (male) professors' attention. Writing on women in French socialism, under the direction of a male historian of Marxism, I shared the motivation described by Iris Marion Young as a "desire to establish a countertheory to Marxism, to develop a feminist theory that would conceive sex or gender as a category with as much theoretical weight as class."[1] Theory, conventionally viewed as masculine, seemed to occupy a privileged place in the academy, and, in order to count, we in women's studies needed some.

Searching in 1970 for a dissertation topic, the first book I had read was August Bebel's *Woman under Socialism*, in a 1904 edition and its thirty-third printing. Bebel declared, "Woman and the workingman have, since old, had this in common—*oppression.* . . . *Woman was the first human being to come into bondage: she was a slave before the male slave existed.*" Hear that, professors of socialism. Bebel's book, originally published in 1879 as *Woman in the Past, Present, and Future* because of the German antisocialist laws, provided my first reading (beyond Simone de Beauvoir) on women in European history. The book devotes only a few pages to women "under socialism" but seemed to provide the basis for a successful theory that would legitimize our work. It would also explain our past and, in some fashion, guide us toward the future.[2]

Materials at hand from the women's liberation movement also portrayed women as an oppressed group. Drawing on women's newly raised consciousness, they affirmed the value of experiential evidence and articulated the realities of personal and (in Kate Millett's provocative new term) "sexual" politics. Added to the older works, such as Bebel's and Beauvoir's, they supplied raw material that stimulated the initial teaching and research in women's studies. The information that Millett's *Sexual Politics*—brought to a vast audience by a *Time* magazine cover story in July 1970—had begun as a doctoral dissertation inspired many feminist students who aspired to become scholars to participate in the invention of "feminist scholarship."[3]

In the early years, historical studies commanded a leading position in the women's studies curriculum. From the women's liberation movement's rediscovery of its nineteenth-century heritage in the struggle for suffrage came a heavy emphasis on nineteenth- and early-twentieth-century history and literature and a tendency to look to history for explanations of women's subordination. Simone de Beauvoir's observation that "one is not born, but rather becomes a woman" also pointed the new scholars toward psychology and sociology; and the humanistic studies were soon supplemented by important, revelatory new work by social scientists. The "eternal feminine" of poetic imagination was seen to be an invention of poets, philosophers, and priests, buttressed by physicians and politicians, as well as by psychologists, physiologists, and biologists, who "naturalized" woman to serve men's interests. Feminist thought in the early years of women's studies reflected the twin goals of exposing the "social construction of femininity" and of explaining its origins. To my knowledge, the first use of this exact term, paraphrasing Beauvoir's notion, was in Jo Freeman's "The Social Construction of the Second Sex," originally written in 1968 and published in 1970. Naomi Weisstein's "Psychology Constructs the Female, or the Fantasy Life of the Male Psychologist," which uses the concept with similar intention, first appeared in 1968 as well.[4] These studies elucidated the meaning of "androcentricity" and "the man-made world," terms retrieved for feminist research from the rediscovered work of the turn-of-the-century American writer Charlotte Perkins Gilman. Later studies would reveal a much longer history of feminist thought.[5]

In the energy-absorbing and exciting work of inventing women's studies courses and founding women's studies programs, abstract questions about theory and the quest for "a theory of one's own" did not immediately claim center stage. Early courses in feminist "thought" (soon to be termed feminist "theory") tended to explain the origins of women's condition on the basis of ideas drawn from familiar explanatory models. Feminist perspectives labeled "liberal" and "socialist" soon emerged, reflecting the influences, respectively, of Mary Wollstonecraft, John Stuart Mill and Harriet Taylor Mill, and Anglo-American suffrage leaders; and of Marx, Engels, Bebel, and other socialist thinkers. Excerpts from their works appeared in several anthologies of historical writings by feminists, including a 1972 collection edited by Miriam Schneir and a 1973 collection edited by Alice S. Rossi. Class analysis was accentuated in American women's history by Gerda Lerner in her 1969 essay "The Lady and the Mill Girl," and was also passed along through the work of the British scholar-activist Sheila Rowbotham, whose 1972 history of women and revolution told of "impudent lasses" of an earlier age and was widely circulated in the United States.[6] The works of contemporary authors such as Shulamith Firestone, Marge Piercy, Susan Brownmiller, and Adrienne Rich traced women's oppression to men's domination of women's bodies in sexual relations, reproduction, marriage, and other realms and provided founding texts for "radical feminism."

All varieties of feminism initially portrayed women chiefly as victims, in some cases of their own bodies, but in others of a "system" grounded in social and economic structures. Each attempted to identify the causes of women's subordinate status and to propose ways to overcome it. Liberal feminism, grounded in Enlightenment thought and "natural rights" philosophy, demanded and anticipated an ever-expanding circumference of democracy, within a contract-based society in which all individuals are treated equally. Socialist feminism located causality in a materialist view according to which women's oppression began in prehistory with the invention of private property and continued because of women's secondary status in economic production. Radical feminism attributed women's subordination to patriarchal structures based on a sexual division of labor in reproduction. None looked deeply into differences among women by race or sexuality. These three models, the "big three," quickly came to dominate feminist thinking, creating an early but persistent scheme for conceptualizing different ways of interpreting women's condition.[7]

A more complex analysis emerged from several developments of the 1970s. The first factor was the tremendous outpouring of feminist scholarship itself. One of the leaders in bringing a new perspective to the male-centered world of scholarship was a historian of Renaissance Italy, Joan Kelly. She had just completed a book on Leon Battista Alberti, a precursor to Leonardo da Vinci whose use of painterly visual perspective she linked to a new "perceptual organization" of the world in the fifteenth and sixteenth centuries. Having studied the intellectual as well as the social, economic, and political transformations marking the transition from feudal into early modern society, Kelly was well prepared to appreciate the potential of a new women's perspective for revising contemporary views of the world.[8]

At the urging of Gerda Lerner, who was then developing, at Sarah Lawrence College, one of the first graduate programs in women's studies (an M.A. program in women's history), Kelly undertook "the most exciting intellectual adventure" of her life. "The change I went through was kaleidoscopic. I had not read a new book. I did not stumble upon a new archive. No fresh piece of information was added to anything I knew. But I knew now that the entire picture I had held of the Renaissance was partial, distorted, limited, and deeply flawed. . . . All I had done was to say, with Leonardo, suppose we look at the dark, dense immobile earth from the vantage point of the moon? . . . Suppose we look at the Renaissance from the vantage point of women?" Kelly went on to publish several influential essays, including "The Social Relation of the Sexes: Methodological Implications for Women's History" (1976), "Did Women Have a Renaissance?" (1977), "The Doubled Vision of Feminist Theory" (1979), and "Early Feminist Theory and the *Querelle des Femmes*" (1982), before her premature death in 1982. Kelly's "vantage point" reappeared somewhat later in the standpoint theory developed by Marxist and other theorists.[9]

New Approaches to the Study of Women in History and Society

A great deal of theory was embedded in the work of other historians as well. An important early contribution came from Gerda Lerner, who in 1969 called for a "new conceptual framework" for writing about women in history. The search for new approaches was underscored by Ann D. Gordon, Mari Jo Buhle, and Nancy Schrom Dye, who, in an essay that had first appeared in 1971, raised the question, "On what bases do women share an historical existence?" This is a question that has continued to resound through the world of women's studies. In the first sentence of the introduction to her 1976 collection *Liberating Women's History: Theoretical and Critical Essays*, Berenice A. Carroll noted, "There has been a recurrent demand for theory in the field of women's history." She attributed it partially to "the disjunctions between the historical experience of this group and the categories, assumptions, and criteria which shape most scholarly writing on history."[10]

That same year, 1976, Natalie Zemon Davis, whose essays "Woman on Top" and "City Women and Religious Change" had appeared in 1975 and stretched common understandings of women's roles, published a review essay, "Women's History in Transition: The European Case," that suggested more complex ways of studying the "significance of the sexes" in the past. Concepts based on traditional interpretations of women's "nature" and "sex roles," and depictions of women that slighted their historical agency, soon gave way to more sophisticated new views.[11]

Anthropologists also played a central role in the early development of feminist theory. From the West Coast came the publication in 1974 by Michelle Zimbalist Rosaldo and Louise Lamphere of *Woman, Culture, and Society*, a set of essays by anthropologists adding to the historical vantage point a cross-cultural perspective that challenged conventional views of women and suggested new models for understanding women and the world. In the development of feminist theory, Gayle Rubin's hypothesis of a "sex/gender system," by means of which the presumably biological given of sex became the base for societally constructed notions of gender, was especially influential. Rubin set the stage for the concepts of femininity and masculinity and all the attitudes, behaviors, laws, and customs related to them to be understood as artifacts created and sustained by patriarchal institutions. After reading these works, from Weisstein and Freeman to Rubin, I personally began to use the word *femininity* in my own work surrounded by quotation marks.[12]

While attacking the androcentricity of traditional disciplines and seeking explanations for women's subordination, women's studies scholars also undertook to learn more about women's experiences in their own right, to explore what women in history had actually done. Many new studies highlighted not women's oppression but women's agency. The anthropologist Sally Slocum demonstrated that "woman the gatherer" had contributed at least as much to human evolution as had "man the hunter." The sociologist Nancy Chodorow reinterpreted Freudian theory to emphasize the role of mothering in creating and maintaining the "social organization of gender." The historian Judith Walkowitz demonstrated female agency as well as social constraints in the lives of prostitutes in Victorian England. The literary scholar Elaine Showalter recommended moving beyond "feminist criticism" of the literary canon to study women as writers and women's writing, proposing a new field that she termed "gynocritics." All demanded that scholars in their respective disciplines rethink conventional wisdom to include female experiences and women-centered perspectives.[13]

The impact was explosive. "The move of women from marginality to the center shatters the system," proclaimed Gerda Lerner. The recognition that old truths and long-accepted interpretations might be different or even false when women's experiences and perceptions were considered led feminist scholars across the disciplines to challenge the conventions of language, categories of analysis, and methods of research that had led to such omission and error. Challenging generic universal abstract Man as a cover for the dominance of men and the exclusion of women, feminist scholars revisited the great men from Aristotle to Marx and Freud, criticized their work and the systems of thought based on it, and began to question the processes through which knowledge is established. The political scientist Susan Moller Okin scrutinized the works of great political philosophers and found the subordination of women to have been assumed, not examined, by them. The philosopher Carol Gould argued against Marxist feminists as well as the tradition of her own field that the "woman question" constituted a "universal" and not a "special" (read, less important) question. The limitations of old explanatory models were exposed and a search for new conceptual schemes began.[14]

While the search for new theory grew out of dissatisfaction with the old models that dominated academic discourse, it emerged simultaneously from the field of feminist practice. In the early 1970s, a group of former staffers from the New Left–oriented, radical feminist news journal *off our backs* (founded in 1970) established *The Furies*, a "lesbian-feminist analytical paper," some of whose members in 1974 founded the journal *Quest*. For Charlotte Bunch, one of its editors and an activist who had come to feminism from the University Christian Movement of the 1960s with experience organizing antiwar and civil rights protests, the founding of *Quest* responded to a felt need for better analysis to inform her movement work. "Theory," she pointed out in the journal's first issue, "enables us to see immediate needs in terms of long-range goals and an overall perspective on the world." She sought in that issue to justify the importance of feminist theory in teaching women "to think systematically about the world" and "to counter women's negativity toward and fear of theory" by showing its importance to their practical concerns. Along with Nancy Hartsock and other members of the *Quest* collective, Bunch sought to educate readers in theoretical issues basic to understanding and effecting political change.[15]

The desire to ground women's studies in theories of knowledge led to an immense development of feminist thought, which came to be termed "feminist epistemology." In a recent collection of essays on the topic, a bibliography of feminist epistemologies (said to be "narrowly" defined) covers six pages. Sandra Harding classifies them in three major groupings: feminist empiricism, feminist standpoint theories, and feminist postmodernism. By feminist empiricism, Harding means the work of scholars for whom "sexism and androcentricism could be eliminated from the results of research if scientists would just follow more rigorously and carefully the existing methods and norms of research"—which, of course, requires adding women and women-oriented perspectives. A more sophisticated form of feminist analysis, "contextual empiricism," also takes into account social factors in science. The prevailing emphasis on epistemology in feminist theory has tended to obscure other work, including work done by historians and social scientists. Similarly, the foregrounding of sex and gender definitions has partially eclipsed analyses of male domination. Since it is not possible here to trace even in summary all of this work, I will focus on questions that have dominated academic feminist discussion about theories and their implications in the 1990s.[16]

Significant early work in the new feminist theory appeared in nonacademic, community-based lesbian journals such as *The Furies* (*Quest's* precursor, founded in 1972), *Sinister Wisdom* (founded in 1976), *Chrysalis* (founded in 1976), and *Conditions* (founded in 1977). Despite the new focus on theory, much of this work comprised personal narratives. Theory is barely mentioned in a 1982 *Signs* review essay on "lesbian identity and community," which draws primarily on social science literature. But it was in "lesbian personal narratives" that Bonnie Zimmerman, author of a follow-up review essay in 1984, said that she found "the free space that nurtures political vision and political change." To illustrate the linkage between personal life and politics, she quoted from Cherríe Moraga and Gloria Anzaldúa's "theory in the flesh." By 1993, the date of the second lesbian issue of *Signs*, lesbianism was viewed as what Shane Phelan termed "a critical site of gender deconstruction rather than as a unitary experience with a singular political meaning."[17] Poststructuralism had quickly complicated the analysis.

The new theory built on Adrienne Rich's now classic 1980 essay "Compulsory Heterosexuality and Lesbian Existence." It reflected as well the articulation of "multiple identities" by women of color such as Anzaldúa, whose "new mestiza," in her view, does not "transcend race but transgresses it, refusing to collude in the homophobic demands of some Chicana/os or in the racist invisibility that is too much a part of white lesbian communities."[18] In this conception, lesbians do not exist with a "fixed external identity"; the idea of "lesbian as being" and "lesbianism as a state of nature" are replaced by "identities [that] rely on politics rather than ontology."[19] It might even mean subsuming lesbianism under a broader rubric, "queer." Rejecting essentialism and fixed identities in favor of sexual pluralism, some postmodernists use the designation *queer* and the term *queer theory* to embrace all "nonnormative sexualities." This is a concept intended to challenge the idea of sexual identity as "monolithic, obvious, and dichotomous." But it may also be interpreted as abandoning the interests of (lesbian) women, under the influence of gay male theories and politics.[20]

The intellectual currents manifested in these changing views had already begun to be felt in the 1970s. By the end of that decade, the dominance of the "big three" had been challenged by a series of works that questioned the validity of earlier categorizations and faulted them for omissions of various kinds, for ethnocentricity, heterosexism, dubious dichotomies, and other unexamined usages. In 1976 *Signs* published an essay in translation by the French author Hélène Cixous, and in 1978 it reported on the work of several French feminists and theorists. Important selections were made available in English by Elaine Marks and Isabelle de Courtivron in 1980. In

1981 *Signs* devoted its fall issue to French feminist theory. *Feminist Studies* published a special issue on deconstruction in the spring of 1988. This importation of French critical theory would ultimately break the already shaken tripartite scheme of feminist theory. It introduced a mode of critical thinking about the nature of women's experience, the origins of female subjectivity and subjection, "difference," and the "social construction" of sexuality which was new to most American feminist scholars.[21]

Women's studies was heavily influenced by work published in Paris in *m/f*, whose first issue had appeared in 1978. The editors of this journal had set out to explore the relationship between feminism and socialism, which was focused at that time, they argued, on a theory of "capitalist patriarchy [that] presupposed a unitary phenomenon of 'women's oppression.'" As Chantal Mouffe explains it, *m/f* rejected any essentialist definition of woman:

> *Legal, medical, political discourses each construct different definitions of women rather than being the expression or representation of pre-given objects, women and men. This means that there can be no "feminine discourse" representing or reflecting a pre-given object, woman. . . . m/f's objective as a feminist journal was to study the construction of the category women within the specific practices that produce sexual difference in many different ways and to scrutinize the way women's subordination was produced in diverse practices, discourses, and institutions. This required analyses of the production of sexual difference in all social practices where the distinction between masculine and feminine existed as a pertinent one, including economic, cultural, political, and legal practices as well as in the family and the specific domain of sexuality. This was quite an original position.*[22]

To a considerable extent (although not exclusively), the turn to post-modernism and the debate over essentialism and constructionism in women's studies have taken place largely among scholars who began in the 1970s as Marxist feminists or were later influenced by Marxist feminism. They were generally more familiar with Continental philosophy and inclined toward theory and poststructuralist thought.[23] Recognition of the failure of the Left to incorporate women as subjects in the development of theory had left many of the feminists who had affiliated with Left-oriented groups frustrated. They had found that it was easier to expose the weakness of Marxian thought in the face of feminism than to solve the problems of patriarchy in capitalism—or anticapitalism. Using Marxist categories of analysis and methodology, some socialist feminists attempted to develop a theory of "capitalist patriarchy and socialist feminism" that would encompass the social relationships of reproduction as well as production. From a different point of view, that of the contract theory that undergirds liberal feminism, Carole Pateman contributed to the analysis of patriarchy by postulating a "sexual contract" embedded in the so-called social contract that is assumed by political theorists to be the foundation of civil society. In her formulation, "The social contract is a fraternal pact that constitutes civil society as a patriarchal or masculine order." The story of how men came to exercise dominion over women had been "repressed."[24] The analysis of patriarchy, however, waned as dialogue within women's studies focused more and more on differences among women.

The quest for feminist theory that could encompass a range of views was advanced by the work of the political theorist Nancy Hartsock. Adapting the Marxian perspective that grounds class in relationships of material life, Hartsock developed a "feminist standpoint theory" that has been very influential. Standpoint theory is a form of feminist historical materialism based in the sexual division of labor. For Hartsock, women's lives, "like the lives of proletarians according to Marxian theory, . . . make available a particular and privileged vantage point on male supremacy, a vantage point which can ground a powerful critique of the phallocratic institutions and ideology which constitute the capitalist form of patriarchy."[25]

Standpoint theory helped to bridge the gap between thought and action by linking the realities of social existence with the workings of the institutional power of both patriarchy and capitalism. It seemed limited, however, when confronted with multiple perspectives of diverse groups of women; Patricia Hill Collins, however, drew on it to account for a black women's standpoint.[26] Theorists have now developed extensive analyses of "partial perspectives" and "situated knowledges." Work on existential and methodological problems of standpoint theory continues, but it seems to be less dominant in the 1990s than various French-influenced discourses. However, these too may be waning, as recognition of the structural parameters of situatedness triggers a movement away from an emphasis on identity (back) toward a materialist, though not necessarily Marxist, analysis.

Who Is Woman and What Is Women's Studies?

A second factor in the emergence of new feminist theory in women's studies was the beginning of self-reflection. As noted in chapter 2, at the first annual meeting of the National Women's Studies Association in 1979 several theory-minded women's studies scholars reflecting on the meaning of their own intellectual enterprise came together to address the question "Is women's studies an academic discipline?" Reviewing definitions of the word *discipline* in several compound forms—*cross-disciplinary, interdisciplinary, transdisciplinary*—Gloria Bowles, then coordinator of women's studies at the University of California, Berkeley, and Sandra Coyner, then women's studies director at Kansas State University (who once described herself as no longer a historian but a "women's studyist"), raised new questions about the nature and the future of women's studies and its place in the academy. Adapting Thomas S. Kuhn's theory of scientific revolutions to their vision, they portrayed women's studies as an emergent discipline, currently in the early stages of developing the paradigms, theories, methods, professional associations, and other accoutrements needed to establish its claim to that status. This new "science of women" would be built upon such paradigms as the social construction of femininity and the sex/gender system. Alternatively, they feared, it might, through curricular transformation projects, be absorbed into other disciplines and disappear.

Renate Klein, then a student of Bowles at the University of California, Berkeley, joined her professor to edit *Theories of Women's Studies* (1983), a collection of essays inspired by the first NWSA meeting. The book sold more than 10,000 copies and is frequently cited. As the forerunner of many successor volumes, this work offers an interesting early model of the state of the art of feminist theory. Its index includes no mention of Derrida or Foucault, difference, essentialism, gender, or "post-" anything. It refers twice to black women and twice to lesbians but offers no entire chapter dealing with either women of color or lesbian identity. Several chapters raise questions about feminist research methodology. One discussion of the use of experience ("Back into the Personal") argues for challenging the positivist dominance in social science research in favor of ethnomethodology. Including an essay entitled "In Praise of Theory," this book paved the way for the emergence of debates over theory as one of the dominant features of women's studies from the mid-1980s until the present. It was an important milestone in the trajectory of debates on methodology and epistemology which were vital to scholars trying to establish and legitimize a new academic field.[27]

A third contribution to the elaboration of the new feminist theory came from the flowering of "women's culture." A catch-all term used to describe women's relationships with women and their activities in women-dominated institutions in historical as well as contemporary societies, it can refer to everything from women's art and literature to communities of religious women, woman-only bookstores, and feminist coffeehouses. As scholars turned from androcentric approaches, which featured women chiefly as secondary figures in male-dominated events or as objects described and images drawn by male authors and artists, and toward gynocentric views, the multiplicity and diversity of women's experiences became more apparent. Talk of "feminism" yielded before recognition of the variety of "feminisms" that constituted many different women's movements, historical and contemporary. New variants of feminism included lesbian feminism, black feminism, a psychoanalytic feminism that draws on but revises Freud, cultural feminism, and many others, all with perspectives centered in the diverse experiences of women. African American women, celebrating their differences, began to substitute Alice Walker's term *womanist* for *feminist* to highlight their position and perspective.[28]

Other women of color likewise redefined feminist words, ideas, and issues in the terms of their own cultures and created portraits in their own images. In response, many practitioners of women's studies recognized the error of generalizing from their own limited experience. Like the men whom they faulted for presuming to include women in putatively generic language, feminists who spoke of "woman" masked differences of race, ethnicity, sexuality, class, religion, and other characteristics of particular individuals or groups. Although the variety of women's experiences had been acknowledged from the beginning of women's studies, and most early anthologies included essays by women of color, the complexities and difficulties of building a diverse movement on the presumption of unity now came rushing to the fore. Who was this "woman" for whom feminism presumed to speak?

The question of "speaking as a woman" had been problematized by the French psychoanalyst Luce Irigaray in *This Sex Which Is Not One* (1977). Her work became the subject of extensive analysis by academic feminists in the United States in the early 1980s, giving rise to heated debate about the influences of biology, language, and "phallologocentricism" on the creation of sexual differences, culture, and the meaning of "woman." Reinforced by this French theory, criticism of faulty generalization about women's experience was captured by the American philosopher Elizabeth Spelman in her tellingly titled 1988 book *Inessential Woman*. Spelman declared speaking "as a woman" to be the "Trojan horse of feminist ethnocentrism." Was the project that was under way truly *feminist* theory, she asked, if it excluded women of color?[29] Yet to speak of women of color also privileged a category of experience whose ontological reality was now challenged. Feminist theory expanded into new space, far past the earlier models (which nevertheless continued to be employed).

As feminism, a discourse that presumed the unity of its object of inquiry, gave way to feminisms to accommodate differences among women, feminist scholars also looked more closely at differences between women and men. What was the significance of sexual differences for the social organization of society? By minimizing differences, feminists demanded equal rights with men—human rights. But could women aspire to equality with men if they emphasized their differences? Women's studies scholars struggled with the question of whether the very concept of woman as the binary (but subordinate, not equal) opposite of man precluded the attainment of equality. Could equal rights with men be attained by (female) individuals who based their collective claim on an assertion of sexual difference? What were the implications of difference—differences between women and men as well as differences among women—for feminist politics? What did "woman" mean? Did it make sense any longer to speak of "woman"? Which woman? "Am I that name?" Denise Riley asked in an influential book of that title. Was women's studies itself misnamed? Should it give way to gender studies?[30]

These new questions required rethinking the very basis on which women's studies had been founded. Since the eighteenth century, feminists arguing for equal rights have grounded their pleas in the abstract notion of the inalienable rights of all beings. The rights of Woman should be recognized as equal and complementary to the rights of Man. For feminism this has been a matter of reason and faith. As a political belief and movement, however, feminism is built upon the notion of women as an existential category of embodied beings who differ from men. In practice, the unproblematic use of the concept "woman" has allowed women to argue for equal rights on the basis of their presumed differences from men and their presumed common female experiences. Many feminists of the nineteenth and early twentieth centuries, including Jeanne Deroin and Aline Valette in France, Louise Otto in Germany, Ellen Key in Sweden, and Anna J. Cooper and Angelina Grimké in the United States, argued for women's rights on the basis of female qualities, duties, and relationships that differed from those of males. They saw themselves as different *and* equal. Concepts such as "Mother-Right," popularized by Friedrich Engels in the late nineteenth century, Jane Addams's "social housekeeping" of the early twentieth century, and Carol Gilligan's more recent "different voice" depend upon the existence of a category of beings who appear—even if constituted through discourse—"different" from a given (male) model.[31]

But so do the most traditional justifications for women's subordination, from Aristotle, Aquinas, and Rousseau to the authors of "protective legislation" and its supporters even among those philosophically opposed to government intervention in economic affairs. In a recent and notorious legal case, *Equal Employment Opportunity Commission v. Sears,* the feminist argument for equality of access to higher-paying jobs lost because of the conviction that women "naturally" prefer different kinds of jobs than men, even if faced with lower compensation. To single out women on the basis of difference as such seemed to court unequal and inferior treatment.[32] The postmodernist historian Joan Scott argues that, as exemplified by this case, feminists have for two centuries been caught between their abstract right to "equality" and their dependence upon the concept of "difference" as the basis of their groups' demands. "Feminism was a protest against women's political exclusion; its goal was to eliminate 'sexual difference' in politics, but it had to make its claims on behalf of 'women'. . . . To the extent that it acted for 'women,' feminism produced 'the sexual difference' it sought to eliminate. This paradox—the need both to accept *and* to refuse 'sexual difference'—was the constitutive condition of feminism as a political movement throughout its long history."[33] (See chapter 7 for further discussion of the Sears case.)

The problem articulated by Scott has provoked a major controversy within feminist theory, one that permeates women's studies. One response to the so-called equality-versus-difference dilemma has been to challenge the terms of the debate, especially the meanings and implications of difference. Riley, Scott, and others query whether "women" constitutes a useful category; they prefer to substitute the concept of gender—gender meant not as merely a synonym for sex, as it is sometimes employed, but to signify a range of sexualities. The increasing focus on gender in feminist theory and women's studies reflects a sensitivity to differences among women which responds to the criticism of lesbians, women of color, and others who have long attacked all "universalizing" tendencies among feminist as well as non-feminist scholars. It demonstrates as well the influence of French theorists. The pervasive presence of the new ideas can be heard in the words of a young Asian American graduate student participating in a discussion about feminism in the 1990s. She asks, "What 'women'? What is this 'women' thing you're talking about? Does that mean me? Does that mean my mother, my roommates, the white woman next door, the check-out clerk at the supermarket, my aunts in Korea, half the world's population?"[34]

One result of the emphasis on difference has been to alter terminology. Acknowledging her somewhat simplistic formulation, Mary Poovey states, "In the first phase of women's studies in the U.S. academy, scholars looked at sex; in the second, they (we) look at gender."[35] But the increasing preference for the term *gender* reflects more than the desire to accommodate a pluralistic understanding of "woman." Self-reflexivity and the quest for new "paradigms" in women's studies emerged concurrently with the "linguistic turn" in history, the rise of the "new historicism" in literary criticism, the burgeoning of cultural studies, and the "interpretive turn" in many liberal arts fields which infused American higher education in the 1980s. This focus on language and discourse highlights the constructed, and hence changeable, experience of gender which feminists have been asserting for a very long time. The change was overdetermined. The relationship between sex and gender, however, remains contested.

Interest in what came to be called "French feminism," although several major French writers did not define themselves as feminist, spread rapidly in women's studies, following the prominent academics who championed it. The hunger for theory found rich nourishment there. Since at least 1982, when the largest session I attended at the NWSA's annual meeting dealt with "feminism and Foucault," women's studies theory has incorporated linguistic analysis and deconstruction. Having criticized dichotomies—later termed binary constructions—that constrain and denigrate women long before they heard of Foucault, Derrida, and other Continental philosophers, women's studies scholars had used gender as a category of analysis from the beginning, but without pursuing its implications for some of their own fundamental assumptions, including the meaning of "woman" and other foundational concepts of women's studies. While deconstructing gender, they have also, sometimes unconsciously, appropriated the methodology employed by Marxists to analyze the constitution of the concept of class. Like Marxists, many feminist theorists assume that material life structures human consciousness, determining the perspective from which a group—in this case, women—apprehend reality.[36]

Implications of Gender Analysis:
The Debate over Postmodernism

Feminist scholars who employed the term *gender* to counter biological determinism and to emphasize cross-cultural and historical variation in women's experience began to focus new attention on the constructed character of relationships between the sexes. As early as 1976, in the same issue with Cixous, *Signs* had published a provocative article in "gender history" which predated the emergence of that concept: Joan Kelly's study of the methodological implications of viewing the past in terms of "the social relations of the sexes." A decade later, when Joan Scott, an American historian of France, published an article entitled "Gender as a Category of Analysis in History" in her profession's leading journal, she achieved new recognition for feminist interpretation and for the French theorists. In her *Gender and the Politics of History* (1988), she demonstrated how to practice gendered analyses, using gender in a series of essays to reveal previously hidden meanings and to revise long-accepted interpretations. Her work seemed to fulfill the promise of women's studies by answering clearly the question, So what? There was far more packed into history than historians acknowledged, including their own role when uncritically accepting at face value documents from an earlier age, as party to past and present politics.[37]

Scott and other scholars, perhaps even more in literature, philosophy, film criticism, and cultural studies than in history, went far beyond the "deconstruction of error"—a term used by Catharine Stimpson in 1978 to explain the first task of feminist scholarship.[38] For poststructuralists and others identified with postmodernism, deconstruction meant to "destabilize" all categories and eclipse foundational theories, to undermine the authority of subjects, to challenge the use of uninterpreted experience as evidence, and ultimately to deny the existence of context-free knowledge and purposeful human agency independent of the discourse that constructed meanings. This has led some contemporary feminists to reject what they see as the limitations of all Enlightenment thought and to question the tenets of a liberalism grounded in an unproblematic view of the human subject as a bearer of rights. The historian Sonya O. Rose provides a clear, succinct explanation of this postmodernist feminist position:

> What postmodernist feminists share is a critique of Enlightenment thought that assumes human beings to be autonomous, stable selves who are capable of producing objective, rational analysis, and of dis- covering generalizable truths, yielding knowledge that exhaustively and completely explains history. Enlightenment ideas, and the knowl- edge generated with these ideas as a foundation, imagine that it is pos- sible to know the truth about the world from an archimedian or God's eye view. Postmodernism eschews the idea that there is a timeless, con- text-free knowledge. Any attempt[s] to theorize the foundations of human existence and use them to explain history are acts of power that pretend to be objective and politically neutral. Heterogeneity, multi- plicity, difference are the stuff of history.[39]

This perspective takes the concept of the "social construction of the second sex" far beyond its meaning of the early 1970s, positing the constituted nature of the concepts "woman" (and "man"), with all their implications and connotations. As Mary Poovey puts it in her excellent analysis of the significance of deconstruction for feminism, "Such a reconceptualization of sex and the individual is the radical—and logical—extension of decon- struction's program. It would challenge the very basis of our current social organization. In doing so, it would necessarily feel like a loss, but it might also create the conditions of possibility for as yet unimagined organizations of human potential."[40] Such ideal visions leave unclear how abstract for- mulations affect material reality.

One vital aspect of women's lives that demands attention in any vision for the future is motherhood. The very common (material) experience of motherhood necessarily affects the perspective (vantage point or standpoint) of women. Historically, maternity has been a source of women's strength and of their vulnerability. Feminists in many eras—such as Hubertine Au- clert, who in late-nineteenth-century France called for a "motherly state"— have grounded their claims in the female capacity for motherhood. This dif- ficult subject, one of feminism's most complex, has not commanded suffi- cient attention in women's studies and feminist theory. Ellen Ross found in a review of recent scholarship on maternity, however, that after a period of negative responses to a mother-blaming culture, feminist scholars turned, in the 1980s and 1990s, toward "reaffirming and celebrating motherhood." A useful project suggested by Jean Bethke Elshtain would be to "trace historically, or better, genealogically paradigms of 'the female' and 'the mother' that have served as catalysts for action and sources of female authority, on the one hand, and, on the other, those paradigms that constrained, inviting privatization and pettiness of purpose. And then, of course, one must go on to offer critical reflection on these exemplars."[41] Ideas about women's capacity for and experiences of childbearing and childrearing are one of many sources of division among feminists in the academy.

When dealing with perplexing problems, including the "equality versus difference" dichotomy, feminists often encounter what Ann Snitow, retracing her personal gender trajectory, terms a "common divide [that] keeps forming in both feminist thought and action between the need to build the identity 'woman' and give it solid political meaning and the need to tear down the very category 'woman' and dismantle its all-too-solid history." Following the trends and influential works of several decades, Snitow locates this division between groups labeled variously as radical feminists and cultural feminists, essentialists and social constructionists, cultural feminists and poststructuralists, "motherists"—defined as "women who present themselves to the world as mothers"—and feminists. Furthermore, she finds that the divide "keeps forming *inside*" the categories. Feminists and others who seek to follow these debates with understanding must become adept at philosophy. It requires, as Hannah Arendt's biographer Elisabeth Young-Bruehl has observed, "the education—the beginning of the education—of women as philosophers."[42]

Essentialism, a term once reserved for philosophers, is now so commonly employed in women's studies that all academic feminists must be prepared to deal with it. Several years ago, at the first class meeting of my course in modern European women's history, I was addressed by a student who, even as she took her seat, asked me, "Are you an essentialist or a constructionist?" It took me a moment to catch on. In 1990, the political theorist Jane Flax drew a parallel between the tension and hostility that greeted her presentation to a group of women's studies faculty of a paper on "the end of innocence" that accompanies the postmodernist perspective, and the experience of 1967, when conflict among black and white allies developed in the civil rights movement. "Postmodernism," Flax explains, "is threatening to some feminists because it radically changes the background assumptions and contexts within which debates about such questions are usually conducted."[43]

In Flax's view, these underpinnings include "Enlightenment discourses of rights, individualism, and equality [which] white-feminist politics in the West since the 1960s have been deeply rooted in. . . . The Enlightenment hope is that utilizing truthful knowledge in the service of legitimate power will assure both freedom and progress. This will occur only if knowledge is grounded in and warranted by a universal reason, not particular 'interests.'" Against the claims of Mary Wollstonecraft, one of the founders of modern feminism, to let reason be women's guide as it was men's, postmodernists deny reason its privileged place, moving it aside in favor of power. For postmodernists, Flax states, "Truth . . . is an effect of discourse"; and there are only interests. Like everything else, gender is variable, contingent on context, and "reflect[s] our questions, desires, and needs." Flax sees no loss to feminism: "What we really want is power in the world, not an innocent truth," and this requires—instead of truth about "women"—entering the political world with self-knowledge, recognizing "differential privileges of race, gender, geographic location, and sexual identities," appreciating the needs of others as well as our own, and taking "responsibility beyond innocence."[44]

In what some feminist scholars see as the end of innocence, others detect the end of feminism. Responding to a 1987 conference on theories of sexual differences, Karen Offen made the point that history sometimes has the "untidy effect of muddying the crystalline waters of theory," and offered a somber view of the effects of postmodern thinking on feminism. In denying that "women" is a meaningful category, postmodernists, in her view, ignored the history of women's protests and achievements in the name of womanhood and women's experiences. Reading the historical record, she finds not only French feminism but feminisms in most of the world to be rooted in assumptions about the complementarity of the sexes and the value of relationships among women, children, and families. In contrast, she argues, the postmodernist critique reveals an "atomistic focus on the liberation of the human individual . . . devoid of distinguishing characteristics." Feminist theory, she believes, must deal with reproduction and motherhood and the real-life experiences of most of the world's women in the past, the present, and—the new reproductive technologies notwithstanding—the foreseeable future. Postmodernist thinking is not supportive of feminism;

instead of "postmodern feminism," Offen would label it "postfeminist post-modernism." In other words, within a postmodernist framework, there can be no political movement for the emancipation of women.[45]

Another historian who is a vocal opponent of the postmodernist per-spective and has vehemently expressed her views is Joan Hoff, former edi-tor of the *Journal of Women's History*. Hoff's essay "The Pernicious Effects of Poststructuralism on Women's History" appeared in several places, in-cluding the *Chronicle of Higher Education*, where it was published in an abbreviated version in 1993. In Hoff's view, poststructuralist theory brings "potentially paralyzing consequences" both to the writing of women's history and to feminist activism. By denying the validity of experience "outside of the ways that language constructs it," poststructuralism, she declares, not only "compromises historians' ability to identify facts and chronological narratives" but also turns women's struggles into "mere sub-jective stories." It would invalidate empirical studies of women who are just beginning to enter historiography as subjects, and it would destroy the basis for a broad-based feminist political movement. Furthermore, she submits that the preference for the term *gender* rather than *woman* masks the per-sonal misogyny of the Continental poststructuralists who inspired post-modernist theory. The poststructuralist historians' "deliberate depoliti-cization of power through representations of the female self as totally diffuse and decentered" threatens women's history with dissolution "in a sea of rel-ativity created on the head of a semiotic pin by deconstructionists."[46]

Hoff singled out Joan Scott, whose work had played such a major role in conveying Continental philosophy to American feminist scholars, for attack. While crediting Scott with good intentions for her concern about the relative lack of impact of more conventional women's history and for her desire to refute stereotypes of women as victims of patriarchal oppres-sion, Hoff termed Scott's solution "no friend of women." For Hoff, the post-structuralist approach to gender moves "beyond the material and cultural representation of sex (biological differences) to a totally abstract represen-tation of sexual and all other kinds of differences between women and men created by society" which fosters what, borrowing from Ronni Sandroff, she termed "phallic drift." It deflects the work of feminist theorists to create a unifying language to express the shared experiences of women across class and race lines, toward the elitist and misogynist theories of "Tootsie" men. Hoff even compared these "postfeminists" to pornographers: like pornog-raphers, they served to "assert male dominance over women by literally and figuratively silencing them by deconstructing (or hacking) them up into smaller fragmented pieces." Postmodernism reduces feminists to what Somer Brodribb has called "ragpickers in the bins of male ideas." In Hoff's opinion, the term *poststructural feminism* is an oxymoron.[47]

While Hoff employs radical rhetoric in her criticism, she is not alone in lamenting the unhappy coincidence of the birth of studies of women and the death of the subject in postmodernist terms. The political scientist Nancy Hartsock writes, "Why is it that just at the moment when so many of us who have been silenced begin to demand the right to name ourselves, to act as subjects rather than as objects of history, that just then the concept of subjecthood becomes problematic? Just when we are forming our own theories about the world, uncertainty emerges about whether the world can be theorized." Hartsock sees these "intellectual moves" as the "transcendental voice of the Enlightenment attempting to come to grips with the social and historical changes of the middle-to-late twentieth century." But she and other theorists also acknowledge the dangers to feminism of abandoning its historical foundations. The political scientist Wendy Brown finds that "postmodernity unsettles feminism because it erodes the *moral* ground that the subject, truth, and normativity coproduce in modernity. When contemporary feminist political theorists or analysts complain about the antipolitical or unpolitical nature of postmodern thought—thought that apprehends and responds to this erosion—they are protesting, *inter alia*, a Nietzschean analysis of truth and morality as fully implicated in and by power, and thereby delegitimated qua Truth and Morality. . . . The question is whether *feminist* politics can prosper without a moral apparatus, whether feminist theorists and activists will give up substituting Truth and Morality for politics. Are we willing to engage in struggle without recrimination . . . ?"[48]

In dividing contemporary feminism into two camps, with a line of separation drawn around the Enlightenment, some theorists implicitly if not explicitly adopt a position that rejects all Enlightenment thought, science, modernism, and everything classified as "Eurocentric." Enlightenment ideas are portrayed as "totalizing," "universalistic," and "hegemonic" and are blamed for consequences that include everything bad about the modern world. A more comprehensive view of the Enlightenment, however, reveals feminism itself (and even postmodernism) to be deeply rooted in aspects of Enlightenment thought. Pointing to "the modernity of feminist postmodernism," Sandra Harding, for one, notes its belief in the "desirability and the possibility of social progress." "It is not clear," she states, how "a specifically feminist alternative to Enlightenment projects . . . could completely take leave of Enlightenment assumptions and still remain feminist. . . . Feminism (also) stands on Enlightenment ground."[49]

Pauline Johnson, an Australian sociologist whose interpretation of feminism as "radical humanism" will be discussed below, also criticizes the readiness of some contemporary feminist theorists to dismiss the Enlightenment and to "jettison the entire legacy" of humanism and rationalism. This is based, in her view, on "a frozen image of seventeenth century rationalism." She suggests that feminists should recognize the Enlightenment as neither a "set of fixed principles" nor an "oppressive, universalising assertion of certain, dogmatically assumed, truth claims" but as a "dynamic, on-going self-critical process" essential to feminism. "To the extent that a contemporary feminism understands itself as an immanent critique which seeks to rescue the emancipatory intent of Enlightenment from the various prejudices which cling to its 'master narratives' I have no argument. My disagreement is, rather, with those for whom this critique of the 'Western paradigm of reason' is seen to impose the necessity for separating contemporary feminism by radical surgery from the influence of Enlightenment thinking."[50]

These feminist scholars point out that feminism is not in competition with the Enlightenment. Returning to the historical documents, Karen Offen peers behind what she terms "the clouded lenses of late twentieth century theoretical concerns, whether post-modernist, post-colonialist, or post-feminist," and shows that "reason provided the essential underpinning for feminist arguments for sexual equality, while pre-Kantian claims for universality of the category 'Man' were repeatedly contested by European Enlightenment feminist theorists." Offen argues that the Enlightenment legacy, with its vocabulary of freedom, equality, and justice, continues to serve feminists well.[51]

The postmodernist perspective on feminism elicits criticism from another direction. Women of color, whose charges against white feminists helped spur the search for a theory to encompass diversity, fear that in its postmodernist guise, the "politics of difference" may also operate to impede the efforts of people of color to be heard. African American scholars, who have participated prominently in the discussion, often criticize the separation of theory from practice, and the exclusionary effects of the strains of theory that came to dominate academic feminism in the 1980s. "The race for theory," Barbara Christian declared in an influential essay, "has silenced many of us." Drawing on her experience of the Black Arts movement of the 1960s, Christian noted the tendency for theory when divorced from practice to become "prescriptive, exclusive, elitist." Feminist theorists, she admits, "do acknowledge that women of color, for example, do exist, then go on to do what they were going to do anyway, which is to invent a theory that has little relevance for us."[52]

Likewise, bell hooks charges that "in some circles, there seems to be a direct connection between white feminist scholars turning towards critical work and theory by white men, and the turning away of white feminists from fully respecting and valuing the critical insights and theoretical offerings of black women or women of color." At a time when black women and men are "yearning," hooks says, to be "critical voices," postmodernism threatens to repudiate as essentialist narratives of African American experience and the "politics of racism." She wants to maintain the "authority of experience," which validates difference, and use it to open up new possibilities beyond one-dimensional "colonial imperialist paradigms of black identity."[53]

The effort required to follow postmodernist arguments, which are often expressed in concepts and language difficult even for scholars to fathom, provokes some of the discomfort; hooks, for one, objects to theory expressed in language that "leaves [women] stumbling bleary-eyed from classroom settings feeling humiliated" because they cannot find meaning in it. She regrets, however, that some feminists respond to "hegemonic feminist theory that does not speak clearly to us by trashing theory, and, as a consequence, further promoting the false dichotomy between theory and practice." Katie King, tracing the history of the "gay/straight split" in United States feminism, criticizes the gatekeeping function of what she terms "the big three—essentializing, universalizing, naturalizing, the 'sins' of feminist theory." The rejection of this "big three" by postmodernist feminist theorists in an effort to respond to criticism by lesbians, women of color, and others who did not see themselves reflected adequately in 1970s feminism may thus further alienate some of those groups. Susan Stanford Friedman finds that the "endless problematization of the ground on which we stand" reinforces a "binary of winners and losers." Is it feminist theory, asks Elizabeth Spelman in a chapter entitled "Now You See Her, Now You Don't," if it privileges white, middle-class women? Mary Maynard agrees that feminist analysts tend to give "lip-service to the significance of racism . . . then fail to give these dimensions sufficient analytical weight." Sharon Sievers, a historian of Japanese feminism, extends the question to a wider cultural context, criticizing the tendency of many feminist scholars "to attach disproportionate weight to western political and philosophical theory." If there is "something universal in feminist experience," then comparative studies are necessary to finding it.[54]

One of the most extended treatments of the divisions over theory appears in the works of the prolific bell hooks. Paralleling the development of women's studies, early work on women by women of color tended toward empirical studies of women's history, literary images of women, and artistic expressions that made visible the hidden, ignored, and suppressed experiences of nondominant groups of women. *Ain't I a Woman?* (1981), hooks' first book, with its provocative title borrowed from Sojourner Truth, began also with (black) women's history but continued beyond what hooks called the "imperialism of patriarchy" into the formulation of feminist theory. *This Bridge Called My Back* appeared the same year, and Gloria Hull, Barbara Scott, and Barbara Smith's important text *All the Women Are White, All the Blacks Are Men, but Some of Us Are Brave* followed in 1982. All contributed concepts to the feminist search for theory.[55]

In hooks's first book, which she began as a nineteen-year-old undergraduate, she challenged not only (white-dominated) patriarchy but also a romanticized black nationalism that, she alleged, sheltered sexism; most important, she criticized racism within feminism. According to hooks, contemporary feminist leaders and the founders of women's studies ignored, when they did not patronize, black women. She nuanced her criticism by acknowledging that "feminism as a political ideology advocating social equality for all women was and is acceptable to many black women." Furthermore, the foundation of separate "black feminist" groups was not. But neither was the "appropriation of feminist ideology by elitist, racist, white women." Instead of rejecting feminism, hooks chose to redefine the term. "To be 'feminist' in any authentic sense of the term," she declared, "is to want for all people, female and male, liberation from sexist role patterns, domination, and oppression." Now the author of more than a dozen books and numerous essays, reviews, and interviews, hooks most consistently criticizes manifestations of any ideology that supports domination of any kind. Her work has won such wide recognition that she has been called a public intellectual, a fact that demonstrates, in her view, a widespread hunger for "theory that engages the concrete." For hooks, the concrete means the daily realities of her own life and other women's lives. One of the

attractions of hooks's work is her willingness to draw on her own experience of private matters to facilitate access to her ideas. However, in contrast
to behavior that she strongly criticizes, hooks takes care not to uncouple
the personal from the political. For example, she uses personal confession,
she argues, "to transgress the public, to disrupt and subvert." Her disclosure
of private life constitutes a "politicized strategic use of private information
that seeks to subvert the politics of domination." The politicization of self,
for hooks, is a means toward theorizing experience.[56]

Black feminism, however, transcends political practice grounded in
daily life. The threat that black feminist criticism might be marginalized
through acceptance of "unstudied distinctions between theory and practice" leads Deborah McDowell to rearrange the usual sequence of terms and
examine "the 'practice' of 'theory.'" She argues that the "theory/practice
opposition is often racialized and gendered, especially in discussions of black
feminist thinking." Challenging both the maternalism she finds demonstrated by some white theorists and the clichéd acceptance by some black
critics of the theory/practice dichotomy, McDowell criticizes the narrow
definition of the former which allows black women's work to be relegated
to the category of "experience," even as the names of black women are
"fetishized" and the authority of experience is denied. One result, she fears,
is that black feminist criticism may be "consigned to the status of the permanent underclass . . . fixed to a reference schemata and a racial stigmata
in a history we've read before." Black feminist thought in fact covers a wide
range of theoretical perspectives, employing a full range of constructionist
and essentialist analyses.[57]

While hooks is probably the most prolific and African Americans are
overall the most prominent theorists among women of color, Asian Americans, Chicanas, Latinas, and others have also drawn on their experience of
ethnic difference to advance feminist theory. Their work responds to what
Elizabeth Spelman calls the "ampersand problem in feminist thought"—the
failure of feminism to conceive of women's oppression and liberation in
terms of both gender and race. In Spelman's view, this reflects a phenomenon
she terms "somatophobia," which is a result of the historically negative attitude toward the body which marks Western culture. The denigration of the
body which led to the close association of bodily functions with the female
sex and with nonwhite races, and to their devaluation, was also responsible, Spelman submits, for the tendency of such liberal feminists as Simone
de Beauvoir and Betty Friedan, and the much-cited radical feminist Shu-

lamith Firestone, to abstract "woman" from her body. "Keep the woman, somehow, but leave behind her woman's body; keep the black person but leave the Blackness behind." Quoting the poet Gwendolyn Brooks, Spelman tells her readers, "The juice from tomatoes is not called merely juice. It is called TOMATO juice." There exists, she concludes, no such creature as "generic woman."[58]

This analogy is problematic, for people do order "juice," refining their selection on second thought. Furthermore, tomatoes appear in many forms, and blackness has many meanings. Nevertheless, Spelman's work has served to awaken awareness and to stimulate further important analysis of difference. When Gloria Anzaldúa notes, in introducing *Making Face, Making Soul*, that "the world knows us by our faces," she adopts Spelman's position. Declaring that we are known by the faces we wear, Anzaldúa draws on Aztec tradition to develop a metaphor for the construction of identity. For Mitsuye Yamada, the masks of Noh theater reveal the multiple uses of "faces" to control, conceal, and permit both endurance and escape. In *Making Face, Making Soul*, Norma Alarcón points out as well the importance of linguistic differences, noting the failure of Anglo-American feminism to recognize that women are "culturally constituted in and through language in complex ways." Joan Scott, attempting to link an affirmation of diversity to postmodernist theory, suggests that "differences may be what we have most in common."[59]

It may be true, as Nellie Y. McKay observes, that "most white feminists no longer universalize the experiences of women . . . not an inconsequential move from where we were a decade and a half ago." But does recognition of differences among women require abandoning commonalities? Do sisters no longer bond? Do mothers share no understandings? Is there no female sex? These questions point to a crucial contest within feminist theory. Awareness of sexual, racial, and ethnic differences among women now seems to define feminism for some feminists. This is a feminism that can be subsumed within "gender studies." The theorist Judith Butler, who repudiates earlier, pre-postmodernist interpretations of the sex-gender system in which "sex is to gender as the natural is to the social," is a leading proponent of "gender" in the contest with "woman/women" as subject. Butler considers sex itself as a cultural construction. In her view, it is through a process of performance that we come to understand sex. Sex is a "postulation" that does not exist prior to language. "This sex posited as prior to construction will, by virtue of being posited, become the effect of that very positing, the construction of construction." For the radical constructivist, the problem next arises: "If the subject is constructed, then who is constructing the subject?" How is sex naturalized? Is there "some part" of sex that is not constructed? What about the body? Everything, in Butler's view, is open, nothing is fixed. Gender is a series of acts, identity an effect.[60]

One great strength of gender analysis is that it defines femininity and masculinity in relationship, as Joan Kelly and Natalie Zemon Davis long ago proposed. The feminist historian Judith Bennett, for example, acknowledges the potential for gender analysis in its postmodernist form to broaden the scope of women's history. She suggests that "we can now look everywhere—even at such traditionally prestigious historical subjects as politics, intellectual discourse, and economics—for gender used as a 'primary signifier of power.'" The historical study of gender might even "demolish entirely the academic 'ghettoization' of women's history." But Bennett also notes the danger that it "ignores women *qua* women . . . evinces very little interest in material reality . . . and . . . intellectualizes and abstracts the inequality of the sexes." It also moves the central focus of women's history away from its feminist goal of historicizing, understanding, and overcoming "patriarchy." Worse yet, others argue that a postmodernist approach might even eclipse feminist scholarship by making women's studies appear essentialist and separatist. "It has become a positive embarrassment to talk about women," lamented the literature scholar Nancy K. Miller in a dialogue about debates in feminist literary criticism.[61]

By emphasizing differences and minimizing commonalities, theorists who deny "woman" a group identity and refuse to grant the authority to speak for "women" are responding to the challenges of lesbians, women of color, women with disabilities, and others who have sharply criticized the privilege assumed by use of the first person plural. But talking to each other in academic language, they may also defer or deter discussion of issues that arise from the daily lives of most women. Some theorists, especially those oriented toward practice and concerned about the realities of women's lives, are very unhappy with the direction of much academic feminist theory. This kind of theory cannot satisfy Charlotte Bunch's quest for theory to guide feminist action. It is "difficult to associate with sexual violence, economic equality, women dying from backstreet abortions. It is gender reinvented as play for those who see themselves far removed from the nitty gritty of women's oppression," says Sheila Jeffreys, referring to the new, postmodernist, "lesbianandgay" theory. Gender as performance, bodies as texts on which gender is enacted, and "postmodern body writing" all appear to the radical feminist Renate Klein to encourage the disembodiment of women; for her, the work of Judith Butler signifies "the body destroyed so that culture can emerge." "But," Klein maintains, "women *are* Our Bodies—Ourselves."[62]

Klein and her co-editor Diane Bell recently published a collection of contributions from sixty-eight authors seeking to recuperate "radical feminism" from the cultural feminism with which it has at times been conflated, to "interrogate" postmodernism, and to "reclaim feminism." In a workshop led by the book's editors and contributors at the 1996 NWSA annual meeting, one sympathizer commented that "postmodernism poses as feminism's smarter, younger sister." It substitutes "high style" for substance.[63] In return, in a review of the Bell and Klein book, the critics of "pomo" feminism have been called "righteous sisters" out to "bludgeon and dismember" their opposition.[64] Joan Hoff, whose attack on postmodernism was reprinted in this collection, was charged with anti-intellectualism, disingenuousness, and sheer "incivility" for having "caricatured and misrepresented the positions gender historians hold."[65]

It is ironic that, despite its potential for radical deconstruction of foundational concepts, "gender studies" continues to be preferred to "women's studies" by some who see it either as a way to reach more students or as an allegedly safer label that appears less threatening to traditionalists, not least because it includes the study of men. It also appeals to scholars who believe that broadening women's studies' scope helps to deny "man" his long-occupied place as universal subject. The labor historian Ava Baron, for example, uses gender analysis to show how male workers' concepts of masculinity, developed in relation to gender as well as to age, level of skill, strength, and other attributes, created the notions of the workplace that until recently were accepted and studied by scholars. The sociologist Michael S. Kimmel, a practitioner of "men's studies," thanks women's studies for having *"made men visible."* He notes that in his discipline, "gender has moved from the margins—Marriage and the Family—to the center." What he formerly perceived as "the Ladies' Auxiliary of Sociology" now constitutes the largest section of the profession. Kimmel credits women's studies for his ability to teach such courses as "Men and Gender Issues" and "Sociology of the Male Experience."[66]

Not all feminist scholars are happy about this development, however. In her 1989 review of eight books in men's studies, Lois Banner finds them to be "informed by feminism [but not] necessarily feminist." Noting their tendency to focus on "how men feel," she suggests that "when sensitivity and personal pain become the modalities of male experience, privilege and domination easily disappear." While the best of the genre contribute useful analyses of the social construction of masculinity, Banner reminds readers that "masculinity is not just an experience, as the men's studies theorists too often seem to view it, it is also an institution." She considers the new field to be misnamed; it is "really a branch of women's studies."[67]

Also observing that "men's studies are primarily concerned with masculine subjectivity" rather than an analysis of "how men gain, maintain, and use power to subordinate women," Diane Richardson and Victoria Robinson suggest that male academics, instead of creating a new field that might divert interest and resources from women's studies, should have "taken on the traditional disciplines." The very name *men's studies*, they fear, contributes to a "deradicalization" of women's studies by suggesting that the two fields are complementary. To illustrate the danger of renaming, Richardson and Robinson conducted a study of the changing nomenclature of publishers' brochures. They reproduce in full-page format the cover for a 1993–94 advertisement entitled "Gender and Women's Studies" which depicts "two bronzed, muscular, naked men, one of whom is worshipping at the feet (and cod-piece) of the other who is standing on a pedestal!" In the authors' view, such "repackaging" dilutes when it does not altogether supersede women's studies and feminism.[68] I have observed that some publishers now offer their works exclusively under the rubric of "gender studies," eliminating women's studies as a separate category. For example, the University of California Press in its late 1996 sale catalog includes "gender studies" but no "women's studies," and Cambridge University Press promotes books on women through its "Gender and Cultural Studies" series.

Nevertheless, some postmodernists argue that far from destroying feminist politics, gender analysis in its new forms provides feminism with a strengthened foundation. Judith Butler insists that rather than destroying the basis for feminist politics along with the stability of its foundational subject, the concept of gender as performance, as verb rather than noun, liberates it. "Paradoxically," she states, "the reconceptualization of identity as an *effect*, that is, as *produced* or *generated*, opens up possibilities of 'agency' that are insidiously foreclosed by positions that take identity categories as foundational and fixed." The deconstructing of the subject opens it to "re-usage or redeployment that previously has not been authorized."[69] But feminists of many persuasions, of course, have long defied authorized behavior.

While postmodernism questions the fixity of gender, it does not negate its reality. Whatever openness may be introduced theoretically by the concept of gender as deed, fixed notions of gender persist in deeply entrenched patterns of behavior. The sociologist Judith Lorber explains that gender operates as a "social institution," a paradigm that provides, in her view, a more comprehensive explanatory model for women's condition than does the "over-used and slippery" concept of patriarchy. Lorber structures her work around various "paradoxes" in the ways in which gender differences function in society. For her, gender constitutes "a process of social construction, a system of social stratification, and an institution that structures every aspect of our lives because of its embeddedness in the family, the workplace, and the state, as well as in sexuality, language, and culture." It is not located in individual or interpersonal relationships but is comprised of "gendered practices [that] produce the social institution of gender, which in turn constrains social practices; structure and practices simultaneously sustain and are legitimized by the micropolitics of everyday life and the macropolitics of state power." Although the institution that exists to create and maintain gender differences is complex, its purpose, in Lorber's view, is simple and insidious: "The point of these differences is to justify the exploitation of an identifiable group—women." It is not easy, Lorber believes, to envision its end.[70]

Feminist theorists adopt many contending positions in the gender debates. The politics of gender analysis within women's studies can be traced in the series of publications that followed Butler's 1990 publication of *Gender Trouble*. Books with titles such as *Conflicts in Feminism* (1990), *Unsettling Relations* (1991), *Feminism without Women* (1991), *Feminism beside Itself* (1995), *Feminist Contentions* (1995), *Who Can Speak?* (1995), and *Radically Speaking: Feminism Reclaimed* (1996) suggest the nature of this contest: they are critical essays by feminist theorists in support of or opposition to some aspect of the new gender analysis. The term *gender* is employed by feminist scholars in many ways. Mary Hawkesworth offers a listing of more than two dozen. While stressing the importance of using gender as a category of analysis, as a "heuristic device" to "denaturalize" gender constructs, she also cautions against using it as a "mode of explanation" to make untenable claims.[71]

Several theorists have sought to resolve conflicts over gender analysis with a "third way," or at least to find a means to answer the charge that feminist theory undercuts feminist politics. Denise Riley believes that theorists can argue that "women" do not exist while engaging in politics as if they do—because the world proceeds as if they did. "Feminism must be agile enough," she suggests, "to say 'Now we will be 'women'—but now we will be persons, not these 'women.'" Diana Fuss urges feminists to "take the risk of essence" (but she argues that "there is no essence to essentialism"—politics is feminism's essence). Donna Haraway agrees that "there is nothing about being 'female' that naturally binds women," but she suggests a way to get beyond "fractured identities." By de-emphasizing the "taxonomies of feminism [that] produce epistemologies to police deviation from official women's experience," even while recognizing the "noninnocence of the category 'woman,'" women can build coalitions on the basis of "affinity, not identity." The film critic Teresa de Lauretis finds a way to reject compromised categories while also avoiding an extreme nominalism by turning to Linda Alcoff's concept of "woman as positionality" and identity as "an emergent projection of a historical experience" rather than a fixed "set of attributes."[72] But in the absence of a collective sense of womanhood, these abstract notions and vague presumptions may be an insufficient counterweight to the pull of particularism.

The philosopher Iris Marion Young, seeking a theory to justify an inclusive practice while also acknowledging differences, draws on Sartre's concept of "serial collectivity." Young assumes with Spelman, Butler, and other feminist theorists that it is impossible to separate gender from other aspects of identity but that broad gender categories serve to homogenize, normalize, exclude, and devalue while obscuring their "constructed, and thus contestable, character." Does this necessarily mean, she asks, that "it makes no sense and is morally wrong ever to talk about women as a group or, in fact, to talk about social groups at all?" What feminists need now, she answers, is "pragmatic theorizing" that addresses the dilemma created by deconstruction of the concept "woman."[73]

Young's solution is to follow Sartre in distinguishing between a social "group" with a fixed set of attributes, common goals, a "self-consciously, mutually acknowledging collective with a self-conscious purpose," and a social "series" that constitutes a collective only in that, while going about their way, a number of individuals find it useful to relate in common fashion to a mutual object or practice. Women do not form a "group," according to this definition; but, like people waiting for the same bus, they do become a "series." "Their actions and goals may be different, and they have nothing necessarily in common in their histories, experiences, or identity. They are united only by their desire to ride on that route." Members of a series may choose to act together, for instance, as bus riders do when they complain about poor service. But since membership in a serial collectivity does not define individual identity, this concept provides a way to envision women as acting collectively without resort to essentialism. "Women need have nothing in common in their individual lives to be serialized as women." As a seriality, Young believes, women can come together as a group, or groups—even in feminism or feminisms—for purposes of coalition politics. However, since the ends of feminist politics are not as singular or as predictable as the route of a bus ride, the usefulness of the concept of seriality as a resolution to feminist contentions is unclear.[74]

Although it is treated somewhat infrequently in feminist theory, the disembodiment that denies fixed gender identity also destabilizes concepts of race, ethnicity, physical ability, and all the other "locations" from which women may speak. The Foucauldian concept of a "body totally imprinted by history," which Judith Butler adopts as the base for her reconceptualization of gender identity, opens up possibilities for (re)constituting other forms of identity as well.[75] Essentialist notions also permeate such group identities as African American, Asian American, and Latino/Latina, all concepts that serve to elide differences and create a sometimes dubious but also undeniable commonality.

For those who, like myself, find the existence of commonalities among women salient to our lives, it is helpful to recall that some conditions of human life affect us all. In the early days of Second Wave feminism, some feminists explained the movement as a form of humanism. Women, after all, are people. Perhaps inchoately, they asserted that "women's rights are human rights." At a time when humanism has fallen, in some feminist thinking, into the dustbin reserved for enemy ideas, Pauline Johnson's effort to restore humanism to feminism provides a welcome antidote. Johnson points out that "modern humanism is not merely a doctrine which asserts the implicit unity of the species. Parallel with the aspiration to consider all humans within these universalising terms has been the equally strong desire to affirm particularity, to raise awareness and respect for the uniqueness of all forms of individuality."[76]

In Johnson's view, the antihumanist thought that appears in some schools of feminism results from a misunderstanding and a one-sided view of humanism. "The tension *within* the cultural ideas of modern humanism [is misinterpreted] as a manifestation of feminism's own struggle *against* humanism." That struggle is based on humanists' long-pervasive assumption of "man" as their model. It is to humanism, however, that feminism owes its own conception of individuals as unique beings endowed with rights, and its concomitant impulse to oppose universalistic categories. "When feminism evokes the ideas of difference and particularity as values which ought to be defended, it speaks precisely in the language of modern humanism. . . . The ideals of self-determining autonomous subjectivity and authentic self-realisation [are] the ideals of modern humanism itself."[77]

Feminism, in this view, is a form of humanism, one that Johnson terms "radical humanism." She intends by this designation to distinguish it from "metaphysical humanism," which she, like many others, criticizes. The essential difference is that radical humanism rejects the "universalising dimension . . . which seeks to abstract from all affiliations and particular integrations," and can be and has been used to oppress. Instead, it recognizes the historical contingency of humanistic ideals and the "paradoxical relation between the universalistic character of its own aspirations and value commitments and the always particularistic, culture-bound terms in which these universalising claims are raised." In other words, there is a conflict at the core of the human condition which must be recognized. Feminism, too partakes of this condition.[78]

It remains unclear whether feminist theory, and with it, women's studies, can transcend differences among women, or whether recognition and accommodation may be sufficient. Feminist theory has come to occupy a privileged place in women's studies, as theory and philosophy long have done in the academy. The stakes of the feminist theory debates in women's studies are high. Everything, including the name of the field itself *(women's studies* or *gender studies)*, the future directions of feminist scholarship in and across the disciplines, relationships within the academy (with ethnic studies as well as with traditional departments), the "politics of identity politics" as they are played out on and off campus, and for some, even the viability of feminism as ideology and as political movement, is affected by theoretical suppositions. These "conflicts in feminism" reflect the growing sophistication of the feminist search for theory, and of the development of the field. Like the earlier schemes that relied on nineteenth-century political economists and sociologists, and the pursuit of new paradigms inspired by Thomas Kuhn, the newer theory draws on the work of male thinkers.

But it differs radically in that it is centered in women's experiences (albeit in a "man-made" world). "Doing theory" complicates feminism but replaces notions of a single sisterhood who would move forward speaking a common language with an enriched and potentially more effective base for broadening its appeal and accomplishing its work. The struggle over theory opens women's studies not only to sectarian division and political polemics but also to intellectual challenges of far-reaching significance for both academic and political work in many countries. It may be, as Marianne Hirsch and Evelyn Fox Keller suggest, that "practicing conflict" itself gives impetus to feminist movement.[79]

Feminist theory has advanced the search for explanations of women's "nature" and "condition" far beyond its origins in the work of philosophers and social scientists of the past who denigrated women in building their theories and defined women as a "problem." Using the master's tools, academic feminists have not only established the legitimacy of women's studies but have moved what the nineteenth century called "the woman question" to the center of discourse in many academic fields. Feminist theorists have contributed to the development of many disciplines. They have proved that theorizing knows neither sex nor race.[80]

Feminist theory remains a work in progress. Theorists have produced no overarching countertheory. On the contrary, they have questioned what is meant by the concept "theory," pondered how empirical studies and experience relate to "doing theory," and sought new ways to enlist theory in the processes of creating and applying knowledge of and in the world. They have criticized the very search for master narratives and all-encompassing frameworks for falsely homogenizing complex experiences. They have historicized feminist theory itself. Because gender is entwined with all other attributes of identity, they have decided that there is no answer to "the woman question."[81] Some, as shown above, would say that there is no "woman." Others, like myself, prefer to elasticize rather than to eliminate the category. It seems to me possible to recognize historical and cultural diversity without denying the basic concept. As Alison Assiter states in her study of "modernist feminism in a postmodern age," the question of defining woman "can and should be separated from the question of whether women are oppressed as women."[82] Feminist theory has other work to do.

While women's studies scholars continue to think, conduct research, write, and teach about how sex and gender matter, they have created a significant if contested role for feminist theory in women's studies and the academy. But whichever side of whatever divide they stand along, they unite in almost unanimous agreement on two issues. One is that gender operates to encode power in society. The other is the purpose of their work. Feminist theories are tools that do not merely mirror reality but seek to transform it. The complex relationship of theory to practice in women's studies remains a hotly debated topic. But few of women's studies' supporters (or detractors) would suggest that doing women's studies is not a political act. Feminist theory offers critical reflections on the politics that it intends to serve. The purpose of deconstruction in women's studies is the transformation of gender relationships. It is the hope of women's studies, through inquiry based on women's experiences, to create new knowledge that will change the world. Although feminist theory criticizes unproblematic uses of "women's experience" and maintains a healthy skepticism of tendencies toward universalism, it nevertheless recognizes the need to continue envisioning a world in which such Enlightenment values as equality, justice, and freedom are extended more broadly and inclusively to all women, and to build a case for feminist agency.

The search for theory has led academic feminists to develop a wide-ranging and profound critique of the Western philosophical tradition and of the academic disciplines and political thought grounded in it. Both liberalism and socialism were found wanting because they relied on assumptions and categories of analysis that ignored sexual and gender difference. A naive universalism underlying some feminist positions was also exposed, and the nature of feminist discourse itself was scrutinized. Poststructuralist thought gave feminist theorists new insight and ways to interpret and express the critique they were developing, and led toward an analysis that clarifies their own quest for theory. It strengthened their critique of the Marxian thought they found wanting, notwithstanding its usefulness as a catalyst and source of methodology, and required feminists of all persuasions to rethink their foundations and their future. Like the Marxian socialists they rightly rejected, academic feminists apply principles to practice. In the world of women's studies, "doing theory" is expected to lead to action. In all their varied aspects, the theories postulated by contemporary academic feminists exemplify the pursuit of knowledge with a constructive purpose.

7

Learning for a Purpose

In August 1974 I went to San Diego State University to take a temporary job teaching women's history and chairing the university's women's studies program. The first person I encountered after signing in, as I hunted in a huge, unfamiliar building for my office, was a longtime staff member who served as a handyman for the college. I said, "Hi, I'm Marilyn Boxer, in women's studies. Can you tell me where to find room 581?" He answered, "Where are the men's studies?" This query, often heard in the early years, was sometimes, as here, an attempt at humor. It probably masked an unconscious fear of the new. But it also harbored an accusation of bias. Many times since then, I have heard the charge that women's studies is "political," an imposter in a university dedicated to the neutral, balanced pursuit of disinterested scholarship. What does it mean to define teaching women's studies as a political act?

This issue of women's studies' political purpose is sometimes raised by opponents of women's studies, and sometimes by its supporters. Inevitably it invokes the relationship between women's studies as an academic field and feminism as an activist movement. Some ask whether women's studies is only politics by another name. Others query instead whether, as it has succeeded in institutionalizing itself, women's studies has lost its activist impulse and become an academic enterprise like others, no longer serving to advance the causes of feminism in its many forms but merely serving to assure career success for a professional elite increasingly given to arcane discussions of theory. Is "academic feminism" an oxymoron? What is the purpose of studies devoted to women? Is knowledge its own end, or does it serve other goals? At the very outset, women's studies practitioners were put on the defensive by these questions. But soon historical perspective led to the realization that the question of purpose is not new, but rather quite old, far older than the quotation from Robert S. Lynd that heads this chapter.

In 1939 Lynd, a sociologist famous for his study *Middletown*, published a series of lectures that he had delivered at Princeton the previous year under the title "Knowledge for What?" It might as well have been called "Beyond Empiricism," for Lynd set out to challenge the social sciences by raising the question of what was to be done with all the knowledge accumulated through research: "No informed person questions nowadays the indispensability of objective data-gathering and of the exhaustive statistical analysis of those data for all they are worth. The only question that is being raised here concerns the need to ask '*What* are they worth for *what?*' Objective empiricism can become as much of a blind alley as can logical speculation."[1]

The value of knowledge for Lynd lay in its application to present problems. Otherwise, he suggested with a mocking reference to the Grand Academy of Lagado in *Gulliver's Travels*, scholarly research was only a "self-justifying pursuit" to keep professionals employed. In a series of what he termed "outrageous hypotheses," Lynd proposed that prior to posing a question, scientists recognize the "constructing frame of its original formulation." They should query themselves about the cultural influences shaping their interests and should select problems "not because they represent interesting moves on an impersonal intellectual chessboard, but because they involve frustrations of the urgent cravings of great masses of the American people." Lynd's goal was "to lessen these frustrations as directly as possible."[2] Half a century later, the feminist scholar Ellen Messer-Davidow put it more succinctly. Entitling her essay "Know-How," she called for academic feminists to "rejoin inquiry and social change," to "make academic change, both intellectual and institutional, instrumental to this goal."[3]

Long before women's studies, academic fields arose out of social concerns. Many of the founders of social science, in the United States as well as in Europe, were social reformers. Auguste Comte, called the father of sociology, created his science of society as a means to replace civil strife with social harmony.[4] The American Social Science Association was founded in

1865 at least partially "to provide a more authoritative basis for dealing with contemporary problems." "Sociology," Lynd declared of his own discipline, "grew up . . . as a form of protest" against abstract studies of individuals and institutions. It had originally had a social mission that now was lost, Lynd suggested, and had been replaced by career ambitions. Just as Lynd's social scientists of the 1930s had "given heavy hostages to fortune," in the form of families supported by incomes that depended on academic success, which was in turn dependent on "productive research," so, too, academic feminists of the 1970s, 1980s, and 1990s required institutional validation that rendered them accountable to university administrators rather than to the "feminist community." Like other members of the professions, some, although politicized by feminist (and other) activist goals and writing and teaching feminist political rhetoric, remained "apolitical" outside the academy, incurring criticism on both scores.[5]

As Lynd's exhortation shows, the linking of academic inquiry to activist goals in American higher education did not commence with the introduction of women's studies. Nor is the question of "advocacy," as activism in the classroom is often termed, germane only to women's studies and other recent scholarship based on "identity politics."[6] A 1995 conference entitled "The Role of Advocacy in the Classroom," sponsored by more than a dozen of the leading national associations of the traditional academic disciplines as well as the American Association of University Professors and the American Council of Learned Societies,[7] testifies to the general importance of the question and to the difficulty of its resolution. The voices of those who still believe in "disengaged," or "disinterested," scholarship, for whom the words *scholar* and *advocate* are necessarily oppositional, were more than balanced by those who would remind us of the link between *professor* and *advocate.* Even if it were possible for faculty to present "balanced" views, as some critics recommend, it is not clear that such neutrality would improve the quality of instruction. On the contrary, as a reporter for the *Chronicle of Higher Education* who attended the conference observed, "Even those on opposite sides of the political spectrum believed that professors who express strong opinions and encourage students to agree are more effective than those who are neutral."[8]

For women's studies, which began academic life intending to serve as the academic arm of the women's liberation movement, the relationship between academic pursuits and advocacy has been the site of internal contestation almost from the start. The goal of women's studies, as it spread quickly through the grassroots—in a process sometimes likened to the springing up of consciousness-raising groups all over the United States in the late 1960s and early 1970s—was not simply to foster among women the "click" experience of feminist conversion but to elicit from new under-standings of their lives a commitment to collective action for change. The women's studies professor, often tellingly called "practitioner,"[9] advocates social change to overcome centuries of the subordination of women by men, based on erroneous assumptions and incomplete knowledge that are now increasingly replaced, and remediated, by the new scholarship on women. According to one instructor in an open university setting, women's studies courses in the 1980s attracted students for "reasons very similar to those that led women to join consciousness-raising groups in the late 1960s." Fearful that women's studies was losing its ties to the women's movement, she cited the concern expressed by the well-known British activist-scholar Sheila Rowbotham that (in Rowbotham's words) women's studies, "which emerged out of arguments and struggle[,] have now begun to grow into a little knowledge industry of their own."[10]

The two parts of the double mission, to educate and to motivate, rested together uneasily from the beginning. The nation's first women's studies program, at San Diego State, split even in its first year, 1970–71, when a conflict over program funding and control led its community activist contingent to move downtown, where they opened a storefront feminist services operation, calling it the Center for Women's Studies and Services.[11] In the fourth year, confronted with a new dean's determination that the program conform to university regulations governing personnel appointments, and anticipating as well a national search for new faculty imposed by the administration, the incumbent faculty—themselves all new that year—resigned en masse. In their view, the administration's decision to cease "rubber stamping" their hiring decisions destroyed their ability to be accountable to their own principles and to their advisory group of community members.[12] Their collective decision-making and teaching practices would be replaced, they believed, by "professionalism," and career interest would overcome political commitment.

The faculty explained their rationale for resigning in a twelve-page brochure entitled *Women's Studies and Socialist Feminism*, dated April 1974. All of them held temporary appointments, the program's earlier tenure-track positions having reportedly been voluntarily abandoned, to facilitate the sharing of teaching duties and salaries. As socialist feminists, they described themselves as "committed to the struggle to end sexism, racism, class oppression and heterosexual dominance in our society." Universities, according to their rationale, existed to perpetuate the privileges of the ruling classes, serving to socialize the managers, professionals, and technicians needed to maintain the system, while also absorbing personnel whose excessive numbers would otherwise overpopulate the capitalist labor market. Ultimately, however, the good jobs would go to white, middle-class men. New programs that responded to poorer people, such as the Educational Opportunity Program (EOP), were actually designed "to placate those agitating for change without really changing the core of the problem—the system."[13] Acting on their ideas would just get protesting students arrested or shot; witness the recent violent confrontations at Augusta State, Jackson State, Kent State, Columbia, and Berkeley. Furthermore, efforts to bring about real change through institutional means absorbed energy better directed elsewhere. The trade-off for the privilege of institutional access was co-optation. In its final statement, the group wrote:

> In the three years of this Women's Studies Program we have found that the university not only absorbs our struggles, our ideas, but it absorbs us, those of us who work here on a day to day basis. It prevents us from raising important political issues on the campus at large that relate directly to women. The incredible paper work and bureaucracy, the deans [sic] meetings, faculty meetings, space (office) allocations, faculty time sheets, on and on the list goes. All of this works to bog us down into the structure of the university and to make us lose sight of our original struggles and demands. This form of bureaucratic bullshit (BB) keeps us from initiating struggle. If we do a lot of BB we can maintain the program, if we don't we lose it. After all, what we really wanted was a Women's Studies Program, wasn't it? Or did we really want women's lives to be dealt with as a reality in every class, in every aspect of the university. Well, after a while you forget what you really wanted, you just work to maintain what you've got.

To these socialist feminists the structure of the university seemed more important than its curriculum. What was taught, in their view, was not for most people primarily preparation for employment. "What you do learn is how to fit into the structure of domination and power hierarchy which is the basis of all institutions of class society." Consistent with their beliefs, the women's studies faculty at San Diego State announced their resignations, predicting that they would be replaced by "professional women who are interested in gaining security in university faculties [and] participate in administration controlled programs."[14]

The question of who teaches in women's studies is closely linked to the field's history and to persisting tensions between its academic and activist goals. The mass resignation of San Diego State's 1973–74 women's studies faculty—none of whom had been there at the program's founding in 1970—allowed the administration to fulfill their prediction, at least partially. New faculty, with Ph.D. degrees, were hired, who were qualified not only by virtue of dissertation research on women but also by interest in feminism demonstrated through prior participation in community women's liberation activities. They were hired into temporary, albeit full-time, positions by an administration wary of committing permanent positions to this troubling and troubled program. Two years later, the two full-time positions were made permanent, and by the end of the 1970s the program had become a department with eight positions and seven tenure lines. I was one of those first hired, and I served as chair for six years.

The experience at San Diego State came earliest but would be repeated elsewhere in some of its aspects. As interest in the new scholarship and teaching mushroomed and students called for and flocked to women's studies classes, other administrators also responded cautiously. The first courses in women's studies were often taught by graduate students, part-time lecturers serving in temporary positions, and junior faculty. Many programs had little choice: they were founded on a shoestring, or less—sometimes by volunteers—and run as a "potluck" operation. In some programs, such as the one at San Francisco State University, a deliberate decision was made to avoid institutionalization and maintain a radical community focus by employing noncredentialed activists as instructors rather than seeking tenure lines for traditionally qualified academicians.[15] While it has become commonplace at colleges and universities across the country to rely extensively on non–tenure line faculty who can be hired, fired, and replaced at will as disciplinary needs change or student enrollment fluctuates, rarely does their role (much discussed in recent literature on higher education) carry the consequences that it has had in women's studies. In several noteworthy cases, the transition from a founding faculty dominated by part-timers to a permanent professoriate has led to bitter and protracted struggles in which faculty qualifications, university expectations and goals, and personal politics combine in always unhappy and sometimes explosive mixtures. In its main outlines, the following scenario is typical.

Gloria Bowles, founding coordinator of women's studies at the University of California, Berkeley, has a Ph.D. degree in comparative literature from Berkeley; she recalls that in 1973 she took seven days of written and three hours of oral exams on the literatures of five languages and never encountered a female author. She began teaching a course on women writers that fall. Joining with three women faculty to develop a major that was instituted in 1976, she was designated as its first coordinator and half-time lecturer. For five years, Bowles developed and managed the program, taught, wrote, and co-edited the first volume to be published on theories of women's studies.[16] In 1983, a tenured faculty member not previously associated with the program was drafted to chair it, in order to push for permanent faculty lines. Bowles continued to teach as a full-time temporary lecturer. In 1985, when the new chair conducted a nationwide search to fill the position, the lectureship was defined as one for a social scientist, thus effectively excluding Bowles from the competition. Although she nonetheless applied and was supported by a number of faculty on the Women's Studies Board, as well as by students, and by scholars around the country who were knowledgeable about her work to define women's studies as a discipline, Bowles was eliminated. The historian who took the lectureship was eventually replaced by other lecturers, who taught the program's core courses as women's studies recruited permanent faculty. The program eventually made several joint appointments of scholars who were outstanding in their own fields but were not known for a central role in developing women's studies.[17]

Joining the Personal, the Political, and the Professional

One important factor in program development is the extent to which women's studies is perceived as just another discipline, an academic subject like others, to be taught by scholars with expertise based on traditional criteria. More than a quarter century after its founding, women's studies now encompasses an extensive literature available to any person who pursues it. Its early development, however, was intertwined with the lives of its creators. Women's studies grew out of the personal and political experiences of university-trained women, many of whom aspired to the professoriate. The intellectual biographies of those who succeeded make fascinating reading for the insight they offer into the formation of an academic field. Weaving together personal, professional, and political threads of women's lives, the anthology *Changing Subjects*, for instance, traces the formation of feminist literary criticism by examining the experiences of a group of feminist students in literature who earned their Ph.D. degrees in the early years of women's studies and achieved academic success in leading universities. Ann Rosalind Jones, who was an undergraduate student at Berkeley when the Free Speech movement began and lived in Paris during the events of May 1968, describes how early feminist literary criticism grew out of the consciousness-raising group she later joined in New York City.

> *We kept planning political interventions, but with the exception of one feeble picket line outside an art film theater, our actions never materialized. Still, we were doing important work: collaborating on the articulation of a felt political knowledge of our being-in-the-world as women. . . . It seems clear to me now that the first stages of feminist literary work corresponded to this process of empathetic analysis. Early critics read women characters in men's books as we read each other in the consciousness-raising group: as women placed in oppressive circumstances. The method was not to blame Shakespeare's Cressida or Thackeray's Becky Sharpe but to understand, perhaps better than their authors, what they were up against. Even more, we read women writers as if they were ourselves: aware of their situation, angry, lucid. Sometimes, of course, this was true: the Redstockings were publishing brilliant polemical pamphlets, Valerie Solanas came out with her "SCUM Manifesto," academics such as Anne Koedt writing "The Myth of the Vaginal Orgasm" showed what committed feminist research could do. The first collections of poetry from the movement stressed genuineness of voice above all, in titles such as* No More Masks *and* I Hear My Sisters Singing. *A title that didn't exist but could have is* Our Voices, Ourselves.[18]

Rachel Blau DuPlessis, then finishing her dissertation at Columbia and beginning her career at Temple University, describes how she co-authored a statement of purpose for the journal *Feminist Studies*, to echo Marx's "Theses on Feuerbach":

The feminist movement has demonstrated that the study of women is more than a compensatory project. Instead, feminism has the potential fundamentally to reshape the way we view the world. We wish not just to interpret women's experiences but to change women's condition. For us, feminist thought represents a transformation of consciousness, social forms, and modes of action.[19]

While black women's studies developed as a separate field only later, partially in response to the relative absence of black women as subjects in both (white) women's studies and (male-dominated) black studies, Alice Walker broke ground in 1972 with her course on black women writers, taught both at the University of Massachusetts at Boston, and at Wellesley College. On the West Coast, Barbara Christian, at the University of California, Berkeley, and Frances Smith Foster at San Diego State offered similar courses, through African American studies and women's studies, in the mid-1970s.[20] Black women's studies, in the words of one of its founders, makes "the real life issues of Black women . . . integral to our conceptions of subject matter, themes, and topics for research." It also requires personal commitment.

To do the work involved in creating Black women's studies requires not only intellectual intensity, but the deepest courage. Ideally, this is passionate and committed research, writing, and teaching whose purpose is to question everything. Coldly "objective" scholarship that changes nothing is not what we strive for. "Objectivity" is itself an example of the reification of white-male thought. What could be less objective than the total white-male studies which are still considered "knowledge"? Everything that human beings participate in is ultimately subjective and biased, and there is nothing inherently wrong with that. The bias of Black women's studies must consider as primary the knowledge that will save Black women's lives.[21]

The Combahee River Collective, whose 1977 "Black Feminist Statement" spurred the development of a distinctive black women's studies, began as a consciousness-raising group of politically active individuals and evolved into a "study group."[22]

Along with the feminist fervor they transferred to learning and teaching about women, the early women's studies faculty generally brought links with community feminist groups and often sponsored or staffed campus student service centers as well. Programs that spanned the academic and activist modes, termed "applied women's studies" by one observer, included workshops in assertiveness training and self-defense, continuing education for second-career or "re-entry" women, in-service sensitivity training on sexism for public employees, and referrals to feminist health care providers.[23] The role of academic women's studies in relation to such extracurricular, co-curricular, and service activities varies widely. In some cases, however, as women's studies programs developed into full-fledged "autonomous" units expected to carry out all the bureaucratic functions lamented by the early San Diego State faculty (such functions were an integral part of that program from the beginning because it was established as a quasi-department with its own faculty, curriculum, and budget), faculty deliberately withdrew from non-academic pursuits on campus, because of lack of time, and/or the desire to legitimize women's studies in the eyes of the academy.[24]

The influence of the early years persists, however. Bonnie Zimmerman, who was a graduate student at the University of Buffalo (now the State University of New York at Buffalo) when she designed her first women's studies class, and who later became chair of the women's studies department at San Diego State University, describes their far-reaching effects—passionately and candidly:

> No body of literature will ever have as strong an impact on my ideas as that produced in the first few years (roughly 1968 through 1972) of the women's liberation movement. Everything we have written since has been a refinement, development, refutation, or reconfiguration of the concepts developed in that pioneering literature. Even the important work on difference that characterizes the feminist theory of the 1980s is not totally new, for the early women's liberation movement had a substantial sensitivity toward class and race oppression that seems to have been muted by later theoretical emphases on "women's nature" and "women's culture."
>
> The generation of feminists that produced these texts—"my" generation—were pioneers. Although isolated individuals preceded us, the wave of political and intellectual activism that began in the late 1960s

was one of the great movements of the century. We broke new ground in virtually every area of society. We took risks and created dazzlingly new ideas and interpretations. Because we were pioneers—because we fervently believed (rightly or wrongly) that we had been born anew— we were also ideologues and fanatics, passionate about our new religion. We believed that we were stripping away the lies and myths of the past to reveal the "real truth" about women and lesbians. We were sweeping the house clean. It was that commitment to truth-telling that made us so intense, and so dogmatic at times.[25]

Today's faculty, in contrast, may enter women's studies teaching with degrees in women's studies—generally not designated as such, but based on substantial coursework or research on women's studies topics. This is one measure of the founders' success. That students can now study "texts without contexts, genders without sexes, and sex without politics" appears to be a mixed blessing.[26] Recognition that the twin goals of intellectual mastery and personal change might not be achieved in equal measure by a women's studies course was reported in *Signs* in 1978. The authors also noted a shift in professorial intentions. "At the inception of the course in 1970, attitude and behavior change was of primary concern while intellectual acquisition and mastery of knowledge were secondary issues. Now that the ideas of the women's movement have become more widely accepted in American society, the instructor of the course emphasizes intellectual mastery."[27]

Academics *versus* Activism

By the mid-1980s, the literature of women's studies began to feature discussions of the allegedly negative consequences of institutionalization. As the number of women's studies courses, programs, faculty, students, publications, and conferences expanded, so did the lament that success would kill its activist—i.e., feminist—political impulse. Even as critics charged women's studies with bringing politics to the campus, academic feminists pointed to the disappearance of politics. Talk of the conflict between the field's twin goals, sometimes expressed as "academics versus activism," became widespread. Renate Klein signaled the concerns of many that, after two decades of rampant growth, women's studies might become purely academic, "spectator knowledge" divorced from affect and action.[28] Annette Kolodny, already well known for her contributions to the field of American studies, brought the issue to a wider audience in 1988 with a backpage essay in the *Chronicle of Higher Education* entitled "Respectability Is Eroding the Revolutionary Potential of Feminist Criticism."[29] Kolodny developed her critique more thoroughly in a *Feminist Studies* article, announcing that a "theory is only as good as its practice." She labeled theory without action "pedantry and moral abdication." Kolodny was concerned about the increasing influence of deconstructionist theory on feminist criticism, finding it "even more problematic . . . that feminist theorizing has emerged as a new *cachet*. Male critics rush to prove that they are at least 'something of a feminist.'" Kolodny detailed a number of instances in which male critics had failed to get the point of, had distorted, or had misappropriated feminist ideas. Her comment about the necessity of linking feminist theory with "visionary politics" was addressed especially to "Ph.D. candidates of the 1980s and 1990s for whom feminism will otherwise become merely another entrée into sophisticated critical theory circles."[30]

In the 1990s, academic feminists published a torrent of self-criticism. For some, institutional structures presented a threat. "Would women's studies lose its critical edge if it had the prerequisites [*sic*] of a department to protect?" asked Duke's Jean Fox O'Barr. Robin Lakoff, from her position as professor of linguistics at the University of California, Berkeley, opined that "feminism, once a stance of radical external critique, can only be compromised by admission to insider status. How can it attack authority when it speaks in the voice of authority?"[31] For others, danger lay in intellectual battles. "Does the price of institutionalization . . . consist of our reduction to a plethora of jostling fields or approaches in which unhappy souls war for precedence with even more ferocity than they do in longer established areas or departments?" worried Susan Gubar, professor of English and women's studies at Indiana University. Ellen Messer-Davidow, professor of English, cultural studies, and women's studies at the University of Minnesota, contrasted women's studies' success in altering the disciplines with its failure to transform academic structures and wondered whether "we have reproduced the academic organization and production of knowledge we once sought to change. . . . Existing both in the disciplines and in opposition to them," academic feminism had made "remarkable gains at a remarkable cost." "Paradoxically, we may have escaped from our domestic enclosures only to find ourselves two decades later ensconced in disciplinary ones."

Cautioning academic feminists against being "preoccupied with discourse," she turned to a highly abstract "structuration theory" for her solution.[32]

The institutionalization of women's studies (and women's centers) at three research universities provided Flora Pearle McMartin with material for a dissertation in higher education which she concluded with the observation that academic feminists had traded "organizational security" for "the problems of co-optation." Posing the question as "institutionalization versus marginalization," McMartin expressed the hope that women's studies faculty would cease to "distance themselves from women's centers," a "tactic" they had employed "to strengthen their image of being an academic discipline" so effectively that "they have alienated themselves from their surrounding feminist community." She also commented on the trend toward departmentalization. "This will provide them with a level of safety because it is more difficult to disband a department than a program. However, women's studies must accept that departmentalization will also pull them further from their roots, and reinforce the perception that they are elitist."[33] Similarly, Paula Rothenberg, director of the New Jersey curriculum transformation project, suggested that women's studies scholars may have "succeeded only in transforming—and isolating—ourselves," even at the "very moment the right wing has decided to connect explicitly the politics of the university with political issues in society at large and is fighting to promote the proliferation of antifeminist, elitist, racist, and heterosexual values."[34] Jerry Anne Flieger, a professor of French literature, reflected on the separation between feminist theory and practice, wondering if it could be attributed to "middle age" as well as to splits between the East and West Coasts or French and Anglo-American thought, along with various other divides: racial differences, differences in sexual orientation, and splits between those with radical and those with liberal sympathies.[35]

Polarization in the debate over issues of political activism often paralleled the separation between a camp that was "*for* theory" and one that was "*against* theory."[36] One refrain running through these comments is the accusation that academic feminists were guilty of "shar[ing] the privilege of the (male) academic elite."[37] In the view of Valeria Wagner, the shift away from politics and action to feminist theory and discourse has created a feminism that exists "for itself," ensconced in a "home" of its own, when it should really remain a nomad. In some instances, disputes over program governance, including the roles to be played by students or community activists, exacerbated the conflict.[38]

It was a rare act to publicly take an opposing stance, calling for academic feminists to loosen the linkage between women's studies and feminist politics and political rhetoric. Jean Bethke Elshtain, a widely known political theorist now teaching at the University of Chicago, suggested in 1987 that the two might be "at odds." She cited a passage from the anthropologist Judith Shapiro's 1981 essay on the study of gender in her discipline: "The danger in too close an association between scholarship and social reformism is not only in the limits it places on intellectual inquiry, but also in the implication that our activities as social, moral, and political beings are dependent on what we are able to discover in our scientific research. Loosening the tie would have liberating consequences . . . [for scholarship] and for feminism as a social movement."[39] Contrasting Shapiro's view with Catharine Stimpson's more positive perspective on the role of passion in feminist criticism, Elshtain ended her call for "an open-textured discursive universe that enables women's studies scholars to live with and within fructifying, desimplifying complexities," by saying that "between Shapiro's voice of caution and Stimpson's voice of passionate, yet dis-illusioned insistence, lies the narrative ground occupied by women's studies at its best."[40]

Locating women's studies' "narrative ground" is no simpler than defining feminism, now routinely referred to as "feminisms."[41] Women's studies exists in thousands of courses, hundreds of programs, myriad publications, and the minds of many academicians, students, activists, and observers of many persuasions. The intersection of academics and activism, with its multiple points of entry, is impossible to place on any grid. How then to determine whether, as so many suggest, women's studies has lost its way? Many would argue that teaching women's studies itself constitutes feminist political action.

The relationship between feminist education and social action has been treated extensively by two well-known feminist writers who seek to link their own academic and activist work. Charlotte Bunch and bell hooks both defend the importance of educating women, as a means to carry forward the spirit of feminism and arm it with new and useful knowledge. Both caution against the anti-intellectualism that sometimes underlies criticism of academic feminism. Bunch, who came to women's studies through "movement" work in the 1960s, and hooks, who took women's studies courses as an undergraduate in the early 1970s and as a graduate student a decade later, have followed very different career paths. Both, however, link women's studies to their personal experiences of sexism; and both consider theory essential to feminist practice.

Charlotte Bunch, having begun political organizing at age nineteen in 1963, declares, "I chose the movement as my career." For her, politics grew out of radical Christianity; it was in church that she first experienced the use of education to create social change. She was a founder of the relatively short-lived but influential journal *Quest* (1974–82), whose purpose was "to create new feminist theory that combines the best of political tracts and academic work." Its staff was "activist in temperament but viewed theory as important to the success of activism. We wanted to articulate a feminist theory out of the daily lives of women and the work of the movement, and we wanted to direct that theory towards a workable strategy for the future." It would be useful theory.[42]

The necessity of linking feminism, inside the classroom as well as out, to the realities of women's lives also motivated bell hooks. On occasion, hooks chided both sides, attacking anti-intellectualism in women's studies as well as arcane theory. For her, feminist awareness and interest in women's studies developed from the "patriarchal tyranny" she and her family experienced as she grew up in a "Southern, black, father-dominated, working-class household . . . where our daily life was full of patriarchal drama." The recognition of sexist oppression and "strategies of resistance" that were useful for her and other black women grew out of her daily life, unlike the feminist analysis based on privileged white women's lives which she feels informed her first women's studies classes. She quotes Bunch approvingly on the importance of education that develops women's capacity for systematic analysis, to prepare them for "the practice of freedom."[43] Either implicitly or explicitly, an additional element linking academic work with feminist action is an "ethic of personal accountability." The sociologist and black feminist theorist Patricia Hill Collins finds a convergence of Afrocentric and feminist values in the application of an "ethic of caring" and in the "interdependence of thought and action."[44]

The words of Bunch and hooks echo in Gloria Anzaldúa's "haciendo teorías" ("making theories"), the explanation (in her introduction to *Making Face, Making Soul*) of the need of women of color for theories that not only explain "what goes on between inner, outer, and peripheral 'I's within a person and between the personal 'I's and the collective 'we' of our ethnic communities" but also point out ways to maneuver in the "'in-between'

Borderland worlds of ethnic communities and academies, feminist and job worlds."[45]

Given the contested definitions of feminist practice and women's experience, it may not be possible to determine whether feminist theory emerges from feminist action or the action from the theory. In defending postmodernist criticism against charges that it undermines feminist politics, Judith Butler (while denying that her work is postmodern) states that "the claim that every political action has its theoretical presuppositions is not the same as the claim that such presuppositions must be sorted out prior to action. It may be that those presuppositions are articulated only in and through that action."[46]

The convergence of women's studies' two objectives, inseparable though they may be, can be observed in two of the institutions through which women's studies exists outside the campus: feminist publishing enterprises and nationwide academic feminist organizations. The processes through which feminist politics and scholarship together helped to shape the development of women's studies is the theme of Patrice McDermott's *Politics and Scholarship.* As mentioned in chapter 1, the major journals in women's studies have played different roles in promoting feminist scholarship. *Feminist Studies* was launched in 1972 as the first academic journal to publish exclusively in the new field; *Signs* was founded in 1975 to become the most scholarly and most prestigious journal in the field; and *Frontiers,* also dating from 1975, was the journal most immediately concerned with bridging academic and community-based feminism. But all illustrate what McDermott calls "the mediation of feminist resistance and patriarchal authority in the production of cultural knowledge." Through these, and many other more specialized or less highly visible academic journals, the research and thought of scholars in women's studies have been institutionalized, legitimized, and presented to a national and international audience. McDermott's primary concerns are "the internal dynamics of the journal (editorial structure, criteria in manuscript selection, and development of alternative forms and conventions), and the external dynamics of the relationship of the journals to the wider women's movement and the university." But she also illuminates the ways in which the journals provide a major site for the interplay of feminist academic work and political activism.[47]

Approaching her subject from a point of view that reflects her multidisciplinary work in the "anthropology of belief systems, the sociology of literature, feminist theory, and discourse analysis," McDermott, a professor of American studies, examines the journals' origins, showing the influence of the underground press of the 1960s. She explores their practices in developing the criteria—both scholarly and political—that determine their selection of manuscripts; contrasts their usage of traditional scholarly conventions and forms; and analyzes their positions in relation to the major controversies and "cultural dramas" that have engaged feminist communities and women's studies. Together, these factors are responsible for what McDermott terms the "social construction of feminist scholarship."[48]

Feminist academic journals—thirty-two of which were founded between 1972 and 1991—reflect the contradictions between the (traditionally defined) political and scholarly cultures whose boundaries women's studies blurs. Where the founders of other academic disciplines sought to distinguish between amateur and professional approaches to their subject area, and to privilege academic over activist goals by standardizing technique, separating fact from interpretation, developing a specialized language, and thereby reducing accessibility to all but their initiates,[49] practitioners of women's studies have endeavored to work in the opposite direction. Striving from within the academy to maintain a "political authenticity" derived from the women's movement, some academic feminists challenge the very institutional ground on which they and other scholars stand.

Feminist academic journals likewise manifest profound ambivalence about the university. The scholars who serve as editors of the major feminist academic journals are now, for the most part, tenured professors at major research universities. Only a handful represent the comprehensive state universities that are defined primarily as teaching institutions, and even fewer speak with non-academic voices. The editors of *Signs* and *Feminist Studies* have been criticized for assuming "gatekeeping positions" that are accused of denying entrance to women of color.[50] Nevertheless, the academic feminist press continues to some extent to reflect the oppositional stance of the underground publications that were its forerunners. While for the most part eschewing their style, feminist publications have absorbed and striven to maintain many of the attitudes and goals characteristic of the socialist, "bohemian," and other alternative publications of the 1930s, 1950s, and 1960s. Opposition to hierarchy, competition, racism, capitalism, imperialism, and elitism can be seen in both their internal dynamics and the criteria they employ for the selection of materials to publish. They vary significantly. *Signs* initially established a typically hierarchical editorial structure, created an editorial board of eminent academics and notable writers, and published only the most scholarly of articles. The very look of the first volume, with its black covers and bold title, announced the seriousness of its intent. It quickly gained a reputation as the most "academic" of the new journals. *Frontiers,* in contrast, adopted a larger, magazine-size format and has always included some manifesto-style, first-person, and creative types of work; it is therefore more open to non-academic voices.[51] But all of the journals have challenged the ideal of value-free scholarship. Whatever their level of insistence on scholarly convention, they seek political relevance. Does this constitute "bias"? Not, their editors would say, in any conventional sense.

At issue, as McDermott points out, is a fundamental disagreement with the conventional academic perspective that scholarly objectivity is possible, or even desirable. The journal editors see their role as publishing oppositional knowledge; along with most feminist scholars, they maintain that the notion of "monolithic truth achieved through abstraction" is a myth.[52] On the contrary, knowledge is "always situated, perspectival, engaged, and involved. It is based on unavoidable prejudgment and is, hence, always 'biased.'"[53] This premise, as noted in chapter 3, puts feminist scholarship and women's studies journals in conflict with the dominant perspective of the academy in the United States. Embodying this contrarian view, women's studies journals serve as vehicles for the diffusion of feminist scholarship throughout the academic world. This is feminist action through the published word. Women's studies seeks to integrate academic knowledge and activism through its publications.

When the editors of *Signs* decided that they wanted to "return to our initial editorial promise . . . to make close connections between feminist theory and feminist practice outside as well as inside of the academy," they could simply announce a call for papers. In the winter 1994 issue, they stated that "in hospitals and schools, in battered women's shelters and abortion clinics, in factories and trade unions, women were constructing practices that were guided by feminist consciousness and feminist goals. And it is these practices, outside the academy just as importantly as inside it, that have constructed our theories." Accordingly, the editors of *Signs* sought submissions for an issue on feminist theory and practice, which appeared in the summer of 1996. This issue features two interviews, one—its lead article— with bell hooks, who suggests that the term *public intellectual,* which has been used increasingly to label her, carries a pejorative cast expressing academics' "hostility to the union of theory and practice," which she is seen to represent.[54] The other, a collective interview with seven participants, all but one of whom were members of a network associated with a women's policy center in Washington, D.C., offers criticism of *Signs* itself. When Charlotte Bunch, suggesting that the journal is irrelevant to feminist action, asks, "Who reads *Signs* anymore?" she is answered, indirectly, by the political theorist Nancy Hartsock, who announces that the journal is moving to her university and "we intend to change that."[55] It is clear from this discussion that after all these years, feminists are still struggling to define feminist practice. Judging from this issue, nevertheless, and despite the Bunch-Hartsock exchange, *Signs* maintains its commitment to politically relevant scholarship. This issue includes articles on queer theory, indigenous Hawaiian nationalism, and recovered memory and sexual abuse, all academic studies of politically controversial topics.

Reflecting on thirteen years engaged in editing and publishing *Frontiers*, that journal's founder, Kathi George, recalls "spen[ding] a lot of time sort of doing intellectual splits. . . . We were trying so hard to bridge the gap between the community and the academy." Determined to include "a non-scholarly voice," George undertook deliberate "author development," actively recruiting and working closely with "non-academic community people." Since her departure in 1987, *Frontiers* has become more scholarly in a conventional sense; it has become, in her view, "a journal you can take to the dean!"[56]

George's personal efforts to balance the tensions between political and scholarly goals represent in microcosm the collective struggle of the membership of the National Women's Studies Association, the field's interdisciplinary, national professional association. Its former national coordinator, Caryn McTighe Musil, has described the struggle to embody in one professional organization academic feminism's multiple goals as a kind of "birthing . . . without anaesthesia."[57]

Looking at the history of this association, it is necessary to recognize that most scholars in women's studies still define themselves largely in terms of the disciplines in which they were trained. As noted in chapter 2, they have established women's caucuses and committees in virtually every field and now play leading roles in the major national organizations of the traditional disciplines.[58] The presence of women scholars and scholarship on women pervades many annual meetings; so much so in some fields, such as modern literature and American studies, that some traditional academics have formed breakaway movements.[59] Since 1977, however, women's stud-

ies practitioners have struggled to organize and maintain an interdisciplinary national organization of their own. It was hoped that the NWSA would
serve to advance the interests of women's studies scholars and scholarship,
teaching, and activities that in other fields might be called "service" but in
women's studies clearly constitute feminist political activism.

The NWSA, founded in San Francisco in 1977, is a professional organization of an unusual kind. While its purpose includes promoting scholarship, and the three program planners for the first annual meeting recall with
pride that the first book on women's studies theory, Bowles and Klein's *Theories of Women's Studies*, grew out of a session at one of its annual meetings, the association does not exist primarily for the purpose of presenting
the latest research in women's studies.[60] The leading edge of feminist scholarship continues its advance mostly at discipline-based meetings of the
American Historical Association, the American Political Science Association, the American Sociological Association, the Modern Language Association, and so forth. Probably the closest event to a national interdisciplinary
conference for the presentation of new scholarship in women's studies is
the triennial Berkshire Conference in Women's History, which also attracts
some scholars of literature, social scientists, and other academic feminists.
The NWSA, however, serves many important functions. It is a place where
women's studies practitioners from different backgrounds meet to exchange
information and spread ideas, to overcome the isolation and alienation that
some face in their own academic environments, to give and to receive inspiration from empathetic others—and sometimes—frequently, in fact—to
confront others and to be confronted about the gap between women's studies' ambitious mission and its accomplishments, which have been limited
by all-too-real problems of both individual and institutional origin. At the
NWSA's annual meetings, the participants, whose numbers have ranged
from a few hundred to several thousand, discuss pedagogy, program administration, professional aspirations, and frustrations. And they wrestle more
or less continuously over political issues. The NWSA also serves to sustain
the activist mission of women's studies.

It is its members' effort to practice feminist principles in their own
professional "home" that has kept NWSA embroiled in controversy and
brought it several times to the brink of destruction. Aspiring to represent
the interests of feminist educators wherever and whoever they might be,
the founders established a governance structure that would, they hoped,
accommodate members who differed in status (students, faculty, staff, and

administrators), in region, in the type of educational institution they represented (primary and secondary schools, community colleges, four-year and
graduate institutions, as well as non-academic community agencies); and
in race or ethnicity, class, religion, sexuality, physical ability, and age. All
conditions and choices would be equally respected. To assure that no individual or group would dominate its proceedings, the Coordinating Council operated initially without a leader, in favor of a "revolving chair" who
would turn by turn recognize the next speaker. No one could speak twice
until everyone had been heard.

Ever since the first annual national conference, where 150 resolutions
were introduced, dealing with matters ranging from ending "world hunger"
to the use of cream of chicken soup in vegetarian casseroles in the dining
halls that served the participants,[61] interest groups have formed and have
demanded to constitute caucuses entitled to special representation. First,
"Third World women" (now termed women of color) and lesbians stepped
forward. By the mid-1980s there were also caucuses representing primary
and secondary school teachers, community college faculty, program administrators, Jewish women, poor and working-class women, women with disabilities, and older women. The list now includes caucuses for a "Catholic
interest" group and for women's centers. Intensely aware of women's long
history and continuing problems of exclusion, the NWSA almost broke its
collective back attempting to offer special treatment to every constituency
that requested it (see chapter 5).

The NWSA's very openness invites challenge. Serving a membership
that is divided, as Deborah Rosenfelt has suggested, between "ideologues"
and "pragmatists,"[62] association leaders and conference convenors have
tried to satisfy everyone. Accepting all forms of feminism and all feminists,
they have at times stretched the NWSA's mission so far as sometimes to
appear to reject its academic and institutional purposes. Initially adopting
language that referred to students and faculty as "learners and practitioners" in lieu of the usual terms, the association sometimes even tends toward
anti-intellectualism. Warnings against professionalism sometimes draw
heavy applause. Program administrators, whose caucus developed spontaneously over a box lunch on the grass at the initial conference in Lawrence,
Kansas, have been criticized as "tools of the patriarchy" for their efforts to
make women's studies work in academic institutions.[63] These and the many
other instances of what most academics would consider to be extreme positions with which the NWSA has had to deal account for the fact that even

long-time devoted members are apt on occasion to think, or even to say, "No way that this will last. They are all too nuts."[64]

But last it has. Despite the pain felt by many and indeed the damage done to some (especially those attempting to provide leadership), the NWSA has been able to revise its constitution, changing the caucus system that skewed representation on the leadership council, and to recover membership lost in the wake of the 1990 debacle. The 1996 conference was able to survive an attack by a group called "Grrls against Professionalism" which objected to the organizers' having scheduled an "embedded conference" dealing with adolescent girls, in a collaboration with a local psychiatric health institution, without consulting with "grrls" in NWSA or "grrls" networks or "psychiatric survivor networks" about the co-sponsorship. NWSA leaders were accused of "adultist and elitist behavior."[65] The NWSA continues to try "to create and practice an ideal model of sisterhood."[66] As a delegate from the Midwest put it in her reflections on the founding years: "Regardless of the utopian, frustrating, hollow, intimidating, and visionary ring of this grand and grandiose plan, we refuse to give it up."[67]

The NWSA encapsulates, in Caryn McTighe Musil's terms, both an *"experiment in structure"* and an *"experiment in purpose."* Writing in 1987 at the group's apogee in membership, when it numbered more than three thousand, Musil, who was then its national coordinator, anticipated a decade of further progress. She found the NWSA to be a unique and singularly vital institution precisely "because we take these kinds of emotional and intellectual risks with each other."[68] A legacy of the 1970s, persisting into the 1990s with its commitment to practice feminist principles, the organization carries a heavy burden. Among its many problems are the dual loyalty of most women's studies practitioners to a home department (or other institution); a lack of resources that has kept it on the edge of insolvency (while it tries to provide access to feminists lacking institutional support or personal funds); the loss of institutional memory (a problem that has hindered feminist progress for centuries), due somewhat to its institutional marginality but also to turnover in leadership; the absence of data concerning its own constituencies; and an all but overwhelming commitment to diversity and radicalism which permits and perhaps fosters what Rosenfelt, referring to the consciousness-raising seminars on racism at Storrs in 1981, called a "necessary, painful, yet productive expression of anger." Perhaps it is at least partially because of the presence of so many first-timers—which Sandra Coyner estimates as 50 percent each year—that attendees tolerate so much emotional intensity and drama at the annual meetings. As Rosen-felt says, we are "so used to opposing and challenging the institutions we work in, we forget sometimes that NWSA is us."[69]

As a laboratory for feminist practice, the NWSA has become a sort of national forum for radical feminism.[70] It overlaps to only a limited extent with what might be called the women's studies professoriate. Most of those who produce the new scholarship on women present their work elsewhere, wanting and needing to adhere to disciplinary professional standards and to fulfill institutional expectations for scholarly achievement.[71] Many early leaders who helped to form the national organization stay away; feminist organizations, reflecting their origins in the anti-authoritarian movements of the 1960s and 1970s, deal poorly with leadership. Nor, despite its toler-ance for extreme expressions of ideology, does the NWSA always admit of unfashionable dissent. As Robin Leidner points out in her thoughtful analy-sis of the NWSA's "constituency, accountability, and deliberation," the or-ganization's struggles provide "ammunition to opponents who charge that women's studies as a field does not encourage open debate . . . [and] see its ideological commitments as antithetical to academic norms of objectivity and falsifiability."[72] It has not been a forum that has always shown acade-mic women's studies at its best.

What influence does the national organization have on the grass-roots? This is hard to assess. Although large numbers of faculty and pro-gram administrators attend its national meetings each year, many others stay away, or having gone once, do not return. But does its commitment to activism also permeate women's studies in colleges and universities? The answer, I think, is yes. The academic feminist commitment to activism is manifested variously in the selection of faculty, the construction of curric-ula, and requirements that encourage internship or student participation in community action projects or extracurricular events.[73] It appears in the teaching of content that is based on research whose questions reflect con-temporary feminist concerns, and in pedagogy that draws students into participating in their own education—claiming rather than receiving it, in Adrienne Rich's phrase.[74] Women's studies faculty combine the roles of scholar and activist through research that seeks to empower the women of the communities whose causes they advocate. The oral historian Sherna Berger Gluck, a longtime political activist most recently doing research on and with Palestinian women, finds that "advocacy scholarship keeps us rooted in the social movement from which we sprang. It retains the potential for informing the movement and for activating the academy." Gluck admits, however, that there are some "contradictions between the two roles that cannot be resolved, but only acknowledged."[75]

The most notorious instance of conflict over the impact of feminist scholarship occurred in the mid-1980s. In a sex-discrimination case brought by the Equal Employment Opportunity Commission (EEOC) against Sears, Roebuck and Company, lawyers for Sears successfully used the historian Rosalind Rosenberg's testimony that history showed patterns of sexual difference in women's choice of employment to support their contention that women had not sought the higher-paying positions that they had allegedly been denied. In developing her case, Rosenberg built on the research of the historian Alice Kessler-Harris. But Kessler-Harris's rebuttal, on behalf of the EEOC, in which she drew counterinferences from data on female labor participation, did not prevail. The judge used the work of feminist historians to decide in favor of Sears. Rosenberg's testimony on behalf of Sears brought her severe criticism and raised troubling questions for some feminist scholars about the political dimensions of their scholarship, in particular about the so-called equality-versus-difference debate that had reached major proportions in that same decade. In *Feminist Studies*, Ruth Milkman concluded an excellent exposition of the evidence and arguments used in this case by suggesting that feminist scholars should recognize the potentially dangerous applications of their work about equality and difference. "That does not mean we must abandon these arguments or the intellectual terrain they have opened up; it does mean that we must be self-conscious in our formulations, keeping firmly in view the ways in which our work can be exploited politically." This is difficult territory for feminist scholars, and Milkman revealed a not uncharacteristic ambivalence.[76] The Sears case highlighted for feminists the importance of ideology in shaping judicial decisions and the difficulty of changing long-entrenched attitudes and behaviors through scholarship.

Women's studies was established by a generation of academic feminists for many of whom political activism was integral to their lives, on and off campus. While some today lament the loss of the activist impulse, others simply wonder whether a feminism learned largely within the academy can fulfill a larger mission of global change. "Perhaps," suggests one of the latter, "the confessional mode in much current feminist theorizing is a needed attempt to find community through theorizing one's experience [and is a response to] their ambivalence about the institutional success."[77]

Charlotte Bunch, in a statement in *Signs* flashed throughout academe by the *Chronicle of Higher Education* on its Internet site, called for "more dialogue between those engaged in trying to make change in the world and those writing theories."[78]

Academics *and* Activism

However, considerable evidence would suggest that the gap is not so wide as these speakers assume, and technology may help to close it. If the thousands of messages sent over the general academic women's studies electronic network, WMST-L—there were 4,316 messages sent on WMST-L between May 1, 1992 and April 30, 1996, and the number is growing—can be viewed as reflecting "the grassroots," then activism is alive out there and is using new as well as time-tested ways to effect change. Despite being considered off limits for this particular forum, the activism recently pursued through or described on the list includes

—*a survey of the treatment of female faculty by their departments;*
—*a call for protest against national welfare reform legislation;*
—*a student protest against naming a building for an early-twentieth-century suffrage leader accused of racism;*
—*a faculty protest against administrative action in a graduate student strike;*
—*a protest against advertisements deemed demeaning to women;*
—*a discussion of internships as providing sites for feminist action; and*
—*a query regarding the affirmative action record of finalists for a college presidency.*

The largest sustained discussion on WMST-L during 1994–96 concerned the question of student attitudes toward feminist activism, with criticism launched in both directions, from faculty toward students, and from students toward faculty, each accusing the other of apathy on feminist issues. Evidence of feminist activism appears frequently on the women's studies list, even despite its intended academic purposes.

One of the problems in maintaining a women's studies electronic list open to thousands of subscribers in a broadly defined field is distinguishing what is appropriate for distribution. The initial message that greets subscribers to WMST-L states that it is "NOT an all-purpose women's studies list" but "focuses only on women's studies teaching, research, and program administration." Given that it has more than four thousand subscribers in more than forty countries, were WMST-L to follow every thread related to all issues of interest to all women, the sheer volume of messages could easily overwhelm the time and computer space available. Joan Korenman, the list monitor, intervenes occasionally: for example, in January 1996 she cut off discussion about the planned May 1 women's and children's march on Washington, D.C., with a reminder that "messages about politics and societal problems lie outside WMST-L's focus." She referred readers to other lists intended for such issues.

The widening use of computer networks offers new opportunities for activists and academics. One index that appeared on the Internet in late 1996 included the titles of eighteen lists devoted to communications about feminist activism. There are at least fifteen lists under the general rubric of women's studies, which is only one of over a dozen categories of lists on women-related topics; in October 1996 one alone, in social science, itself offered a choice of twenty individual lists. As a means of connecting the grassroots, the women's studies electronic lists may fulfill a function missing since the waning of the well-publicized community groups that comprised the women's liberation movement of the 1960s and 1970s. They may also serve, as more women's studies faculty along with other instructors integrate information technology into course design, to facilitate feminist work. According to bell hooks, women's studies should "promote anew the small group setting as an arena for education for critical consensus." She wants women and men in their neighborhoods to talk about feminist issues. For this purpose, the Internet may provide a virtual living-room (or storefront).[79]

The debate over the balance between the academic and activist goals of women's studies arises not only from the feminist content of women's studies and its origins in the women's liberation movement, but also from its form. As an interdisciplinary field seeking to engage questions dealing with the whole of women's experiences (however defined), it belongs to the genre that Julie Thompson Klein, in her treatise on the history, theory, and practice of interdisciplinary studies, calls "critical interdisciplinarity." In this view, interdisciplinarity implies a "new way of knowing." It may also signify, Klein points out, "an instrumental alignment of knowledge and action," in which "analysis [is] considered a purposeful activity," and interdisciplinarity "a means of reuniting action and thought." One result is "an intermixing of values," which challenges the "way disciplinary and cultural knowledge has been circumscribed by authoritative categories and specious dichotomies. The interdisciplinary critique was, therefore, a disciplinary, and epistemological, *and* a cultural critique" (emphasis in original).[80] But women's studies is not alone in this critical posture. Anthropology, ethnic studies, public history, philanthropy studies, and even American studies (whose development was spurred by nationalism during the World War II era and by anti-Communism in the 1950s) have all been cited as new fields that depart from a model of disinterested academic endeavor.[81]

For some women's studies scholars, the constant posing of their academic work and activism as a dichotomy or an oxymoron and the insistent call to feminist accountability reflects a sense of loss, self-accusation, and recrimination.[82] Others stress the positive. I recently put the question "Is teaching women's studies a political act?" to several acquaintances of mine who have served as chairs of women's studies programs. All answered in a split second and with a resounding "Yes!" One woman of color modified her initial answer with a more hesitant, "Yes, if. . . ." But in light of the current condition of women across class, color, and the globe, I think a simple "yes" will do. Knowledge empowers, and education—all education, if it "takes"—produces change. The fact that feminism is not dead but on the contrary continues to expand is surely to some extent due to the reach of women's studies, not only its teaching but also the testimony of its experts in cases less famous than *EEOC v. Sears*.[83]

Feminist activity made women's studies possible, and women's studies continues to take many of its questions from the women's movement, although it does not always answer in language accessible to that community. Charlotte Bunch has quoted Catharine Stimpson's statement "I'd really like feminists to draw up an agenda and say, 'Here is what we need to learn from women's studies.'" That might be useful. I think that in a less direct way it does work like that. The historian Estelle Freedman has pointed out that "the scholarly project of questioning gender salience follows the lead of activist feminist politics. . . . What activists first acknowledged, scholars soon translated into theories that invoked postmodern and deconstructionist concepts in attempts to 'go beyond' gender." Freedman locates the impulse of scholars to connect gender analysis with race, class, age, and other human differences in experiences of the social world outside academia.[84]

Scholars talk about theories as "instruments for transforming reality." Perhaps one way it works is that faculty who teach women's studies

give students "walking shoes." This phrase is borrowed from a women's
studies student, and is taken from a presentation she gave jointly with her
instructor at a regional women's studies association meeting. The student
describes how she was sitting on her sofa reading a book on women's work
in the nineteenth-century shoemaking industry for her women's history
course when she was informed that her sister's boyfriend, the father of her
sister's baby, had just been shot and killed. The book, she says, became "a
weight on my lap." Let the student speak for herself:

> *The juxtaposition was jarring. Another young black man had been mur-*
> *dered by his peers. Another young black woman, my baby sister, had*
> *been left with a fatherless child. And I was reading about white women*
> *making shoes in the nineteenth century. I was bewildered, frustrated,*
> *furious. My life didn't make sense. I asked myself what I was doing read-*
> *ing about shoes, preparing for a [college teaching] career that could not*
> *have saved my sister from this tragedy. What did Women's Studies mat-*
> *ter to my sister and other young women like her? What did shoes matter?*
>
> *. . . A prose poem written by Ruth Forman that I came upon in*
> *Women's Studies Quarterly helped me think things through. In "Trav-*
> *elin' Shoes," Forman honors and thanks her teacher, June Jordan. For-*
> *man writes that in June Jordan's class, "in the middle of all that theory*
> *and ivory tower . . . something real was going on. Something magical."*
> *She observes that Jordan helped her validate her voice, helped her*
> *make connections between herself and a history of struggle, helped her*
> *move from one place to another. "In that room in Barrows, you brought*
> *me close to that place. Challenged my fingers to touch that tree . . . find*
> *the heavy grooves of my people, the beauty and resistance and lan-*
> *guage of [Langston] Hughes, Angelina Grimké, Phillis Wheatley, and*
> *countless others. I know I am part of the roots with no beginning and*
> *no end. . . . Thank you for the shoes."*

"In this piece," the student concludes, "Forman suggests that teachers give students walking shoes, the means to move inside the self and outside of the self, the means to make connections, find sites of power and
resistance, see context, locate meaning. Teachers give students tools for
travel."[85] One need only skim the first book about women's studies graduates to learn how far they go in those shoes.[86]

Women's studies need not indoctrinate. It is sufficient that it empower students with the passion to learn and to utilize their learning in living. If politics is about power, in that sense, women's studies is indeed political. Many thoughtful and informed academics today agree that teaching is a political act in the broadest sense of the word. It allows faculty to make choices that reflect their interests and values. One need not be a postmodernist to see that courses and curricula, even the subjects that are considered to constitute legitimate fields of knowledge, are selected—or "constructed," as Jane Roland Martin points out (see chapter 3). Nevertheless, the continuing effort to connect academic endeavors and activism in women's studies provokes substantial criticism from outside women's studies as well as concern within (see chapter 8). It contributes to an ongoing identity crisis in the NWSA, discussed above. Perhaps on all sides it would be useful to recollect that teaching has long been connected with preaching, and that not every tension needs to be resolved through elimination of one side. Women's studies at its best offers instead original, provocative thought and action.

The problem of purpose for women's studies must be set in a larger context. If women's studies is one of the major intellectual currents of the twentieth century, and I believe it is, then it cannot escape the difficult complexities that such currents entail. As Thomas Mann observed long ago, "The wholeness of the human problem permits nobody to separate the intellectual and artistic from the political and social and to isolate himself [or herself] within the ivory tower of the 'cultural' proper."[87] Hannah Arendt declared that humanity "can be achieved only by one who has thrown his [or her] life and his [or her] person into 'the venture into the public realm.' . . . Speaking is also a form of action. That is one venture. The other is: we start something. We weave our strand onto a network of relations. What comes of it we never know."[88] We can never know completely, or in advance, where women's studies students—or faculty—will go in the "travelin' shoes" women's studies gives them.

Academic feminists struggle to integrate many conventionally dichotomous or discordant facets of life. Tracing her own intellectual and political trajectory, Ann Snitow, a professor of literature, finds it essential, if difficult, to accept the paradoxes and to live with contradictions. "There is no marriage of theoretical mind and activist brawn to give us New Feminist Woman," she declares. "Activism requires of feminists that we elaborate the fiction 'woman' as if she were not a provisional invention at all but a person we know well, one in need of obvious rights and powers. Activism and theory weave together here, working on what remains the same basic cloth, the stuff of feminism." Snitow notes that the pace of change is slow: "Mass feminist consciousness has made a great difference; we have created not only new expectations but also new institutions. Yet, inevitably, the optimism of activism has given way to the academic second thoughts that tell us why our work is so hard. For even straightforward, liberal changes— like equal pay or day-care—are proving far more elusive than feminists dreamed in 1970. We are moving more slowly than Western women of the late twentieth century can easily accept—or are even likely to imagine."[89] Taking a longer, historical view, however, one observes an accelerating pace of change, and tendrils spread, by the power of modern communications, far more widely than those of earlier feminist movements. The stems of feminism are now deeply planted throughout the terrain of higher education.

The successful institutionalization of women's studies means that the historical memory of this generation's work will survive. Unlike many feminist efforts of previous eras, their progress will not be lost but, on the contrary, will provide a legacy on which future generations of activists and scholars can build. It is in the context of world historical change that the new knowledge produced in women's studies, about and largely by women, to answer women's questions, serves its many purposes. It provides one answer to the handyman's question with which this chapter began. By including women as producers and as subjects of knowledge, women's studies seeks to expand the knowledge base of the traditional accumulation of pre–women's studies learning, so that it will no longer constitute a virtual domain of men's studies. It will make complete what has heretofore been partial, in both senses of the word. It serves also to re-engage the worlds of learning and life. Seeking and telling many truths about many women, and about their perceptions of the world, academic feminists hope to transform women's condition and, by empowering women with knowledge, to change the world. For these aspirations the proponents of women's studies stand accused of "putting scholarship and teaching into the service of politics."[90] Those on both sides often seem to lack a historical perspective on the very old question of whether knowledge is its own end. Periodically, the argument over women's studies hits the headlines, and occasionally it produces best-sellers. But feminist critics and critics of feminism rarely talk with each other. The following chapter will look at both sides of the missing critical dialogue about some of the issues in contention.

8

Sources of Criticism

Are the practitioners of women's studies "all advocates who resent that name, and for the most part even wily spokesmen for their prejudices which they baptize 'truths'?" The conservative member of the National Council of the National Endowment for the Humanities (NEH) who declared, "What I truly believe is that second-rate traditionalist scholarship is ultimately more valuable to the country than first-rate feminist works," would likely answer this question in the affirmative. So might other critics of women's studies, from "neocons" to "neofems," as Susan Faludi terms them in the subtitle of her chapter "The Backlash Brain Trust," part of her study of a recent widespread tendency to blame feminism for cultural changes of the past century. From its beginnings, women's studies has been a frequent target of criticism by opponents both outside and within the academy. As the objects of attack, advocates of women's studies find themselves in interesting company. For it was Friedrich Nietzsche, inveighing against fellow philosophers in his critique of the "will to truth" a hundred years ago, who brought the charge cited above. History is replete with attacks against intellectuals by thinkers of a different mind. As Faludi's nicknames suggest, over the decades the identity of the critics has changed. However, Catharine R. Stimpson graphically points out that "despite these mutations, the opposition has had a constant theme: women's studies is the monster mother of gender rebellion and mindlessness. . . . Academic feminism betrays the free market, the free world, free and objective inquiry, the family, and heterosexuality without tears. Religious fundamentalists chime in that women's studies/academic feminism is ungodly, too."[1]

While its virulence has sometimes been surprising, controversy over women's studies was inevitable. Women's studies entered the academy at a time of significant change in the church, the family, and the world economy. Following the pattern of other historical manifestations of feminism, it gained a foothold only when fractures had already appeared in previously solid walls of resistance to women's historical claims. It is understandable, therefore, that women's studies, which introduced feminist issues into higher education, would be perceived by opponents of changes in gender relations as one of the causes of those changes and would be accused accordingly. To understand the nature of much of the criticism, it is important to keep in mind developments not only in higher education but also in society as a whole. Some of the hostile language and angry tone of the attacks may reflect discomfort with women's changing roles. It may also be explicable to some degree as a Reagan-era rebellion against the counterculture of the 1960s and 1970s. Attacks on women's studies form part of what Ellen Messer-Davidow, in a heavily documented essay, describes as a well-funded and carefully "manufactured" campaign against "liberalized higher education."[2]

One major source of criticism, mostly internal to the academy or at least to the intellectual community, is dissatisfaction with post–World War II phenomena affecting higher education, including increasing specialization as well as a countertrend toward interdisciplinary research and teaching. The lowering of the barriers that formerly kept "nontraditional" groups of students and faculty, as well as the "town" (of "town/gown" infamy), outside the ivied walls has also provoked profound change that some traditionalists find disturbing. Other intellectual challenges are posed by changing curricular content, new methods of teaching, new subjects for research, and new fields of knowledge, such as women's studies.

Academic feminism introduces a new approach to previously hidden knowledge. One of the bases of feminist analysis is a recognition of subjectivity, of the ways in which one's personal past influences one's politics and one's scholarship. Because they are often accustomed to self-analysis— "Why do I feel this way?"—feminists also tend to ask this question of their critics. Lynne Cheney and Allan Bloom claim "objectivity" while denying any subjective basis for their sometimes malicious attacks on feminism, in the academy and beyond.[3]

Finally, academic feminists themselves argue with their putative sisters about truth and error in the time-honored manner of scholars seeking to promote their own views over those of colleagues. In the process, they provide strong ammunition for antifeminist attackers, some of whom assert that feminism is a monolithic movement whose adherents silence dissent, and others of whom claim that it is rife with conflict and internal dissension. Critics seem not to be able to read the words *feminisms* and *women's studies* in the plural. As they have evolved from an earlier defensiveness, however, academic feminists have manifested greater confidence in dealing with intellectual and political quarrels.

Women's studies is criticized on numerous grounds. These include its advocacy of new subject matter and its refusal to reserve canonical status for traditional works; its questioning of the concept of objectivity; its criticism of male-dominated, hierarchical institutional structures; its presentation of women as victims of subordination and oppression; its introduction of new pedagogical practices; its existence outside traditional departmental administrative units; and—whether the separation is due to the preference of women's studies faculty or to their exclusion by others—the interdisciplinary location and separate program focus that is often the result. Each of these is a large topic, often intertwined with others. These issues, which have been addressed in other chapters, will be taken up here as they appear in the works of such well-known critics of academic feminism and women's studies as Allan Bloom, Lynne Cheney, Gertrude Himmelfarb, Roger Kimball, Karen Lehrman, John Leo, Michael Levin, Camille Paglia, Daphne Patai and Noretta Koertge, and Christina Hoff Sommers. Other criticism of women's studies, especially internal criticism, will be addressed as well.

Throughout this book, I have alluded to problems faced by women's studies, some imaginary, others real, of varying degrees of seriousness. I hope that I have already laid to rest the allegation that voices of dissent are completely stifled. If women's studies is still struggling to create a tradition of self-criticism and live comfortably with dissent, it is often the fear of feeding antifeminism that leads to self-censorship. With more than a quarter of a century of success behind it, and continuing growth evident, supporters are now learning to deal with the intellectual and political challenges they face, on grounds both spurious and serious; and to do so without denying a feminist commitment, however defined. Like Joan Korenman monitoring the WMST-L mailing list and trying to separate the discussion of women's issues in society from specific concerns about teaching, research, and administration in academic women's studies programs, I will focus on criticism that is aimed primarily at the *academic* feminist experience.[4]

This is a tricky task. Criticism of women's studies draws much of its energy from dissatisfaction with developments in the larger social context. Women's studies is a favorite target in the prevailing "culture wars." At least since the early 1980s, members of numerous groups whose work has been funded by the political Right have accused academics who lean to the Left of creating what the sociologist Birgitte Berger, in the pages of a National Association of Scholars (NAS) journal, calls a "travesty of the intellect." Berger presents a sociological analysis of the origins of academic feminism, situating women's studies amid a left-wing politics divided between a Marxist "Hard Left" and a "Soft Left" comprised of advocates of environmentalism, peace movements, cultural pluralism, holistic medicine, and alternative education. In Berger's view, academic feminism pushes a "New Class" agenda that propels the women's movement, both off-campus and on. Oddly, in a piece that argues that feminism is *sui generis,* she declares that "most [academics], men as well as women, subscribe to New Class culture and ideology." But academic feminism brings a uniquely dangerous potential to the "strangely opaque and susceptible—dare one say, effeminate?—intellectual climate" of today's academy. Berger approves of some of the new scholarship on women, which she terms "feminist empiricism" (based presumably on "hard data"), leveling her heaviest cannon against the "gender subjectivism" of the "imperial feminism" that she believes dominates women's studies. Now, she declares, it is time to "declare war." In fact, the war was announced long ago, for her "New Class," a sociological term with origins in late-nineteenth-century European thought, referring to a knowledge-based cultural group, is an old Cold War formulation. Rather intriguingly, Berger distinguishes her "New Class" feminists from other "professional" feminists, who, she finds, "march to a different drummer." But in the ensuing discussion she does not make clear where her parade of feminist enemies is divided.[5]

In any case, the war was already well under way by the late 1970s or early 1980s, or even as early as the 1950s, depending on which source one credits. A number of today's anti–women's studies warriors are associated with the National Association of Scholars or with one of its parent or fraternal organizations. Ronald Reagan's appointees as head of the NEH, notably William Bennett and Lynne Cheney, both included women's studies on their lists of cultural enemies. The NEH's support for scholarship on women declined drastically during the 1980s; by one account, from up to 10 percent of both awards and funds at mid-decade to only 2 percent of funds by the early 1990s.[6] The "Back to Basics" movement of that decade tended to count women's studies among its antagonists, even though many courses on women included heavy reading assignments in literature, history, philosophy, and sociology, through which students encountered, often for the first time, the works of major figures (including the dead white European males who dominate traditional reading lists) and thereby learned much of "the basics."

Attacks by Outsiders

The major success story of the 1980s for the conservative forces came not through the acts of federal agencies, however. It was the surprise best-seller by Allan Bloom, *The Closing of the American Mind: How Higher Education Has Failed Democracy and Impoverished the Souls of Today's Students*. Bloom's book achieved a place on the *New York Times* best-seller list for thirty-six weeks and sold eight hundred thousand copies in its first year. The book attacks virtually every cultural shift in American society since the 1960s, including increased extramarital sex, divorce, and rock music, attributing to feminism responsibility for changes in family and interpersonal relationships. In its academic guise, feminism had become for Bloom "the latest enemy of the vitality of the classic texts," which Bloom believed should themselves "dictate what the questions are and the method of approaching them." They should be read, he declared, "as their authors wished them to be read."[7]

Feminist scholars, it seems, were asking questions "dictated" neither by the authors themselves nor by Bloom. For example, Kathleen B. Jones, a professor of political theory and women's studies, compares her reading of Rousseau's *Emile* with Bloom's. In passages where Bloom reads Rousseau to find support for the naturalness of female subordination in family life as necessary to social harmony, Jones finds justification for wife abuse. "Nature should be the standard by which we judge our own lives and the lives of peoples," opined Bloom, apparently oblivious to his role in interpreting its meanings. In his lament for the loss of "moral restraints" on sexual behavior, Bloom alludes to the most famous of female sexual sinners in modern European literature. "Anna Karenina and Madame Bovary are adulteresses, but the cosmos no longer rebels at their deed." Bloom conveniently ignores the death penalty imposed on them by their creators, presumably writing for the "cosmos."[8]

Defense of the canon against "ideologically motivated assaults on the intellectual and moral substance of our culture" provided the rationale for a series of successor volumes to Bloom's, including Roger Kimball's *Tenured Radicals*, whose subtitle, "How Politics Has Corrupted Our Higher Education," clearly echoes Bloom's. Presenting "radical feminism" as "the single biggest challenge to the canon as traditionally conceived," Kimball quotes approvingly Berger's view that it constitutes "an imperialism of feminist sentiments." Kimball objects especially to academic feminism's alliance with deconstructionist theory and its insistence on employing gender as an analytical category. "If gender is a 'crucial element in the way we all read and write' then why not sexual orientation, race, and class?" he notes, deriding feminist efforts to interpret women's experiences as part of a more complex structure of meaning. Drawing on another article in the NAS journal, Kimball envisions a dystopic academic future in which "every course will be Oppression Studies."[9]

Ultimately it is against pluralism in the academy and society, which he characterizes as a new ideological orthodoxy, that Kimball levels his own cannon. In his view, deconstructionists, multiculturalists, and feminists have turned literature into "political propaganda and virtue mongering." Tenured radicals, whom he describes as "the privileged beneficiaries of the spiritual and material achievements of our history who, out of perversity, ignorance, or malice, have chosen to turn their backs on the culture that nourished them and made them what they are," have rejected not only traditional values but all appreciation for any moral values. Without citing any source, Kimball asserts that critics of the traditional literary canon have "often rejected" the notion that Shakespeare's works are superior to Bugs Bunny cartoons. Alluding to an infamous Central Park assault case of 1989, he finds an association between English professor Stanley Fish's rejection of the concept of "disinterested judgment" and (positively) "sanctioned rape and brutality." It is hard to avoid agreeing with Nancy Baker Jones, who characterizes Kimball, along with Bloom and others, as authors of "reactionary assault literature" filled with hyperbole and reductionism, in the "paranoid-style" of American anti-intellectualism.[10]

In a less personalized, more temperate, and balanced analysis of the culture wars, David Bromwich criticizes both the "antiquarian-reactionary and the academic-radical ideas of tradition." Opposing "group thinking" in higher education as "politics by other means," Bromwich focuses on those who use the concepts of "culture as social identity," "community," and "professionalism" to demand intellectual conformity. While many advocates of opening the curriculum and the university to pluralistic views might agree with him—as I do—that using intimidation to obtain adherence to any particular point of view in the pursuit of knowledge is anathema, he unfortunately selects as his one example of a "faculty loyalty oath" a case involving Christina Hoff Sommers (whose work will be treated below). In this instance, the alleged offense was a question posed by a women's studies curriculum committee to Sommers regarding how, to the extent "relevant to the content of the course," she would introduce "pluralistic views." For Sommers and Bromwich, this invitation to multiculturalism, despite the qualification "insofar as it might be relevant," signified a violation of "faculty autonomy" with regard to course content. Ideally, course descriptions and content follow from consensual agreement among faculty colleagues about curricular goals. As is well known, however, academics often—perhaps beneficially, given their mission to advance new knowledge—quarrel over what is the appropriate scope and content for courses and curricula. However, Bromwich's main point, of the dangers of political pressure toward intellectual conformity, is one with which most feminist scholars, in my experience, would agree. The power that women's studies pursues is the power to create knowledge. New schools of thought that challenge older ways of thinking do not necessarily equate to "group-think."[11]

The assertion that feminist attempts to broaden the scope of the curriculum transform scholarship into politics, but that the "traditional" curriculum is "sex-neutral" despite its omissions, undergirds much criticism of women's studies. For example, Michael Levin, whose 1987 book *Feminism and Freedom* is an unrelenting diatribe against feminism, asserts that the women's movement is based on an erroneous assumption about "the social determinativeness of innate sex differences" and hence is "bound to be wrong about everything else." After dismissing studies of women based on differing social experiences of the sexes as no more important than "left-handed studies," Levin aims his strongest attack at the feminist critique of objectivity. "Without question," he declares, "the illusoriness of objective truth is the discovery that feminist scholars themselves regard as their most significant." While alluding briefly to a "long tradition of epistemological relativism" in his own field of philosophy, Levin declares that "its arguments have nothing to do with the genitals of inquirers and are consequently unavailable to feminist relativists"—he rather than they making that judgment. Nor in his criticism of feminist scientists does Levin acknowledge any of the recent reassessments of science coming from outside feminist scholarship, such as the works of Thomas S. Kuhn, Paul Feyerabend, Bruno Latour, and others. Levin ignores the major works of feminist scholars in the humanities and the social science disciplines. It is hard to take seriously anyone whose "operational definition" of a feminist is "anyone who takes seriously the analogy between Blacks and women."[12]

Dismissing women's studies as "ersatz scholarship," Levin joins Peter Shaw, the NEH council member who declared that he "fundamentally do[es] not respect feminist scholarship," in trivializing it. Similarly, William H. Honan, in a *New York Times* column, points to an article in *Women's Studies Quarterly* (a journal with a heavy emphasis on pedagogy) on helping math-anxious individuals succeed in studying statistics as an example of the trivia responsible for the allegedly declining value of scholarly publications.[13] Journalistic attacks such as these appear regularly in popular periodicals. For example, one article alluding to women's studies as "the finishing school of the '90s" draws from course descriptions for Cornell's "The Sociology of Reproduction," Columbia's "The Invisible Woman in Literature: The Lesbian Literary Tradition," and Dartmouth's "Women and Religion: New Explorations" the peevish inference that women's studies majors "have spent four years doing little else than blathering about gender and feeling their way around in the discrete world of feminist ideology." Illustrated by a group of four booted women marching in regimental order, the article cited the study at Wellesley College (mentioned in chapter 4, above) in which 30 percent of women's studies students felt unable to express unpopular opinions in class compared to 14 percent in a control group; and two professors at Oberlin College who found women's studies overly political. The author's conclusion—that feminist educators were depriving women of both the critical thinking skills and the career preparation needed to "assume leadership in the economic and political arenas"—might have differed had she extended her research to the actual postgraduation employment of women's studies graduates.[14]

Despite the successes reported by women's studies alumnae, many journalists continue to deny the value of knowledge about women. "Undergraduates today have no business focusing on feminist theories of literature. The problem is not that the theories are warping their values," says an English professor who doubles as a writer for major national, opinion-making reviews. "It is that such tasks are simply a waste of time."[15] Other critics, including Levin, allege that women's studies courses are "easy." The fact that students who major in women's studies, half of whom continue on to graduate school, themselves report the opposite seems to go unheard. Without evidence of grading practices in women's studies, Lynne Cheney links feminist criticism of male-dominated standards in "the world in general and schools in particular" with grade inflation.[16]

Clearly, women's studies makes some people uncomfortable. For detractors of women's studies, criticism of sexism in social institutions quickly becomes evidence of "male-bashing" and the practice of "victim-ology." John Leo, another highly visible journalist, trivializes serious feminist work when he declares the concept of phallologocentrism to be "a complicated way of saying men are bad." Feminist scholars talk openly about issues formerly reserved for gossip or "woman-talk," if considered mentionable at all. A case in point is Eve Kosofsky Sedgwick's paper "Jane Austen and the Masturbating Girl," and what Sedgwick calls "the phrase's career in journalism." As soon as the title appeared in the program of a forthcoming convention of the Modern Language Association, it elicited a storm of disapproval—becoming, in Sedgwick's words, "the Q.E.D. of phobic narratives about the degeneracy of academic discourse in the humanities." This is notwithstanding, she points out, "the half-century-long normalizing rehabilitation of this common form of isometric exercise." For Sedgwick, a rereading of *Sense and Sensibility* in the context of a nineteenth-century masturbation phobia and the reaction to her study demonstrate "how profoundly, how destructively twentieth-century readings are already shaped by the discourse of masturbation and its sequelae: *more* destructively than the novel is, even though onanism per se, and the phobia against it, are living issues in the novel as they no longer are today." Sedgwick's primary interest lies in the development of concepts of sexual identity and the formative role of the identity of the masturbator in the "triumph of the heterosexist homo/hetero calculus." She may also, along with some other feminist critics, intend to be provocative.[17]

To some extent, however, it may be less Sedgwick's content and style than her experimental and "new historicist" approach that were responsible for what she calls "the depredations of the press around my title." Even while eliciting intense internal criticism that belies the very common assertion that women's studies follows one party line, the rise to prominence of many scholars influenced by postmodernism has encouraged detractors to identify academic feminism with the "linguistic Left." One critic of American studies sums up his view of the latter's wrongheaded development similarly as "the absolutist, ironic privileging of race, class, and gender in the new orthodoxy of poststructuralist cultural studies [that] too often creates a patronizing calculus of victimization, a formulaic demand for reversibility, and a clannish standard of political correctness."[18] Academic feminism is deemed guilty by association.

The "new orthodoxy" received nationwide notoriety in the revision (widely denounced by William Bennett and others) of the core curriculum at Stanford University which culminated in the replacement of a "Western Civilization" requirement with "Cultures, Issues and Values (CIV)," and the institution in 1991 of a general education requirement in gender studies. (The latter was made optional in 1995.) Along with a celebrated case involving the use of a textbook on race and gender in an English class at the University of Texas in 1990, the Stanford debate fueled a far-reaching controversy over "political correctness" in the curriculum in which women's studies was frequently indicted—not least by John Leo, whose book gave *Newsweek* a cover story on "Thought Police." By 1993, the literature had grown to fill a (fairly selective) bibliography of 150 items. Despite gross generalizations based on small numbers and limited evidence, the critics of gender—and multicultural—studies won widespread attention and support. The distinguished philosopher Richard Rorty, while reviewing a book with the inflammatory title *Dictatorship of Virtue* and disagreeing with its diagnosis of a cultural crisis due to multiculturalism, conceded success to the opposition. He termed it a "well-organised, well-financed and very energetic religious Right [which] is a hundred times more threatening to free speech and genuine diversity of opinion than all the multiculturalists put together. This Right has made clever and effective use of the widespread suspicion of multiculturalism. A large portion of the American middle class has been brought to believe that the universities are under the control of a 'political correctness police.'" For Rorty, the multiculturalism debate was a "sideshow" that served to divert attention from the social and economic problems facing the nation.[19]

Internal Debates

In its summer 1992 edition, *Signs* devoted its forum section to the "PC" debate. The philosopher Marilyn Frye used the occasion to argue with other academic feminists against what she considered "politically correct" positions in women's studies. Against those who favor affirmative action and its curricular form of integration or transformation, which she sees as "annihilative assimilation" and "cultural colonialism," she advocated a more radical notion of restructuring the university. The historian Alice Kessler-Harris portrayed "the view from women's studies" as one that recognizes the multiplicity signified by the contested category "woman" as partisan to multiculturalism, but she offered a carefully balanced view, cautioning against accepting "excesses that admittedly have been perpetrated in the name of multiculturalism." Kessler-Harris hoped to use the debate as a catalyst to avoid "our own form of political correctness." She cited as potential hazards overemphasis on "how we learn over what we learn" and excessive deference to experience, which she judged "by itself a problematic basis for action." She warned as well against the overemphasis on resisting institutionalization, pointing, for example, to the threat it posed to junior faculty. "We stand or fall on [women's studies'] contributions to the intellectual discourse around which our institutions of higher education are constructed," she said. While calling for unity, Kessler-Harris cautioned against internal pressure toward political correctness. "Insofar as we allow the 'politically correct' label to inhibit our efforts to achieve a multicultural education, we need to oppose it. And insofar as we use multiculturalism to stifle conversation in our own programs, we need to recognize the importance of dialogue in creating change."[20]

One danger of extremist attacks is that they may elicit extreme responses. This measured statement from Kessler-Harris, the director of the women's studies program at Rutgers University and an American women's historian who is known for her role as an expert witness on women's work for the plaintiff in the EEOC case against Sears (see chapter 7), is evidence against the charge that women's studies suppresses dissent. Her own testimony, however, acknowledges the kernel of truth in the accusation. The tendency toward "narrow politics" and "political correctness," which has on occasion led to extremes in women's studies settings that range from program staff meetings to national conferences, clearly exists.

The difficulty feminists face in criticizing one another is also recognized, at least tacitly, in the forums on feminist book reviewing that appeared in *Feminist Studies* in 1988 and in the *Women's Review of Books* in 1994. In a symposium in the former journal, five scholars, including the book review editor of the *Women's Review of Books*, discussed whether women had a "special responsibility as reviewers to be more understanding, more charitable." According to Natalie Zemon Davis, who was then professor of history at Princeton University and who in 1987 had been president of the American Historical Association, the informants to whom she had put the question had "snorted, 'Absolutely not.' You call it as it is." The discussants here agreed with Donna Haraway's comment that "feminists are better served by engaged criticism than by automatic praise." They seemed to agree with Davis that intellectual quarrels serve an important function in advancing scholarly thinking. Davis herself, however, would opt even in the case of a "hopelessly, pig-headedly bad" book to find "one positive thing" to say.[21]

In this forum, the historian Cynthia Neverdon-Morton, addressing reviews of books about African American women, drew attention to the importance of providing sufficient context for uninformed readers and of opening opportunities for reviewing to all qualified people—"women, men, blacks, whites." Linda Gardiner, editor-in-chief of the *Women's Review of Books*, views feminist reviewing as "by nature oppositional." She challenged reviewers to "remember the reader," as she denied the idea that "it's unfeminist to criticize your sisters in public," a position that she felt "unfairly favors author over reader." She would replace "support" and "community" as goals of feminist readers with "responsibility," "construction," and "self-consciousness."[22]

It is possible to read works about women's studies in search of pressure toward conformity, a task facilitated by the very openness of debate that tells it frankly, warts and all. Studies of teaching in women's studies are particularly good sources, for most reports on feminist pedagogy in practice cite examples of resistance as well as of receptivity. But it is also possible to distort the prevalence and impact of the negative and use it to rationalize opposition to all feminist-inspired education. Examples of this behavior pervade the works of a series of writers whom Patrice McDermott identifies as the "new critics." Unlike the earlier attacks of Bloom, Cheney, and others whose work was "framed in moral terms, judging what students 'ought' to be taught for the good of the national character but not scrutinizing the theoretical and methodological merits of the disciplines involved ... [the new critics] claim to be engaged in a highly rational, rather than moral, debate about the intellectual validity of feminist education. . . . This new, specific attack on women's studies classrooms and research is politically more, and intellectually less, than it seems."[23]

The new critics named by McDermott include Karen Lehrman, Wendy Kaminer, and Christina Hoff Sommers. A "media history" of these attacks, however, might open with the flash across the headlines of the publicity-loving Camille Paglia, whose "personal, inflammatory presence in the media," as she herself puts it, began in late 1990. Portrayed on her book covers as "America's premier intellectual renegade" and "our foremost intellectual provocateur," Paglia is a professor of the humanities, and a specialist in literature and art history, with a gift for invective. She has garnered immense attention by lashing out with what Ellen Willis terms "baroque eloquence and passionate conviction" in language that makes her work, however superficial or wrong-headed, fun to read. On closer review, however, there may be little reason to dwell on her in a discussion of women's studies, for most of the diatribes she directs at academic feminism contain little or nothing of substance. Her primary complaint against contemporary feminism, and against women's studies by extension, though not by analysis of evidence, is that it is hostile to sexual activity. Feminism and women's studies, in Paglia's view, are guilty of helping to deflect the sexual revolution of the 1960s and 1970s, by focusing on its dangers rather than its pleasures.[24]

On the whirlwind tour of mostly Ivy League colleges where she gathered the headlines reprinted in her "media history," Paglia repeatedly offered one prescription: replace women's studies with sex studies. Beyond denigrating the search for women's lost heritage in art and literature, she has nothing to say about the rest of women's studies: nothing on women in history or cross-cultural studies, on women's work, women's health issues, or politics. Yet she dismisses it all. Much of her argument is lodged against academic professional associations, especially the Modern Language Association (whose annual conferences she would abolish). She protests against the academy itself. It is hard not to agree with Susan Faludi's characterization of Paglia as a "faux-feminist" motivated by a desire for attention. Whatever truth is contained in Paglia's campaign of condemnation, and there is some, it is lost in the dense swamps of her intemperate verbiage.[25]

The biggest anti–women's studies headlines of 1993 appeared in the back-to-school issue of *Mother Jones*, alongside a cover photograph of a woman college student, captioned "Our Minds, Our Selves: Is Feminist Education Limiting Her Potential?" The reporter Karen Lehrman visited classes and talked with students and faculty at the University of California, Berkeley; the University of Iowa; Smith College; and Dartmouth College, emerging with a scathing tale of "discussions [that] alternate between the personal and the political, with mere pit stops at the academic." She asserted that the "vast majority [of faculty] rely . . . on a common set of feminist theories," and she attested that she had "waded through the more popular reading materials." Unfortunately for the reader seeking to find substantive criticism in her article, she attends to no feminist theory—only the "guiding principle" that women are oppressed; and she refers to only a single, introductory text, although she does cite the opinions of a number of women's studies faculty. Her main concerns seem to center on pedagogy and politics. Lehrman acknowledges that "the field has generated a considerable amount of first-rate scholarship on women." But she fails to mention any of it, and apparently she did not visit any of the thousands of classes where it is taught. Perhaps, as Pauline Bart has suggested, Lehrman did not bother to do so because she was too eager for the "instant stardom for women criticizing feminist endeavors." Lehrman's poorly researched article generated far greater response than it merited. A useful contrast is offered by Paula Kamen in her 1991 book *Feminist Fatale,* which includes an account of her visits to a much wider range of women's studies classes taught at a set of very different institutions, including the University of California, Santa Cruz; Brooklyn College; and an outpost of Northeastern Illinois University in a Latino section of Chicago.[26]

It was Christina Hoff Sommers's *Who Stole Feminism?* that won the publicity prize of 1994, drawing intense attention from press and television. Purporting to warn readers of the alleged dangers of what she names "gender feminism," Sommers debunks women's studies and the work of contemporary women's organizations in the community. She discredits as "noble lies" several highly visible reports about anorexia, girls' self-esteem and school achievement, and the incidence of rape. Probably her most notable achievement was exposing as gross error the annual number of deaths from anorexia in the United States as reported in a popular book on the dangers of women's compliance with the dictates of fashion. However, Sommers failed to temper the criticism in her own book, despite the prompt correction made by the author she criticizes, even though the author's acknowledgment of error appeared in a paperback edition published before

Sommers's book appeared. Sloppy scholarship is one point among several for which she was taken to task by members of her own scholarly community, the American Philosophical Association.[27] Sommers's defense in this instance was that the damage had already been done.

The coverage of Sommers's book in the press and on television was impressive. Patrice McDermott reports that it was reviewed in publications including the *Wall Street Journal*, the *New York Times*, the *New York Daily News*, the *New York Post*, the *Los Angeles Times*, the *Boston Globe*, the *Washington Post*, *Newsweek*, the *National Review*, *U.S. News and World Report*, the *Chicago Tribune*, and the premiere American issue of *Marie Claire*. It was discussed on television and radio talk shows including ABC's *Nightline*, the *McLaughlin Group*, CNN's *Crossfire*, and CBS's *Eye to Eye with Connie Chung*. Commentators applauded Sommers for her courage, promoting her views and characterizing reaction to her work as a "vitriolic response," the latter being the opening words of an interview with Sommers that appeared in the *San Francisco Examiner* a year later. As McDermott notes, this put feminists on the defensive. Had the *San Francisco Examiner*'s reporter labored through the charges and countercharges in letters from more than fifty individuals that appeared in the *Proceedings and Addresses of the American Philosophical Association*, she might have written a more balanced account.[28]

Balance, however, had nothing to do with it. Beginning with her subtitle, "How Women Have Betrayed Women," Sommers makes categorical statements and uses terms intended to inflame rather than illuminate. To suit her purpose, she lumps together all women, all feminists, all men, all women's studies courses, gliding across vast rhetorical spaces on the carpet of a single instance or one report. While Sommers did expose major errors in several highly publicized reports critical of women's condition in the contemporary United States, she did not practice what she preached in preparing her own work. Her academy, "colonized" by "gender feminists" who employ neologisms such as *ovular, thealogian,* and *herstory,* and by men who deliberately hire weaker female colleagues to protect their own mediocrity from exposure by competition, is unlike any that responsible researchers are likely to encounter. Sommers also gets her facts wrong. "Twenty years ago," she announces, "the nation's academies offered fewer than twenty courses in women's studies." But in fact, San Diego State alone offered a list of ten different women's studies courses twenty-five years before Sommers's book appeared; by the mid-1970s, the number of institutional *programs* had reached 150, with courses a multiple of that—added to which were classes scattered across many campuses that lacked officially organized units. This information is readily available.[29]

Sommers acknowledges that there is "interesting" scholarly work being done in women's studies. However, she pays little attention to academic feminist scholarship. Instead she points to some of the sillier instances of feminist excess in language usage, and she finds her errors in what is primarily non-academic feminist work. She offers anecdotal impression rather than systematic analysis of her subject. Had Sommers read the history of feminism before setting out to attack it, she would have discovered scholarship dealing with many forms of feminism and numerous intelligent, illuminating ways to interpret them. For example, the historian Karen Offen, in her 1988 article "Defining Feminism," a much-cited and often reprinted study now available in French, German, Spanish, and Japanese, mentions more than two dozen versions of feminism that she has noted. The philosopher Sandra Lee Bartky, in a letter refuting charges brought against her by Sommers, mentions about twenty varieties, a list that overlaps little with Offen's. There is no single feminism to be "stolen."[30]

Most significantly, had Sommers done her homework she would have learned that the very kind of feminism she praises, which she designates "equity feminism," is precisely that type often criticized as the most "individualistic," in the least attractive sense of that word. This is a feminism that Offen finds much less pervasive historically than a more "relational" kind of feminism advanced by persons concerned to improve women's status as members of families and societies. Ironically, Elizabeth Fox-Genovese, a historian and former women's studies director sometimes associated with Sommers as a critic of feminism and women's studies, herself published a book charging feminists with too individualistic a vision. But thoughtful discussion about feminism hardly appears to be Sommers's goal. *Who Stole Feminism?* has been described as "the opening shot in a much larger campaign against feminism, directed this time by antifeminist women." There is a great appetite for work by women who criticize other women—"Traitor to Her Sex?" headlined the *San Francisco Examiner* interview with Sommers in letters an inch high, lending credence to Patrice McDermott's observation that "debunking feminist contentions that gendered relations of unequal power are structural and systemic features of contemporary society" is the main objective of such press attention. Furthermore, antifeminism, especially when purveyed by self-styled feminists and proffered in snazzy sound bites, sells.[31]

And sell these books must, if the reports of the very large advances paid to their authors are correct. According to one source, for writing her book Sommers garnered $110,000 in support from three foundations (all noted in Messer-Davidow's analysis of the right-wing campaign); another commentator placed this figure at "at least $164,000"; a third source noted that the foundation grants came "on top of a reported 'six-figure' advance" from her publisher. Sylvia Hewlett is reported also to have received a six-figure advance for *A Lesser Life*, her recent book attacking feminism. Despite disappointing sales, she attracted invitations to appear on more than one hundred talk shows. As Susan Faludi points out, "Revisionism as a marketing tool" works.[32]

While the media made Sommers a celebrity, she lent her support to a group of academics and journalists who in 1993 founded a national organization called the Women's Freedom Network (WFN). Placing the WFN somewhere between Phyllis Schlafly's Eagle Forum and the National Organization for Women, they described themselves as "seeking alternatives to both extremist and ideological feminism and antifeminist traditionalism." The WFN's first national meeting, held in Washington, D.C., in October 1994, was billed as "Reclaiming Feminism: Voices in Dialogue." Sommers provided the opening plenary address. Speaking after dinner the first evening to an audience of about sixty people, she summarized the contents of her book, stressing the "epidemic of hoaxes" she had exposed, calling for a counterpresence to feminism in the media, and citing a number of instances of women's studies gone astray. She pointed to a class assignment that required students to "do an outrageous act" and to a "bleed-in" sponsored by a women's center, a reference that elicited the loudest laughter of the evening. A "healthier alternative" would disavow "radical ideologies," avoid "PC," and "not compare its scholars to Copernicus, Darwin, and Freud."[33]

Asked by the journalist Wendy Kaminer what constituted her definition of a "feminism that is nonideological," Sommers replied, "I don't know. . . . Advocates are in the way. . . . I can't get to the truth." She repeated this comment when Kaminer, whose participation in the national meeting I found informed, thoughtful, and nuanced, asked Sommers if she felt that there were any remaining structural or other barriers that disadvantaged women. Sommers offered no other answer. Another member of the audience, Joan Mandle, women's studies director at Colgate University in New York State, after agreeing with Sommers about the importance of exposing bad research, questioned her about her own. "I have trouble understanding how you know this is dominant in academia. I teach women's studies—not in the way you describe as dominant." She might have pointed out that Sommers had reported on her visit to a National Women's Studies Association conference but had apparently made no effort to seek information about feminist scholarship at the American Historical Association, the American Sociological Association, the American Political Science Association, or the Modern Language Association, or at the other major disciplinary meetings where most feminist scholars present their work.

Attracted to this WFN meeting myself by the presence on the program announcement of Jean Bethke Elshtain and Elizabeth Fox-Genovese, two women's studies scholars whose work I had read and respected, I attended the meeting and was disappointed when neither appeared as scheduled. However, aware of the justness of some criticism of women's studies, I sought to learn at the WFN meeting whether the new organization would in fact offer a balanced and centrist agenda helpful to academic feminists. I heard no "dialogue." Instead I observed a barrage of attacks on feminism, "balanced" only by one presentation about bias in the media by Deirdre English, former editor of *Mother Jones*, who suggested that one reason readers tend to believe even poorly grounded research reports depicting women as victims is that the "damsel in distress is consistent with patriarchy and male domination. . . . The feminist image overlaps the patriarchal image." English also pointed to the continuing reality of women's needs in employment, child care, health care, and family support. Criticizing Sommers's presentation of the previous evening, English declared that it was "much too early to declare victory and go home." Like Kaminer, she sought a balance. English hoped to see the WFN "emerge with a profeminist agenda."

This has not happened. What I have found in the WFN's subsequent communications and publications is a continual attack on feminists and feminism. The *Women's Freedom Network Newsletter* seems to delight in debunking feminist reports, ranging from the politics of the gender gap to sexual harassment. It reads as if its title were "Freedom *from* Feminism." The reader seeks in vain for positive coverage of any topic related to improving the status of women in the United States. (The summer 1996 issue included one article supporting women's claims, an excerpt from a speech given in London dealing with the condition of Iranian women.) Other issues have featured interviews with dissatisfied women's studies students, attacks on affirmative action, discussions of "fathers' rights," and selections from books critical of feminism and women's studies. The WFN provides evidence to document Patrice McDermott's contention that the "new critics" proffer "a version of women's studies that trivializes feminist analyses of power, undermines attempts to effect social change, and casts feminism as a hegemonic bully on American campuses. In this popular press scenario, exaggerated feminist propaganda, not material inequity, is responsible for the oppression of women in contemporary society." The WFN's third annual conference in October 1996 was entitled "Rethinking Sexual Harassment."[34]

It is the "bully on campus" image that provides a place on this critical agenda for Daphne Patai and Noretta Koertge's *Professing Feminism*, with its lurid subtitle, "Cautionary Tales from the Strange World of Women's Studies." Its publication coincided with the WFN's first annual meeting, where Patai filled in for Fox-Genovese at the scheduled session on women and scholarship. Drawing on her own experience as professor of women's studies and Brazilian literature at the University of Massachusetts at Amherst, Patai focused her remarks on two of her objections to women's studies: its "academic separatism" and its "deference to political activism." The "separatist mentality" reflected, she felt, an "inability to deal with men" (and, incidentally, gave her the subject of her next book, which attacks male-bashing—which she also calls "heterophobia"—in feminism). She was less concerned, she said, with the intellectual substance of women's studies and more with how the content was used by faculty who were teaching material outside their areas of expertise because of the interdisciplinary structure of most women's studies programs. Presumably this encourages the dominance of politics over academic pursuits.[35]

Like Lehrman's article and Sommers's book, the work of Patai and Koertge indicts women's studies broadly on the basis of a few selected instances. Unfortunately, they tend to tar all of women's studies with a wide brush, when carefully drawn lines of criticism would do—and perhaps also do some good. The authors' use of phrases such as "cautionary tales," "oppression sweepstakes," "proselytizing and policing," and "semantic sorcery" for chapter titles seems unlikely to elicit constructive change. They also fail to distinguish important and serious issues from trivial ones, and commonly accepted views from hotly contested ones. They do not appreciate the necessity of inclusive language if girls and women are ever to achieve equal opportunity; few are the Sarah Grimkés who could as early as 1853 envision a woman occupying the chair of the chief justice of the U.S. Supreme Court, in the story told today by Justice Ruth Bader Ginsburg. Most of us would need some visual or aural cue. Nevertheless, in view of the authors' other contributions to women's studies, this work calls for analysis and response.[36]

Where Lehrman visited four programs from among more than six hundred, Patai and Koertge interviewed thirty out of many thousands who teach women's studies courses. They base their strongest criticism on the testimony of *three* "who walked away." Patai and Koertge have stretched testimony from these three into what they consider "a coherent picture of the unhealthy conditions and self-destructive tendencies that appear to be intrinsic to many Women's Studies programs." These are described as "students who stomp in seminars" and become "ideologically inflamed Stepford Wives," "belligerent anti-intellectualism" on the part of faculty, who practice "maternalism" in lieu of fostering open and critical thinking, and themselves "'rush to a kind of groupthink,'" an example of which is the "privileging of racial categories." While allowing that "much research inspired by feminist commitments has been eminently worthwhile," the authors join their "three" in questioning whether women's studies programs are an appropriate site for this work. Because women's studies "has never developed a clear view of itself as an academic discipline," one informant stated that she preferred to focus her work in her "own department," and the authors agree.[37]

After offering a number of possible explanations for the problems they perceived, including the "growing pains" of programs and "a lifetime of experience in dysfunctional nuclear families" on the part of students and faculty, Patai and Koertge settle on feminist ideology as the fundamental factor that subverts what might otherwise, in their view, be an "interesting debate." They state that they deliberately prefer the term *ideology* to *worldview* or *philosophy of life*, to emphasize the "unacknowledged" and "self-serving" aspects of the beliefs underlying women's studies. This becomes, for the authors, "IDPOL," or identity politics. Patai and Koertge practice a rhetorical strategy much like that which they accuse academic feminists of using. A glaring example of this is their charge that feminists play word games, practicing "WORDMAGIC." Patai and Koertge identify as feminist magic not only "Phony Philology," which has led some feminists to substitute such terms as *ovular* for *seminal*, or *herstory* for *history*, but also several other types of alleged attempts to change society by manipulating language. "Metaphor Madness" is their term for seeking clitoral imagery in female poetry or finding misogynist intent in scientific discussions of penetrating nature. "Linguistic Litmus Tests" is their label for feminists' insistence that adult human females be called women rather than girls and demands for clarity in language referring to either or both sexes. Worst of all, the authors find, is the practice they call "Accordion Concepts," by which "concepts are stretched so wide that crucial distinctions are obliterated"; examples include Adrienne Rich's notion of a lesbian continuum that includes women who are not homosexual but focus their energies on women-related activities, and the idea that all heterosexual intercourse may be defined as rape because of the power differential between men and women in society. I suspect that few feminist academics utilize the neologisms; I personally know of none. I find their illustrations unconvincing, either because they are based on superficial understandings of the underlying points or because they refer to much-argued positions taken by a limited number of individuals. Apart from providing no evidence on how widespread such views and practices might be, the authors themselves play silly word games throughout their book. *Professing Feminism* is replete with cutesy neologisms, all presented in upper case: IDPOL for identity politics, BIODENIAL for social construction, GENDERAGENDA for insistence on precision in terminology, authorship, and interpretation, TOTAL REJ for the reappraisal of history in quest of women's experience. Who's playing with language?[38]

Patai and Koertge point to real problems that exist in some women's studies courses and programs. It is true that an emphasis on consensus has tended to suppress criticism from within women's studies. It is true that the field's important constructive critique of traditional disciplines and creation of new knowledge have been accompanied by impossibly grand goals. Democratic impulses and suspicion of authority, which women's studies faculty share with many others, sometimes do shade into anti-intellectualism or irresponsible attacks on individuals of achievement. Attempts to establish parameters for women's studies courses and curricula, a task important to a new and broadly based field, may tend to close some doors prematurely. There *is* too much focus on differences and not enough on commonalities among women. As Patai courageously pointed out in a 1992 essay on "ideological policing" in women's studies, deference to identity politics could threaten the credibility of women's studies.[39] It is foolish for feminists, however few, to dismiss as Eurocentric the powerful insights and courageous work of men and women, dead or alive, who have struggled to develop and to practice the great and liberatory principles that—however inadequately realized to date—are part of the European legacy. It is self-defeating for feminist ideologues to alienate feminist scholars, many of whose works fill the reading lists of women's studies courses, because the latter lack interest in or patience with the long discussions of non-academic issues that the former sometimes enjoy, whether in staff meetings or national conferences. These are not good practices.

However, many of the problems that Patai and Koertge lay at the door of women's studies plague other academic programs as well. Other faculty besides those in women's studies tend to overpersonalize; other courses sometimes offer academic credit for service learning of dubious scholarly merit; other course outlines and classroom discussions promote political causes. If the "new critics" are truly feminists, as many of them claim, they should not be so quick to attribute to the feminism of women's studies faults that, however lamentable, are endemic in the academy. The solution is not inflammatory denunciation but informed debate, not gross generalizations offered in antifeminist venues, but open discussion in academic forums where constructive criticism could do some good.

Even a cursory survey of women's studies literature demolishes the myth of a monolithic movement closed to criticism. But it may be, as McDermott suggests, that empirical evidence is irrelevant, for the new critics' intention is a "moral attack on feminist cultural authority." Attempting to undermine the access of women's studies to power in the academy, they exaggerate to the point of absurdity. Patai and Koertge, for example, evoke the dangers of feminist ideology by alluding to "the Aryan university of Nazi Germany; Stalinism and Maoism; lily-white institutions in the pre-1960s U.S. South; the purges provoked by McCarthyism; East German universities whose faculties first had to embody Marxist-Leninist truths and were then removed wholesale when that ideology folded; ethnically pure enclaves in the former Yugoslavia." They destroy their own potential for credibility.[40]

Far from annihilating their opponents, women's studies scholars today invite their criticism—and the critics publish on the front pages of feminist journals. In my review of internal criticism within women's studies, I found many instances of academic feminists challenging each other's work. They argue about the balance between academic work and activism; show concern lest "dogma" obscure feminism's multiplicity of perspectives; question the validity of "nurturance" in the classroom and of the concept of feminist pedagogy altogether, denying "women's ways of knowing"; debate separation from the disciplines versus integration into them; call for less self-examination and reduced emphasis on difference; challenge the language, philosophy, and uses of postmodernism; recognize the need for more, and more positive, discussion of heterosexuality as well as of mothering; and generally welcome dialogue on every point beyond a basic "feminist" acknowledgment of the historical subordination of women and commitment to working to overcome it.

A number of the contentious issues within women's studies have been discussed in earlier chapters and the debate need not be repeated here; so a few points must suffice. Against charges that women's studies silences critics, many important voices stand out. Some, such as Jean Bethke Elshtain and Catharine Stimpson, have for years challenged some feminist political rhetoric and have continued to earn respect for their views. Elshtain, an early critic of male-biased norms in political science, has criticized radical feminism, liberal feminism, and socialist feminism, as well as any feminist drive toward a single, simple truth. She challenges a feminist classic, Simone de Beauvoir's *Second Sex*, the works of Betty Friedan and Shulamith Firestone, and many other foundational women's studies texts. Elshtain is probably best known for her criticism of feminist views of the family.

In her 1981 book *Public Man, Private Woman*, Elshtain charges feminists with reducing "the realm of intimacy" to a "world of reproduction, an analogy of the productive process," thereby neglecting the importance and denigrating the positive aspects of traditional female concerns. Intent on attaining access to the professional and political world, they also underestimate its "darker realities." Elshtain cautions against the type of feminism, grounded in liberalism, that would reabsorb the private into the public. In her view, it fails to deal adequately with such large issues of life as motherhood, family, and human relations. "Too often," she wrote in 1981, "feminist utopians and revolutionists throw out not the baby *with* the bathwater, but the baby *rather than* the bathwater. That is, they junk all notions of what is essential, of limiting conditions, in the creation of the future by concentrating exclusively on what must, they believe, change in order for women to be 'free.' They will brook no disagreement for to disagree is to exhibit the poison of 'male identification.'"[41]

Reminding feminists that "tradition does have claims on us, history does limit us," Elshtain suggests that, while taking care to avoid "senti-mentalization," women might unite around the "moral and political im-perative" of a feminism committed to "maternal thinking." She terms it "social feminism."[42] She also reconsiders the feminist proposition that "the personal is political," in which she discerns a harmful erosion of the dis-tinction between private and public spheres, which tends to dissolve the world of intimate and caring relationships and open them to state intru-sion; her feminism would seek a public voice through which women might express an ethic of care. Elshtain grounds her analysis of feminist claims in practice—a term she uses not, as some feminist theorists do, in the sense of "activism," but as it applies to the practical considerations of human exis-tence, including motherhood and family life. She would like to see more of what she feels feminism has suppressed: "open reflective discussion of heterosexual ties and eroticism, the needs and identities of children con-sidered as ends-in-themselves and not merely as means, and accounts of the normative meaning and richness of being a parent."[43]

It is true that Elshtain brings to feminism a dimension that has tended to be slighted. In their mission to repair the world so as to make it safer and more equitable for women, feminists have sometimes avoided dealing with women's important traditional concerns. Using a very powerful example, Sophocles' *Antigone*—"the woman who throws sand in the machine of arro-gant public power"—Elshtain reminds other feminists that public and pri-vate obligations are not easily reconciled, as Antigone's fate demonstrates. For Elshtain, "Antigone embodies a civic revolt, action undertaken in de-fense of exigencies that emerge from the private sphere. The entire history of feminism is in part a story of such forms of revolt."[44]

Elshtain is not alone among feminists in recognizing that conflicts involving moral claims are part of what it means to be human. While some have rejected her analysis as "maternalist," others have cited her work in their own efforts to create a more nuanced understanding of mothering, family, and "empathetic caregiving." Since the 1980s, numerous feminist writers have celebrated maternity and motherhood, so much so that Ellen Ross, in a review essay on what she terms "the oldest vocation," notes a tendency to neglect "the ways in which the love and care of children is, for everyone, an open invitation not only to unending hard work but also to trouble and sorrow, if not usually [as in Ross's case] to tragedy."[45]

What Ross found important to feminist scholarship on mothering was recognition of the full scope of its impact on women. She states,

Looking at mothers as "subjects" means learning about the details of their daily material work; about the quality of their feelings for their children; about changes mothering brings in relationships with jobs, men, friends, and lovers; about the public activities and political positions stimulated by women's experiences as caretakers of children; about the survival and nurturing skills of single mothers, mothers of big families, and those with very sick or disabled children; about styles of child care and the meaning of mothering and fathering in different regions, cultures, and communities; about the tangle of social and legal rights and needs dividing biological and foster mothers in a national system that is growing exponentially. And what does motherhood signify to women who have had a period of infertility, who have experienced the death of a child . . . or whose children arrived through adoption? Without full recognition of the phenomenology of mothering the ability of feminist scholarship to comprehend the scope of women's lives today is much diminished.[46]

Even while questioning Elshtain and other "conservative feminists," leading feminist academics such as Judith Stacey have attempted to respond constructively to the problems they identify. While interpreting Elshtain's work as part of a "great leap backwards," an "internal backlash" that strengthens antifeminism, Stacey notes that such criticism "speaks from and to a reservoir of unmet needs for intimacy, nurturance, and security that feminists experience as much as other women and men." Stacey also rejects the view of female socialization that, to her mind, "Elshtain and others criticize correctly for portraying women only as victims, robots or fools." She, too, recognizes that, "resenting the transhistoric female responsibility for unilateral nurturance of children," feminists have given insufficient attention to the question of children's needs.[47]

In a 1987 review essay on "postfeminism" and antifeminism, Stacey and Deborah Rosenfelt acknowledged the "divide between single feminists and those in couples, between parents and those without children." It was not enough for feminists to focus on an economic agenda; they needed also to "develop cultural forms that fill some of the same longings for intimacy, interdependency, and emotional security that most heterosexuals try to satisfy in marriage, however oppressive to women its unequal relations of power." They called for more attention to "forms of committed human relations," within a "feminism neither afraid to exercise its capacity for self-criticism nor forgetful of its liberating vision."[48] Feminist scholars have responded abundantly.

However sympathetic to maternalism and so-called "difference feminism," feminist theorists do not want the promotion of an ethic of care to undermine their argument for changing the social structures and family relations that have served women badly. Kathleen Jones, for example, comments that Elshtain tends to focus only on the positive aspects of the family. In her proposal for democratizing relations of authority by developing a new form of "compassionate authority," Jones points to the need for "reworking both the structure and the ethos of intimate relations, including 'the family.'" Birte Siim chides Elshtain for envisioning an "ideal type" of family and failing to analyze "the everyday life of concrete families as institutions full of contradictions and inequalities." But both she and Jones, along with Kathy Ferguson and others, share Elshtain's concern for the intrusion of economic institutions and bureaucratic state power on individuals and families. My own hope is that the work of Elshtain and other critics mindful of the importance of familial relations will serve to bring public discourse to bear on the interdependence of all human beings. The rugged individual, or self-made person, is a myth, whatever his or her sex. Changes in gender-defined family and societal arrangements that reflect this reality are essential. Selective use of "sex-responsive" as well as "sex-blind" ways of pursuing sexual equality, as Alison Jaggar suggests, can offer feminists the possibility of "having it both ways"; that is, of demanding "a fair share of the pie, carcinogenic though it ultimately may be," while also seeking transformation toward healthier fare.[49]

The controversy over Elshtain and the complicated reception of her work and that of other "difference feminists" provide evidence against the myth of a monolithic ideology of women's studies.[50] Numerous other academic feminists call for more internal criticism and proceed to offer it. Susan Stanford Friedman calls for rejecting orthodoxy in teaching and in building theory. Feminist principles should include "resisting the temptation to impose a feminist orthodoxy that students do not feel free to critique." Feminist practice should extend to pluralism in the historiography of feminism itself. In a study of competing narratives of feminist history, Friedman does not refrain from identifying the "will-to-power," reductionism, and/or contradictions she finds in the work of such highly regarded scholars as Toril Moi, Joan Scott, and Gayatri Spivak. Her conclusion is a call for a pluralism that encompasses both "the need to make history by writing history as a political act; and the need to problematize that activity so as to avoid the creation of grand narratives that reproduce the totalizing histories of winners in which the stories of losers are lost. . . . I promote both/and." It is important, in Friedman's view, for multiple histories of multiple feminisms to be written, for this historiography will help to shape feminism's future. Another well-known women's studies scholar, Elaine Marks, grounding her critique in French studies, declares that she would like to "displace a fundamentalist, literal, and political feminism by a more heretical, imaginative, and poetical-ontological feminist inquiry."[51]

The feminist theorist bell hooks, in *Talking Back*, discusses the daring it takes to disagree and the importance of "defiant speech" in making growth possible. Calling for more feminist scholarship and open discussion about men and masculinity, she notes the tendency of feminists either to silence themselves or to "raise these issues in ways that alienate, that convey ridicule, contempt, or our own uncertainty." She would like to see feminist scholars "mapping out a terrain where women can speak to and about men in ways that challenge but do not diminish." She also "talks back" to other feminists on the topic of identity politics. She questions the "focus on self" not only of "privileged white women" but also of women of color, who "began to focus attention on identity in static and non-productive ways." She risks calling the foundational statement of the Combahee River Collective on radical black women's politics "very problematic." Quoting Jenny Bourne, who took Jewish women (a group with whom she associates herself) to task for permitting the "discovery of identity" itself to become an end, hooks challenges feminists of all colors to use "confession and memory" as means to political awareness, without "getting trapped in identity politics."[52]

The writer Michele Wallace also points out the difficulty of differing publicly with a sister feminist. Criticizing hooks in the *Women's Review of Books*, she admits the pressure toward silence, which stems from fear of unintended consequences. "Could the exposure of the excesses of one prominent black feminist scholar call into question the intentions of all other black feminists?" Wallace takes the chance of "sacrific[ing] the questionable solidarity of black feminist discourse" and suggests that hooks's work is both superficial and self-serving.[53]

Feminist fault-finding targets other intellectual flaws as well. Identifying one of the potential problems in interdisciplinary studies, the political scientist Virginia Sapiro chides some feminist scholars for using the terminology of political theory as "symbolic flags" rather than "analytical concepts." She also charges them with demonstrating insufficient interest in the work of feminist political scientists and the social sciences generally. "Political science–based feminist theorists often voice frustration with feminist theory that ignores the knowledge gained from the long-standing debates in political theory, even within the 'male-stream.'" Author of an introductory text for women's studies, Sapiro has wrestled with the challenge of "competing explanations" and distinguishes between interdisciplinary and multidisciplinary work. Sapiro's criticism of her colleagues appears in one of many books that capture the spirit of the statement "Practicing conflict is also practicing feminism."[54] Like other academic endeavors, women's studies advances through challenge and response.

Looking back from the 1990s, Marianne Hirsch recalls hearing a colleague at a women's studies conference in 1982 declare, "It is so gratifying to see that feminism has evolved to the point where feminists can criticize each other." Linda S. Kauffman agrees, commenting that "feminism's greatest strength has always been its capacity for self-critique, and it would be a great pity to see that capacity muted by the insistence on consensus." She remarks that "sexism infects both genders; as a discursive construct, can't we finally put to rest that *bête noire*, 'the white male'?" Other feminist scholars call for recuperation of the nondiscursive white male and heterosexual relationships as well. Elshtain calls for a revision of both public and private life, for *"the redemption of everyday life,"* which would include the "transformation of men as well as women" and the reconstruction of human relationships. Arguing that "physiological sexual difference will always dictate a differential cultural construction of gender until such time as the reproduction of the species within a given culture ceases to be an issue," Karen Offen calls for "rethinking and reclaiming sexual difference— and the category women—in a way that avoids the construction of dominance/subordination hierarchies." In an essay entitled "Politics of Intimacy: Heterosexuality, Love, and Power," Robyn Rowland—after acknowledging her awareness of the continuing violence against women—seeks to envision "strategies for living a radical feminist heterosexuality. Feminism is not just critique. We are also involved in 'anticipatory vision'; in constructing a new kind of society with feminist ethics and politics as its base. Part of that vision must include healthy, loving relationships with men."[55] As suggested also in chapter 6, theorizing about "difference" increasingly includes efforts to understand the social construction of masculinity, and the diverse "positionalities" of men. It is also important to acknowledge the positive changes already made in men's behavior.

The charge of "man-hating" in women's studies is just one of the criticisms that Carol Sternhell addresses in a front-page review in the *Women's Review of Books*. Discussing the works of Patai and Koertge and Sommers, as well as Maher and Tetreault's study of the dynamics of the feminist classroom, Sternhell begins by establishing her credentials as a feminist through her years as a student, then a professor of journalism, and later a director of a women's studies program. She conveys well the sense of exhilaration she found in the "intellectually rigorous" courses that propelled her into a career as a feminist scholar, and her dismay over the "oppression olympics, the identity politics promenade" she encountered at a meeting of the NWSA. This organization, she states, "depresses all the feminists I know. The mind-numbing litany of race/class/gender/sex-preference/age/ethnicity/ability/weight/dry-cleaning-fluid allergy often seems to substitute both for serious thought and for serious political action." This is hardly mindless praise for feminist dogma, and its prominence helps to disprove Patai and Koertge's assertion that "reforms are not likely to come from within."[56]

While facing up to these academic feminist flaws, Sternhell finds in the books under review a "portrait [that] is unrepresentative, partial, a series of snapshots taken on a very bad day." One book (Sommers's) she found "so mean-spirited and dishonest it's easy to dismiss"; the Patai and Koertge at times accurate but "lopsided, incomplete." Pointing out that "women's studies, like any academic field, can be mined for closed-mindedness and infighting, but also for evidence of brilliant scholarship and great teaching," she counters point after point in the two censorious books. While finding herself "stunned" by Sommers's depiction of university life, which portrays the inverse of her own experience, Sternhell suffers the greatest "discomfort" with Maher and Tetreault's endorsement of "positional pedagogy." Acknowledging that the "more interactive, less hierarchical" teaching that they recommend is admirable, she also points out that "these methods, and the understanding that all knowledge is partial, are familiar to anyone concerned with progressive education." It is their apparent approval of a classroom where learning was seen not as individual achievement but as validation of personal experience, where "all anyone seems to talk about . . . is race/class/gender, etc.," that, Sternhell declares, "left me feeling depressed. . . . If I really thought women's studies could be reduced to a sharing and sparring of 'positions,' I swear I'd give it all up tomorrow. Maybe today."[57] Academic feminist criticism of women's studies is alive and well in the field's leading organ for substantial book reviews.

Feminist criticism of women's studies is not confined to feminist journals, however. Catharine Stimpson, a leader in the field for over two decades, nationally known as a literary critic, novelist, and public intellectual, and founding editor of *Signs*, has shared her concerns widely. Writing for nonspecialists in *dissent*, Stimpson followed a sketch of more than two decades of women's studies' development with a candid portrait of her "doubts and worries" about its future. "Women's studies has made mistakes," she admits, "that have left it open to doubt. To its unheralded credit, analyzing them is a feature of the serious feminist literature. I am unquenchably in debt to feminism for a moral vision, blueprints for social change, psychological support, and vitality. However, academic work demands the interrogation of moral visions, blueprints for change, and ideas. A syllabus cannot be an agenda. . . . Women's studies falters when it gives up the necessary tension between the academy and any social and political movement, and baldly subordinates 'studies' to 'women.'"[58]

Stimpson identifies a number of problematic tendencies in women's studies. These include the oversimplification of complex historical and social phenomena into such categories as "patriarchy" or the "iron triangle, 'race/class/gender,'" as well as overreliance on anecdote, experience, and nurturance in the classroom. Critics fault women's studies, she notes, for having "ignored and evaded the power of nature in the construction of gender" and for "refus[ing] to admit how necessary to society the legal, heterosexual family is." She calls for more open discussion of these issues. Questioning the prevalence of identity politics that divides women, Stimpson regrets that "very few claim a place in the center." Describing herself as a Second Waver and a centrist, she attributes more nuanced views to her current students, who she anticipates will work out many feminist complexities in the generational succession to a "Third Wave." Despite her concerns, Stimpson is optimistic about the future of the younger cohort, whose lives in a global information society include a legacy from women's studies which gives them access to ideas and options denied to earlier generations of women: "I retain my faith that women's studies is helping to redesign democracy and the mind."[59]

The Importance of a Longer View

Generational succession is driving numerous feminist scholars to rethink the "paradigms" of women's studies in new contexts. As women's studies programs and their faculty mature, there is greater tolerance for living with paradox. The books of the 1990s devoted to exploring contentions within feminism demonstrate that it is now easier to be a centrist and that self-censorship has declined. Even Andrea Dworkin, often cited as the author of extreme views on female sexuality, has called for a more balanced view, citing the need for a feminist "middle." "I am a radical, but I'm a radical who believes that you have to have the whole spectrum of people. You need your mainstream feminists."[60]

Like Dworkin, women's studies practitioners need to contextualize their own claims and to help students overcome their own sometimes over-personalized and presentist tendencies to rush to judgment of people and positions without adequate knowledge of the past, or without supporting evidence. A lot more history would help. Studies of subjectivity and sexuality are obviously vital in a field that seeks to understand and enhance linkages and interdependence among disparate aspects of life. It is also understandable that students today are attracted to studies of reproductive technologies, fluid sexualities, popular culture, and spirituality, to repeat a list presented in a discussion of "generations of feminism" led by Ruth Perry, women's studies director at the Massachusetts Institute of Technology.[61] But these topics, too, must be contextualized within the history of women. Women's studies is an important part of the history of feminism, and history is essential to understanding feminism in all its diverse aspects.

One of the problems of women's studies is that its field is so large. The image evoked by the metaphor of a blind person describing an elephant does not even approach its scope. Everyone touches some part of the body of women's studies; everyone feels qualified to speak and even to teach: an applicant for a faculty position in the program I once chaired actually offered as his chief qualification the statement "My wife is a woman." Probably a little more humility before the immensity of the territory and the task would do us all good. It is of questionable value to encourage an undergraduate student without training in history or philosophy to think up "a theory of her own."[62] Feminism is a world historical movement, and women's studies, as its academic expression, faces a vast and vital task that will absorb generations of scholars in research and produce scholarship beyond our imagining today.

The other necessary charge requires change on everyone's part: It is critical that scholars in women's studies speak more often *with* and not *past* their opponents—and vice versa. This need is increasingly voiced; it remains a challenge important to the future of women's studies and higher education. Ignorance represents perhaps a greater problem for women's studies than does open hostility, which can be answered with intellectual tools, traditional and new.[63]

As I have tried to show throughout this book, women's studies is anything but single-minded. In the face of evidence to the contrary, the continuing charge that it is can only reflect the limited knowledge, narrow focus, or hostile intentions of the observer. Problems can be acknowledged with understanding and regret, or with satisfaction and anger. The tone of the work is revealing. I know that I, too, risk having my words lifted from their context and quoted with intent to harm. But I am convinced that women's studies is fundamentally sound and resilient. As Susan B. Anthony said of the movement for woman suffrage: "Failure is impossible." The institutionalization of women's studies and the serious scholarship of its practitioners assure its future, despite current battles.

The culture wars, of which many attacks on women's studies from the outside constitute only a part, have a long history. The historians Joyce Appleby, Lynn Hunt, and Margaret Jacob, cited in the discussion of objectivity in chapter 3, trace them back to the Enlightenment. A historian of the twentieth-century United States, William Issel, places the disavowal of feminism that gained prominence in the mid-1980s in the context of the rise of a conservative political movement traceable to controversies of the 1920s, buoyed by 1930s criticism of the New Deal, laissez-faire traditionalist opposition to twentieth-century liberalism, the politics of anti-Communism and the Cold War, Barry Goldwater, condemnation of the 1960s counterculture, and ultimately, Phyllis Schlafly and the political action committees that defeated the Equal Rights Amendment. The conservative agenda in national politics for much of this century has coalesced over cultural as much as economic issues. Ellen Messer-Davidow argues convincingly that the conservative critique today is less a defense of tradition than a concerted "attack on liberalized higher education [manufactured] by means of a right-wing apparatus dedicated to making radical cultural change." Its goal is to "impose its vision of America on all of us," she declares. To this end, it has done precisely what it accuses Left-oriented scholars—including academic feminists—of doing; that is, it has created (through its think tanks) "'expert' knowledge" explicitly to advance its political purposes.[64]

Antifeminism is as old as the "woman question," as is the history of denunciation of movements advocating women's rights as separatist, man-hating, and decadent. Mary Louise Roberts has shown how the perception in World War I France that "this civilization . . . no longer has sexes" became a "primary referent for the ruin of civilization itself." Contests within feminist movements themselves, especially on grounds of class, also have a long heritage. Feminism was castigated by major socialist figures as a "deviation" in the class struggle of the late nineteenth and early twentieth century. Socialist women leaders devoted themselves to "tear[ing] socialist and proletarian women away from feminist confusionism." It is also useful, as a corrective to current concern about generational conflict over the "f-word," to recall the reaction against feminism in the interwar period. No less a feminist hero than Virginia Woolf, as Karen Offen notes, found *feminism* a troubling term. In 1938 Woolf suggested "incinerating" the word *feminist*, which she described as "an old word, a vicious and corrupt word that has done much harm in its day and is now obsolete." She went on, Offen points out, to write "one of the most unequivocally radical 'feminist' tracts of all time, a work which joined the issue of sex discrimination in the professions with that of racism and other forms of discrimination all as mutually-reinforcing sources of war."[65] A long perspective is essential to appreciation of the condition of women, feminism, and women's studies in higher education.

Separating criticism of women's studies from the many challenges to feminism generally and to the sociopolitical context in which it has developed and flourished is no less difficult than assessing its impact on the university. The latter will be the theme of the next, and final, chapter of this book. Women's studies attempts to "tell the truth" about women. It thereby runs head-on into an offensive by traditionalists, as they are labeled by Appleby, Hunt, and Jacob in their defense of the discipline of history against the "all-out war on multiculturalism and the democratization of the university." "Demanding a return to the old days when truth was absolute and dissent adjudicated by those like themselves," the opponents of new ideas see women's studies as a threat. As these authors say of postmodernists: "One man's truth is another woman's falsity."[66]

The opponents of women's studies would close the many windows it opens, allowing winds of change to enter. Women's studies has participated in the transformation of understanding about the nature of knowledge. If a new consensus should emerge from the knowledge wars, it seems likely that scholars who study women and gender will contribute greatly to its formulation. This is only one of the many changes attributable to the presence of new women, new questions, new scholarship, and the new field of women's studies in the academy.

9

Perspective and Purpose

Asked to reflect on the successes and future prospects of women's studies, the historian Gerda Lerner declared in 1988 that "trying to pin the field down at this juncture 'would be like trying to describe the Renaissance— ten years after it began. It's a gigantic intellectual transformation.'" Whether alluding to the Renaissance or the Enlightenment, to Copernicus or Darwin, several scholars have compared the impact of women's studies to the major intellectual transformations that mark human history. In the sense that such great moments in human experience give rise to an immense flowering of art, literature, and science, and to the challenging of previously accepted authorities of text or tradition, these comparisons are apt. The term *feminist enlightenment*, first suggested by the late sociologist Jessie Bernard, is appropriate to those meanings, although not insofar as it may evoke a search for universal laws or rules to define the world. Feminist enlightenment stands instead for the mental "click," the spiritual conversion, the realization of a new capacity for vision that illuminates the dark and enlarges the landscape. By posing new questions and seeking answers that place women in the center, it allows altogether new ways of viewing women and the world to emerge. An important question about women's studies is the extent to which this light penetrates academic and public cultures.[1]

In 1963, when Clark Kerr told his Godkin Lecture audience at Harvard University that "universities in America are at a hinge of history: while connected with their past, they are swinging in another direction," he was concerned with the effects of the relatively recent recognition that "new knowledge is the most important factor in economic and social growth." As a direct result, the university was assuming a new role in society. It was being called upon to educate a much larger proportion of the population than ever before. There is no indication, in the first edition of the publication that resulted from Kerr's lectures, that he foresaw that a quarter century later women would constitute more than half of that enlarged student body. Nor did he envision that within a very few years, new faculty specializing in studies for and about women would claim a place in the future "City of Intellect." In a 1982 postscript to the book's third edition, he noted that a higher proportion of students were then women or minorities; but he added, speaking of this and other recent developments, that "none of these is a fundamental change." Quoting the comment of an English classicist from turn-of-the-century Cambridge that "nothing should ever be done for the first time," Kerr predicted that the faculty's "guild mentality" meant that they would resist change. He hoped, however, that the great universities would adapt to three significant new conditions, which he identified as "growth, shifting academic emphases, and involvement in the life of society."[2]

There was nothing in the history of the modern university that prepared it for the qualitative changes that vast quantitative demographic shifts in the composition of its student body and faculty, innovative intellectual inquiry, and new engagement in the community would entail. In concluding this study, this final chapter will assess the impact of academic feminism, or women's studies—a notable component of these developments which attracted many of the new faculty and students—on the current and future purposes of American colleges and universities. It will look at the influence of women's studies and its advocates on academic culture, on faculty, students, and pedagogy, and on the curriculum, the "canon," and liberal education, noting as well its repercussions in the public intellectual community. Finally, it will attempt to assess the longer-range influence of the very savvy, sometimes sassy, and always serious and scholarly feminist women associated with women's studies.

In 1983, when *Academe*, the publication of the venerable American Association of University Professors, devoted its back-to-school issue to "feminism in the academy," the lead editorial observed that "the new feminism has already changed the way the academy must think about all sorts of important topics—politics, children, wages, morality, thinking itself."

The issue was dedicated to "that revolution." *Academe* observed that "this new feminism—like any other major structure for thinking about our world—has begun to break down and reorganize old intellectual categories and disciplinary boundaries." *Academe* anticipated that the academy would change directions "after the academic disciplines absorb the implications of this important contribution to our intellectual history."[3]

The changing directions of the academy have been the subject of much contention since Kerr gave his lectures on its "uses." Allan Bloom and his sympathizers and successors notwithstanding, the dominant voices of higher education in this country have applauded the democratization of higher learning and have contributed heavily to achieving that end. Taking as indicative one of the first promotional pieces at hand as I write—the winter 1996 list of publications of the Association of American Colleges and Universities (AACU)—I count, among the nine new or recent "releases" featured on its cover, seven that present some visual or verbal cue to changes congenial to if not directly influenced by the new demographics, among which the rapid increase of women in virtually all capacities stands out.[4]

In 1986 the Carnegie Foundation for the Advancement of Teaching published an important report based on a survey of colleges and universities in the United States. Its dominant theme was the conflicts it found in all areas of academic life between individual interests and community needs. The tensions which the Carnegie Foundation found pervasive in higher education reflected a "decline in 'cultural coherence'" that accompanied increasing diversity in American society. The confusion over goals which the Carnegie report noted reflected a conflict over purposes. It was alleged that a new careerism and diminished interest in the liberal arts had accompanied the shift from elite to mass higher education. But while women students have swelled enrollments in undergraduate business majors, they have also flocked to courses in the humanities and social sciences, not least those that incorporate new perspectives and new knowledge about women. (In the late 1970s at San Diego State, we found that the largest number of women's studies students by major came from the business school.) The Carnegie report called for making connections between education for competency and "commitment to community," for "balance . . . between individual interests and shared concerns." Its author hoped to see a revised general education with a strong liberal arts core, including a section entitled "Identity: The Search for Meaning." As reports from women's studies students and faculty show, this is precisely what women's studies offers. In academic feminist jargon, this constitutes the "connected learning" that is said to be a primary attraction of the field to its students. It signifies learning that is connected meaningfully to women's lives.[5]

What feminism claims for women is justice and the social changes necessary to make the attainment of justice a practical possibility. What women's studies asks from the university is for women to be heard in the processes and places where knowledge is created, taught, and preserved. This requires a university that accepts the feminist perspective, with its moral claim and political stance, as a legitimate contribution toward understanding the universe. To place academic feminism within the history of higher education, I find it useful to refer to the philosopher Alasdair MacIntyre's conception of three stages in the development of the university, which parallel his "three rival versions of moral enquiry." In this scheme, the modern university began, especially in Scotland and the United States, as a "preliberal" institution, devoted to rational inquiry and to preparing an educated (male) public, but requiring as a "precondition a high degree of homogeneity in fundamental belief." By deliberately excluding potential dissenters, it could pursue rational inquiry justified by consensus on its moral (and religious) purpose. "In the United States formal and informal pressures ensured that in the antebellum colleges no nontheological utilitarian was appointed to a teaching position." "Preferments and promotions" were used to "ensure that upholders of the consensus . . . occupied the relevant professorial chairs."[6]

In MacIntyre's history, the preliberal university of "constrained agreements" gave way to the liberal university. The liberal university was shaped by a corrective argument about the injustice of its exclusions but also by the "false premises . . . that human rationality is such . . . that, if freed from external constraints and most notably from the constraints imposed by religious and moral tests, it will produce not only progress in enquiry but also agreement among all rational persons as to what the rationally justified conclusions of such enquiry are." The result of "institutional tolerance of limitless disagreement encounters in the areas of morality and theology standpoints" has been excluding "substantive moral and theological enquiry" from the liberal university. Lacking consensus on moral philosophy, and unable to "appeal to some specific rational understanding of how human goods are to be ordered and the place within that ordering of the goods of enquiry," the university is in "disarray" and cannot respond to its critics. Once again, fundamental change is needed.[7]

What to do? MacIntyre notes the prescriptions of Bennett, Bloom, and company, especially the recommendation that a curriculum of great books be restored, but points out that this recommendation is flawed on at least two grounds. One is the fact that these texts can be read many ways, and "until the problems of how they are to be read have received an answer, such lists do not rise to the status of a concrete proposal." But making his point in another way that is especially relevant to the contemporary university, MacIntyre notes that advocates of the "Great Books curriculum often defend it as a way of restoring to us and to our students what they speak of as *our* cultural tradition; but we are in fact the inheritors, if that is the right word, of a number of rival and incompatible traditions and there is no way of either selecting a list of books to be read or advancing a determinate account of how they are to be read, interpreted, and elucidated which does not involve taking a partisan stand in the conflict of traditions." Not only does a fair reading require recognition of past disagreements of interpretation, but "there is no way of reading them in terms of the conflicts in which they participate independently of the reader's participation in these same conflicts or at least in the analogous conflicts of the present."[8]

MacIntyre does not make explicit the ironic point that the very timelessness that the traditionalists associate with "great books" makes them participants in today's disagreements over great issues. He goes on, however, to situate those conflicts within the context of the three versions of moral inquiry that are the central topic of his work—the encyclopaedist tradition of the eighteenth- and nineteenth-century Enlightenments, the genealogical tradition associated with Nietzsche, and the Thomistic "tradition-informed dialectical enterprise"—pointing out that texts read from these differing perspectives would present conflicting views of the nature of truth, being, and the self and its identity and place, as well as competing concepts of how the world and its goods are to be ordered. These conflicts could and should be taught.[9]

In MacIntyre's formulation, it is time for the emergence of a third type of university, which would become a "place of constrained disagreement, of imposed participation in conflict, in which a central responsibility of higher education would be to initiate students into conflict." Instead of trying to provide a neutral, objective, or balanced professorial presentation, each faculty member would take part "as the protagonist of a particular point of view." While "advanc[ing] enquiry from within that particular point of view," the intellectual rivals would contend with each other and "test and retest" their own theses. Students in this new university of constrained disagreement would learn to "read scrupulously and carefully in order to possess a text in a way which enables them to arrive at independent interpretative judgments," ideally also learning to "protect themselves against too facile an acceptance of—or indeed too facile a rejection of—their teachers' interpretations." (This type of institution supposedly existed once, MacIntyre argues, pointing to the thirteenth-century University of Paris.)[10]

Defending himself against anticipated charges of utopianism, MacIntyre goes on to show how the form of the lecture as well as the lecturer might also be changed in a university reconceptualized along these lines. It is past time, he argues, to recognize that the revolt of students in the 1960s and early 1970s, with its call for relevance, was a "response to the barrenness of a [liberal] university which had deprived itself of substantive moral enquiry, a barrenness already diagnosed in the nineteenth century by Nietzsche" and others.[11] I have borrowed from MacIntyre because I find that his work advances our understanding of the crisis of meaning in today's university, of what women's studies can bring to higher education, and of why its antagonists object so strongly to its offerings.

For feminists, discussion of moral purpose must recognize that notions of morality have historically been formulated in ways that supported male dominance. As a result, feminist theorists are rightly cautious about its usage, sometimes preferring the term *ethical*. Nevertheless, "making moral problems public," as Kathryn Pyne Addelson notes, can lead to action to bring about change, within the academy and within the community.[12] The historical subordination of women, I believe, is an *ethical* problem that women's studies raises. Women's studies, in my view, is trying to restore a form of moral inquiry to the university. Reforming our conceptualization of basic moral and political values is a central theme of academic feminism. Like Olympe de Gouges, in the language of liberal humanism, it adds "the rights of women" to the "rights of man." Like Angelina Grimké, in the pursuit of justice for all, it asserts that "human beings have *rights*, because they are *moral* beings." Along with women at the Fourth World Conference on Women at Beijing in 1995, it declares that women's rights are human rights.[13]

From the point of view of some feminists (as discussed in chapter 6), liberal humanism necessarily precludes attainment of equality, unless women were to become men. For Man, the abstract individual of the Declaration of the Rights of Man and Citizen, turns out on analysis to have been—in the eighteenth century and ever after—embodied as male. Failing that, they argue, women face an impossible paradox in claiming their rights.[14] What is required is to reconceive the notion of the individual, of liberalism and liberal institutions, and to transform the university and society into a pluralistic community that cares for human brings in their embodied diversity. In MacIntyre's university of "constrained disagreement," women's studies would be one among many (more or less) equal participants. Students would get the preparation they need to think critically about the difficult and complex issues they face as citizens of a diverse and rapidly changing global society. This would put a stop to the pretense of some critics that ideologies had been eliminated from the university until brought back illegitimately by Marxists or feminists or the proponents of multiculturalism.

Jaroslav Pelikan, in his 1992 reexamination of Cardinal Newman's classic nineteenth-century work *The Idea of the University*, quotes the famous theologian as warning, "Great minds need elbow room. . . . If you insist that in their speculations, researches, or conclusions in their particular science . . . they must get up all that divines have said or the multitude believed upon religious matters, you simply crush and stamp out the flame within them and they can do nothing at all." The university must also provide an environment supportive of diverse collegial communities, including those on the borders between conventional disciplines, among which Pelikan cites women's studies as well as biochemistry, mathematical economics, and comparative literature. Offering his "idea of the university" as an intellectual community that transcends traditional boundaries, he comments on Newman's discourses, putting each in a contemporary context, reassessing such notions as "knowledge its own end" in the light of the Holocaust, and adding to the virtues of "imperial intellect" a "dimension of personal caring" and a concern for moral consequences.[15] These represent traditional concerns of women. They are also goals for an academic field that seeks to demonstrate connections between intellectual, personal, and community lives.

Countering Dominant Intellectual Trends

This objective, however, contravenes the dominant trends in many disciplines, which for half of the twentieth century developed in an antithetical direction. In a review of what he terms "the new rigorism in the human sciences" during the middle decades of the century, the historian Carl E. Schorske states that "ethics, aesthetics, metaphysics, and politics were all for a time equally excluded as the source of pseudo-problems that could not be formulated or addressed with the rigorous canons of epistemological reliability developed by and out of science." Schorske refers here specifically to the discipline of philosophy but finds similar tendencies in other branches of the humanities and social sciences. Overall, the "passage [was] from range to rigor," and the disciplines "rebuilt their foundations and postwar professional identities on analytic methods, if to differing degrees. To do so, they had shrunk, marginalized, or extruded some of the value concerns of their traditional subject matter."[16]

When waves of discontent with such truncated, scientized fields of study began to surface in the 1960s and 1970s, women, although slowly at first, caught the current. It is easy for those of us who are intellectual "women of a certain age" to recall when the greatest compliment we might hear was "You think like a man." In 1970, when F[lorence] N[ightingale] David, a British-born professor of statistics at the University of California, told a group of female graduate students that they could safely ignore "sexual politics" in the university because all it took for success was "being two hundred percent as good as a man," and that they could do it because she had done it (receiving honors from the king for statistical work that helped England defend against Nazi rockets), she represented the thinking of the second stage in women's higher education, its "coeducation" phase. Give us access to the men's curriculum and we can do it, maybe even better, they said. "Getting gendered" in those days meant becoming an "honorary male." We "thought like a man" and were expected to do so. (Sometimes, as the philosopher of education Jane Roland Martin recalls, we were even addressed as men. The card accompanying a bouquet she received on being elected president of the Philosophy of Education Society was addressed to Dr. James Martin.) In the third stage, introduced by women's studies, gender awareness means challenging received intellectual authority rather than identifying with it, and claiming it for women.[17]

Historians have pointed out how the presence of women as college and university faculty declined between the early and middle periods of the twentieth century and began to increase again only after the resurgence of feminism in the late 1960s. Major gains showed up in the mid-1970s, as the cohort of 1960s graduate students entered the professorial ranks. The proportion of women students at all levels rose steadily. By 1994 it was reported that women constituted 59 percent of undergraduates, outnumbered males among students seeking advanced degrees, and received about 44 percent of all doctorates awarded to United States citizens—compared to only 19 percent in 1973. The proportion of women among full-time faculty and administrators rose significantly. In the nation's largest system of four-year higher education, the California State University, between 1975 and 1995 women increased from 25 to 38 percent among faculty and from 34.6 to 53 percent in the professional and administrative ranks. According to one report, between 1976 and 1993 the number of women among full-time faculty in the United States rose by 70 percent.[18]

Not all the new women were New Women—that is, women who manifested a changing consciousness and behavior. Some, however, did fit Roger Kimball's definition of "tenured radicals."[19] Whether women were representing or challenging the traditional dichotomous definitions of femininity, their increasing visibility on campus brought new interests to bear in the teaching, research, and service dimensions of university life, affecting important aspects of educational and institutional policy and practice. Women began to address in new ways long-accepted, and often hierarchical, dichotomous concepts, including those of mind/body, theory/practice, personal/professional, competitive/collaborative, senior/junior faculty, departmental/interdisciplinary, faculty/student, and, in particular, women/men. To cite a few examples mentioned by feminist scholars, bell hooks argues against the mind/body split, calls for more passion in the classroom, and takes "radical" faculty to task for failing to practice the engagement they preach. Carol Thomas Neely describes the intellectual process of analyzing anew male and female characters in Shakespeare in order, for instance, to "disrupt the neat division between good women and bad men" in *Othello*. Madelon Sprengnether explores how her observation that women faculty were "wildly unmentored" led her to rethink competition and collaboration in peer professional relationships. Martha A. Ackelsberg and Kathryn Pyne Addelson reject altogether the liberal acceptance of competition. Well-known academics lead national efforts to influence legislation on welfare reform. Dale Bauer speaks of the feminist use of the personal voice in the academy as "driving up the stakes of professional commitment." As the writer Nora Ephron put it in a commencement speech at Wellesley College in 1996, many academic feminists say, "Take it personally."[20]

The academy today provides tens of thousands of women an opportunity to speak from the platform; and women's studies offers a singularly receptive ambiance and audience for their messages. No longer are women in the academy required to look on "through the tiny, narrowing slits of the outer gallery walls," as if segregated from the men in an Orthodox Jewish synagogue—an image evoked by Andrew Lakritz in his study of identity and the authority to speak. More and more women possess what he calls "the chutzpa of an ambassador" needed to "storm the inner circle." Some speak in a voice that violates academic traditions of social decorum.[21]

Good girls no longer, feminist scholars may even, along with Barbara Tomlinson, advocate open expression of "textual vehemence," legitimizing language uncommon in academic usage as necessary to overcome conventions that have served to "deny them the dignity and moral force of being angry." Matters previously dismissed as "women's issues" have become important ingredients in university debate. Women's studies scholars pursue research on such topics as abused children and battered wives, which requires, as Jessie Bernard puts it, "the reintroduction of the blacked-out suffering." Borrowing terms from Robert Merton, Bernard notes that "sociological euphemisms" can no longer hide the "social sadisms" that occur as realities of women's (and men's) daily lives.[22]

Campus-wide and system-wide committees did not begin to undertake serious efforts to develop "family-friendly" policies to facilitate the combining of academic work and family life until a generation after the sociologist Arlie Russell Hochschild had compared the differing impacts of university expectations on the struggles of young academic women and of their male counterparts. Reflecting on the university's "imperial relation to the family," she argued that the latter served as the former's "welfare agency." By the 1990s, many colleges and universities not only provided childcare facilities but had also started to create "designer clocks for academic careers." These actions are signals of a sea change in academic culture brought about by its changing sex ratio and feminist claims. The new knowledge and new attitudes introduced by women's studies have encouraged expectations that women's issues should be a normal part of the discussions in the academy. "Work-family issues, dependent care, and a more flexible definition of family are now on the table," states Donna Shavlik, director of the Office of Women in Higher Education of the American Council on Education. Mariam Chamberlain sees the emergence of women's studies as the "most powerful force affecting women in higher education."[23]

Shavlik and Chamberlain speak from positions of institutional leadership. The journalist Paula Kamen, traveling about the country talking about feminism with more than two hundred diverse women and men, mostly members of the "twentysomething" generation, suggests that women's studies serves as "the reproductive organ of the women's movement." Women seeking "empowerment"—a key motivation for students—look to women's studies instructors as advocates and exemplars. Despite continuing warnings about a "chilly climate" for women on campus, and allegations that women may be "marooned on Gilligan's Island" by the work of "difference feminists" such as Carol Gilligan and Sara Ruddick, the influence of women on the academic culture is widely felt.[24]

In an engagingly frank study of institutional change in an elite law school, Julius Getman characterizes the effects of admitting women to the "company of scholars" as part of a "struggle for the soul of higher education." Beginning his tale in the 1960s, Getman describes an academic world in which there were no women faculty, in which women were assumed not to be "serious scholars," and in which, if they tried to prove otherwise, they would have been expected to meet greater demands than their male predecessors. "It was not that most male faculty thought themselves prejudiced or that they openly discriminated; it was more that they thought female faculty were a challenge to existing standards of excellence" as well as a threat to the reputations of elite institutions. Some feared that women's presence would diminish a school's "status." Others resisted the personal or familial effects of women's changing roles.[25]

Getman's candid account neatly complements Hochschild's 1973 essay, for he relates how women's new aspirations to academic careers affected marital relationships and departmental manners. Recalling a dinner party at a midwestern university in 1969, Getman quotes a chemistry professor as commenting "during dessert" that "the women's movement is going to destroy scholarship in America. We're a perfect example. I am on the verge of a major conceptual breakthrough that I could achieve soon if only Ginny wouldn't keep insisting that I look after the children all the time." Another guest, a professor of English, lamented that he thought that his wife wanted him "to stop working on my novel so that she can get her B.A." Getman now realizes that "the comfortable, male-dominated world in which we dwelt was soon to become a thing of the past. . . . Within a short time, all of the couples present that evening were separated, divorced, or struggling to restructure their marriages." The changes in academic life necessary to facilitate combining career and marriage for both partners have not been easy, concludes Getman, for "colleges and universities have not learned to accommodate the special needs of families. It is not clear whether they will."[26]

One of the most ingrained aspects of academic life is its individualism. This plays out in many ways, of course, including disciplinary specialization and deference to expertise, fragmentation of the curriculum, and social isolation. At the worst, it results in what David Damrosch, in his study of academic culture, terms "departmental nationalism." While his most extreme example of "protectionistic nationalism" concerns a bitter battle over departmental ownership of the territory covered in a course on American black politics at San Francisco State University, Damrosch discusses as well his own experience of curricular conflict between English literature and religious studies at Columbia University. Damrosch fears more of the same as studies of race, class, and gender lead into what he terms a "sort of biofeedback loop" in which "a small-group identity literally becomes a scholarly speciality." Especially in an era of scarcity, this could aggravate the "archaic hyperindividualism of our prevailing academic ethos" and the "alienating aggression" that he seeks to overcome.[27]

Unfortunately, women's studies figures little in Damrosch's interesting study (although he does cite women's studies as an example of the faculty commitment needed for an interdisciplinary program to thrive). He criticizes the individualism of both faculty and academic departments. Since his main purpose is to advocate greater collaboration within institutions and to suggest ways in which a "culture of cooperation can grow up alongside the culture of isolation, not replacing it but providing a livelier cultural landscape than now exists" and changing scholarly practices that inhibit "intellectual sociability," he might well have devoted some sustained attention to the countertrends exhibited by women's studies scholars.[28] Instead of seeing scholarship as an isolated activity, many academic feminists see it as a collaborative effort. Feminist scholars often share not only course syllabi and bibliographies but documentary sources and early drafts of their work, when they do not publish jointly, as many have done even in fields where this is not a common practice. In women's studies, making connections also means linking subjects across disciplinary lines and linking intellectual concerns with personal ones, as well as working together despite differences in professional or personal status. The extent to which women scholars are changing the culture of the university in the sense of community Damrosch envisions is still uncertain; but many of them are clearly encouraging that trend. As women move through the ranks, their increasing and inevitable accession to the higher rungs of faculty and administrative ladders means that the full impact of the changes wrought by the "gendering" of the academy will be felt for many years to come.

The increasing presence of women is probably responsible for putting certain issues previously relegated to "private life" before the academic community. In other instances, women's voices amplify those of men who have been calling for change for a very long time. Taking pedagogy seriously, women's studies instructors have made a significant impact on students, as chapter 4 has shown. Those students in turn effect change elsewhere in the academy. The "most powerful witness" to this influence is, as Caryn McTighe Musil points out, the number of students of all ages and ethnicities, and increasingly, of varying political perspectives, who enroll in women's studies classes even when they fear incurring a stigma thereby. Given "voice" in these classes, some will test it beyond that setting. Jean O'Barr attests to this potential with her tale of a graduate seminar paper entitled "'Sir'Vey or 'Madam'Vey?" in which students reported on systematically collected data comparing female and male graduate students' experience in two science departments at Duke University. Circulated among senior administrators and presented at a seminar sponsored by the two departments which was attended by more than fifty students and a few faculty, the students' report of prejudicial treatment against women appeared to have brought about noticeable change within the next two years. The Musil and O'Barr and Wyer studies of student impact are complemented by reports such as one that appeared in the *New York Times* on feminist women challenging traditional teaching methods in the nation's leading law schools.[29]

Teaching methods that employ both cognitive and affective modalities, including those that resemble consciousness-raising sessions, remain the subject of controversy, even in women's studies. But their presence seems to be growing, along with the recognition of the intricate relationships among authority, knowledge, culture, and power. Frank H. T. Rhodes, in an essay on the "place of teaching in the research university" which he wrote while president of Cornell University, acknowledged that "effective teaching involves the personal engagement of teacher and pupil. . . . It is, in current jargon, both cognitive and affective in its components." Teaching is increasingly viewed as a social practice that belies a "two cultures" mode of university life, in which faculty and students rarely intersect. Women's studies expects its faculty to be accessible and accountable teachers who mentor their students. Furthermore, rather than engage in territorial struggles over academic turf, women's studies faculty have tended to celebrate the spread of courses on women throughout the curriculum. In some cases, they have adopted an explicit policy of developing courses that are first taught in a women's studies program and then transferred to the curriculum of one of the traditional departments. Women's studies could be prescribed as a remedy to many of the ills that such critics as Rhodes and Damrosch detect in the contemporary academy.[30]

The Impact of Women's Studies on the Disciplines

The diminishing role of teaching and the disciplinary isolation of which Rhodes, Damrosch, and many other critics complain is reflected in the fragmented curriculum that women's studies seeks to transform. How effective the attempts at transformation have been remains hard to assess at this time. Not only does the influence of women's studies vary from field to field and from place to place, but it cannot be isolated from many other intellectual and political tendencies that affect what material is taught and what classes are taken. Whether lauding or lamenting the emergence of a "plurality of truths" within the academy, many observers agree that women's studies, by embracing diversity and broadening the context of many questions, has played a role in the declining dominance of intellectual influences of European origin. Its effects may be seen positively as renovating the disciplines and saving the liberal arts from increasing isolation from contemporary concerns, or negatively, as both a symptom and a cause of the decline of the West. The highly publicized debates over the changing of general education requirements at Stanford University helped to focus national attention on what students read. How they read it—the "politics of interpretation"—also figures in the "culture wars" to which women's studies is a party. Calling for enlargement of the canonical literature, women's studies argues that "our various canons have been established by men, reading books written mostly by men for men, with women as eavesdroppers; and now it is time for men to join in working at the vast project of reeducating our imaginations." This is the statement not of a feminist scholar but of Wayne Booth, a well-known literary critic and commentator on higher education from the University of Chicago, the home of the late Allan Bloom and of a newly established gender studies center.[31]

That the new scholarship is finding its way into the classroom is suggested in a report of the Higher Education Research Institute at the University of California, Los Angeles. In 1995 it found that among the 34,000 faculty included in its annual survey, 37 percent agreed that many courses at their institutions included feminist perspectives; this figure was up from 29 percent in 1989. Marilyn Schuster and Susan Van Dyne may have exaggerated when they suggested that "the impact of scholarship about women throughout all academic disciplines and on our pedagogy ... may have an even more profound effect than the computer revolution on how we understand human experience, how we organize knowledge, and how we teach our students." But as we approach the year 2000, it is undeniable that women's studies has planted sprouting seeds throughout universities across the nation and around the world. Competency in feminist scholarship is increasingly expected at the doctoral level in English, history, sociology, and many other fields.[32]

The generative energy of women's studies, according to women's studies director Ruth Perry of the Massachusetts Institute of Technology, has also contributed to the rise of gay and lesbian studies, queer studies, cultural studies, and postcolonial studies. "For me," declares one instructor of composition and literature who teaches at two midwestern universities, "cultural studies is a branch of women's studies." Gender has become for him an "effective pedagogical tool, a part of the foundation of every course I will teach whose goal has anything to do with thinking and writing critically about culture." Historians of cultural studies trace its genealogy further back than the advent of academic feminism, however, to the 1950s or earlier. But they do credit women's studies for its role in expanding definitions of politics to include a "radically deinstitutionalized understanding of the political process," which includes personal relationships and other experiences of everyday life.[33]

Women's studies does provide a point of entry for scholars across a wide range of fields, as it did for the historian I quoted in the Introduction, who said of his work in history and cultural studies, "It all started with women's studies." In the eyes of advocates of women's studies, this is as it should be. Women's studies is, or should be, everywhere, inspiring and invoking fresh perspectives. Because it is assumed to be impossible to add women and stir—to add a round-world view to a flat-world view—they believe that inclusion of women will reshape the curriculum, the university, and society. In light of Gerda Lerner's admonition, it is probably much too early to assess the extent to which this transformation is likely to happen. One might well retort, why not just add women? By ignoring contradictions, a person can hold mutually contradictory thoughts in a single head. Academic specialization probably facilitates this type of compartmentalization. Rather than changing the foundations, women's studies may contribute to the kind of alteration that Virginia Smith describes in her study of developments in general education. The tendency, she notes, is to "find today's coherence by using yesterday's patterns let out a bit at the seams because we've grown a little, inserting a gore here and there to accommodate non-Western culture, including in the syllabus a female writer, but essentially keeping the same pattern." Even if women's studies required a whole new dress, it might be a special gown worn only at designated events—a result analogous to the fate of home economics, which caused some of the earliest academic feminists to fear for the future if women's studies developed as a separate field. Even in the mid-to-late 1990s, the old refrain that women's studies is a "passing fad" can be heard. Is women's studies an artifact of the mid-twentieth-century rebirth of feminism? Will it be forgotten? Or will the "feminist enlightenment" ultimately force a "reevaluation of the whole of higher education," as Page Smith anticipated? The answer lies in passing the torch to a new generation and in institutionalizing, while keeping the "freshness" of outsider status.[34]

The impact of women's studies on the disciplines varies tremendously, of course. Carolyn Heilbrun compares feminist criticism in her field to "dropping a bomb into the stable world of literary masterpieces." Judith Zinsser notes the introduction of women's history to the staid, venerable International Congress of Historical Sciences (ICHS) in 1980. Three scholars of European women's history served sequentially as chairs of the American Historical Association committee representing the United States at the international congresses of 1990 and 1995 and the forthcoming congress of 2000, helping to bring to ICHS programs major themes and multiple sessions on women and gender. The program for the Berkshire Conference in Women's History, held at Chapel Hill, North Carolina, in 1996, indicated that the University of North Carolina, which had begun offering a doctorate in women's history in 1991, counted fourteen faculty who teach and publish in the field. Nearby Duke University listed thirteen members of its thirty-eight-member history department as having that specialization. The production of historical literature has mushroomed. According to Zinsser, writing in 1993, a reference guide to articles in American history which in 1968–69 devoted one-fourth of one column to the category "women" required more than four pages to cover the topic in its 1989–90 edition. For a period of *six months* in 1995, the number of theses in history listed in a subject catalog for UMI Dissertation Services under the heading "Women's Studies" was 119; 92 of these were doctoral dissertations. This contrasts with a cumulative total of 16 reported for *eighty-seven years* in the early development of the historical profession, and it represents only a portion of the dissertations and theses indexed under the subjects of women's studies and history. Even though their influence in some fields remains very limited, these figures substantiate academic feminists' claims about the magnitude of the changes under way.[35]

Because, as an administrator and a scholar, I have observed women's studies' expanding presence across a broad educational landscape, I was astonished to find so little notice taken of it in the recent survey of "American academic culture in transformation" which appeared in the winter 1997 issue of *Daedalus*, the journal of the American Academy of Arts and Sciences. In a series of articles reviewing changes over the period 1945–95 in economics, literary studies, philosophy, and political science, women's studies is scarcely mentioned. To test against some "hard" data my sense that the authors had missed a major phenomenon, I undertook a search of *Dissertation Abstracts Ondisc* for those four fields plus my own discipline of history. Given the many ways in which academic feminist studies may be reported, it is difficult to classify women's studies with precision; and the rubric "women's studies" as an indexing field was initiated only in 1978.[36] Some of the titles listed, largely from Canadian institutions, are master's rather than doctoral studies. Nevertheless, the numbers I found reported for new research in women's studies are remarkable.

Because of the complications of classification, and the fact that dissertations may, by the request of an author or the decision of an indexing editor, be listed in two or more fields, the prevalence of women's studies dissertations in specific disciplines may be overstated in the figures in table 2. The numbers for the overall category "women's studies," however, should be accurate, for no title is listed there more than once. What is of considerable interest is to note the steady acceleration in the numbers of dissertations and theses in women's studies over the latter part of the fifty years in

Table 2. Dissertations and Theses in Women's Studies as Reported in *Dissertation Abstracts Ondisc* by Selected Discipline and Year, 1980–1995

Year	Economics	History	Literature	Philosophy	Political Science	Total Women's Studies (All Fields)
1980	6	23	36	2	4	126
1985	6	42	39	4	3	174
1990	53	289	318	42	43	1,246
1995	77	658	806	97	115	2,478

Source: Dissertation Abstracts Ondisc (Ann Arbor, Mich.: University Microfilms International, n.d.), data for 1980, 1985, 1990, 1995.

which the *Daedalus* authors took such little notice of its impact in their four fields.

These, of course, are figures in each case for one year only. The use of "women's studies" as an indexing category was instituted by *Dissertation Abstracts International* in 1978, and the cumulative total of graduate degrees reported under that rubric from 1978 through 1995 is 13,084![37] Women's studies thus constitutes a major countertrend to the dominant intellectual tendencies within higher education on which the *Daedalus* authors focus, the "new rigorism" of Carl Schorske, mentioned above. It also contravenes a concurrent trend toward vocational and professional studies. Surely these data suggest that fifty years from now, a comparable survey will take far more notice of what women have wrought in the academy.

Achieving Cultural Authority

Three decades after the "rebirth of feminism," feminist consciousness has seeped so deeply into the soil of American society that even women and men who reject the designation "feminist" express, as their own, ideas that derive from this women's movement. Journalists and scholars such as Paula Kamen and Rose Glickman, who have talked at length with the younger generation, have found that mainstream America now expects its daughters to enjoy opportunities and to assume responsibilities reserved to men only a generation ago. Two men, well-known in journalism and scholarship, who agree with Kamen and Glickman about the power of feminism are Garry

Wills and Richard Rorty, who have termed it, respectively, "the greatest change in our lifetime—the women's movement freeing the talents of half the human race," and (along with gay liberation) one of the "lasting and significant moral achievements of the twentieth century."[38] In women's studies, feminism has a curricular base from which new ideas can be generated to add to the intellectual reservoirs that supply the university, culture, and society. Even if women's studies has not yet impelled a reevaluation of higher education, women and gender now appear across the curriculum. Academic feminists have pulpits from which to speak. Transformation projects carry the new scholarship beyond women's studies classrooms.

What is needed now is debate. Women's studies should not be dismissed without a hearing by those who assume that because of its political goals it is only (in the dichotomy suggested by the philosopher John Searle) a *"cause to be advanced"* rather than a *"domain to be studied."* Women's studies today offers an avenue to the exploration of important questions about the nature of human existence, the quality of human life, and the sources of human knowledge. Like Searle, I note the absence of "debate about the presuppositions of the traditional university and the alternatives." I believe that critics of women's studies as well as advocates of the field should be heard, in settings where partisans of rival views try to understand what thinkers of a different mind are saying. Academic feminists must gain a place in the intellectual contests where serious attention is paid. Their adversaries must pay attention to the substance of their work. This is the opportunity that MacIntyre's university of "constrained disagreement" would offer.[39]

Catharine Stimpson remarks, "Under a variety of rubrics, 'women's studies' is a force." It is a force embodying women's power to bring about change in the university. But can it, will it, bring corresponding change to public as well as to intellectual life? Can academic feminists gain the cultural authority necessary to translate intellectual expertise into public knowledge? Works by feminist scholars such as Patrice McDermott and Kathleen Jones show the difficulties facing women who seek authority in a society that has no tradition of accepting women as "civic humanists." Although generally he neglects women in his otherwise interesting study of the social history of American intellectuals, Thomas Bender has traced the process whereby the authority of the "learned circle[s]" that dominated a male civic culture in the mid–nineteenth century gave way to the authority of expertise and an increasingly distant university culture by the early twentieth. This has led, in his view, to an "impoverished public culture"; he sees "little in the culture of academe to suggest any lessening of the commitment to academic autonomy." Radical scholars concerned with social problems he finds to be no exception: "Scholars who pronounce themselves uncompromising radicals have produced some of the most relentlessly academic writing" about social concerns. "Yet there is an enormous gulf between their scholarship and the social life where men and women and children feel the effects of these evils."[40]

Bender should have looked at women's studies. His prescription for the academy in the next decade—"the opening up of the disciplines, the ventilating of professional communities that have come to share too much and that have become too self-referential"—is an agenda familiar to those of us in women's studies. "Breaking the disciplines," promoting interdisciplinarity, building bridges to the community, these are the heart and soul of women's studies. After helping to usher in what Bender elsewhere terms an "era . . . of remarkable intellectual invention," women's studies is poised also to play a leading role in "restoring a place for academic knowledge in the public culture and a role for public discussion in academic culture."[41]

For women's studies, translating academic expertise into public knowledge and "political truth"—which Bender finds "not to be fundamentally different" from "academic truth"—will be a difficult task. It is not simply a matter of restoring a lapsed public role. "No woman could be a civic humanist," writes Bender, even though "women trained in the social sciences at the turn of the century could be and were very prominent in public life."[42] Nor is it only a matter of providing a new vocabulary for formerly closeted experience. To a considerable extent, women's studies has already done this. In alliance with feminism, women's studies has infiltrated into the larger culture. A post-1970 lexicon of terms that now pervade the language of both academia and the press might include, besides several varieties of feminism itself, such expressions as *androcentricity, androgyny, consciousness raising, date rape, displaced homemaker, domestic violence, family leave, female genital mutilation, feminization of poverty, gender, gender gap, homophobia, patriarchy, phallocentricism, rape crisis center, reproductive rights, sexism, sexual harassment,* and *sexual politics*. These and many other now-common terms entered the culture from feminism, often through women's studies. They appear as the focus of major public policy debates. But the persisting sense, in some circles within women's studies as well as beyond it, that women's studies is or should be the "academic arm" of feminism—not its brain—tends to obscure the discipline's purpose of recovering historical knowledge and producing new knowledge. It hinders the accession of women's studies scholars to positions as "civic humanists" and perhaps tends to reduce their effectiveness as expert witnesses in contests that hinge on new ways of thinking about women's roles.[43]

As the role of the university in society continues to evolve, the distinction between academic work and activism is likely to diminish, tending, in Bender's terms, toward a "blending of the university into society (or vice versa)."[44] Similarly, as more students seek higher education, with an increasing proportion of women among them, the reduction of the historic town/gown split means that more women's studies students will themselves become civic practitioners of feminism. Much remains to be added by new scholarship, and they will accomplish it. There are many missing words about women: unknown names to be discovered; concepts and theories to be revised as "unisexual" databases are expanded; new questions to be asked; new sources to be examined; and new answers to be postulated, evaluated, and promulgated. There remains much work for the next generation.

Still, the sheer volume of what we have learned so far has surprised us all. It constitutes a legacy to be applauded and to be passed on. We now know so much more about the sexes in society than we could have imagined: the language inclusive of women (no longer are women lost in the generic); the lives and work of women worthies and women warriors as well as unknown women of all ages, races, and places; the ways women have thought and acted—or, for lack of opportunity, have failed to think and act; and the ways in which the doubled vision of women's studies stimulates new thought and action. We now know that the task will never end: not in ten years (a guess ventured by one of the administrators at San Diego State in 1974 when I first interviewed for that temporary position there), not in twenty or thirty, and, I expect, not as long as scholars and thinkers retain a passion to know and to interpret the world. Feminist scholars continue to pose new questions, and as yet, women's studies generates far more questions than definitive answers. This is appropriate, for much serious, scholarly work lies ahead, both on campus and in the culture.

In this view, the work of women's studies is an integral part of an intellectual revolution that women's studies helped to inspire. The originality and contributions of women's studies and of feminist theory are not sufficiently recognized by scholars in other fields who are only recently discovering what feminist scholars already know. The sheer intellectual energy contained in the concept "women's studies"—or rather, released through it—can scarcely be described, although I have attempted a beginning in this book. As Marilyn Schuster and Susan Van Dyne point out, to enter this world is to "experience a liberating intellectual excitement, a sense of expanding possibilities. For teachers, whole new fields of inquiry are opened; new areas for research, publication, and professional renewal become available. The compelling motivation most frequently described by teachers who have entered this stage is a voracious intellectual appetite." Even administrators find themselves moving "just a bit further toward enlightenment" when they delve into the substance of women's studies, as one wrote to Jean O'Barr after participating in a seminar as part of a team of two deans and a provost at Duke University. When Jill Ker Conway in 1974 expressed her fear that women's studies might become a "decorative frill," she could not have anticipated the extent of the enhancement it would provide.[45] Still, it may be argued that feminism has flourished many times in the past, only to fade for long periods. With the changing of the guard, what are the chances that the next generation will pursue it with inherited zest?

The success of women's studies in gaining not only a toehold but tenure in the conservative institution of higher education, however ambivalent some academic feminists may be about it, offers grounds for belief that it would survive even in a "postfeminist" world, to keep alive the feminist impulse. In the past, feminism often failed, and even faded from memory, for lack of institutionalization. The extent to which women's studies has now infiltrated the academy, and the power of its presence, is expressed well by Michael Awkward in his article "A Black Man's Place(s) in Black Feminist Criticism":

> I believe that we must acknowledge that feminism represents, at least in areas of the American academy, an incomparably productive, influential, and resilient ideology and institution which men, no matter how cunning, duplicitous, or culturally powerful, will neither control nor overthrow in the foreseeable future, one whose perspectives have proven and might continue to prove convincing even to biological males. . . . We must be honest about feminism's current persuasiveness and indomitability, about its clarifying, transformative potential. . . . Surely it is neither naive, presumptuous, nor premature to suggest that

feminism as ideology and reading strategy has assumed a position of exegetical and institutional strength capable of withstanding even the most energetically masculinistic acts of subversion.[46]

Focusing on its intellectual contributions, Awkward, a professor of English and Afro-American studies, makes clear his belief that women's studies is likely to survive even in a postfeminist world.

Other observers, however, continue to stress institutional dangers. Alice Kessler-Harris and Amy Swerdlow, after evaluating the twenty-year history of dissertation awards for research in women's studies by the Woodrow Wilson National Fellowship Foundation, preliminary to a decision to terminate that program, sounded a note of concern: a report on their work in the *Chronicle of Higher Education* was entitled "Despite Success, Women's Studies Faces Uncertain Future." Kessler-Harris and Swerdlow expressed fear that too much was now being taken for granted. The history of the "intellectual and political battles" required to establish women's studies needed to be told. They stressed the challenges remaining: minimal faculty, limited financing, insufficient support staff, dependence on goodwill, and politically motivated attacks that especially threaten junior faculty. Among the Woodrow Wilson fellowship recipients they polled, one out of five considered women's studies "still at a 'critical stage.'" Some informants feared a backlash, which might come with the "postfeminism" that assumes a kind of feminist critique but domesticates it, "delivering us back into a prefeminist world," as Tania Modleski puts it her *Feminism without Women.* Alternatively, women's studies could be lost by being subsumed into gender studies, which Modleski fears "might prove yet to be the phaseout"; or antifeminism in the academy might take the form that Annette Kolodny terms "intellectual harassment," creating an environment in which feminists' academic freedom is constrained and their work is discouraged or devalued.[47] A long-constrained job market creates conditions that may exacerbate these problems.

Bearing in mind both Gerda Lerner's reservation on too early an assessment and the columnist Ellen Goodman's observation that "in any period of change, people can get hit by a swinging pendulum,"[48] I would venture an optimistic prediction about the future of women's studies. Certainly, many problems exist, and even some of the original questions—especially those involving interdisciplinarity and institutional structure—

remain to be worked out over time. But if we think back almost thirty years, survey the length of the roads traveled, and eschew the totalizing goals and millenarian attitudes that sometimes beset women's studies, then I think that we can gain inspiration from its successes and anticipate a future in which women's studies continues to flourish both in the United States and around the world. The great proliferation of knowledge that has been taking place means that as traditional or postmodernist criticism breaks open closed categories, knowledge about women is available to be inserted into the fissures. The empowerment of women, which surely includes the increasing attainment of doctoral degrees, means that with every new cohort of faculty, feminist scholars win appointments in the universities; whether or not they are actively engaged in non-academic feminism, they bring about change in disciplines, departments, and academic culture, and they reach more students. As these faculty are increasingly diverse, the study of gender without race or class analysis will diminish and the enrollment of a wider range of students will increase. It is clear that women's studies no longer belongs to its founders but belongs to all who claim an education for and about women, and beyond that, to all who bring a commitment to change toward a more open, egalitarian, and humane society. In the process, the definition of what constitutes higher education is changing and ultimately will alter the definition of an educated person.

One way to assess the impact of women's studies is by studying the progress it has made in changing the bodies of knowledge transmitted by university faculty. As noted in chapter 3, the focus here has not been on feminist work within individual fields; in any case, feminist influence varies greatly across the disciplines comprising the liberal arts and sciences and the professions. Some, no doubt, remain at "phase one," with a "womanless" curriculum, while others have advanced further along the continuum toward integrating all human experience, reaching stage 5 of Schuster and Van Dyne's six-phase scheme.

I have often been asked by academic administrators as well as non-academic acquaintances—not just in the early days, when many expected women's studies to disappear shortly, but more recently as well—whether women's studies is likely to remain a separate field, with its work to be completed at some future date; or alternatively, whether it is to be subsumed within gender studies or transcended through assimilation into traditional disciplines in a transformed curriculum. Despite some reservations about the application of "phase theory" to such a complex process, one way in which I might respond is simply to defer: to point out that so much research remains to be done in the first stages of transformation—the search for missing women, the challenge to existing interpretations, the development of new perspectives—that only a future generation will be able to decide. A more adventurous and probably useful reply begins with an analogy: although economic issues and philosophical perspectives are taught in courses in history, political science, sociology, and elsewhere, no one suggests eliminating the economics or philosophy departments. Similarly, women's studies needs a place where women are the primary focus of research and teaching; where there is room in the curriculum for many and wide-ranging topics; and where the work of women's studies specialists generates material to be included elsewhere. Without a faculty for whom work on women is the basis of their professional careers, the field will not develop adequately. The answer to all "either/or" questions, then, is "both/ and." The state of the art will change over time, as it does in all disciplines and interdisciplinary areas. Come back with that question in a hundred years. Meanwhile, support this vital and creative intellectual endeavor.

Another measure of academic feminist influence is the interest demonstrated by university alumnae, and the tangible support that alumnae have provided for women's studies, as the new scholarship has been made available to them. For example, in one instance of what Jean Fox O'Barr calls "educating beyond the walls," the Duke University women's studies program offered alumnae educational programs through which they could become acquainted with feminist scholarship as well as with women's studies faculty and students. Over a five-year period, Duke was able to create a million-dollar endowment from female graduates who had a minimal history of donating to the university. O'Barr attributes her and her colleagues' success to their having engaged this new community in the educational process. "Raising funds from women for feminist educational projects requires that alumnae themselves come to see what was missing in their own education, learn how the new scholarship on women fills in gaps that they had not previously named, and believe that younger women and men will begin their adult lives better equipped than they were. Like feminist scholars, alumnae learn to observe, to give voice, and to act."[49]

Raising funds to enrich curricular offerings, endow fellowships, and support research is common to academic programs, and academic feminists are finding success in these endeavors at many public as well as private universities, including the University of Cincinnati, Indiana University, Stanford University, the University of South Carolina, and the University of Southern California. A second major purpose for creating "friends of women's studies" groups is to bring the new scholarship to a broader public. The Institute for Research on Women and Gender at Stanford University is notably successful in this effort. It sponsors Bay Area Associates, Los Angeles Associates, New York Associates, and Corporate Associates, all of which meet periodically for presentations and seminars offered by feminist scholars and business and professional leaders. New groups are being developed in Chicago and San Diego. In the fall of 1996, more than two hundred attended a panel discussion entitled "Girls in Gangs: Coming from What, Going to Where, and Why?" organized by the Los Angeles group. The IRWG also maintains a national advisory panel and has several times presented a summer institute on women and leadership for executive women from leading companies around the country. It recently concluded a successful campaign to raise over a million dollars to endow the position of its director and a dissertation fellowship program. Working with a recent challenge grant, it expects to raise substantial additional funds. According to its director, Dr. Iris Litt, the institute has raised more funds from non-alumnae and alumnae with no history of giving to the university than has any other unit on campus.[50]

Like Duke University, Stanford University provides continuing education in women's studies for members of its public community. At the University of Cincinnati, Laura Struminger Schor, who directed the women's studies program there in the 1980s, also engaged the participation of major civic institutions whose staff performed duties affected by new understandings of women's experience. While building a group of "Friends of Women's Studies" and seeking funds for program enhancement, she recruited groups such as the Domestic Relations Committee of the Cincinnati Bar Association and the Cincinnati Historical Society to co-sponsor programs on women and public policy and women in local history. In one instance, she reports, the county's domestic relations court closed for the day so that its staff could participate in a women's studies symposium dealing with divorce issues. New information and new ideas about women also sparked local efforts to change public policies and brought members and funds to the outreach group. So many small donors gave money to build a half-million-dollar endowment fund for the Cincinnati program that someone suggested naming the fund for "Anon." On the other hand, at Indiana University, women's studies received from one donor an unsolicited million-dollar gift. At the University of Southern California, a major donor provided funding for two endowed women's studies chairs.[51]

The education promoted by women's studies engages its public because it promises to enhance—or rather, to restore—the role of the university in giving meaning to people's lives and moral direction to society. The arguments for sex equity are ethical as well as legal and economic. While gender differences in moral development remain a subject of research and feminists debate the origins and implications of an "ethic of care," a new discussion has begun about the role of education in the formulation and transmission of social and cultural values.[52] Women's studies gives new meaning to lives of its students, faculty, and community associates, and it brings to higher education new possibilities for questions, answers, and interpretations of personal and social relationships. No "feminist enlightenment" is needed and one need not be a postmodernist to recognize human beings as social creatures "constituted in conversation."[53] One need only observe carefully the growth and development of an infant, as I have watched my newborn granddaughter in recent months. But prior to women's studies, few philosophers felt the need to notice young children, and scientific studies of infants remained the specialty of a few subdisciplines falling outside the interests of most liberal education. For feminist scholars, studies of interpersonal subjective processes in diverse settings are essential to understanding "femininity" and "masculinity," as well as power relations and social structures.

Jane Roland Martin, whose work on constituting curricula is discussed above in chapter 3, offers from her own life a striking example of the broadening impact of feminist analysis. Already an "accomplished, tough-minded philosopher of education," Martin began to study the place of women in educational thought only while preparing her presidential address to the Philosophy of Education Society. She describes the experience of working on a paper on Rousseau's *Emile:* "One Friday afternoon, I was electrified by the thought that if Sophie is brought into the equation, the standard interpretation of Rousseau's philosophy of education is proven wrong." Soon after, Martin reports, she "discovered that if the education of women is taken seriously, the ways in which our culture's concept of what it is to be an educated person must be redefined." Although she was a woman working in a traditional woman's field with sufficient success to have attained her professional society's highest office, it was only in her presidential presentation that she departed from her field's methodological norms and dared to assert her view that "an adequate ideal of the educated person must give the reproductive processes of society their due."[54]

Incorporating Martin's three C's—care, concern, and connection—into higher education would mean no longer "relegating home and family to the 'ontological basement,'" but re-opening the disciplines to matters of value, and creating spaces both within and between them in which new questions about personal, social, and cultural problems can emerge. In this "radical future of gender enrichment," Martin foresees the fulfillment of John Dewey's lifelong efforts to integrate in the educational process mind and body, head and heart, reason and emotion, self and other, and thought and action. Beyond dissolving these dichotomies, a future enriched by women's studies would require erasing the distinction between the productive and reproductive processes of society and paying attention, in all the theories and practices of society, to what it takes to form and sustain human beings in all their diversity.[55]

In the university that I envision, adopting the three C's is not a matter of adding women's traditional concerns to men's. The three C's would not replace reading, writing, and arithmetic, or economics, philosophy, and political science. But they would require asking how the "subject-entities" of those disciplines affect, and are affected by, the lives of women and men of diverse peoples and circumstances. In this new context, higher education would connect what scholars and students study with the lives they lead, and would offer inspiration to all who seek more than instrumental knowledge. Liberal education might truly liberate people from the narrow constraints of their lives.

This is a promise that education could offer, if it were to take seriously the insights and claims of women's studies. It is a prospect certain to disturb the defenders of tradition, but it is not inconsistent with academic excellence and it can satisfy the longings of those who seek to use the new knowledge to connect the personal, the political, and the professional parts of their lives and to fashion a meaningful place for themselves with others in a less fragmented world. The "feminist enlightenment" brings this vision to the university and to society.

Before concluding this study, I want to say what women's studies and its vision have brought to me. Women's studies has helped me to understand the meaning of the struggle that has defined my life: my devotion to motherhood, which came early to me, and my passion for learning, which was there from the beginning of my conscious life. For any human being, it is not easy to make connections and resolve conflicts among countless needs, interests, and desires. But women with powerful drives in the direction of both family and professional vocations face an inordinate burden in a society that has historically found it simpler to treat them as separate and unequal; women have often been punished for their desire to live fully. Feminism, in its insistence on making connections between the personal and the political, and women's studies, which expresses both the personal and the political in the professional, seek to make whole what the world takes apart. Throughout this book, I have spoken of linking, connecting, and integrating. I have quoted students and faculty, a few among many thousands, who turn to women's studies because it turns them on intellectually—the light bulb is powered by the energy of fusion. It is a kind of fusion that blends together the parts of a life they want to live whole. It takes a lot of energy to practice women's studies. But as it satisfies the longing for meaning of questing minds and helps to integrate divided lives, it gives back in full measure. I hope that this study returns to readers some of what women's studies has given to me.

In the notes, references to edited volumes that are listed in the bibliography are given in shortened form. See the bibliography for complete information.

Introduction: Speaking of Women's Studies

1. Author's personal notes on meeting of American Historical Association, San Francisco, Calif., Jan. 1994.
2. Audre Lorde, "The Master's Tools Will Never Dismantle the Master's House," in *Sister Outsider: Essays and Speeches* (Freedom, Calif.: Crossing Press, 1984).
3. Elisabeth Young-Bruehl, "The Education of Women as Philosophers," in Minnich, O'Barr, and Rosenfeld, eds., *Reconstructing the Academy*, 10.
4. Sheila Tobias, who later served as associate provost at Wesleyan University, in Connecticut, and for the last seventeen years has been a self-described "free-lance scholar-activist," has become well known for her many contributions on subjects ranging from "math anxiety" to the military. Her latest book is *Faces of Feminism: An Activist's Reflections on the Women's Movement* (Boulder, Colo.: Westview Press, 1997).
5. Toril Moi, *Sexual/Textual Politics: Feminist Literary Theory* (London: Methuen, 1985), 142.
6. Judith Butler, "Contingent Foundations: Feminism and the Question of 'Postmodernism,'" in Seyla Benhabib et al., *Feminist Contentions: A Philosophical Exchange* (New York: Routledge, 1995), 48.
7. Caren Kaplan terms the "politics of location" a "particularly North American feminist articulation of difference . . . [emphasizing] the privilege of whiteness." Kaplan, "The Politics of Location as Transnational Feminist Critical Practice," in Grewal and Kaplan, eds., *Scattered Hegemonies*, 137–52, quotation on 139. The source of the phrase is Adrienne Rich, "Notes toward a Politics of Location," in *Blood, Bread, and Poetry: Selected Prose* (New York: W. W. Norton, 1986), 210–31.
8. Linda Alcoff, "The Problem of Speaking for Others," in Roof and Wiegman, eds., *Who Can Speak?*, 97–119, quotation on 111.
9. Chamberlain, ed., *Women in Academe*, 137.
10. Page Smith, *Killing the Spirit: Higher Education in America* (New York: Viking, 1990), 291–92. Had Smith looked into the content of women's studies, he might have been able to connect his negative and positive observations about it.
11. On "caring, concern, and connection," I borrow from Jane Roland Martin,

Changing the Educational Landscape: Philosophy, Women, and Curriculum (New York: Routledge, 1994); see chaps. 3 and 9, below.

12. Karen Offen, "'What! Such Things Have Happened and No Women Were Taught about Them': A Nineteenth-Century French Woman's View of the Importance of Women's History," *Journal of Women's History* 9, no. 2 (summer 1997): 147–53.

Chapter 1: Feminist Advocacy, Scholarly Inquiry, and the Experience of Women

This chapter is based on my "Advocacy, Inquiry, Experience: Building Women's Studies Together" (keynote address presented on Nov. 4, 1995, at symposium celebrating the twenty-fifth anniversary of the founding of a women's studies program at San Diego State University in 1970).

1. "Women's Studies," *Newsweek*, Oct. 26, 1970, 61.

2. The early history and development of women's studies is traced in detail in my review essay "For and about Women: The Theory and Practice of Women's Studies in the United States," *Signs* 7, no. 3 (spring 1982): 661–95. See also Florence Howe, *Seven Years Later: Women's Studies Programs in 1976*, Report of the National Advisory Council on Women's Educational Programs (Washington, D.C.: U.S. Department of Education, June 1977); idem, "Introduction: The First Decade of Women's Studies," *Harvard Educational Review* 49, no. 4 (1979): 413–21; Catharine R. Stimpson with Nona Kressner Cobb, *Women's Studies in the United States*, Report to the Ford Foundation (New York: Ford Foundation, 1986); and the National Institute of Education's Women's Studies Monograph Series, 1980, which includes eight reports based on recommendations in Howe, *Seven Years Later.*

3. On "female revolution," see Janice Law Trecker, "Woman's Place Is in the Curriculum," *Saturday Review*, Oct. 16, 1971, 83–86, 92, quotations on 86. For an early account of the emergence of the first courses and programs on women, see Florence Howe and Carol Ahlum, "Women's Studies and Social Change," in Alice S. Rossi and Ann Calderwood, eds., *Academic Women on the Move* (New York: Sage, 1973), 393–423; the essay also appears in Florence Howe, *Myths of Coeducation: Selected Essays, 1964–1983* (Bloomington: Indiana University Press, 1984), 78–110. Howe is currently professor of English at the City College of New York and continues to direct the Feminist Press.

4. Based on "Women's Studies Programs—1994," *Women's Studies Quarterly* 22, nos. 1 and 2 (spring–summer 1994): 141–75; for an updated list (which arrived too late for my use here), see ibid., 25, nos. 1 and 2 (spring–summer 1997): 422–55. For a study of the origins and development of four programs based on 167 interviews with faculty, students, and staff, see Barbara Scott Winkler, "A

Comparative History of Four Women's Studies Programs, 1970–1985" (Ph.D. diss., University of Michigan, 1992).

5. Roberta Salper, "Women's Studies," *Ramparts* 10, no. 6 (Dec. 1971): 56–60, quotation on 57. See also *Women's Studies Program: Three Years of Struggle* (San Diego: Inside the Beast, May 1973), 4.

6. Ann Calderwood, revised 1977 editorial statement for *Feminist Studies*, quoted in Patrice McDermott, *Politics and Scholarship: Feminist Academic Journals and the Production of Knowledge* (Urbana: University of Illinois Press, 1994), 80.

7. Elaine Showalter, "Introduction: Teaching about Women, 1971," in Showalter and Ohmann, eds., *Female Studies IV*, iii.

8. On *Female Studies I* and the rest of the ten-volume *Female Studies* series published between 1970 and 1976, see Boxer, "For and about Women," 664–65.

9. Kay Boals, "The Politics of Male-Female Relations," in Sheila Tobias, ed., *Female Studies I*, 57a.

10. Judith Grant, *Fundamental Feminism: Contesting the Core Concepts of Feminist Theory* (New York: Routledge, 1993), 4.

11. For the range and the incidence by topic of articles in women's history published in the 1980s, see Joan Hoff, "Introduction: An Overview of Women's History in the United States," in Gayle V. Fischer, comp., *Journal of Women's History, Guide to Periodical Literature* (Bloomington: Indiana University Press, 1992), 9–11.

12. Susan Groag Bell and Mollie Schwartz Rosenhan pointed out that "'women's studies' is a "misnomer . . . grammatically incorrect and conceptually imprecise." They stated a preference for "women studies" or "feminist studies." See Bell and Rosenhan, "A Problem in Naming: Women Studies—Women's Studies," *Signs* 6, no. 3 (spring 1981): 540–42. Several universities, including the University of Missouri, San Francisco State, and the University of Washington, did adopt the name "women studies"; Stanford University chose "feminist studies." That the "elision of studies by women and studies about women" is possible in English but not in other languages is noted by Elizabeth Bird in "Women's Studies in European Higher Education: Sigma and Coimbra," *European Journal of Women's Studies* 3, no. 2 (May 1996): 151–65, quotation on 154. For a response to Bell and Rosenhan and a positive view of the ambiguity inherent in the "apostrophe" formation, see Jane Gallop, *Reading Lacan* (Ithaca: Cornell University Press, 1985), 13–18. On naming as a "slippery business" and on "the dangers of fetishization," see Toril Moi, *Sexual/Textual Politics: Feminist Literary Theory* (London: Methuen, 1985), 160; on naming and criticizing as a "slippery, perilous business," see Susan Bordo, "Feminism, Postmodernism, and Gender-Skepticism," in Nicholson, ed., *Feminism/Postmodernism*, 133–56, quotation on 135. Florence Howe reports not being allowed to use the word *women* in a course description in 1970; see her

"Women and the Power to Change," in Howe, ed., *Women and the Power to Change*, 150. On "hegemonic" and "homogenizing norms," see Kathleen B. Jones and Anna G. Jónasdóttir, "Introduction: Gender as an Analytic Category in Political Theory," in Jones and Jónasdóttir, eds., *Political Interests of Gender*, 27.

13. On naming, see also Boxer, "For and about Women," 664–65 n. 11; Howe, ed., *Female Studies II*; cf. Vivian P. Makosky and Michele A. Paludi, "Feminism and Women's Studies in the Academy," in Paludi and Steuernagel, eds., *Feminist Restructuring of the Academic Disciplines*, 6. On shared concerns, see Kirstie McClure, "The Issue of Foundations: Scientized Politics, Politicized Science, and Feminist Critical Practices," in Butler and Scott, eds., *Feminists Theorize the Political*, 349.

14. Preamble to the constitution of the NWSA, drafted at the founding convention in San Francisco in January 1977 and published in *Women's Studies Newsletter* 5, nos. 1–2 (winter–spring 1977): 6–18.

15. Robin Leidner, "Stretching the Boundaries of Liberalism: Democratic Innovation in a Feminist Organization," *Signs* 16, no. 2 (winter 1991): 263–89.

16. Patrocinio Schweickart, quoted in McDermott, *Politics and Scholarship*, 164.

17. On beating the academics, see ibid., 163. On editorial policy, see Catharine R. Stimpson et al., "Editorial," *Signs* 1, no. 1 (autumn 1975), v–viii, quotation on viii. Barbara Gelpi discussed the care with which the journal's relationship to feminism was handled when she sought top administrators' support for bringing it to Stanford in 1980 in "Reflections on *Signs* at Stanford, 1980–85" (presentation in Jing Lyman lecture series, Stanford University, Apr. 30, 1997).

18. McDermott, *Politics and Scholarship*, 124.

19. Virginia Woolf, *Three Guineas* (New York: Harcourt, Brace, 1938), esp. 60–62.

20. In 1996, one women's studies list alone, WMST-L, which began in 1991 and is monitored by Joan Korenman at the University of Maryland, Baltimore County, reported 4,127 subscribers in forty-two countries (the report was made by Korenman on May 16, 1996). For information on subscribing to the list and on obtaining archived materials, obtain Korenman's "WMST-L User's Guide" by sending an e-mail message to listserv@umdd.umd.edu with the message "get guide wmst-l" (without the quotation marks). Those with access to the World Wide Web can obtain instructions on searching the WMST-L archives at http://www.umbc.edu/wmst/simplesearch.html. Bibliographic information appears regularly on WMST-L, the women's history listserv H-WOMEN, and many other women-oriented discussion groups. An outstanding bibliographical source is the University of Wisconsin System Library, whose publications include *Feminist Collections*, *Feminist Periodicals*, and *New Books on Women and Feminism*. Its website is http://www.library.wisc.edu/libraries/WomensStudies/. For information on more than two hundred women-related e-mail lists, see http://www.umbc.edu/wmst/forums.html. See also Joan

Korenman, *Internet Resources on Women: Using Electronic Media in Curriculum Transformation* (Baltimore, Md.: Towson State University, National Center for Curriculum Transformation Resources on Women, 1997).

21. Hartman and Banner, eds., *Clio's Consciousness Raised*, xi. For other specific references, see Marilyn J. Boxer, "Women's Studies, Feminist Goals, and the Science of Women," in Pearson, Shavlik, and Touchton, eds., *Educating the Majority*, 184–204, esp. 201 n. 5.

22. O'Barr and Wyer, eds., *Engaging Feminism*, 29.

23. See also Louise Bernikow, "Political Matricide: Feminism's Second Wave, Third Wave, and the Amnesia Problem" (plenary session on "Generations," National Women's Studies Association annual meeting, Norman, Okla., June 15, 1995).

24. Susan Stanford Friedman, "Beyond White and Other: Relationality and Narratives of Race in Feminist Discourse," *Signs* 21, no. 1 (autumn 1995): 1–49, quotations on 18, 30, 39, 40.

25. Caryn McTighe Musil, "Foreword," in Albrecht and Brewer, eds., *Bridges of Power*, vi.

26. See Frances A. Maher and Mary Kay Thompson Tetreault, *The Feminist Classroom: An Inside Look at How Professors and Students Are Transforming Higher Education for a Diverse Society* (New York: BasicBooks, 1994), esp. chap. 1.

27. Margo Culley and Catherine Portuges, "Introduction," in Culley and Portuges, eds., *Gendered Subjects*, 1–7, quotation on 5–6.

28. Carol Gilligan, *In a Different Voice: Psychological Theory and Women's Development* (Cambridge: Harvard University Press, 1982); Mary Field Belenky et al., *Women's Ways of Knowing: The Development of Self, Voice, and Mind* (New York: BasicBooks, 1986). For a collection of essays on the occasion of the tenth anniversary of the latter book's publication, Frances Maher and Mary Kay Thompson Tetreault contributed a study of this book's influence on women's studies; see Maher with Tetreault, "*Women's Ways of Knowing* in Women's Studies, Feminist Pedagogies, and Feminist Theory," in Goldberger et al., eds., *Knowledge, Difference, and Power*, 148–74.

29. Maher and Tetreault, *Feminist Classroom*, esp. ix.

30. Denise Riley, *"Am I That Name?" Feminism and the Category of "Women" in History* (Minneapolis: University of Minnesota Press, 1988).

31. Dominick LaCapra, "History, Language, and Reading," *American Historical Review* 100, no. 3 (June 1995): 799–828, quotation on 822.

32. Judith Grant, "I Feel Therefore I Am: A Critique of Female Experience as the Basis for a Feminist Epistemology," in Falco, ed., *Feminism and Epistemology*, 99–114, quotation on 106.

33. Jane Roland Martin, "Methodological Essentialism, False Difference, and

Other Dangerous Traps," *Signs* 19, no. 3 (spring 1994): 630–57, quotation on 637.

34. Joan W. Scott, "The Evidence of Experience," *Critical Inquiry* 17 (1991): 773–97, quotation on 777.

35. Robert Coles, "The Disparity between Intellect and Character," *Chronicle of Higher Education* 41, no. 48 (Sept. 22, 1995).

36. See Alasdair MacIntyre, *Three Rival Versions of Moral Enquiry: Encyclopaedia, Genealogy, and Tradition* (Notre Dame, Ind.: University of Notre Dame Press, 1990); and chap. 9, below.

Chapter 2: Constituting a New Field of Knowledge

1. Tom Wolfe, *The Electric Kool-Aid Acid Test* (New York: Bantam, 1969), 93.

2. Jo Freeman, *The Politics of Women's Liberation: A Case Study of an Emerging Social Movement and Its Relation to the Policy Process* (New York: David McKay, 1975).

3. Preamble to the constitution of the NWSA, *Women's Studies Newsletter* 5, nos. 1–2 (winter–spring 1977): 6.

4. Chamberlain, ed., *Women in Academe*, esp. 275–89. For a case study of the impact of women and feminism on teaching, research, professional organizations, and academic institutions in one discipline, see Judith P. Zinsser, *History and Feminism: A Glass Half Full* (New York: Twayne, 1993).

5. A later version of this paper appeared as Linda Gordon et al., "Historical Phallacies: Sexism in American Historical Writing," in Carroll, ed., *Liberating Women's History*, 55–74.

6. Clifford Adelman, *The New College Course Map and Transcript Files: Changes in Course-Taking and Achievement, 1972–1993* (Washington, D.C.: Office of Educational Research and Improvement, U.S. Department of Education, Oct. 1995), 255, 262.

7. Books that analyze traditional disciplines from a women's studies perspective include Ellen Carol DuBois et al., *Feminist Scholarship: Kindling in the Groves of Academe* (Urbana: University of Illinois Press, 1987); Farnham, ed., *Impact of Feminist Research*; Hartman and Messer-Davidow, eds., *(En)Gendering Knowledge*; Kramarae and Spender, eds., *Knowledge Explosion*; Paludi and Steuernagel, eds., *Feminist Restructuring of the Academic Disciplines*; Sherman and Beck, eds., *Prism of Sex*; Spender, ed., *Men's Studies Modified*; and Stanton and Stewart, eds., *Feminisms in the Academy*. Several of these include analysis of professional studies such as engineering, law, library science, medicine, and nursing, as well as liberal arts fields. See also Hull, ed., *State of the Art in Women's Studies*, which includes essays on eleven disciplines.

8. Frank B. Morgan and Susan G. Broyles, *Degrees and Other Awards Conferred by Institutions of Higher Education, 1992–93* (Washington, D.C.: Office of

Educational Research and Improvement, U.S. Department of Education, Mar.
1995), 36. Morgan provided by telephone the following additional information
on degrees awarded in women's studies, pointing out that prior to 1991–92,
women's studies was listed in the Multi/Interdisciplinary Area, not the Ethnic
and Cultural Studies Area:

	Totals	B.A.	M.A.	Ph.D.
1986–87	130	119	9	2
1987–88	158	148	8	2
1988–89	170	157	12	1
1989–90	219	202	16	1
1990–91	274	261	13	0
1991–92	354	330	24	0
1992–93	444	411	33	0

On the structure of the women's studies major, see Johnnella E. Butler et al.,
Liberal Learning and the Women's Studies Major (n.p.: National Women's
Studies Association for the Association of American Colleges, 1991), 6–12;
Marcia Westkott and Gay Victoria, "A Survey of the Women's Studies Major,"
NWSA Journal 3, no. 3 (autumn 1991): 430–35.

9. Jo Freeman, personal communications, Jan. 26, Apr. 17, 1997; idem, ed.,
   Women: A Feminist Perspective (Palo Alto, Calif.: Mayfield, 1975); later editions of *Women* appeared in 1979, 1984, 1989, and 1995.
10. Freeman, ed., *Women* (1975), xvi; Rosalyn F. Baxandall, "Who Shall Care for
    Our Children? The History and Development of Child Care in the United
    States," in Freeman, ed., *Women* (1975), 88–102, quotation on 88.
11. Freeman, ed., *Women*, 3d ed. (1984), xi.
12. Freeman, ed., *Women*, 5th ed. (1995), viii.
13. Hunter College Women's Studies Collective, *Women's Realities, Women's
    Choices: An Introduction to Women's Studies* (New York: Oxford University
    Press, 1983), ix, xiii.
14. Hunter College Women's Studies Collective, *Women's Realities, Women's
    Choices*, 2d ed. (New York: Oxford University Press, 1995), xii–xiii, 16.
15. Ibid., 4, 13, 14. I thank Dorothy Helly for the figure on sales, as of winter 1996.
16. The idea of women's studies as moral inquiry is discussed in chap. 9. I would
    like to acknowledge here the awareness demonstrated by the editors of the
    Encyclopedia of Bioethics, revised edition, who, recognizing the historical
    condition of women as a bioethical issue, invited me to contribute an essay on
    women's history for that publication. See Marilyn J. Boxer, "Women: Histori-
    cal and Cross-Cultural Perspectives," *Encyclopedia of Bioethics*, 5 vols., rev.
    ed., Warren T. Reich, editor-in-chief (New York: Simon and Schuster Macmil-
    lan, 1995), 5:2554–60.
17. Sheila Ruth, *Issues in Feminism: A First Course in Women's Studies* (Boston:

Houghton Mifflin, 1980), xi; idem, *Issues in Feminism: An Introduction to Women's Studies*, 3d ed. (Mountain View, Calif.: Mayfield, 1995), xii.

18. Cf. Barbara Hillyer Davis, "Teaching the Feminist Minority," in Bunch and Pollack, eds., *Learning Our Way*, 89–97; this essay is also in *Women's Studies Quarterly* 9, no. 4 (winter 1981).

19. Anita Clair Fellman and Barbara A. Winstead, "Old Dominion University: Making Connections," in Musil, ed., *Courage to Question*, 85–86.

20. Abby Markowitz, Towson State University, quoted in Caryn McTighe Musil, "Conclusion," in Musil, ed., *Courage to Question*, 197.

21. Florence Howe, "Toward Women's Studies in the Eighties: Part 1," *Women's Studies Newsletter* 8, no. 4 (fall 1979): 2.

22. Quoted in Butler et al., *Liberal Learning*, 3.

23. Author's notes on program administrators' preconference meeting, National Women's Studies Association annual meeting, University of Oklahoma, Norman, June 21, 1995.

24. Nina Ayoub, comp., "New Scholarly Books," *Chronicle of Higher Education*, May 26, 1995, A13, and Feb. 7, 1997; book review section, *San Francisco Examiner*, July 24, 1994, 6.

25. "Professor Elizabeth Fox-Genovese Interviewed by Carol Iannone," *Academic Questions* 5, no. 3 (summer 1992): 56–65, quotation on 56.

26. Project on the Status and Education of Women, Association of American Colleges, "Evaluating Courses for Inclusion of New Scholarship on Women," May 1988, 1.

27. For WMST-L discussion between March 1992 and May 1995 of policies on crosslisting of courses with women's studies, send message "get crosslst policies" (without the quotation marks; note the shortened form of the word "crosslist") to listserv@umdd.umd.edu. Original query, Donna Phillips, Morehead State University (Kentucky), "We are new at this!," WMST-L, Mar. 27, 1992; on the distinction between "core" and "affiliated," see Jean L. Potuchek, Gettysburg College (Pennsylvania), "We are new at this!," WMST-L, Mar. 27, 1992.

28. Joan Korenman, University of Maryland, Baltimore County, "We are new at this!," WMST-L, Mar. 27, 1992.

29. Vivian P. Makosky and Michele A. Paludi, "Feminism and Women's Studies in the Academy," in Paludi and Steuernagel, eds., *Foundations for a Feminist Restructuring*, 1–37, table on 17–18.

30. Joyce Trebilcot, Washington University (St. Louis), "Criteria or policy statement," WMST-L, May 12, 1995.

31. For Howe, Lerner, and San Francisco State, see Boxer, "For and about Women," 688–89.

32. Adrienne Rich, "Conditions for Work: The Common World of Women," foreword to Ruddick and Daniels, eds., *Working It Out*, xiii–xxiv, quotation on xv.

33. Marge Piercy, "Friedan," WMST-L, May 14, 1995.
34. At San Diego State University, women's studies was originally designated a "program." But since, from the beginning, it had its own faculty lines, course rubric, and enrollment-based budget, and its chair reported directly to a dean, it was a department in all but name. It became a department in name too in about 1977, but its status as an academic unit did not change.
35. Author's notes on "The Next Twenty-five Years," women's studies program administrators conference, Arizona State University, Tempe, Feb. 14, 1997.
36. The list of departments is mostly from Ruth Dickstein (at University of Arizona library), "Women's Studies Departments," WMST-L, Nov. 28, 1995; on the power of departments, Ellen Berry (director of women's studies at Bowling Green State, in Ohio) wrote to WMST-L on Oct. 22, 1995, "Power still basically resides within the departmental structure—interdisciplinary programs of all kinds often fall through the cracks because they are not integrated into the decision-making structures in the same way departments are"; on trivialization, see Beatrice Kachuck, "WS and alliances," WMST-L, Sept. 10, 1995.
37. Diana Scully, "Overview of Women's Studies: Organization and Institutional Status in U.S. Higher Education," NWSA Journal 8, no. 3 (fall 1996): 124.
38. Jill Ker Conway, True North: A Memoir (New York: Vintage Books, 1994), 218.
39. Nancy Cott, quoted in Gloria Bowles and Renate Duelli Klein, "Introduction: Theories of Women's Studies and the Autonomy/Integration Debate," in Bowles and Klein, eds., Theories of Women's Studies, 1–26, quotation on 7. Barbara Miller Solomon describes how home economics "foreshadowed" women's studies in In the Company of Educated Women: A History of Women and Higher Education in America (New Haven: Yale University Press, 1985), 87.
40. Sandra Coyner, "Women's Studies as an Academic Discipline: Why and How To Do It," in Bowles and Klein, eds., Theories of Women's Studies, 46–71, quotations on 47, 59, 60.
41. Jean Fox O'Barr, Feminism in Action: Building Institutions and Community through Women's Studies (Chapel Hill: University of North Carolina Press, 1994), 283.
42. Claire Moses, personal communication, Feb. 14, 1997.
43. Kidd and Spencer, eds., Guide to Graduate Work in Women's Studies.
44. Ann B. Shteir, "The Women's Studies Ph.D.: A Report from the Field," Women's Studies Quarterly 25, nos. 1–2 (spring–summer 1997): 388–403, quotation on 388. Information on "The Next Twenty-five Years," women's studies program administrators conference, Arizona State University, Tempe, Feb. 1997, is from my personal notes. See also Shteir, ed., Graduate Women's Studies; and Claire G. Moses, "Looking Back, Looking Ahead," Bridging (University of Maryland, College Park), Sept. 1996, 1.

45. Women's Studies Program, University of Iowa, "Proposal for a Ph.D. in Women's Studies," submitted Sept. 1994, revised Feb. 1996, typescript.

46. Jessie Bernard, "Re-Viewing the Impact of Women's Studies on Sociology," in Farnham, ed., *Impact of Feminist Research*, 193–216, quotation on 198; Marilyn J. Boxer, "A Course in 'Feminology': Women's Studies in France circa 1902," *Women's Studies Quarterly*, International Supplement no. 1 (Jan. 1982): 24–27.

47. Quotation from Mary Ellen S. Capek, executive director, NCRW, undated letter received 1994; on resources, see Chamberlain, ed., *Women in Academe*, 299–300.

48. Linda Eisenmann, "Weathering 'A Climate of Unexpectation': Gender Equity and the Radcliffe Institute, 1960–1995," *Academe* 81, no. 4 (July-Aug. 1995): 21–25.

49. Chamberlain, ed., *Women in Academe*, 295.

50. Ibid., 306; on 308–10, Chamberlain provides a chronological listing of specialized libraries and research centers founded between 1943 and 1987.

51. "How SIROW Can Serve You," *SIROW: Newsletter of the Southwest Institute for Research on Women* 50 (Mar. 1995): 1; Leslie I. Hill, "The Ford Foundation Program on Mainstreaming Minority Women's Studies," *Women's Studies Quarterly* 18, nos. 1–2 (spring–summer 1990): 24–38.

52. Mariam K. Chamberlain and Alison Bernstein, "Philanthropy and the Emergence of Women's Studies," *Teachers College Record* 93, no. 3 (spring 1992): 556–68.

53. Stimpson with Cobb, *Women's Studies in the United States*, 43; "Give and Take," *Chronicle of Higher Education*, July 14, 1995, A27. For detailed information on external funding of women's studies in the 1980s, see Caryn McTighe Musil and Ruby Sales, "Funding Women's Studies," in Butler and Walter, eds., *Transforming the Curriculum*, 21–34. Musil and Sales stress the point that, overall, women's studies is poorly funded; furthermore, according to one survey, a large majority (79%) of programs received no outside funds.

54. Brown et al., eds., *W.I.S.H.*, 1–8; Burton Bollag, "Women's Studies Programs Gain a Foothold in Eastern Europe," *Chronicle of Higher Education*, Dec. 13, 1996, A14; Beverly Guy-Sheftall with Susan Heath, *Women's Studies: A Retrospective*, report to the Ford Foundation (New York: Ford Foundation, 1995), 19–21. See also "Women's Studies in Europe," special issue of *Women's Studies Quarterly* 20, nos. 3 and 4 (fall–winter 1992); "Women's Studies: A World View," special issue of ibid., 22, nos. 3 and 4 (fall–winter 1994); and "Beijing and Beyond: Toward the Twenty-first Century for Women," special issue of ibid., 24, nos. 1 and 2 (spring–summer 1996). In their first issue, the editors of the *European Journal of Women's Studies* state: "From Vilnius to Dublin, from Thessalonika to Coimbra, women's studies has become part of the European academic landscape." *European Journal of Women's Studies* 1, no. 1 (spring 1994): 99. Reports on the development of women's studies in different coun-

tries appear frequently in the journal's "State of the Art" section; for Turkey, see Marianne Grünell and Anneke Voeten, "Feminism in Plural: Women's Studies in Turkey," ibid., 4, no. 2 (May 1997): 219–33. On the politics and impact of women's education in Asia, Africa, and Latin America, see Conway and Bourque, eds., *Politics of Women's Education*.

Chapter 3: Challenging the Traditional Curriculum

1. Florence Howe, "Feminism and the Education of Women (1975)," in *Myths of Coeducation: Selected Essays, 1964–1983* (Bloomington: Indiana University Press, 1984), 175–205; and idem, "Myths of Coeducation (1978)," in ibid., 206–20; Linda Kerber, "'Why Should Girls Be Learn'd and Wise?': Two Centuries of Higher Education of Women as Seen through the Unfinished Work of Alice Mary Baldwin," in Faragher and Howe, eds., *Women and Higher Education in American History*, 18–42, quotation on 20. On the history of black women's education in the United States, see Linda M. Perkins, "The Education of Black Women in the Nineteenth Century," in ibid., 64–86; and Jeanne Noble, "The Higher Education of Black Women in the Twentieth Century," in ibid., 87–106. See also Barbara Miller Solomon, *In the Company of Educated Women: A History of Women and Higher Education in America* (New Haven: Yale University Press, 1985).
2. Annette Kolodny, "Dancing through the Minefield: Some Observations on the Theory and Practice of a Feminist Literary Criticism," *Feminist Studies* 6, no. 1 (spring 1980): 1–25, quotation on 6; Elisabeth Young-Bruehl, "The Education of Women as Philosophers," in Minnich, O'Barr, and Rosenfeld, eds., *Reconstructing the Academy*, 9–23, quotation on 11; originally published in *Signs* 12, no. 2 (winter 1987): 207–21.
3. On questions and perception, see Neil Postman and Charles Weingartner, *Teaching as a Subversive Activity* (New York: Delta, 1969), 121; Audre Lorde, "The Master's Tools Will Never Dismantle the Master's House," in *Sister Outsider: Essays and Speeches* (Freedom, Calif.: Crossing Press, 1984), 110–13.
4. Patricia Meyer Spacks, "The Difference It Makes," in Langland and Gove, eds., *Feminist Perspective in the Academy*, 7–24, quotation on 7–9, 17; originally published in *Soundings: An Interdisciplinary Journal* 64, no. 4 (winter 1981): 343–60.
5. Gayle Greene and Coppélia Kahn, "Introduction," in Greene and Kahn, eds., *Changing Subjects*, 1; William Butler Yeats, "The Choice," in *Selected Poems and Three Plays*, 3d ed. (New York: Macmillan, 1962), 138.
6. Nannerl O. Keohane, "Speaking from Silence: Women and the Science of Politics," in Langland and Gove, eds., *Feminist Perspective in the Academy*, 86–100, quotations on 86, 89, 98.
7. Claire Sprague, editor of the Twayne series, in foreword to Judith P. Zinsser,

History and Feminism: A Glass Half Full (New York: Twayne, 1993), vii; see also Sue V. Rosser, *Biology and Feminism: A Dynamic Interaction* (New York: Twayne, 1992).

8. For a typical anthology, see Farnham, ed., *Impact of Feminist Research*, vii, viii; on lack of objectivity in science, see Christie Farnham, "Introduction: The Same or Different?," in ibid., 1–8, quotation on 2. For collection of essays, see Stanton and Stewart, eds., *Feminisms in the Academy*, v, vi; on fields transformed and paradigm shift, Domna C. Stanton and Abigail J. Stewart, "Introduction: Remodeling Relations: Women's Studies and the Disciplines," in ibid., 1–16, quotations on 5, 7; Rosser, *Biology and Feminism*, 133. On the resistance of science to women's studies, see Helen E. Longino and Evelynn Hammonds, "Conflicts and Tensions in the Feminist Study of Gender and Science," in Hirsch and Keller, eds., *Conflicts in Feminism*, 164–83.

9. "'In' Box," *Chronicle of Higher Education*, Feb. 14, 1997, A10.

10. Ellen Carol DuBois et al., *Feminist Scholarship: Kindling in the Groves of Academe* (Urbana: University of Illinois Press, 1987), 157–94, data on 165–70. On anthropology, see also di Leonardo, ed., *Gender at the Crossroads of Knowledge*. More recently, Susan Christopher reports working with her thesis advisor, Patricia Gumport, at Stanford's School of Education to collect content analysis data from two "gatekeeping" journals each in history, philosophy, and sociology for the period 1960–90; this study remains incomplete. Susan Christopher, personal communication, Nov. 18, 1996.

11. Claire Goldberg Moses and Leslie Wahl Rabine, *Feminism, Socialism, and French Romanticism* (Bloomington: Indiana University Press, 1993), 2; Page Smith, *Killing the Spirit: Higher Education in America* (New York: Viking, 1990), 19, 289–92.

12. Florence Howe, "Breaking the Disciplines: In the Nineteenth Century and Today (1978)," in *Myths of Coeducation*, 221–30.

13. Jane Roland Martin, *Changing the Educational Landscape: Philosophy, Women, and Curriculum* (New York: Routledge, 1994), 188–91.

14. Ibid., 208–9, 211, 229–31.

15. Bunch explains her meaning as follows: "Another view of feminism that has limited us is what Mary Hunt and I labeled the 'add women and stir' approach to change. I do believe in adding women and stirring, in many situations, but the women added have to be willing to stir up the mix so that it no longer looks the same, so that we are reorienting whatever we've been stirred into. Feminism must be more than adding women into structures as they are; it must also be about transforming those institutions, making them more humane." Bunch, *Passionate Politics: Feminist Theory in Action* (New York: St. Martin's Press, 1987), 140; the volume contains her collected essays, 1968–1986.

16. In her original statement, Janice Monk, addressing an audience of geographers

on the necessity of curriculum transformation, said, "As an analogy, consider integrating the concept of a round earth into a course that assumes a flat earth." Monk, "Integrating Women into the Geography Curriculum," *Journal of Geography* 82, no. 6 (1983): 271–73, quotation on 271.

17. On the early study of the impact of women's studies, see Chamberlain, ed., *Women in Academe*, 156.

18. Betty Schmitz et al., "Women's Studies and Curriculum Transformation," in Banks and Banks, eds., *Handbook of Research on Multicultural Education*, 708–28. See also Friedman et al., eds., *Creating an Inclusive College Curriculum*.

19. Chamberlain, ed., *Women in Academe*, 158; Ellen Messer-Davidow, "Know-How," in Hartman and Messer-Davidow, eds., *(En)Gendering Knowledge*, 281–309, quotation on 281.

20. Schmitz et al., "Women's Studies and Curriculum Transformation," 720.

21. Elizabeth Kamarck Minnich, *Transforming Knowledge* (Philadelphia: Temple University Press, 1990), 2, 37–38, 177, 178, 181; for Copernicus and Darwin, see idem, "Friends and Critics: The Feminist Academy," in Beth Reed, ed., *Toward a Feminist Transformation of the Academy: Proceedings of the Fifth Annual GLCA [Great Lakes Colleges Association] Women's Studies Conference, Nov. 2–4, 1979* (Ann Arbor, Mich.: Great Lakes College Association Women's Studies Program, 1980), 1–11, quotation on 7.

22. For McIntosh, see Betty Schmitz, *Integrating Women's Studies into the Curriculum: A Guide and Bibliography* (Old Westbury, N.Y.: Feminist Press, 1985), esp. 26. See also Mary Kay Thompson Tetreault, "Feminist Phase Theory," *Journal of Higher Education* 56 (July–Aug. 1985): 363–84. Tetreault also identified five phases, which she termed "male scholarship, compensatory scholarship, bifocal scholarship, feminist scholarship, and multifocal or relational scholarship" (367). Several of the schemes are reviewed and discussed in relation to liberal arts and sciences disciplines by Margaret L. Andersen, "Changing the Curriculum in Higher Education," *Signs* 12, no. 2 (winter 1987): 222–54. For Lerner, see Gerda Lerner, "New Approaches to the Study of Women in American History," *Journal of Social History* 3, no. 1 (fall 1969): 53–62; and idem, "Placing Women in History: Definitions and Challenges," *Feminist Studies* 3, no. 1–2 (fall 1975): 5–14, both also in her *The Majority Finds Its Past: Placing Women in History* (New York: Oxford University Press, 1979). For the use of phase theory in a study of incorporating gender into a required core curriculum, see Susan Christopher, "Gendered Knowledge in the Core Curriculum" (paper presented at National Women's Studies Association annual meeting, Skidmore College, New York, 1996); the paper is based on idem, "Required Knowledge: Incorporating Gender into a Core Curriculum" (Ph.D. diss., Stanford University, 1995).

23. See also Marilyn R. Schuster and Susan R. Van Dyne, "Stages of Curriculum

Transformation," in Schuster and Van Dyne, eds., *Women's Place in the Academy*, 13–29, chart on 16. In 1996, Schuster and Van Dyne updated their chart on curriculum transformation, which now appears as "Stages of Change in the Curriculum and the Classroom," reprinted here as table 1, from Elaine Hedges, *Getting Started: Planning Curriculum Transformation* (Towson, Md.: National Center for Curriculum Transformation Resources on Women, 1997), 92.

24. Marilyn R. Schuster and Susan R. Van Dyne, "Changing the Institution," in Schuster and Van Dyne, eds., *Women's Place in the Academy*, 91–97, quotation on 97.

25. Susan Hardy Aiken et al., "Trying Transformations: Curriculum Integration and the Problem of Resistance," *Signs* 12, no. 2 (winter 1987): 255–75, quotations on 258, 261–64, 273.

26. See Lynne Goodstein, "The Failure of Curriculum Transformation at a Major Public University: When 'Diversity' Equals 'Variety,'" *NWSA Journal* 6, no. 1 (spring 1994): 82–102; and "Lynne Goodstein Responds," ibid., 6, no. 2 (summer 1994): 308–13, quotation on 311; and the forum on that project in ibid., 6, no. 2 (summer 1994): 291–313, especially Paula Rothenberg, "Rural U.: A Cautionary Tale," ibid., 6, no. 2 (summer 1994): 291–98.

27. Ellen G. Friedman of Trenton State College, quoted in Joye Mercer, "Curricular Project in New Jersey Faces an Uncertain Future," *Chronicle of Higher Education*, Nov. 23, 1994, A26.

28. Lynne V. Cheney, *Telling the Truth: Why Our Culture and Our Country Have Stopped Making Sense—and What We Can Do about It* (New York: Simon and Schuster, 1995), 97, 101, 106. Cheney refers to Anne Fausto-Sterling, "Race, Gender, and Science," *Transformations* 2, no. 2 (fall 1992): 5–6.

29. Andersen, "Changing the Curriculum," 228–30; see also the discussion of terminology in Schmitz, *Integrating Women's Studies*, 7–8.

30. Sandra Coyner, *Transforming the Knowledge Base: A Panel Discussion at the National Network of Women's Caucuses, First Biennial Meeting, 1989* (New York: National Council for Research on Women, 1990), 6–7.

31. Sandra Coyner, "Women's Studies as an Academic Discipline: Why and How to Do It," in Bowles and Klein, eds., *Theories of Women's Studies*, 46–71, quotation on 46; idem, "The Ideas of Mainstreaming: Women's Studies and the Disciplines," *Frontiers VIII*, no. 3 (1986): 87–95. For other views on the question of autonomy, see Deborah Rosenfelt, "What Women's Studies Professors Do That Mainstreaming Can't," *Women's Studies International Forum* 7, no. 3 (1984): 167–75; Peggy McIntosh and Elizabeth Kamarck Minnich, "Varieties of Women's Studies," ibid., 7, no. 3 (1984): 139–48. These issues have been articulated more recently by Domna Stanton and Abigail Stewart in "Remodeling Relations: Women's Studies and the Disciplines," in Stanton and Stewart, eds., *Feminisms in the Academy*, 1–16, esp. 10.

32. Coyner, "Women's Studies as an Academic Discipline," 59, 64, quotation from Stimpson on 57.

33. Myra Dinnerstein, "Questions for the Nineties," *Women's Review of Books* 6, no. 5 (Feb. 1989), 13. See also Marilyn Strathern, "An Awkward Relationship: The Case of Feminism and Anthropology," *Signs* 12, no. 2 (winter 1987): 276–92.

34. Evelyn Torton Beck, "Asking for the Future," *Women's Review of Books* 6, no. 5 (Feb. 1989): 22; Bonnie Zimmerman, presentation on "Curricular Issues for the Twenty-first Century," at "The Next Twenty-five Years," women's studies program administrators' conference, Arizona State University, Tempe, Feb. 13–15, 1997.

35. Sandra Harding, "Introduction: Is There a Feminist Method?," in Harding, ed., *Feminism and Methodology,* 1–14. See also idem, *The Science Question in Feminism* (Ithaca: Cornell University Press, 1986); and idem, *Whose Science? Whose Knowledge? Thinking from Women's Lives* (Ithaca: Cornell University Press, 1991). For Evelyn Fox Keller, see her "Feminism and Science," in Keller and Longino, eds., *Feminism and Science,* 28–40, quotation on 38.

36. Joyce McCarl Nielsen, "Introduction," in Nielsen, ed., *Feminist Research Methods,* 1–37, quotations on 12–13, 20. See also Keller and Longino, eds., *Feminism and Science.*

37. Coyner, *Transforming the Knowledge Base,* 16; Harding, *Science Question in Feminism,* 228–29. For "conscious partiality," see Maria Mies, "Toward a Methodology for Feminist Research," in Bowles and Klein, eds., *Theories of Women's Studies,* 117–39, quotation on 122.

38. Judith A. Cook and Mary Margaret Fonow, "Knowledge and Women's Interests: Issues of Epistemology and Methodology in Feminist Sociological Research," in Nielsen, ed., *Feminist Research Methods,* 69–93, quotations on 72–73; idem, "Back to the Future: A Look at the Second Wave of Feminist Epistemology and Methodology," in Fonow and Cook, eds., *Beyond Methodology,* 1–15.

39. Judith Stacey, "Disloyal to the Disciplines: A Feminist Trajectory in the Borderlands," in Stanton and Stewart, eds., *Feminisms in the Academy,* 311–29, quotations on 316–18, 320, 324–25.

40. Christine de Pizan, quoted in Boxer and Quataert, eds., *Connecting Spheres,* 9.

41. Farnham, "Introduction," 1–8, quotation on 2; Leslie W. Rabine, "Stormy Weather: A Memoir of the Second Wave," in Greene and Kahn, eds., *Changing Subjects,* 216; Margaret L. Andersen, *Thinking about Women: Sociological and Feminist Perspectives* (New York: Macmillan, 1983), 232.

42. Carol P. Christ, "Toward a Paradigm Shift in the Academy and in Religious Studies," in Farnham, ed., *Impact of Feminist Research,* 53–76, quotations on 54, 55–56; Norma Alarcón, "The Theoretical Subject(s) of *This Bridge Called*

My Back and Anglo-American Feminism," in Anzaldúa, ed., *Making Face, Making Soul,* 363–64.

43. Peter Novick, *That Noble Dream: The "Objectivity Question" and the American Historical Profession* (New York: Cambridge University Press, 1988), quotation on 40. See also Mark C. Smith, *Social Science in the Crucible: The American Debate over Objectivity and Purpose, 1918–1941* (Durham, N.C.: Duke University Press, 1994).

44. Donna Haraway, "Situated Knowledges: The Science Question in Feminism and the Privilege of Partial Perspective," *Feminist Studies* 14, no. 3 (1988): 575–99, quotations on 581, 584.

45. John R. Searle, "Rationality and Realism, What Is at Stake?," in Cole, Barber, and Graubard, eds., *Research University in a Time of Discontent,* 55–83, quotations on 68, 81. For a good example of feminist redefinition, challenging the "Western Rationalistic Tradition" (Searle's capitals), see Toril Moi, "Representation of Patriarchy: Sexuality and Epistemology in Freud's Dora," *Feminist Review* 9 (Oct. 1981): 60–74. For new ways to conceptualize objectivity, see Sandra Harding, "Rethinking Standpoint Epistemology: What Is 'Strong Objectivity'?," in Alcoff and Potter, eds., *Feminist Epistemologies,* 49–82.

46. Searle, "Rationality and Realism," 71; Joyce Appleby, Lynn Hunt, and Margaret Jacob, *Telling the Truth about History* (New York: W. W. Norton, 1994), quotations on 276, 309.

47. Messer-Davidow, "Know-How," 289. On marginality, see Stanton and Stewart, "Remodeling Relations," 3.

48. Messer-Davidow, "Know-How," 307 n. 53.

49. The team charged with curriculum transformation at Lewis and Clark College in Oregon defined their task as "gender-balancing" for reasons of strategy as well as theory, explaining, "We needed an unthreatening term to designate our comprehensive concerns." Susan Kirschner, Jane Monnig Atkinson, and Elizabeth Arch, "Reassessing Coeducation," in Schuster and Van Dyne, eds., *Women's Place in the Academy,* 36.

50. Postman and Weingartner, *Teaching as a Subversive Activity,* 16–24.

51. For reports on the 1975 Sagaris Institute in Vermont, the Califia Communities of 1976–83, and the Feminist Studies Workshop in Los Angeles in 1973 which led to the L.A. Women's Building and several other alternative structures, see "Alternative Structures for Feminist Education," pt. 2 of Bunch and Pollack, eds., *Learning Our Way,* 113–245; Ruth Iskin, "Feminist Education at the Feminist Studio Workshop," in ibid., 169–86, quotation on 169. For a women's studies movement that developed largely outside of institutions of higher education, see Ann Taylor Allen, "Women's Studies as Cultural Movement and Academic Discipline in the United States and West Germany: The Early Phase," *Women in Germany Yearbook* 9 (1993): 1–25; and idem, "The March

through the Institutions: Women's Studies in the United States and West and East Germany, 1980–1995," *Signs* 22, no. 1 (autumn 1996): 152–80.

Chapter 4: Changing the Classroom

1. Important reports that document the concern with reformation of teaching in higher education include Study Group on the Conditions of Excellence in American Higher Education, *Involvement in Learning: Realizing the Potential of American Higher Education* (Washington, D.C.: National Institute of Education, 1984); *Integrity in the College Curriculum: A Report to the Academic Community* (Washington, D.C.: Association of American Colleges, 1985); Ernest L. Boyer, *College: The Undergraduate Experience in America* (New York: Harper and Row, 1987); *A New Vitality in General Education* (Washington, D.C.: Association of American Colleges, 1988); *Campus Life: In Search of Community* (Princeton: Carnegie Foundation for the Advancement of Teaching, 1990); and *The Challenge of Connecting Learning: Liberal Learning and the Arts and Sciences Major* (Washington, D.C.: Association of American Colleges, 1991).
2. Allan Bloom, *The Closing of the American Mind: How Higher Education Has Failed Democracy and Impoverished the Souls of Today's Students* (New York: Simon and Schuster, 1987); Adrienne Rich, "Claiming an Education," in *On Lies, Secrets, and Silence: Selected Prose, 1966–1978* (New York: W. W. Norton, 1979), 231–35.
3. Paulo Freire, *The Pedagogy of the Oppressed* (New York: Continuum, 1970); Jerry Farber, "The Student as Nigger" (1967), in *The Student as Nigger: Essays and Stories* (New York: Pocket Books, 1970), 90–100. See also Carmen Luke and Jennifer Gore, eds., *Feminisms and Critical Pedagogy* (New York: Routledge, 1992); and Henry Giroux, *Border Crossings: Cultural Workers and the Politics of Education* (New York: Routledge, 1992), 39–88.
4. Jean MacGregor and Roberta S. Matthews, "The Challenge of Collaborative Learning: Creating Bridges between Communities," *Change* 26, no. 5 (Sept.–Oct. 1994), 53; and editorial by AAHE president Russell Edgerton and other articles in same issue. See also Kenneth A. Bruffee, *Collaborative Learning: Higher Education, Interdependence, and the Authority of Knowledge* (Baltimore: Johns Hopkins University Press, 1995).
5. Linda Woodbridge, "The Centrifugal Classroom," in Deats and Lenker, eds., *Gender and Academe*, 133–51, quotation on 150.
6. Marilyn J. Boxer, "Women's Studies, Feminist Goals, and the Science of Women," in Pearson, Shavlik, and Touchton, eds., *Educating the Majority*, 184–204, quotation on 184.
7. Carolyn M. Shrewsbury, "What Is Feminist Pedagogy?," *Women's Studies Quarterly* 21, nos. 3 and 4 (fall–winter 1993): 8–16, quotation on 8.

8. See Mary Kay Schleiter, director, Women's Studies, University of Wisconsin—
   Parkside, WMST-L, Oct. 23, 1995, who said that the women's studies steering
   committee decided against sharing with other faculty its description of feminist pedagogy because it "would sound so radical to them." Most early publications about women's studies tended to focus on course and curriculum content. Two important collections dealing with feminist teaching appeared in
   1985: Culley and Portugues, eds., *Gendered Subjects;* and Barbara Hillyer
   Davis, ed., "Feminist Education," special issue of *Journal of Thought* 20, no. 3
   (fall 1985). For a succinct and thoughtful summary of the issues, see also
   Renate D. Klein, "The Dynamics of the Women's Studies Classroom: A
   Review Essay of the Teaching Practice of Women's Studies in Higher Education," *Women's Studies International Forum* 10, no. 2 (1987): 187–206. For
   more recent work, see "Feminist Pedagogy: An Update," special issue of
   Women's Studies Quarterly 21, nos. 3 and 4 (fall–winter 1993).
9. See Elaine Showalter, "Introduction: Teaching about Women, 1971," in
   Showalter and Ohmann, eds., *Female Studies IV,* i–xii. Showalter is now
   Avalon Foundation Professor of Humanities and professor of English at Princeton University. The quotations are from Gerda Lerner, in ibid., vii–viii. Lerner
   is now Robinson-Edwards Senior Distinguished Professor Emerita of History at
   the University of Wisconsin.
10. Woodbridge, "Centrifugal Classroom," 133–34.
11. Barbara Omolade, "A Black Feminist Pedagogy," *Women's Studies Quarterly*
    21, nos. 3 and 4 (fall–winter 1993): 31–38.
12. Susan Stanford Friedman, "Authority in the Feminist Classroom: A Contra-
    diction in Terms?," in Culley and Portugues, eds., *Gendered Subjects,* 203–8,
    quotation on 205.
13. Ibid., 206–7.
14. Kathleen B. Jones, *Compassionate Authority: Democracy and the Representa-
    tion of Women* (New York: Routledge, 1993), 23.
15. Nancy Schniedewind, "Teaching Feminist Process in the 1990s," *Women's
    Studies Quarterly* 21, nos. 3 and 4 (fall–winter 1993): 17–30, quotation on 19;
    see also Frances Maher, "Pedagogies for the Gender-Balanced Classroom,"
    Journal of Thought 20, no. 3 (fall 1985): 48–64; and Nancy Schniedewind,
    "Cooperatively Structured Learning: Implications for Feminist Pedagogy," in
    ibid., 74–87.
16. On "process and content," see Nancy Schniedewind and Frances Maher, eds.,
    "Feminist Pedagogy," special issue of *Women's Studies Quarterly* 15, nos. 3
    and 4 (1987): 4, quoted in Jean O'Barr and Mary Wyer, "Introduction," in
    O'Barr and Wyer, eds., *Engaging Feminism,* 10; on "orthodoxy," see O'Barr and
    Wyer, "Reassessing Classrooms," in ibid., 73. O'Barr is director of the wom-
    en's studies program at Duke University, where Wyer also teaches women's
    studies.

17. Mary Field Belenky et al., *Women's Ways of Knowing: The Development of Self, Voice, and Mind* (New York: BasicBooks, 1986), 6. The authors also acknowledge their debt to the earlier work of William Perry.

18. Goldberger et al., eds., *Knowledge, Difference, and Power.* Nancy Rule Goldberger, "Introduction: Looking Backward, Looking Forward," in ibid., 2, lists "psychology, philosophy, education, women's studies, diversity and culture studies, humanities, law and feminist jurisprudence, nursing, theology, and communications" as fields in which interest has been expressed; and Ann Stanton, "Reconfiguring Teaching and Knowing in the College Classroom," in ibid., 26, refers to a citation index of more than five hundred listings. On how *WWK* influenced curriculum redesign at one liberal arts college, see Rosemarie Carfagna, "Creating Gender Equity in the College Classroom," *College Board Review* 172 (summer 1994): 8–13, 28.

19. Belenky et al., *Women's Ways of Knowing,* 3, 40, 74, 102. For a one-page outline of the five "ways," see Stanton, "Reconfiguring Teaching," 31.

20. Belenky et al., *Women's Ways of Knowing,* 124, 134, 152.

21. Joan E. Hartman points out that class influences "ways of knowing" as well, declaring that "at my institution, where I teach less privileged students, I encounter diffidence regardless of gender, and I need to empower men as well as women." Hartman, "Telling Stories: The Construction of Women's Agency," in Hartman and Messer-Davidow, eds., *(En)Gendering Knowledge,* 11–34, quotation on 24.

22. For a critique of pedagogy based on postmodernism, see Susan Johnston, "Not for Queers Only: Pedagogy and Postmodernism," *NWSA Journal* 7, no. 1 (spring 1995): 109–22, quotation on 120.

23. Goldberger, "Introduction," 7, 11; Stanton, "Reconfiguring Teaching," 35, 39, 45.

24. Frances A. Maher with Mary Kay Tetreault, "*Women's Ways of Knowing* in Women's Studies, Feminist Pedagogies, and Feminist Theory," in Goldberger et al., eds., *Knowledge, Difference, and Power,* 152.

25. Frances A. Maher and Mary Kay Thompson Tetreault, *The Feminist Classroom: An Inside Look at How Professors and Students Are Transforming Higher Education for a Diverse Society* (New York: BasicBooks, 1994), 9, 224.

26. Ibid., 89, 130–39. Scholars in fields other than women's studies are also concerned, of course, with the authenticity of subjective experience; see, for instance, Luise White, "'They Could Make Their Victims Dull': Genders and Genres, Fantasies and Cures in Colonial Southern Uganda," *American Historical Review* 100, no. 5 (Dec. 1995): 1379–1402.

27. The use of journal writing as a teaching device has been common in women's studies since the beginning; see Showalter, "Introduction." For recent criticism of requiring self-disclosure by students, see Susan Swartzland, Diana Pace, and Virginia Lee Stamler, "The Ethics of Requiring Students to Write

about Their Personal Lives," *Chronicle of Higher Education*, Feb. 17, 1993, B1–B2.

28. Carol Mattingly, "Valuing the Personal: Feminist Concerns for the Writing Classroom," in Deats and Lenker, eds., *Gender and Academe*, 153–66, quotation on 155; Caryn McTighe Musil, "Introduction," in Musil, ed., *Courage to Question*, 1.

29. Mary Belenky, quoted in Mattingly, "Valuing the Personal," 156.

30. Kathleen Weiler, "Revisioning Feminist Pedagogy," *NWSA Journal* 7, no. 2 (summer 1995): 100–106, quotation on 104.

31. bell hooks, *Teaching to Transgress: Education as the Practice of Freedom* (New York: Routledge, 1994), 39–40, 83–84.

32. Victoria Steinitz and Sandra Kanter, "Becoming Outspoken: Beyond Connected Learning," *Women's Studies Quarterly* 19, nos. 1 and 2 (1991): 138–51, quotation on 139.

33. O'Barr and Wyer, "Introduction," 7, 8; Charles Paine, "The Personal Is Problematic," in O'Barr and Wyer, eds., *Engaging Feminism*, 115. The sixty students included forty-two graduate students and eighteen undergraduates, among whom were nine women of color, five men, and six returning students. For examples of students learning to think critically about texts read in other classes, see Jean Fox O'Barr, *Feminism in Action: Building Institutions and Community through Women's Studies* (Chapel Hill: University of North Carolina Press, 1994), 62–63.

34. O'Barr and Wyer, "Introduction," 10.

35. Barbara Hillyer Davis, "Teaching the Feminist Minority," in Culley and Portugues, eds., *Gendered Subjects*, 245–52, quotation on 252. On "conversion," see Estelle B. Freedman, "Small-Group Pedagogy: Consciousness Raising in Conservative Times," in Garber, ed., *Tilting the Tower*, 35–50, quotations on 36, 39–40. For O'Barr, see her *Feminism in Action*, 239. See also a recent discussion on the "H-NET list for Women's History," H-WOMEN@h-net.msu.edu, Jan. 8–10, 1995.

36. On the origins and structure of the assessment project, see Caryn McTighe Musil, "Relaxing Your Neck Muscles: The History of the Project," chap. 1 of Musil, ed., *Students at the Center*, 3–16. The results are reported in Musil, ed., *Courage to Question*.

37. Musil, "Introduction," 1, 14.

38. Pat Hutchings, "The Assessment Movement and Feminism: Connection or Collision?" in Musil, ed., *Students at the Center*, 17–25, quotation on 22.

39. Musil, ed., *Students at the Center*, 7–8; Musil, "Relaxing Your Neck Muscles," 13.

40. Caryn McTighe Musil, "Conclusion," in Musil, ed., *Courage to Question*, 197–213, quotation on 201.

41. Marcia Westkott and Gay Victoria, "University of Colorado: Personalized

Learning," in Musil, ed., *Courage to Question*, 17–42, quotation on 29; Musil, "Conclusion," 200.

42. Laurie Finke et al., "Lewis and Clark: A Single Curriculum," in Musil, ed., *Courage to Question*, 43–81, esp. 59–66; Anita Clair Fellman and Barbara A. Winstead, "Old Dominion University: Making Connections," in ibid., 83–108, quotations on 95, 96, 104.

43. Rosanna Hertz and Susan Reverby, "Wellesley College: Counting the Meanings," in Musil, ed., *Courage to Question*, 109–129, quotations on 113, 115–17.

44. Michele Paludi and Joan Tronto, "CUNY–Hunter College: Feminist Education," in Musil, ed., *Courage to Question*, 133–55, quotation on 143; Linda R. Silver, "Oberlin College: Self-Empowerment and Difference," in ibid., 157–77, quotations on 158, 166; Mary Jo Neitz with Michelle Gadbois, "University of Missouri-Columbia: For Women's Sake," in ibid., 179–96, quotations on 187, 194.

45. Barbara F. Luebke and Mary Ellen Reilly, *Women's Studies Graduates: The First Generation* (New York: Teachers College Press, 1995); for demographics, see 3–10, quotations on xii, 12, 26, 33, 40, 53, 57.

46. Alexander W. Astin, "The American Freshman: National Norms for Fall 1986," *Chronicle of Higher Education*, Jan. 14, 1987. Astin's report surveyed 204,491 first-year students at 372 institutions.

47. Luebke and Reilly, *Women's Studies Graduates*, 33, 65, 129; Westkott and Victoria, "University of Colorado," 33–34.

48. Luebke and Reilly, *Women's Studies Graduates*, quotations on 18, 19; Maher and Tetreault, *Feminist Classroom*, 96–101.

49. Maher and Tetreault, *Feminist Classroom*, 200.

50. For a discussion of two cultures, see Westkott and Victoria, "University of Colorado," 21–23; and *The Challenge of Connecting Learning* (Washington, D.C.: Association of American Colleges, 1991); for student praise, see Westkott and Victoria, "University of Colorado," 24.

51. Anne Statham, Laurel Richardson, and Judith A. Cook, *Gender and University Teaching: A Negotiated Difference* (Albany: State University of New York Press, 1991), 21, 125, 126, 128.

52. Ibid., 153.

53. The "midwife-teacher" model is opposed to a "banker-teacher" model. Belenky et al., *Women's Ways of Knowing*, 217–18. For dissent on grounds of class, see Steinitz and Kanter, "Becoming Outspoken," 138–53. For problems of feminist pedagogy in relation to race, see Susan Geiger and Jacqueline N. Zita, "White Traders: The Caveat Emptor of Women's Studies," *Journal of Thought* 20, no. 3 (fall 1985): 106–21.

Chapter 5: Embracing Diversity

1. Jane Roland Martin, "Methodological Essentialism, False Difference, and Other Dangerous Traps," *Signs* 19, no. 3 (spring 1994): 630–57, quotation on 646.

2. Morgan, ed., *Sisterhood Is Powerful*, xxvi.

3. Alice Echols, *Daring to Be Bad: Radical Feminism in America, 1967–1975* (Minneapolis: University of Minnesota Press, 1989), 203; Gloria Bowles, personal communication, Mar. 29, 1997.

4. Audre Lorde's comment is in "The Master's Tools Will Never Dismantle the Master's House" (comments given Sept. 29, 1979, at a Second Sex Conference in New York City), *Sister Outsider: Essays and Speeches* (Freedom, Calif.: Crossing Press, 1984), 110–13, quotation on 112. Beale's essay was reprinted in other anthologies of that era; see, e.g., *Liberation Now! Writings from the Women's Liberation Movement* (New York: Dell, 1971), 185–97.

5. On white feminists "becoming haole," see Sylvia Yanagisako, "What You Call West Looks East to Me: A Far East Perspective on West Coast Feminism" (presentation in Jing Lyman lecture series on "West Coast Feminism: Theory and Practice in Academe," Stanford University, Feb. 26, 1997). On Black Sisters, see WMST-L, Mar. 22, 1996.

6. Christina Crosby, "Dealing with Differences," in Butler and Scott, eds., *Feminists Theorize the Political*, 130, 131, 136.

7. "Celebrating Difference / Exploring Commonality: Women's Studies in the '90s," Conference of the South Central Women's Studies Association, at the University of Oklahoma in Norman, May 29–30, 1996; "Complicating Categories: Women, Gender, and Difference," Berkshire Conference in Women's History, at the University of North Carolina, Chapel Hill, June 7–9, 1996. For one analysis of the "dilemmas," see Georgia Warnke, "Discourse Ethics and Feminist Dilemmas of Difference," in Meehan, ed., *Feminists Read Habermas*, 247–61.

8. Sara Evans, *Personal Politics: The Roots of Women's Liberation in the Civil Rights Movement and the New Left* (New York: Vintage, 1980), 51. A flyer advertising the women's studies program at San Diego State in the fall of 1970 was illustrated with seven women's faces; six of those portrayed were clearly women of color.

9. Berenice A. Carroll, "International Trends: Scholarship and Action. CCWHP and the Movement(s)," *Journal of Women's History* 6, no. 3 (fall 1994): 79–96, quotation on 79. The six "generative works" are Cellestine Ware, *Woman Power: The Movement for Women's Liberation* (New York: Tower, 1970); Kate Millett, *Sexual Politics* (Garden City, N.Y.: Doubleday, 1970); Morgan, ed., *Sisterhood Is Powerful*; Cade, ed., *Black Woman*; Shulamith Firestone, *The Dialectic of Sex: The Case for Feminist Revolution* (New York: Bantam, 1970); Tanner, ed., *Voices from Women's Liberation*.

10. Helen Hacker, "Women as a Minority Group," *Social Forces* 30 (1951): 60–69; Vivian Gornick, "The Next Great Moment in History Is Ours," in *Liberation Now!*, 25–39; Naomi Weisstein, "Woman as Nigger," *Psychology Today*, Oct. 1969, reprinted in Tanner, ed., *Voices from Women's Liberation*, 296–303.

11. On the "vicious campaign" of Susan B. Anthony and Elizabeth Cady Stanton to gain suffrage, see Paula Giddings, *When and Where I Enter: The Impact of Black Women on Race and Sex in America* (New York: William Morrow, 1984), 66. Giddings bases her account on the work of Rosalyn Terborg-Penn, which includes "The Historical Treatment of the Afro-American in the Woman's Suffrage Movement, 1900–1920: A Bibliographical Essay," *Current Bibliography on African Affairs* 7 (summer 1974): 245–59; idem, "Nineteenth-Century Black Women and Woman Suffrage," *Potomac Review* 7:3 (spring–summer 1977): 13–24; idem, and "Discrimination against Afro-American Women in the Woman's Movement, 1830–1920," in Harley and Terborg-Penn, eds., *Afro-American Woman*, 17–27. The quotation from Mary Astell is from the preface to the 1706 edition of her *Serious Proposal to the Ladies* [1670], quoted in Hilda L. Smith, *Reason's Disciples: Seventeenth Century English Feminists* (Urbana: University of Illinois Press, 1982), 132. For a historian's view of the power of the analogy between sex and race, see Lisa Maria Hogeland, "*Invisible Man* and Invisible Women: The Sex/Race Analogy of the 1970's," *Women's History Review* 5, no. 1 (1996): 31–53.

12. For an extensive discussion of this point, see bell hooks, *Ain't I a Woman: Black Women and Feminism* (Boston: South End Press, 1981), esp. chap. 4, "Racism and Feminism: The Issue of Accountability," 119–58. On limitations of the "double jeopardy" concept, see Margaret L. Andersen, *Thinking about Women: Sociological and Feminist Perspectives* (New York: Macmillan, 1983), 290–92, quotation on 290; and especially Deborah K. King, "Multiple Jeopardy, Multiple Consciousness: The Context of a Black Feminist Ideology," *Signs* 14, no. 1 (autumn 1988): 42–72.

13. Joreen, "The 51 Percent Minority Group: A Statistical Essay," in Morgan, ed., *Sisterhood Is Powerful*, 46.

14. Mary Wollstonecraft, *A Vindication of the Rights of Woman*, ed. Carol H. Poston (New York: W. W. Norton, 1975), 57.

15. Toni Cade, "Preface," in Cade, ed., *Black Woman*, quotations on 9, 10, 11; on black women's studies, see Gloria T. Hull and Barbara Smith, "Introduction: The Politics of Black Women's Studies," in Hull, Scott, and Smith, eds., *But Some of Us Are Brave*, vii–xxxi, quotation on xxvi; on intolerance, see Cherríe Moraga and Gloria Anzaldúa, "Introduction," in Moraga and Anzaldúa, eds., *This Bridge Called My Back*, xxiii–xxvi, quotation on xxiii; on heterosexism, see Margaret Cruikshank, "Introduction," in Cruikshank, ed., *Lesbian Studies*, ix–xviii.

16. Florence Howe, *Seven Years Later: Women's Studies Programs in 1976*, Report

of the National Advisory Council on Women's Educational Programs (Washington, D.C.: U.S. Department of Education, June 1977), 31, 83–104.

17. Florence Howe, "A Symbiotic Relationship," *Women's Review of Books* 6, no. 5 (Feb. 1989): 15; Gerda Lerner, ed., *Black Women in White America: A Documentary History* (1972; New York: Vintage, 1973); Carolyn Rodgers, "It Is Deep," in Bell, Parker, and Guy-Sheftall, eds., *Sturdy Black Bridges*, 376. See also *Civil Rights Digest* 6, no. 3 (spring 1974), which featured articles on U.S. women of color and offered feminist perspectives on sexism and racism.

18. Toni Cade Bambara, "Foreword," in Moraga and Anzaldúa, eds., *This Bridge Called My Back*, vi–vii, quotation on vi; Moraga and Anzaldúa, "Introduction," xxiii–xxvi, quotation on xxvi; Gloria Anzaldúa, "Speaking in Tongues: A Letter to Third World Women Writers," in Moraga and Anzaldúa, eds., *This Bridge Called My Back*, 165–73, quotation on 167. See also Albrecht and Brewer, eds., *Bridges of Power.*

19. Norma Alarcón, "The Theoretical Subject(s) of *This Bridge Called My Back* and Anglo-American Feminism," in Anzaldúa, ed., *Making Face, Making Soul*, 356–69, quotation on 357.

20. Ibid., 357, 360.

21. Bonnie Zimmerman, "One Out of Thirty: Lesbianism in Women's Studies Textbooks," in Cruikshank, ed., *Lesbian Studies*, 128–31, quotation on 130; Kathy Hickok, "Lesbian Images in Women's Literature Anthologies," in ibid., 132–47.

22. Hull and Smith, "Introduction," xvii–xxxi, quotation on xvii; Moraga and Anzaldúa, "Introduction," xxvi. Audre Lorde's "The Master's Tools Will Never Dismantle the Master's House" is included in Moraga and Anzaldúa, *This Bridge Called My Back*, 98–101. See also Barbara Grier, *The Lesbian in Literature: A Bibliography* (Tallahassee, Fla.: Naiad Press, 1981).

23. King, "Multiple Jeopardy," 42–72, quotation on 45; on identity, see hooks, *Ain't I a Woman*, 7, quoted in King, "Multiple Jeopardy," 45.

24. Evelyn Brooks Higginbotham, "Beyond the Sound of Silence: Afro-American Women in History," *Gender and History* 1, no. 1 (spring 1989): 50–67, quotation on 52; Patricia Hill Collins, "Learning from the Outsider Within: The Sociological Significance of Black Feminist Thought," in Fonow and Cook, eds., *Beyond Methodology*, 35–59, quotations on 53. For a short summary of black feminism as a means toward human empowerment, see idem, "Defining Black Feminist Thought," chap. 2 in *Black Feminist Thought: Knowledge, Consciousness, and the Politics of Empowerment* (New York: Routledge, 1990), 19–39.

25. bell hooks, *Teaching to Transgress: Education as the Practice of Freedom* (New York: Routledge, 1994), 53.

26. Cruikshank, ed., *Lesbian Studies*, x.

27. Cherríe Moraga and Barbara Smith, "Lesbian Literature: A Third World Femi-

nist Perspective," in Cruikshank, ed., *Lesbian Studies*, 55–65, quotations on 62, 63, 64.

28. Adrienne Rich, "Compulsory Heterosexuality and Lesbian Existence," *Signs* 5, no. 4 (summer 1980): 631–60, quotations on 648.

29. Marilyn Frye, "A Lesbian Perspective on Women's Studies," in Cruikshank, ed., *Lesbian Studies*, 194–98, quotations on 195, 196.

30. Mohanty, Russo, and Torres, eds., *Third World Women and the Politics of Feminism*, ix–xi. On "systems of domination" and "relations of rule," see Chandra Talpade Mohanty, "Introduction: Cartographies of Struggle: Third World Women and the Politics of Feminism," in ibid., 1–47, esp. 13–15. See also Maria Anna Jaimes Guerrero, "Civil Rights versus Sovereignty: Native American Women in Life and Land Struggles," in Alexander and Mohanty, eds., *Feminist Genealogies, Colonial Legacies, Democratic Futures*, 101–21.

Although they stress differences based on personal identity, Third World women also sometimes object to the reactions provoked by this very differentiation. Accusing white feminists of using them as token women, for example, Trinh Minh-ha said, "It is as if everywhere we go, we become Someone's [sic] private zoo." Gayatri Chakravorty Spivak found "cardcarrying listeners, the hegemonic people, the dominant people" too ready to accept whatever was offered by "national informants" under the rubric of cultural differences. Minh-ha also challenged the motivation behind the "sense of specialness" and "planned authenticity" that, she felt, sometimes became substitutes for efforts to understand and willingness to share power. The ultimate goal, in her view, should be to "dismantle the very notion of core (be it static or not) and identity." This is hard to do in a context dominated by identity politics. See Trinh Minh-ha, *Woman, Native, Other: Writing Postcoloniality and Feminism* (Bloomington: Indiana University Press, 1989), 79–116, quotations on 82, 96; for Spivak, see Sabina Sawhney, "The Joke and the Hoax: (Not) Speaking as the Other," in Roof and Wiegman, eds., *Who Can Speak?*, 208–20, quotation on 209.

31. Freeman, ed., *Women* (1st ed.); Sheila Ruth, *Issues in Feminism: A First Course in Women's Studies* (Boston: Houghton Mifflin, 1980); Hunter College Women's Studies Collective, *Women's Realities, Women's Choices: An Introduction to Women's Studies* (New York: Oxford University Press, 1983); see chap. 2, above, nn. 10–14, for later editions.

32. Richardson and Taylor, eds., *Feminist Frontiers*; Richardson and Taylor, eds., *Feminist Frontiers III*, quotation on xi; Kesselman, McNair, and Schniedewind, eds., *Women*; for hooks, see "Talking Back," in ibid., 13–16; quotation, Lucita Woodis, "What Women's Studies Has Meant to Me," ibid., 24–25, quotation on 24. For a recent collection about Asian American women, see Asian Women United of California, *Making Waves: An Anthology of Writings by and about Asian American Women* (Boston: Beacon Press, 1989). Other texts

for a multicultural introduction to women's studies include Andersen and Collins, eds., *Race, Class, and Gender;* and Disch, ed., *Reconstructing Gender.*

33. Linda Garber, "Introduction," in Garber, ed., *Tilting the Tower,* ix; Toni A. H. McNaron and Bonnie Zimmerman, "Introduction," in McNaron and Zimmerman, eds., *New Lesbian Studies,* xiii–xix, quotation on xiv.

34. Mariam K. Chamberlain, "Preface," in Fiol-Matta and Chamberlain, eds., *Women of Color and the Multicultural Curriculum,* xi.

35. McNaron and Zimmerman, eds., *New Lesbian Studies,* xv. See also Tamsin Wilton, *Lesbian Studies: Setting an Agenda* (London: Routledge, 1995).

36. Wilkinson and Kitzinger, eds., *Heterosexuality.*

37. Anita Silvers, "'Defective' Agents: Equality, Difference, and the Tyranny of the Normal," *Journal of Social Philosophy,* 25th-anniversary special issue (1994): 154–75, quotation on 155; also idem, personal communication, May 1996.

38. Evelyn Torton Beck, "The Politics of Jewish Invisibility," *NWSA Journal* 1, no. 1 (1988): 93–102, quotation on 101. For a discussion of the "Europeanness" of Jews, see WMST-L, Jan. 24–25, 1996.

39. Barbara Smith, "Between a Rock and a Hard Place: Relationships between Black and Jewish Women," in Elly Bulkin, Minnie Bruce Pratt, and Barbara Smith, *Yours in Struggle: Three Feminist Perspectives on Anti-Semitism and Racism* (Brooklyn, N.Y.: Long Haul Press, 1984), 85; Elly Bulkin, "Hard Ground: Jewish Identity, Racism, and Anti-Semitism," in ibid., 150.

40. Smith, "Rock and a Hard Place," 85.

41. Bulkin, "Hard Ground," 128, 132.

42. Robin Leidner, "Constituency, Accountability, and Deliberation: Reshaping Democracy in the National Women's Studies Association," *NWSA Journal* 5, no. 1 (spring 1993): 4–27, quotations on 13, 19; see also Jennie Ruby, Farar Elliott, and Carol Anne Douglas, "NWSA: Troubles Surface at Conference," *off our backs* 20 no. 8 (Aug.–Sept. 1990): 1, 10ff.

43. Bethania Maria (Gonzalez), letter to former NWSA members, Oct. 28, 1994; Kris Anderson, WMST-L, July 18, 1994.

44. See Elizabeth V. Spelman, *Inessential Woman: Problems of Exclusion in Feminist Thought* (Boston: Beacon Press, 1988), 162; and Deborah McDowell, "Transferences: Black Feminist Discourse. The 'Practice' of Theory," in Elam and Wiegman, eds., *Feminism beside Itself,* 97.

45. hooks, *Teaching to Transgress,* 104; Mary Childers and bell hooks, "A Conversation about Race and Class," in Hirsch and Keller, eds., *Conflicts in Feminism,* 60–81.

46. Susan Stanford Friedman, "Beyond White and Other: Relationality and Narratives of Race in Feminist Discourse," *Signs* 21, no. 1 (autumn 1995): 1–49, quotations on 3, 7, 13, 17, 18.

47. Friedman, "Beyond White and Other," 18; Martin, "Methodological Essentialism," 630–57, quotations on 632, 646, 648. See also Teresa de Lauretis, "The

Essence of the Triangle; or, Taking the Risk of Essentialism Seriously: Feminist Theory in Italy, the U.S., and Britain," *differences* 1, no. 2 (summer 1989): 3–37.

48. Susan Bordo, "Feminism, Postmodernism, and Gender-Skepticism," in Nicholson, ed., *Feminism/Postmodernism*, 133–56, quotation on 139; Crosby, "Dealing with Differences," 137.

49. The phrase "race, class, gender (or sexuality)" is sometimes referred to—variously with anger, irony, or regret—as an "iron triangle," "holy trinity," or "mantra" that must be invoked in feminist rhetoric. For concern about its use by friends of women's studies, see Catharine R. Stimpson, "Women's Studies and Its Discontents," *dissent* 43, no. 1 (winter 1996): 71; Inderpal Grewal and Caren Kaplan, "Introduction: Transnational Practices and Questions of Postmodernity," in Grewal and Kaplan, eds., *Scattered Hegemonies*, 1–33, quotations on 17, 19, 20; Inderpal Grewal, "Autobiographical Subjects and Diasporic Locations: *Meatless Days* and *Borderlands*," in ibid., 231–54, quotation on 250. For global perspectives on postcolonial feminism, see also Nupur Chaudhuri and Cheryl Johnson-Odim, eds., "Global Perspectives," special issue of *NWSA Journal* 8, no. 1 (spring 1996).

50. Barbara Christian, "But Who Do You Really Belong to—Black Studies or Women's Studies?," *Women's Studies* 17 (1989): 17–23; Stephanie Riger, Carrie Brecke, and Eve Wiederhold, "Dynamics of the Pluralistic Classroom: A Selected Bibliography," *NWSA Journal* 7, no. 2 (summer 1995): 58–75, quotations on 59–60. See also Joanna de Groot and Mary Maynard, "Facing the 1990s: Problems and Possibilities for Women's Studies," in de Groot and Maynard, eds., *Women's Studies in the 1990s*, 171; and Karen E. Rowe, "Shifting Models, Creating Vision: Process and Pedagogy for Curriculum Transformation," in Fiol-Matta and Chamberlain, eds., *Women of Color and the Multicultural Curriculum*, 25–36, esp. 30–31; Warnke, "Discourse Ethics," 247–61; and Iris Marion Young, "The Ideal of Community and the Politics of Difference," in Nicholson, ed., *Feminism/Postmodernism*, 300–323.

51. Evelyn Nakano Glenn, "White Women/Women of Color: The Social Construction of Racialized Gender, 1900–1940" (paper presented at "The Feminist Future: A Transnational Perspective from California," conference, Lake Arrowhead Conference Center in Southern California, Nov. 1993), 3; Gerda Lerner, "Rethinking the Paradigm," in *Why History Matters: Life and Thought* (New York: Oxford University Press, 1997), 148–84; Tessie Liu, "Teaching the Differences among Women from a Historical Perspective: Rethinking Race and Gender as Social Categories," *Women's Studies International Forum* 14, no. 4 (1991): 265–76; Rose M. Brewer, "Theorizing Race, Class, and Gender: The New Scholarship of Black Feminist Intellectuals and Black Women's Labor," in James and Busia, eds., *Theorizing Black Feminisms*, 13–30; Bonnie Zimmerman, "Seeing, Reading, Knowing: The Lesbian Appropriation of Literature," in

Hartman and Messer-Davidow, eds., *(En)Gendering Knowledge*, 85–99, quotation on 97.

52. Frances A. Maher and Mary Kay Thompson Tetreault, *The Feminist Classroom: An Inside Look at How Professors and Students Are Transforming Higher Education for a Diverse Society* (New York: BasicBooks, 1994), 223. For a discussion of the uses of "self-deconstruction" in the academy, see Dale M. Bauer, "Personal Criticism and the Academic Personality," in Roof and Wiegman, eds., *Who Can Speak?*, 56–69.

53. Author's notes taken during membership assembly and small group discussions, National Women's Studies Association annual meeting, University of Oklahoma, Norman, June 21–25, 1995.

54. Diana Fuss, *Essentially Speaking: Feminism, Nature, and Difference* (New York: Routledge, 1989), 20, 101–2, 115–17.

55. Jenny Bourne, "Homelands of the Mind: Jewish Feminism and Identity Politics," *Race and Class* 29: 1 (summer 1987): 1–24, quotations on 1, 2, 14, 15.

56. hooks, *Teaching to Transgress*, 81, 83, 85, 86, 90; idem, "Black Students Who Reject Feminism," *Chronicle of Higher Education*, July 13, 1994, A44; Tiya Miles, "Lessons from a Young Feminist Collective," in Findlen, ed., *Listen Up*, 167–76, esp. 172–73. For a sensitive, complex analysis of who is authorized to write and teach on the experience of one cultural group, see Ann duCille, "The Occult of True Black Womanhood: Critical Demeanor and Black Feminist Studies," *Signs* 19, no. 3 (spring 1994): 591–629.

57. hooks, *Teaching to Transgress*, 126.

58. Lauri Umansky, "'The Sisters Reply': Black Nationalist Pronatalism, Black Feminism, and the Quest for a Multiracial Women's Movement, 1965–1974," *Critical Matrix* 8, no. 2 (1994): 19–50, quotations on 24, 38.

59. Lisa Albrecht and Rose M. Brewer, "Bridges of Power: *Women's Multicultural Alliances for Social Change*," in Albrecht and Brewer, eds., *Bridges of Power*, 2–22, quotation on 18.

60. For alliances between people who are different, see Judit Moschkovitz, quoted in Gloria Anzaldúa, "Bridge, Drawbridge, Sandbar, or Island: *Lesbians-of-Color Hacienda Alianzas*," in Albrecht and Brewer, eds., *Bridges of Power*, 220.

61. Anzaldúa, "Bridge, Drawbridge," 228–29.

62. See, e.g., Norma Alarcón, quoted in "Introduction," in de la Torre and Pesquera, eds., *Building with Our Hands*, 3–4.

63. Kolmar and Vogt, eds., *Selected Syllabi for Women's Studies Courses*.

64. Gail Pheterson, "Alliances between Women: Overcoming Internalized Oppression and Internalized Domination," *Signs* 12, no. 1 (autumn 1986): 146–60.

65. Kathleen Weiler, "Revisioning Feminist Pedagogy," *NWSA Journal* 7, no. 2 (summer 1995): 101.

66. Kesselman, McNair, and Schniedewind, eds., *Women;* see also Fiol-Matta and Chamberlain, eds., *Women of Color and the Multicultural Curriculum.*

67. One example of a highly publicized joint appointment is that of Paula J. Giddings in both African American studies and women's studies at Duke University. See also Deborah S. Rosenfelt, "'Definitive' Issues: Women's Studies, Multicultural Education, and Curriculum Transformation in Policy and Practice in the United States," *Women's Studies Quarterly* 22, nos. 3 and 4 (fall–winter 1994): 26–41. For earlier collaborative projects, see Nancy Hoffman, "Black Studies, Ethnic Studies, and Women's Studies: Some Reflections on Collaborative Projects," ibid., 14, nos. 1 and 2 (spring–summer 1986): 49–53. On San Francisco State, see Barbara Scott Winkler, "A Comparative History of Four Women's Studies Programs, 1970–1985" (Ph.D. diss., University of Michigan, 1992), 274.

68. Lynne Goodstein and LaVerne Gyant, "A Minor of Our Own: A Case for an Academic Program in Women of Color," *Women's Studies Quarterly* 18, nos. 1 and 2 (1990): 39–45; on "normative," see Karen E. Rowe, "Shifting Models," in Fiol-Matta and Chamberlain, eds., *Women of Color and the Multicultural Curriculum,* quotation on 35. On feminist self and other, Liu borrows from Aihwa Ong. Liu, "Teaching the Differences among Women," 265–76, quotation on 267. See also Elizabeth Higginbotham, "Designing an Inclusive Curriculum: Bringing All Women into the Core," *Women's Studies Quarterly* 18, nos. 1 and 2 (1990): 19.

69. Teresa de Lauretis, "Upping the Anti (sic) in Feminist Theory," in Hirsch and Keller, eds., *Conflicts in Feminism,* 255–70, quotation on 263. On experience, identity, and authority, useful works include Biddy Martin and Chandra Talpade Mohanty, "Feminist Politics: What's Home Got to Do with It?," in de Lauretis, ed., *Feminist Studies / Critical Studies,* 191–212; and Roof and Wiegman, eds., *Who Can Speak?*

70. On individual dilemmas, see Leslie Bow, "'For Every Gesture of Loyalty, There Doesn't Have to Be a Betrayal': Asian American Criticism and the Politics of Locality," in Roof and Wiegman, eds., *Who Can Speak?,* 30–55, quotation on 44–45; de Lauretis, "Upping the Anti," 265.

71. *On Campus with Women* (Association of American Colleges and Universities), 24, no. 2 (fall 1994): 3; ibid., no. 4 (spring 1995): 5.

72. Jodi Dean, *Solidarity of Strangers: Feminism after Identity Politics* (Berkeley: University of California Press, 1996), 1, 3–4.

73. Johnnella E. Butler, "Transforming the Curriculum: Teaching about Women of Color," in Butler and Walter, eds., *Transforming the Curriculum,* 67–87, quotations on 70, 75, 86 n. 12.

74. On relational feminism, see Karen Offen, "Defining Feminism: A Comparative Historical Approach," *Signs* 14, no. 1 (autumn 1988): 119–57; and chap. 6, below. See also the analysis developed by Leonard Fein to explain the problem

of the universal and particular in "Jewish continuity": Leonard Fein, *Smashing Idols and Other Prescriptions for Jewish Continuity* (New York: Nathan Cummings Foundation, 1994), discussed in Elizabeth K. Minnich, *Liberal Learning and the Arts of Connection for the New Academy* (Washington: Association of American Colleges and Universities, 1995), 16–17.

75. Johnnella Butler, quoted in Liza Fiol-Matta, "Litmus Tests for Curriculum Transformation," in Fiol-Matta and Chamberlain, eds., *Women of Color and the Multicultural Curriculum*, 141.

Chapter 6: The Quest for Theory

1. Iris Marion Young, "Gender as Seriality: Thinking about Women as a Social Collective," in Nicholson and Seidman, eds., *Social Postmodernism*, 191.

2. August Bebel, *Woman under Socialism* (New York: New York Labor News, 1904), 9, emphasis in original.

3. For autobiographical reconstructions of this process, see Rachel Blau DuPlessis, "Reader, I Married Me: A Polygynous Memoir," in Greene and Kahn, eds., *Changing Subjects*, 97–111; Carolyn Porter, "Getting Gendered," in ibid., 168–79; Bonnie Zimmerman, "In Academia and Out: The Experience of a Lesbian Feminist Literary Critic," in ibid., 112–20; and other essays in ibid. DuPlessis, then a Columbia University graduate student, recalls her response to Millett and also notes the large number of feminist critics who emerged from Columbia's English and French departments (100–101 and 109 n. 6).

4. Naomi Weisstein's "Psychology Constructs the Female, or the Fantasy Life of the Male Psychologist" was described as "a standard text for the study of Women's Liberation" when it was reprinted in Adams and Briscoe, eds., *Up against the Wall, Mother*, 176–92; its early publication history appears on 176. Both Weisstein's article and Jo Freeman's "The Social Construction of the Second Sex" were reprinted in Garskof, ed., *Roles Women Play*, 68–83, and 123–41, respectively.

5. Charlotte Perkins Gilman, *The Man-Made World; or Our Androcentric Culture* (New York: Charlton, 1911). Gilman credited the American sociologist Lester F. Ward for the concept of androcentrism and gynaecocentric theory developed in his book *Pure Sociology* (New York: Macmillan, 1903).

6. Schneir, ed., *Feminism*; Rossi, ed., *Feminist Papers*; Gerda Lerner, "The Lady and the Mill Girl: Changes in the Status of Women in the Age of Jackson, 1800–1840," *Midcontinent American Studies Journal* 10, no. 1 (spring 1969): 5–15. "Impudent Lasses" is the title of chap. 1 in Sheila Rowbotham, *Women, Resistance, and Revolution: A History of Women and Revolution in the Modern World* (1972; New York: Vintage, 1974).

7. Mary Maynard points out that this formulation appeared in 1975 in Gayle

Yates, *What Women Want: The Ideas of the Movement* (Cambridge: Harvard University Press, 1975); and in Barbara Deckard, *The Women's Movement* (New York: Harper and Row, 1975). See Maynard's very interesting study "Beyond the 'Big Three': The Development of Feminist Theory into the 1990s," *Women's History Review* 4, no. 3 (1995): 259–81. For a typical use of the "big three," see Margaret L. Andersen, *Thinking about Women: Sociological and Feminist Perspectives* (New York: Macmillan, 1983). For an in-depth analysis of these conceptions of feminism and political philosophy, see Alison M. Jaggar, *Feminist Politics and Human Nature* (Totowa, N.J.: Rowman and Allanheld, 1983).

8. Joan Kelly, *Women, History, and Theory: The Essays of Joan Kelly* (Chicago: University of Chicago Press, 1984), xii. The four essays cited appear in this volume.

9. Ibid., quotation on xiii.

10. Gerda Lerner, "New Approaches to the Study of Women in American History," *Journal of Social History* 3, no. 1 (fall 1969): 333–56; this essay is also in Carroll, ed., *Liberating Women's History*, 349–56; Ann D. Gordon, Mari Jo Buhle, and Nancy Schrom Dye, "The Problem of Women's History," in ibid., 75–92; Berenice A. Carroll, "Introduction," in ibid., ix, xi.

11. Natalie Zemon Davis, "City Women and Religious Change," in *Society and Culture in Early Modern France: Eight Essays by Natalie Zemon Davis* (Stanford: Stanford University Press, 1975), 65–95; and idem, "Women on Top," in ibid., 124–51.

12. For the contribution of anthropologists, see Rosaldo and Lamphere, eds., *Women, Culture, and Society*; and Reiter, ed., *Toward an Anthropology of Women*; the latter volume includes Gayle Rubin, "The Traffic in Women: Notes on the 'Political Economy' of Sex," 157–210. For an excellent recent review of feminism and anthropology, see Micaela di Leonardo, "Introduction: Gender, Culture, and Political Economy. Feminist Anthropology in Historical Perspective," in di Leonardo, ed., *Gender at the Crossroads of Knowledge*, 1–48.

13. Sally Slocum, "Woman the Gatherer: Male Bias in Anthropology," in Reiter, ed., *Toward an Anthropology of Women*, 36–50; Nancy Chodorow, *The Reproduction of Mothering: Psychoanalysis and the Sociology of Gender* (Berkeley: University of California Press, 1978); Judith R. Walkowitz, *Prostitution and Victorian Society: Women, Class, and the State* (Cambridge: Cambridge University Press, 1980); Elaine Showalter, "Feminist Criticism in the Wilderness," in Abel, ed., *Writing and Sexual Difference*, 9–35, esp. 14–15. Chodorow's work, which includes *Feminism and Psychoanalytic Theory* (New Haven: Yale University Press, 1989), has generated a wealth of other works investigating gender differentiation and inequality as the results of both psychological and cultural influences within family settings. For a critique of Chodorow and

other theorists which emphasizes the infant as an active meaning maker in the development of social relations, see Maureen A. Mahoney and Barbara Yngvesson, "The Construction of Subjectivity and the Paradox of Resistance: Reintegrating Feminist Anthropology and Psychology," *Signs* 18, no. 1 (autumn 1992): 44–73. For guidance regarding this literature, see two review essays: Judith Kegan Gardiner, "Psychoanalysis and Feminism: An American Humanist's View," *Signs* 17, no. 2 (winter 1992): 437–54; and Michèle Barrett, "Psychoanalysis and Feminism: A British Sociologist's View," ibid., 17, no. 2 (winter 1992): 455–66.

14. Gerda Lerner, "Placing Women in History: A Theoretical Approach" (paper delivered to the Organization of American Historians, 1980), quoted in Gloria Bowles and Renate Duelli Klein, "Introduction: Theories of Women's Studies and the Autonomy/Integration Debate," in Bowles and Klein, eds., *Theories of Women's Studies*, 1–26, quotation on 12; Susan Moller Okin, *Women in Western Political Thought* (Princeton: Princeton University Press, 1979); Carol C. Gould, "The Woman Question: Philosophy of Liberation and the Liberation of Philosophy," in Gould and Wartofsky, eds., *Women and Philosophy*, 5–44. For a concise summary of some important early contributions to rethinking conventional wisdom in the disciplines, see Marilyn J. Boxer, "Women's Studies, Feminist Goals, and the Science of Women," in Pearson, Shavlik, and Touchton, eds., *Educating the Majority*, 184–204, esp. 185–90.

15. Patrice McDermott, *Politics and Scholarship: Feminist Academic Journals and the Production of Knowledge* (Urbana: University of Illinois Press, 1994), 34–35; Charlotte Bunch, "Not by Degrees: Feminist Theory and Education," reprinted in Bunch and Pollack, eds., *Learning Our Way*, 248–60, quotations on 249, 256; idem, "Building Feminist Theory: The Story of *Quest*," in *Passionate Politics: Feminist Theory in Action. Essays, 1968–1986* (New York: St. Martin's Press, 1987), 230–39, quotations on 232–33. For a sampling of articles from *Quest*, see *Quest* Staff, *Building Feminist Theory: Essays from "Quest"* (New York: Longman, 1981). See also Nancy Hartsock, "Feminist Theory and the Development of Revolutionary Strategy," in Eisenstein, ed., *Capitalist Patriarchy*, 56–77.

16. "Bibliography of Feminist Epistemologies," in Alcoff and Potter, eds., *Feminist Epistemologies*, 295–301; Sandra Harding, "Rethinking Standpoint Epistemology: What Is 'Strong Objectivity'?," in ibid., 49–82, quotation on 51. See also Mary E. Hawkesworth, "Knowers, Knowing, Known: Feminist Theory and Claims of Truth," *Signs* 14, no. 3 (spring 1989): 533–57.

17. Susan Krieger, "Lesbian Identity and Community: Recent Social Science Literature," *Signs* 8, no. 1 (autumn 1982): 91–108; Bonnie Zimmerman, "The Politics of Transliteration: Lesbian Personal Narratives," ibid., 9, no. 4 (summer 1984): 663–82, quotation on 678; Moraga and Anzaldúa, eds., *This Bridge*

Called My Back, 23; Shane Phelan, "(Be)Coming Out: Lesbian Identity and Politics," *Signs* 18, no. 4 (summer 1993): 765–90, quotation on 766.

18. Anzaldúa, quoted in Phelan, "(Be)Coming Out," 781.

19. Phelan, "(Be)Coming Out," 773, 777, 779.

20. Suzanna Danuta Walters, "From Here to Queer: Radical Feminism, Postmodernism, and the Lesbian Menace (or, Why Can't a Woman Be More Like a Fag?)," *Signs* 21, no. 4 (summer 1996): 830–69, quotations on 832; Sheila Jeffreys, "Return to Gender: Postmodernism and Lesbianandgay [sic] Theory," in Bell and Klein, eds., *Radically Speaking*, 359–74.

21. Hélène Cixous, "The Laugh of the Medusa," *Signs* 1, no. 4 (summer 1976): 875–93; Elaine Marks, "Women and Literature in France," ibid., 3, no. 4 (summer 1978): 832–42; and Carolyn Greenstein Burke, "Report from Paris: Women's Writing and the Women's Movement," ibid., 3, no. 4 (summer 1978): 843–55; Marks and Courtivron, eds., *New French Feminisms;* see also Nancy Fraser, "Introduction: Revaluing French Feminism," in Fraser and Bartky, eds., *Revaluing French Feminism*, 1–24.

22. Chantal Mouffe, "The Legacy of *m/f*," in Adams and Cowie, eds., *Woman in Question*, 3–4.

23. The debate may also reflect the criticism by former Marxist feminists who became postmodernists of the (male) "unencumbered self" of Marxist (and liberal) theory from the perspective of a (female) "situated self." See Seyla Benhabib and Drucilla Cornell, "Introduction: Beyond the Politics of Gender," in Benhabib and Cornell, eds., *Feminism as Critique*, 10–13.

24. Eisenstein, ed., *Capitalist Patriarchy;* idem, *The Radical Future of Liberal Feminism* (New York: Longman, 1981); Carole Pateman, "The Fraternal Social Contract," chap. 2 of *The Disorder of Women: Democracy, Feminism, and Political Theory* (Stanford: Stanford University Press, 1989), 33–57, quotations on 33–34; see also idem, *The Sexual Contract* (Stanford: Stanford University Press, 1988).

25. Nancy C. M. Hartsock, "The Feminist Standpoint: Developing the Ground for a Specifically Feminist Historical Materialism," in Harding, ed., *Feminism and Methodology*, 157–80, quotation on 159. For a summary and critique of standpoint theory and several responses to it, including comments by Hartsock, Patricia Hill Collins, and others, see Susan Hekman, "Truth and Method: Feminist Standpoint Theory Revisited," *Signs* 22, no. 2 (winter 1997): 341–65; and "Comments and Reply," ibid., 22, no. 2 (winter 1997): 366–402.

26. Patricia Hill Collins, "Learning from the Outsider Within: The Sociological Significance of Black Feminist Thought," *Social Problems* 33, no. 6 (1986): 14–32; idem, "Comment on Hekman's 'Truth and Method,'" *Signs* 22, no. 2 (winter 1997): 375–81.

27. Liz Stanley and Sue Wise, "'Back into the Personal'? or, Our Attempts to Construct 'Feminist Research,'" in Bowles and Klein, eds., *Theories of Women's*

Studies, 192–209; Mary Evans, "In Praise of Theory: The Case for Women's Studies," in ibid., 219–28.

28. For Walker's explanation of *womanist,* see Alice Walker, "Definition of Womanist," in Anzaldúa, ed., *Making Face, Making Soul,* 370.

29. Luce Irigaray, *This Sex Which Is Not One,* trans. Catherine Porter with Carolyn Burke (Ithaca: Cornell University Press, 1985); Elizabeth V. Spelman, *Inessential Woman: Problems of Exclusion in Feminist Thought* (Boston: Beacon Press, 1988), x, 167, 185.

30. Denise Riley, *"Am I That Name?" Feminism and the Category of "Women" in History* (Minneapolis: University of Minnesota Press, 1988).

31. On the "relational feminism" of such figures, see Karen Offen, "Defining Feminism: A Comparative Historical Approach," *Signs* 14, no. 1 (autumn 1988): 119–57.

32. See Ruth Milkman, "Women's History and the Sears Case," *Feminist Studies* 12, no. 2 (summer 1986): 375–400.

33. Joan Wallach Scott, *Only Paradoxes to Offer: French Feminists and the Rights of Man* (Cambridge: Harvard University Press, 1996), 3–4.

34. JeeYeun Lee, "Beyond Bean Counting," in Findlen, ed., *Listen Up,* 205–11, quotation on 211.

35. Mary Poovey, "The Differences of Women's Studies: The Example of Literary Criticism," in Stanton and Stewart, eds., *Feminisms in the Academy,* 135–56, quotation on 135.

36. On Marxian methodology, see Hartsock, "Feminist Standpoint."

37. Joan Kelly-Gadol, "The Social Relations of the Sexes: Methodological Implications of Women's History," *Signs* 1, no. 4 (summer 1976): 809–23; Joan W. Scott, "Gender: A Useful Category of Historical Analysis," *American Historical Review* 91, no. 5 (Dec. 1986): 1053–75; idem, *Gender and the Politics of History* (New York: Columbia University Press, 1988).

38. Catharine R. Stimpson, "Women's Studies: An Overview," *University of Michigan Papers in Women's Studies,* May 1978, 14–26.

39. Sonya O. Rose, "Gender History / Women's History: Is Feminist Scholarship Losing Its Critical Edge?" *Journal of Women's History* 5, no. 1 (spring 1993): 89–101, quotation on 97 n. 14.

40. Mary Poovey, "Feminism and Deconstruction," *Feminist Studies* 14, no. 1 (spring 1988): 51–65, quotation on 60.

41. On motherhood, see the essays in "Maternity, Equality and Difference in Historical Contexts," pt. 2 of Bock and James, eds., *Beyond Equality and Difference.* For Auclert, see Karen Offen, "Minotaur or Mother: The Gendering of the State in Early Third Republic France," in *Gender and the Origins of the Welfare State: Conferences at the Center for European Studies, 1987–88* (Cambridge: [Harvard] Center for European Studies, n.d.); Ellen Ross, "New Thoughts on 'the Oldest Vocation': Mothers and Motherhood in Recent Femi-

nist Scholarship," *Signs* 20, no. 2 (winter 1995): 397–413, quotation on 398; Jean Bethke Elshtain, "The Power and Powerlessness of Women," in Bock and James, eds., *Beyond Equality and Difference*, 110–25, quotation on 118. See also Bock and Thane, eds., *Maternity and Gender Policies;* and Glenn, Chang, and Forcey, eds., *Mothering.*

42. Ann Snitow, "A Gender Diary," in Scott, ed., *Feminism and History*, 505–44, quotations on 505–6, 515, 519; Elisabeth Young-Bruehl, "The Education of Women as Philosophers," in Minnich, O'Barr, and Rosenfeld, eds., *Reconstructing the Academy*, 9–23, quotation on 15.

43. Jane Flax, "The End of Innocence," in Butler and Scott, eds., *Feminists Theorize the Political*, 445–63, quotation on 446.

44. Ibid., 446–47, 452, 454, 458, 460.

45. Karen Offen, "Feminism and Sexual Difference in Historical Perspective," in Rhode, ed., *Theoretical Perspectives on Sexual Difference*, 13–20, quotations on 16, 19.

46. Joan Hoff, "The Pernicious Effects of Poststructuralism on Women's History," in Bell and Klein, eds., *Radically Speaking*, 393–412, quotations on 393, 394, 396; also see *Chronicle of Higher Education*, Oct. 20, 1993, B1–B2. A longer version appeared as Joan Hoff, "Gender as a Postmodern Category of Paralysis," *Women's History Review* 3 (1994): 149–68.

47. Hoff, "Pernicious Effects," 399–400, 405–7; Somer Brodribb, "Nothing Mat(t)ers," in Bell and Klein, eds., *Radically Speaking*, 297–310, quotation on 305. Hoff borrows the term *phallic drift* from Ronni Sandroff, who defines it as "the powerful tendency for public discussion of gender issues to drift, inexorably, back to the male point of view." Hoff, "Pernicious Effects," 406.

48. Nancy Hartsock, "Foucault on Power: A Theory For Women?," in Nicholson, ed., *Feminism/Postmodernism*, 157–75, quotations on 163–64; Wendy Brown, *States of Injury: Power and Freedom in Late Modernity* (Princeton: Princeton University Press, 1995), 48. Marion Smiley points out that other theories, including Marxism, also deny women the right to define their own identity, finding only the class aspect of identity formation significant; see her "Feminist Theory and the Question of Identity," *Women and Politics* 13, no. 2 (1993): 91–122.

49. For a discussion of this tendency, see Sandra Harding, "Feminism, Science, and the Anti-Enlightenment Critiques," in Nicholson, ed., *Feminism/Postmodernism*, 83–106, quotation on 99. Harding also discusses the links between feminism and postmodernism in "Feminist Epistemology in and after the Enlightenment," chap. 7 of *Whose Science? Whose Knowledge? Thinking from Women's Lives* (Ithaca: Cornell University Press, 1991), 164–87.

50. Pauline Johnson, *Feminism as Radical Humanism* (Boulder, Colo.: Westview, 1994), 26, 30.

51. Karen Offen, "Reclaiming the European Enlightenment for Feminism; or Prol-

ogomena to Any Future History of Eighteenth Century Europe," in Akkerman and Stuurman, eds., *Feminist Political Thought in European History*, 85–103, quotations on 99.

52. Barbara Christian, "The Race for Theory," *Feminist Studies* 14, no. 1 (spring 1988): 67–79, quotations on 69, 74–75.

53. bell hooks, *Teaching to Transgress: Education as the Practice of Freedom* (New York: Routledge, 1994), 63. See also idem, "Postmodern Blackness," in *Yearning: Race, Gender, and Cultural Politics* (Boston: South End Press, 1990), 23–31.

54. hooks, *Teaching to Transgress*, 65; Katie King, "Producing Sex, Theory, and Culture: Gay/Straight Remapping in Contemporary Feminism," in Hirsch and Keller, eds., *Conflicts in Feminism*, 82–101, quotation on 89; Susan Stanford Friedman, "Making History: Reflections on Feminism, Narrative, and Desire," in Elam and Wiegman, eds., *Feminism beside Itself*, 11–53, quotations on 26, 35; Elizabeth Spelman, "Now You See Her, Now You Don't," in *Inessential Woman*, 160–87; Maynard, "Beyond the 'Big Three,'" 259–81, quotation on 265; Sharon Sievers, "Six (or More) Feminists in Search of a Historian," *Journal of Women's History* 1, no. 2 (fall 1989): 319–30, quotations on 323–24.

55. See, e.g., Harley and Terborg-Penn, eds., *Afro-American Woman*; Moraga and Anzaldúa, eds., *This Bridge Called My Back*; Hull, Scott, and Smith, eds., *But Some of Us Are Brave*; and bell hooks, *Ain't I a Woman: Black Women and Feminism* (Boston: South End Press, 1981), quotation on 87.

56. hooks, *Ain't I a Woman?*, 148, 150, 189, 195; bell hooks with Tanya McKinnon, "Sisterhood: Beyond Public and Private," *Signs* 21, no. 4 (summer 1996): 814–29, quotations on 819, 823. On "politicization of self," see bell hooks, *Talking Back: Thinking Feminist, Thinking Black* (Boston: South End Press, 1989), 109.

57. Deborah McDowell, "Transferences: Black Feminist Discourse: The Practice of Theory," in Elam and Wiegman, eds., *Feminism beside Itself*, 93–118, quotations on 94, 101, 107, 111. See also Patricia Hill Collins, *Black Feminist Thought: Knowledge, Consciousness, and the Politics of Empowerment* (New York: Routledge, 1990), 19–40; and Freida High W. Tesfagiorgis, "In Search of a Discourse and Critique/s that Center the Art of Black Women Artists," in James and Busia, eds., *Theorizing Black Feminisms*, 228–66.

58. Spelman, *Inessential Woman*, 126–28, 186–87.

59. Gloria Anzaldúa, "Haciendo Caras, una Entrada," in Anzaldúa, ed., *Making Face, Making Soul*, xv; idem, "La Conciencia de la Mestiza: Towards a New Consciousness," in ibid., 377–89; Mitsuye Yamada, "Masks of Woman," in ibid., 114–16; Norma Alarcón, "The Theoretical Subject(s) of *This Bridge Called My Back* and Anglo-American Feminism," in ibid., 356–69, quotation on 363–64; Joan W. Scott, "The New University: Beyond Political Correctness," *Perspectives* 30, no. 7 (Oct. 1992): 18.

60. Nellie Y. McKay, "Acknowledging Differences: Can Women Find Unity through Diversity?," in James and Busia, eds., *Theorizing Black Feminisms*, 267–82, quotation on 279; Judith Butler, *Gender Trouble: Feminism and the Subversion of Identity* (New York: Routledge, 1990), 146, 147; idem, *Bodies That Matter: On the Discursive Limits of Self* (New York: Routledge, 1993), quotations on 5, 6, 11.

61. Judith M. Bennett, "Feminism and History," *Gender and History* 1, no. 3 (autumn 1989): 251–72, quotations on 258; Nancy K. Miller, in Jane Gallop, Marianne Hirsch, and Nancy K. Miller, "Criticizing Feminist Criticism," in Hirsch and Keller, eds., *Conflicts in Feminism*, 349–69, quotation on 351.

62. Jeffreys, "Return to Gender," 359–74, quotation on 359; Renate Klein, "(Dead) Bodies Floating in Cyberspace: Post-Modernism and the Dismemberment of Women," in Bell and Klein, eds., *Radically Speaking*, 346–58, quotations on 356, 357.

63. Bell and Klein, eds., *Radically Speaking*; workshop reported by Carol Anne Douglas, *off our backs* 24, no. 8 (Aug.–Sept. 1996): 20.

64. Elayne Rapping, "Politics and Polemics," review of *Radically Speaking*, ed. Diane Bell and Renate Klein, *Women's Review of Books* 14, no. 1 (Oct. 1996): 9. For "A Po-mo Quiz," see Bell and Klein, eds., *Radically Speaking*, 558–61.

65. Susan Kingsley Kent, "Mistrials and Diatribulations: A Reply to Joan Hoff," *Women's History Review* 5, no. 1 (1996): 11–12.

66. Ava Baron, "On Looking at Men: Masculinity and the Making of a Gendered Working-Class History," in Shapiro, ed., *Feminists Revision History*, 146–71; Michael S. Kimmel, "Men and Women's Studies: Premises, Perils, and Promise," in Hewitt, O'Barr, and Rosebaugh, eds., *Talking Gender*, 153–66, quotations on 154, 156.

67. Lois Banner, review of eight books in men's studies, *Signs* 14, no. 3 (spring 1989): 703–8, quotations on 705, 707–8. Banner has also written about the Program for the Study of Women and Men in Society at the University of Southern California; see her "Women's Studies and Men's Studies: An Alternative Approach," *Women's Studies International Forum* 9, no. 2 (1986): 141–44.

68. Diane Richardson and Victoria Robinson, "Theorizing Women's Studies, Gender Studies, and Masculinity: The Politics of Naming," *European Journal of Women's Studies* 1, no. 1 (spring 1994): 11–27, quotation on 24–25; idem, "Repackaging Women and Feminism: Taking the Heat Off Patriarchy," in Bell and Klein, eds., *Radically Speaking*, 179–87, illustration on 181, quotation on 180.

69. Butler, *Gender Trouble*, 147; idem, "Contingent Foundations: Feminism and the Question of 'Postmodernism,'" in Seyla Benhabib et al., *Feminist Contentions: A Philosophical Exchange* (New York: Routledge, 1995), 49.

70. Judith Lorber, *Paradoxes of Gender* (New Haven: Yale University Press, 1994), quotations on 5, 8.

71. Mary Hawkesworth, "Confounding Gender," *Signs* 22, no. 3 (spring 1997): 649–85, esp. 650–51, quotation on 655. See also replies to Hawkesworth, ibid., 22, no. 3 (spring 1997): 685–713.

72. Riley, *"Am I That Name?,"* 112–13; Diana Fuss, *Essentially Speaking: Feminism, Nature, and Difference* (New York: Routledge, 1989), xii, 18, 37; Donna Haraway, "A Manifesto for Cyborgs: Science, Technology, and Socialist Feminism in the 1980s," in Nicholson, ed., *Feminism/Postmodernism*, 190–233, quotations on 196–99; Teresa de Lauretis, "The Essence of the Triangle or, Taking the Risk of Essentialism Seriously: Feminist Theory in Italy, the United States, and Britain," *differences* 1, no. 2 (summer 1989): 11–12, citing Linda Alcoff, "Cultural Feminism versus Poststructuralism: The Identity Crisis in Feminist Theory," *Signs* 13, no. 3 (spring 1988): 405–36.

73. Young, "Gender as Seriality," 187–215, quotations on 188, 190–92.

74. Ibid., 199, 209.

75. Butler, *Gender Trouble*, 128–30.

76. Johnson, *Feminism as Radical Humanism*, viii.

77. Ibid., 19, 20.

78. Ibid., 10–12, 20. Johnson draws on the work of Ferenc Feher and Agnes Heller.

79. Marianne Hirsch and Evelyn Fox Keller, "Introduction: January 4, 1990," in Hirsch and Keller, eds., *Conflicts in Feminism*, 1–5; idem, "Conclusion: Practicing Conflict in Feminist Theory," in ibid., 370–85; Rapping, "Politics and Polemics," 9–10.

80. See Laurie Finke's rebuttal to the association between masculinity and theory, "The Rhetoric of Marginality: Why I Do Feminist Theory," *Tulsa Studies In Women's Literature* 5, no. 2 (fall 1986): 251–72.

81. On the importance of historicizing feminist theory, see Maynard, "Beyond the 'Big Three,'" 270, 277; Antoinette Burton, "'History' Is Now: Feminist Theory and the Production of Historical Feminisms," *Women's History Review* 1, no. 1 (1992): 25–39.

82. Alison Assiter, *Enlightened Women: Modernist Feminism in a Postmodern Age* (London: Routledge, 1996), 112.

Chapter 7: "Knowledge for What?"

Some of the material in this chapter was included in my paper "Is Teaching Women's Studies a Political Act?" (presentation in Jing Lyman lecture series, Stanford University, Jan. 15, 1997).

1. Robert S. Lynd, *Knowledge for What? The Place of Social Science in American Culture* (Princeton: Princeton University Press, 1939).

2. Ibid., 128–29.

3. Ibid., 202, 208; Ellen Messer-Davidow, "Know-How," in Hartman and Messer-Davidow, eds., *(En)Gendering Knowledge*, 281–309, quotation on 300.

4. Mary Pickering, *Auguste Comte: An Intellectual Biography*, vol. 1 (Cambridge: Cambridge University Press, 1993).

5. Dorothy Ross, "The Development of the Social Sciences," in Oleson and Voss, eds., *Organization of Knowledge in Modern America*, 109, quoted in Gloria Bowles, "Is Women's Studies an Academic Discipline?," in Bowles and Klein, *Theories of Women's Studies*, 33; Lynd, *Knowledge for What?*, 10, 14; Russell Jacoby, "America's Professoriate: Politicized, Yet Apolitical," *Chronicle of Higher Education*, Apr. 12, 1996, B1–B2. Jacoby accuses many Left-oriented faculty of "inflating the most modest activity with global significance" (B2). On the split between academics and activism as it developed along gender lines in sociology at the University of Chicago, see Sara Delamont, "Old Fogies and Intellectual Women: An Episode in Academic History," *Women's History Review* 1, no. 1 (1992): 39–61.

6. See, for example, the discussion of "philanthropy studies" in Peter Dobkin Hall, *Inventing the Nonprofit Sector and Other Essays in Philanthropy, Voluntarism, and Nonprofit Organizations* (Baltimore: Johns Hopkins University Press, 1992), 233–42; and the discussion of public history in Peter Novick, *That Noble Dream: The "Objectivity Question" and the American Historical Profession* (New York: Cambridge University Press, 1988), 510–21.

7. The sponsors included the American Academy of Religion, the American Anthropological Association, the American Association of University Professors, the American Council of Learned Societies, the American Historical Association, the American Philosophical Association, the American Society for Aesthetics, the American Sociological Association, the American Studies Association, the Association of American Geographers, the Association of American Law Schools, the College Art Association, the Middle East Studies Association, the Modern Language Association of America, and the Organization of American Historians. For the conference proceedings, see Spacks, ed., *Advocacy in the Classroom*. For contrasting views of the "scholar," the "professor," and the "advocate," see Gertrude Himmelfarb, "The New Advocacy and the Old," in ibid., 97; and Andrea A. Lunsford, "Afterthoughts on the Role of Advocacy in the Classroom," in ibid., 433.

8. Robin Wilson, "Teacher or Advocate?," *Chronicle of Higher Education*, June 16, 1995, A18.

9. On the early goals and the use of this term, see Renate D. Klein, "Passion and Politics in Women's Studies in the 1990's," *Women's Studies International Forum* 14, no. 3 (1991): 125–34, esp. 125–26 and 131 n. 3.

10. Rowbotham is quoted in Susan Lees, "Feminist Politics and Women's Studies: Struggle, Not Incorporation," in Aaron and Walby, eds., *Out of the Margins*, 90–104, quotations on 90, 92.

11. Carol Rowell [Council], "General Reflections on Funding and Our Movement," typed manuscript (San Diego: Center for Women's Studies and Ser-

vices, 1974). See also Marilyn J. Boxer, "For and about Women: The Theory and Practice of Women's Studies in the United States," *Signs* 7, no. 3 (spring 1982): 670. The center continued to offer noncredit classes taught by volunteers through its "Feminist Free-You."

12. Diane Clark, "Entire SDSU Women's Studies Faculty to Quit," *San Diego Union*, Feb. 26, 1974. "[The dean's] regime has eliminated any space that existed for women's studies based on students needs and socialist feminist politics," they declared. Neysa Gelfan, "Women's Studies Faculty Quits Department," *Daily Aztec* (San Diego State University), Feb. 22, 1974.

13. Women's Studies Board, *Women's Studies and Socialist Feminism* (San Diego: Fanshen Printing Collective, Apr. 20, 1974), quotations on 1, 3.

14. Ibid., 3, 6, 8.

15. On San Francisco State, see Barbara Scott Winkler, "A Comparative History of Four Women's Studies Programs, 1970–1985" (Ph.D. diss., University of Michigan, 1992), 43–51. On potluck: "Women's studies programs, like their social gatherings, are run on a potluck basis." Ruth Perry et al., "Inventing a Feminist Institution in Boston: An Informal History of the Graduate Consortium in Women's Studies at Radcliffe College," *NWSA Journal* 8, no. 2 (summer 1996): 62.

16. Bowles and Klein, eds., *Theories of Women's Studies*. Bowles later published *Louise Bogan's Aesthetic of Limitation* (Bloomington: Indiana University Press, 1987). See also idem, ed., *Strategies for Women's Studies in the Eighties*, originally an issue of *Women's Studies International Forum*, which Bowles edited to air divergent views after the eruption of the "autonomy/integration" debate. It includes articles by scholars both praising and questioning integration projects. See also three interviews: Deborah Rosenfelt, "Ethnic Studies and Women's Studies at UC Berkeley: A Collective Interview," special California issue of *Radical Teacher* 14 (Dec. 1979): 12–18; Lisa Harrington, "California Q&A: An Interview with Gloria Bowles," *California Monthly* 92, no. 3 (Jan.–Feb. 1983): 8–11, 30; and Walter Goodman, "Women's Studies: The Debate Continues," *New York Times Magazine*, Apr. 22, 1984.

17. Gloria Bowles, "Creating Women's Studies: University of California Berkeley, 1973–1985" (paper delivered at conference on "The History of Women and California: The First 125 Years," Apr. 28, 1995); idem, personal communication, Aug. 7, 1996. I am personally familiar with similar cases at California State University, Long Beach; Stephens College, in Missouri; Kansas State University, in Manhattan, Kansas; and San Francisco State University. On the use of temporary faculty, see Gappa and Leslie, eds., *Invisible Faculty*.

18. Ann Rosalind Jones, "Imaginary Gardens with Real Frogs in Them: Feminist Euphoria and the Franco-American Divide, 1976–88," in Greene and Kahn, eds., *Changing Subjects*, 64–82, quotation on 68–69.

19. Rachel Blau DuPlessis, "Reader, I Married Me: A Polygynous Memoir," in Greene and Kahn, eds., *Changing Subjects*, 97–111, quotation on 104.

20. On the early development of black women's studies, see Gloria T. Hull and Barbara Smith, "Introduction: The Politics of Black Women's Studies," in Hull, Scott, and Smith, eds., *But Some of Us Are Brave*, xxv–xxviii.

21. Ibid., xxii, xxv.

22. Ibid., 19–20; also see Jaime Grant, WMST-L, May 29, 1996. For a perceptive student's account, see bell hooks, *Teaching to Transgress: Education as the Practice of Freedom* (New York: Routledge, 1994), 119–27.

23. For example, I offered workshops on "Women's Rights and Social Change" for employees of the Cleveland National Forest in 1976 and 1977.

24. According to one recent study, "Women's studies sought to avoid identification with the [women's] center in order to improve their own status in the university." Flora Pearle McMartin, "The Institutionalization of Women's Centers and Women's Studies Programs at Three Research Universities" (Ed.D. diss., University of California, Berkeley, 1993), 71–72.

25. Bonnie Zimmerman, "In Academia and Out: The Experience of a Lesbian Feminist Literary Critic," in Greene and Kahn, eds., *Changing Subjects*, 112–20, quotation on 115.

26. Somer Brodribb, quoted in Klein, "Passion and Politics in Women's Studies in the 1990s," 130.

27. Lorelei R. Brush, Alice Ross Gold, and Marni Goldstein White, "The Paradox of Intention and Effect: A Women's Studies Course," *Signs* 3, no. 4 (summer 1978): 870–83, quotation on 882.

28. Marie Mies, quoted in Renate D. Klein, "The Dynamics of the Women's Studies Classroom: A Review Essay on the Practice of Women's Studies in Higher Education," *Women's Studies International Forum* 10, no. 2 (1987): 187–206, quotation on 199 n. 25.

29. Annette Kolodny, "Respectability Is Eroding the Revolutionary Potential of Feminist Criticism," *Chronicle of Higher Education*, May 4, 1988, A52.

30. Annette Kolodny, "Dancing between Left and Right: Feminism and the Academic Minefield in the 1980s," *Feminist Studies* 14, no. 3 (fall 1988): 453–66, quotations on 457, 461, 465.

31. Jean Fox O'Barr, *Feminism in Action: Building Institutions and Community through Women's Studies* (Chapel Hill: University of North Carolina Press, 1994), 282; Robin Lakoff, *Talking Power: The Politics of Language in Our Lives* (New York: BasicBooks, 1990), 209.

32. Susan Gubar, "Feminist Misogyny: Mary Wollstonecraft and the Paradox of 'It Takes One to Know One,'" in Elam and Wiegman, eds., *Feminism beside Itself*, 133–54, quotation on 147; Messer-Davidow, "Know-How," quotations on 281–82, 289, 301.

33. McMartin, "Institutionalization of Women's Centers and Women's Studies Programs," 249, 254, 258–59.
34. Paula Rothenberg, review of *Unsettling Relations: The University as a Site of Feminist Struggles*, by Himani Bannerji et al., *(En)Gendering Knowledge: Feminists in Academe*, ed. Joan E. Hartman and Ellen Messer-Davidow, and *Gender and University Teaching: A Negotiated Difference*, by Anne Statham, Laurel Richardson, and Judith A. Cook, *Signs* 19, no. 2 (winter 1994): 559–63, quotations on 559, 563.
35. Jerry Anne Flieger, "Growing Up Theoretical: Across the Divide," in Greene and Kahn, eds., *Changing Subjects*, 253–66, esp. 253–54.
36. Teresa de Lauretis, "Upping the Anti (sic) in Feminist Theory," in Hirsch and Keller, eds., *Conflicts in Feminism*, 255–70, quotation on 264.
37. Lees, "Feminist Politics and Women's Studies," 90–104, quotation citing Maria Mies, 95; Maria Mies, "Toward a Methodology for Feminist Research," in Bowles and Klein, eds., *Theories of Women's Studies*, 117–39. Cf. Ailbhe Smyth, who disassociates herself from "[women's studies], its stars, its gurus, and its power-brokers" in "A (Political) Postcard from a Peripheral Pre-Postmodern State (of Mind) or How Alliteration and Parentheses Can Knock You Down Dead in Women's Studies," *Women's Studies International Forum* 15, no. 3 (1992): 331–37, quotation on 332.
38. Valeria Wagner, "In the Name of Feminism," in Elam and Wiegman, eds., *Feminism beside Itself*, 119–30, quotations on 122, 123, 125. On governance conflict, see references to the University of Minnesota and San Francisco State in Winkler, "Comparative History," 43–51.
39. Judith Shapiro, "Anthropology and the Study of Gender," in Langland and Gove, eds., *Feminist Perspective in the Academy*, 110–29, quotation on 126–27, quoted in Jean Bethke Elshtain, "Feminist Political Rhetoric and Women's Studies," in Nelson, Megill, and McCloskey, eds., *Rhetoric of the Human Sciences*, 319–40, quotation on 336.
40. Elshtain, "Feminist Political Rhetoric," 320, 337.
41. See, e.g., Karen Offen, "Defining Feminism: A Comparative Historical Approach," *Signs* 14, no. 1 (autumn 1988): 119–57.
42. Charlotte Bunch, *Passionate Politics: Feminist Theory in Action. Essays, 1968–1986* (New York: St. Martin's Press, 1987), 4, 220, 232–33, 240.
43. On "patriarchal tyranny" and "strategies of resistance," see bell hooks, *Feminist Theory: From Margin to Center* (Boston: South End Press, 1984), 10; on "anti-intellectualism" and Bunch, see 112–15. On "patriarchal drama" and early interest in women's studies, see idem, *Teaching to Transgress*, 119–27.
44. Patricia Hill Collins, *Black Feminist Thought: Knowledge, Consciousness, and the Politics of Empowerment* (New York: Routledge, 1990), 28, 215–19.
45. Gloria Anzaldúa, "Haciendo Caras, Una Entrada," in Anzaldúa, ed., *Making Face, Making Soul*, xxv–xxvi.

46. Judith Butler, "For a Careful Reading," in Seyla Benhabib et al., *Feminist Contentions: A Philosophical Exchange* (New York: Routledge, 1995), 127–43, quotations on 129, 133. For insight into contemporary feminist perspectives on these definitions, see Heidi Hartmann et al., "Bringing Together Feminist Theory and Practice: A Collective Interview," *Signs* 21, no. 4 (summer 1996): 917–51.

47. Patrice McDermott, *Politics and Scholarship: Feminist Academic Journals and the Production of Knowledge* (Urbana: University of Illinois Press, 1994), 1, 9.

48. Ibid., 10.

49. See Novick, *That Noble Dream.*

50. Maxine Baca Zinn et al., "The Costs of Exclusionary Practices in Women's Studies," in Minnich, O'Barr, and Rosenfeld, eds., *Reconstructing the Academy*, 128; this essay was also published in *Signs* 11, no. 2 (winter 1986): 290–303.

51. For an account of the founding of *Frontiers*, with "no funding . . . no financing, [and] no national organization," and of that journal's successful struggle to be both "editorially and financially independent" for thirteen years under the leadership of Kathi George, its initial editor and publisher, see "On the Fringes of Academe: Creating the Pathway. Panel Conversation at the Tenth Anniversary Celebration of San Diego Independent Scholars, October 10, 1992," *Journal of Unconventional History* 4, no. 2 (winter 1993): 7–27, quotation on 12.

52. McDermott, *Politics and Scholarship*, 154.

53. Susan Hekman, "The Feminization of Epistemology: Gender and the Social Sciences," *Women in Politics* 7, no. 3 (fall 1987): 65–83, quotation on 69.

54. bell hooks with Tanya McKinnon, "Sisterhood: Beyond Public and Private," *Signs* 21, no. 4 (summer 1996): 814–29, quotation on 821.

55. Hartmann et al., "Bringing Together Feminist Theory and Practice," 917–51, quotations on 923.

56. George, "On the Fringes," 17, 25.

57. Caryn McTighe Musil, quoted by Patrice McDermott in "The Risks and Responsibilities of Feminist Academic Journals," *NWSA Journal* 6, no. 3 (fall 1994): 373–83, quotation on 380.

58. As noted in chap. 2, four women served as president of the American Historical Association between 1987 and 1997. Yolanda Moses, an early activist in the NWSA and now president of the City College of New York, served as president of the American Anthropological Association in 1996. Women now occupy positions of leadership in many other scholarly associations as well as educational institutions.

59. The Association of Literary Scholars and Critics, organized by dissidents from the Modern Language Association, opposes what they consider the politicization of literary studies. This group is said to have two thousand members. See

William C. Dowling, "Let's Get the MLA Out of the Hiring Process," *Chronicle of Higher Education*, Feb. 7, 1997, A60.

60. For their recollection and a collective attempt at assessing the NWSA's first decade, see Towns, Cupo, and Hageman, comps., *Re-Membering*. The three program planners are Emily Abel, Deborah Rosenfelt, and Peg Strobel; see their "'Toto, I Think We're No Longer in Kansas': Reflections on the 1979 Conference," in ibid., 69–72.

61. There was a protest over this occurrence at the 1979 meeting in Lawrence, Kansas.

62. Deborah Rosenfelt, "A Time for Confrontation," *Women's Studies Quarterly* 9, no. 3 (fall 1981): 10–12.

63. Sandra J. Coyner, "Program Administrators," in Towns, Cupo, and Hageman, comps., *Re-Membering*, 110–13, quotation on 111.

64. Patricia A. Gozemba, "The First Three Years, but Who's Counting?," in Towns, Cupo, and Hageman, comps., *Re-Membering*, 76–81, quotation on 76.

65. Beth [Ribet], "Recommended Action for NWSA," WMST-L, Dec. 29, 1995. For postconference reports, see *off our backs* 26, no. 8 (Aug.–Sept. 1996): 14–17.

66. Judith A. Sturnick, "Remembering the First Coordinating Council," in Towns, Cupo, and Hageman, comps., *Re-Membering*, 57–59, quotation on 59.

67. Dorothy Haecker, "Feminists in the Midwest: Connections and Courage," in Towns, Cupo, and Hageman, comps., *Re-Membering*, 61–63, quotation on 63.

68. Caryn McTighe Musil, "Life in the Experimental Lane: A National Coordinator's View, 1984–1987," in Towns, Cupo, and Hageman, comps., *Re-Membering*, 135–40, quotations on 135, 138.

69. Rosenfelt, "Time for Confrontation," 10, 12.

70. I owe this observation to Bonnie Zimmerman.

71. Cf. Susan Stanford Friedman, "Making History: Reflections on Feminism, Narrative, and Desire," in Elam and Wiegman, eds., *Feminism beside Itself*, 18.

72. Robin Leidner, "Constituency, Accountability, and Deliberation: Reshaping Democracy in the National Women's Studies Association," *NWSA Journal* 5, no. 1 (spring 1993): 4–27, quotation on 25 n. 16. On early leadership problems, see Jo Freeman, "The Tyranny of Structurelessness," *Berkeley Journal of Sociology* 17 (1972–73): 151–64, reprinted in Jaquette, ed., *Women in Politics*, 204–14.

73. See, e.g., Susan S. Arpad, "Burnout," *Women's Studies International Forum* 9, no. 2 (1986): 208.

74. See, e.g., Jennifer Scanlon, "Keeping Our Activist Selves Alive in the Classroom: Pedagogy and Political Activism," *Feminist Teacher* 7, no. 2 (1993): 8–13.

75. Sherna Berger Gluck, "Advocacy Oral History: Palestinian Women in Resistance," in Gluck and Patai, eds., *Women's Words*, 205–19, quotations on 214, 218.

76. Ruth Milkman, "Women's History and the Sears Case," *Feminist Studies* 12, no. 2 (summer 1986): 375–400, quotation on 394–95; on its relation to "equality and difference," see Joan Wallach Scott, "The Sears Case," chap. 8 of *Gender and the Politics of History* (New York: Columbia University Press, 1988), 167–77. On conflicts faced by individual faculty, see Barrie Thorne, "Contradictions, and a Glimpse of Utopia: Daily Life in a University Women's Studies Program," *Women's Studies International Quarterly* 1 (1978): 201–5.

77. Dale M. Bauer, "Personal Criticism and the Academic Personality," in Roof and Wiegman, eds., *Who Can Speak?*, 56–69, quotation on 66.

78. Excerpt from Hartmann et al., "Bringing Together Feminist Theory and Practice," *Signs* 21, no. 4 (summer 1996), in the *Chronicle of Higher Education*'s electronic "Daily Report from Academe Today," Aug. 21, 1996.

79. bell hooks, "Feminism: A Transformational Politic," in Rhode, ed., *Theoretical Perspectives on Sexual Difference*, 185–93, quotation on 190. One report counted more than two hundred women-related e-mail lists. On March 18, 1997, Joan Korenman reported that WMST-L had 4,207 subscribers in forty-five countries.

80. Klein follows Arthur Kroker; see Julie Thompson Klein, *Interdisciplinarity: History, Theory, and Practice* (Detroit: Wayne State University Press, 1990), 96–98. Klein discusses black studies and other ethnic studies fields as well.

81. On public history, see Peter Novick, "Every Group Its Own Historian," chap. 14 of *That Noble Dream*, esp. 510–21; on nonprofit organizations and scholarship, see Hall, *Inventing the Nonprofit Sector*, esp. chap. 7, "Obstacles to Nonprofits Teaching and Research," and chap. 8, "Dilemmas of Research on Philanthropy, Voluntarism, and Nonprofit Organizations"; on American studies, see Kermit Vanderbilt, *American Literature and the Academy* (Philadelphia: University of Pennsylvania Press, 1986); and Linda Kerber's presidential address, "Diversity and the Transformation of American Studies," *American Quarterly* 41, no. 3 (1989): 415–31. Carl E. Schorske sees American studies as "an offspring of Progressivist academic culture" in which literary scholars foreshadowed the role they have in cultural studies, including feminist and gender studies, today. Schorske, "The New Rigorism in the Human Sciences, 1940–1960," *Daedalus* (winter 1997): 302–3.

82. On the need for and the problem of accountability in the context of black studies, see Johnnetta Cole, "Black Studies in Liberal Arts Education," in Butler and Walter, eds., *Transforming the Curriculum*, 137–38. The poet Adrienne Rich argues that feminist literary criticism "implies continuous and conscious accountability to the lives of women," and not just academic women. Rich, "Toward a More Feminist Criticism" (1981), in *Blood, Bread, and Poetry: Selected Prose, 1979–1985* (New York: W. W. Norton, 1986), 88. On accountability and black women's studies, see Hull and Smith, "Introduction," xxi–xxiii.

83. See, e.g., the testimony of the feminist economist Myra Strober, cited in chap. 9, below, n. 43.
84. Catherine Stimpson, quoted in Bunch, *Passionate Politics*, 130; Estelle Freedman, "Theoretical Perspectives on Sexual Difference: An Overview," in Rhode, ed., *Theoretical Perspectives on Sexual Difference*, 259–60.
85. Tiya Miles, in Kathleen B. Jones and Tiya Miles, "Risking Integrity: Political Responsibilities of Women's Studies to Changing Communities (A Dialogue in Several Acts)" (paper presented at Pacific Southwest Women's Studies Association meeting, Apr. 1996), 4–5.
86. Barbara F. Luebke and Mary Ellen Reilly, *Women's Studies Graduates: The First Generation* (New York: Teachers College Press, 1995).
87. Thomas Mann, quoted by Marjorie Garber, "Back to Whose Basics?," *New York Times Book Review*, Oct. 29, 1995, 55.
88. Hannah Arendt, "What Remains? The Language Remains: A Conversation with Günter Gaus," in *Essays in Understanding, 1930–1954*, ed. Jerome Kohn (New York: Harcourt Brace, 1994), 1–23, quotation on 22–23.
89. Ann Snitow, "A Gender Diary," in Scott, ed., *Feminism and History*, 505–43, quotation on 517–18.
90. Lynne V. Cheney, *Telling the Truth: Why Our Culture and Our Country Have Stopped Making Sense—and What We Can Do about It* (New York: Simon and Schuster, 1995), 106. On "knowledge [as] its own end" in contemporary perspective, see the discussion of John Henry Newman's principles in Jaroslav Pelikan, *The Idea of the University: A Reexamination* (New Haven: Yale University Press, 1992).

Chapter 8: Critics Inside and Outside the Academy

1. Nietzsche, quoted in Judith Grant, *Fundamental Feminism: Contesting the Core Concepts of Feminist Theory* (New York: Routledge, 1993), 138; Peter Shaw, quoted in Stephen Burd, "Ready to Cry Foul: Defiant Conservative Relishes the NEH Fights to Come," *Chronicle of Higher Education*, June 29, 1994, A25; Susan Faludi, *Backlash: The Undeclared War against American Women* (New York: Crown, 1991), 281; Catharine R. Stimpson, "Women's Studies and Its Discontents," *dissent* 43, no. 1 (winter 1996): 72.
2. Ellen Messer-Davidow, "Manufacturing the Attack on Liberalized Higher Education," *Social Text* 36 (fall 1993): 40–80, quotation on 43.
3. I want to thank Gloria Bowles for sharing this observation.
4. An example of this practice is the criticism that Sylvia Ann Hewlett directs at feminists who were her colleagues in the early 1980s for having given her inadequate support, when she attempted unsuccessfully to combine an academic career with childbearing, a decade before family leave policies began to take hold in business, industry, government, and education. Hewlett, *A Lesser*

Life: The Myth of Women's Liberation in America (New York: William Morrow, 1986); Marilyn J. Boxer, "Designer Clocks for Academic Careers," *History Teacher* 29, no. 4 (Aug. 1996): 471–81.

5. Birgitte Berger, "Academic Feminism and the 'Left,'" *Academic Questions* 1, no. 2 (spring 1988): 6–15, quotations on 10, 11, 14, 15.

6. Elaine Ginsberg and Sara Lennox, "Antifeminism in Scholarship and Publishing," in Clark et al., eds., *Antifeminism in the Academy,* 169–99, quotation on 183.

7. Allan Bloom, *The Closing of the American Mind: How Higher Education Has Failed Democracy and Impoverished the Souls of Today's Students* (New York: Simon and Schuster, 1987), 65, 344. This passage is singled out in a discussion of Bloom's "propensity for making sweeping claims without even a shred of evidence" and his concern for the "reproduction of elites," by Stanley Aronowitz, in his "Schooling, Culture, and Literacy in the Age of Broken Dreams: A Review of Bloom and Hirsch," *Harvard Educational Review* 58, no. 2 (May 1988): 173; and by Kathleen B. Jones, in her "Le Mal des Fleurs: A Feminist Response to *The Closing of the American Mind*," *Women and Politics* 9, no. 4 (1989): 7.

8. Bloom, *Closing of the American Mind,* 38, 108; Jones, "Mal des Fleurs," 12–13.

9. Roger Kimball, *Tenured Radicals: How Politics Has Corrupted Our Higher Education* (New York: HarperCollins, 1991), 15, 19. *Oppression studies* is a term that Kimball owes to Thomas Short, "'Diversity' and 'Breaking the Disciplines': Two New Assaults on the Curriculum," *Academic Questions* 1, no. 3 (summer 1988): 24.

10. Kimball, *Tenured Radicals,* xii, 155–56, 193, 207; Nancy Baker Jones, "Confronting the PC 'Debate': The Politics of Identity and the American Image," *NWSA Journal* 6, no. 3 (fall 1994): 388–89.

11. David Bromwich, *Politics by Other Means: Higher Education and Group Thinking* (New Haven: Yale University Press, 1992), xi, 26–27.

12. Michael Levin, *Feminism and Freedom* (New Brunswick, N.J.: Transaction Books, 1987), ix, 179–80, 187–88. According to Levin, "Once all nonanatomical sex differences are taken to be social in origin, an analogy between women and racial minorities is inevitable" (23). For a succinct statement on feminism, science, and objectivity, see Evelyn Fox Keller and Helen E. Longino, "Introduction," in Keller and Longino, eds., *Feminism and Science,* 1–14.

13. Levin's discussion of women's studies in *Feminism and Freedom* is a revised version of his "Women's Studies, Ersatz Scholarship," *New Perspectives* 17, no. 3 (summer 1985): 7–10. Shaw, quoted in Burd, "Ready to Cry Foul," A25; William H. Honan, "Acorns Sprout Where Mighty Oaks Grew," *New York Times,* Oct. 16, 1994, E3.

14. Michelle Easton, "The Finishing School of the '90s," *Wall Street Journal,* Mar.

12, 1996, A14. On women's studies graduates, see Barbara Luebke and Mary Ellen Reilly, *Women's Studies Graduates: The First Generation* (New York: Teachers College Press, 1995).

15. Louis Menand, quoted in Robin Wilson, "Professor, Critic, Professional Gadfly," *Chronicle of Higher Education*, Mar. 22, 1996, A16, A19.

16. Levin, *Feminism and Freedom*, 178; Lynne V. Cheney, *Telling the Truth: Why Our Culture and Our Country Have Stopped Making Sense—and What We Can Do about It* (New York: Simon and Schuster, 1995), 38.

17. John Leo, interview by news commentator Pete Wilson on Channel 35, San Francisco, Sept. 1, 1995; and idem, on *The McLaughlin Group*, Sept. 4, 1994; Eve Kosofsky Sedgwick, "Jane Austen and the Masturbating Girl," in James Chandler, Arnold I. Davidson, and Harry Harootunian, eds., *Questions of Evidence: Proof, Practice, and Persuasion across the Disciplines* (Chicago: University of Chicago Press, 1994), 105–24, quotations on 105 n. 2, 106, 113, 123.

18. Eve Kosofsky Sedgwick, "Against Epistemology," in Chandler, Davidson, and Harootunian, eds., *Questions of Evidence*, 132–36, quotation on 134; Steven Watts, "The Idiocy of American Studies: Poststructuralism, Language, and Politics in the Age of Self-Fulfillment," *American Quarterly* 43, no. 4 (Dec. 1991): 625–60, quotation on 653.

19. John Leo, *Two Steps Ahead of the Thought Police* (New York: Simon and Schuster, 1994); Richard Rorty, "A Leg-Up for Oliver North," review of *Dictatorship of Virtue: Multiculturalism and the Battle for American's Future*, by Richard Bernstein, *London Review of Books*, Oct. 20, 1994, quotation on 15. For bibliography, see Nancy Baker Jones, "The PC 'Debate': A Selected Bibliography," *NWSA Journal* 6, no. 3 (fall 1994): 404–12.

20. Marilyn Frye, "Getting It Right," *Signs* 17, no. 4 (summer 1992): 781–93, quotations on 790; Alice Kessler-Harris, "The View from Women's Studies," ibid., 17, no. 4 (summer 1992): 794–805, quotations on 795, 803, 804, 805.

21. Natalie Zemon Davis et al., "Feminist Book Reviewing: A Symposium," *Feminist Studies* 14, no. 3 (fall 1988): 601–25; Davis, "On Reviewing," in ibid., 602–6, quotations on 602, 605. "Women Reviewing / Reviewing Women" was the title of a November 1993 tenth-anniversary conference sponsored by the *Women's Review of Books*; keynote speeches and panel presentations from this conference were published in the journal in vol. 11, nos. 4–7 (Jan.–Apr. 1994).

22. Cynthia Neverdon-Morton, "Through the Looking Glass: Reviewing Books about the Afro-American Female Experience," in Davis et al., "Feminist Book Reviewing," 612–17, quotation on 616; Linda Gardiner, "Remember the Reader," in ibid., 617–22, quotations on 617, 621–22.

23. Patrice McDermott, "On Cultural Authority: Women's Studies, Feminist Politics, and the Popular Press," *Signs* 20, no. 3 (spring 1995): 668–84, quotation on 671. For frank discussion, see, e.g., Culley and Portugues, eds., *Gendered Sub-*

jects; Frances A. Maher and Mary Kay Thompson Tetreault, *The Feminist Classroom: An Inside Look at How Professors and Students Are Transforming Higher Education for a Diverse Society* (New York: BasicBooks, 1994).

24. Camille Paglia, *Sex, Art, and Culture: Essays* (New York: Vintage, 1992), 301; Ellen Willis, "Notes on Camp," *dissent*, spring 1993, 251–54, quotation on 254. On media attention, see also Faludi, *Backlash*, 31; and idem, "I'm Not a Feminist, but I Play One on TV," *Ms.* magazine, Mar.–Apr. 1995, 30–39. The term *media history* is Paglia's.

25. Faludi, "I'm Not a Feminist," 30.

26. Karen Lehrman, "Off Course," *Mother Jones*, Sept.–Oct., 1993, 45–51, 64, 66, 68; Pauline Bart, letter to the editor, *Mother Jones*, Nov.–Dec. 1993, 5; Paula Kamen, *Feminist Fatale: Voices from the "Twentysomething" Generation Explore the Future of the Women's Movement* (New York: Donald I. Fine, 1991).

27. Christina Hoff Sommers, *Who Stole Feminism? How Women Have Betrayed Women* (New York: Simon and Schuster, 1994), 22 (on "gender feminism"), 12 (on incorrect figure), 188 (on "noble lies"). For reviews of *Who Stole Feminism?*, see Nina Auerbach, "Sisterhood Is Fractious," *New York Times Book Review*, June 12, 1994, 13; letters to the editor, ibid., July 3 and 17, 1994, and Apr. 30, 1995; also Laura Flanders, "The 'Stolen Feminism' Hoax: Anti-Feminist Attack Based on Error-Filled Anecdotes," *Extra!* Sept.–Oct. 1994; Susan Stanford Friedman, "Making History: Reflections on Feminism, Narrative, and Desire," in Elam and Wiegman, eds., *Feminism beside Itself*, 16–18; Carol Sternhell, "The Proper Study of Womankind," *Women's Review of Books* 12, no. 3 (Dec. 1994): 1, 3–4; and McDermott, "On Cultural Authority." Sommers's behavior was the subject of extensive debate in dozens of letters, some supportive but mostly negative, published in the *Proceedings and Addresses of the American Philosophical Association* 65, nos. 5 and 7 (1992); ibid., 66, nos. 5 and 7 (1993); ibid., 67, no. 1 (1994). On failure to adequately acknowledge correction, see Naomi Wolf's letter to the editor, *Time*, Aug. 22, 1994, 9–10; and Sommers's letter to the editor and Rebecca Pepper Sinkler's reply, *New York Times Book Review*, Apr. 30, 1995, 39.

28. McDermott, "On Cultural Authority," 670; the phrase "vitriolic response" is from Joan Smith, "Christina Hoff Sommers: Traitor to Her Sex?," *San Francisco Examiner*, May 28, 1995, C-15.

29. Sommers, *Who Stole Feminism?*, 134–35 (on gender feminism and colonizing), 50 (on neologisms and number of courses); see Marilyn J. Boxer, "For and about Women: The Theory and Practice of Women's Studies in the United States," *Signs* 7, no. 3 (spring 1982): 661–95, reprinted in 1982 and 1989 and referenced widely.

30. Sommers, *Who Stole Feminism?*, 63; Karen Offen, "Defining Feminism: A Comparative Historical Approach," *Signs* 14, no. 1 (autumn 1988): 119–57;

Sandra Lee Bartky, letter to the editor, *Proceedings and Addresses of the American Philosophical Association* 65, no. 7 (1992): 57.

31. Offen, "Defining Feminism." See Elizabeth Fox-Genovese, *Feminism without Illusions: A Critique of Individualism* (Chapel Hill: University of North Carolina Press, 1991); Smith, "Christina Hoff Sommers," C-15; on "opening shot," see Ginsberg and Lennox, "Antifeminism in Scholarship and Publishing," 169–99, quotation on 189; on debunking, see McDermott, "On Cultural Authority," 673.

32. For the $110,000 figure, see Alison M. Jaggar in *Proceedings and Addresses of the American Philosophical Association* 65, no. 7 (1992): 70; for $164,000, see McDermott, "On Cultural Authority," 669 n. 1; for the six-figure contract, see Flanders, "'Stolen Feminism' Hoax," 6–9, quotation on 8, originally reported by Anthony Flint, "Ivy League Could Come Clean," *Boston Globe*, May 17, 1992, B33. On Hewlett, see Faludi, *Backlash*, 314; on marketing tool, see 318.

33. Here Sommers alludes to Elizabeth K. Minnich but misinterprets the meaning of the reference; see chap. 3 above. The comparison is not between feminist scholars and the great figures of science, but between the effects of changing world-views: androcentricity and geocentricity, respectively. My account of "Reclaiming Feminism: Voices in Dialogue," Women's Freedom Network National Conference, first annual meeting, American University, Washington, D.C., Oct. 1–2, 1994, is based on my recollections; quotations are from my notes. For a selection of papers presented at the conference, see Simon, ed., *Neither Victim nor Enemy*.

34. *Women's Freedom Network Newsletter* 3, no. 3 (summer 1996): 5, 13; McDermott, "On Cultural Authority," 669 n. 2, 671.

35. Daphne Patai and Noretta Koertge, *Professing Feminism: Cautionary Tales from the Strange World of Women's Studies* (New York: BasicBooks, 1994), 5, 54; also, author's notes, WFN conference, n. 33. For a thoughtful, balanced review of this book, see Sternhell, "Proper Study of Womankind," 1, 3–4.

36. Patai and Koertge, *Professing Feminism*, ix; for Ginsburg story, see Jeffrey Rosen, "The New Look on the Court," *New York Times Book Review*, Oct. 5, 1997, 90, 96.

37. Patai and Koertge, *Professing Feminism*, 11, 13, 17, 22, 29, 32, 38, 42, 43.

38. Ibid., 45, 48, 50, 120. Another neologism, apparently the authors', is *gendelirium* (155). Their term "TOTAL REJ" won a place in Gerald Parshall's "Buzzwords: The Language That Will Shape Our World in 1995," *U.S. News and World Report*, Dec. 26, 1994–Jan. 2, 1995, 79.

39. Daphne Patai, "The Struggle for Feminist Purity Threatens the Goals of Feminism," *Chronicle of Higher Education*, Feb. 5, 1992, B1–B2. For Patai and Koertge's criticism of one set of criteria suggested for crosslisting, see Patai and Koertge, *Professing Feminism*, 177–82.

40. McDermott, "On Cultural Authority," 676; Patai and Koertge, *Professing Feminism*, 214–15.

41. Jean Bethke Elshtain, *Public Man, Private Woman: Women in Social and Political Thought* (Princeton: Princeton University Press, 1981), 320–21; idem, "Antigone's Daughters," *Democracy* 2, no. 2 (Apr. 1982): 46–59, quotations on 48, 50.

42. Elshtain, *Public Man, Private Woman*, 321–23, 332–33, 336. Elshtain cites Sara Ruddick's "Maternal Thinking," *Feminist Studies* 6, no. 2 (summer 1980): 342–67. Maternal feminism resembles "social feminism," a term long used to describe the work of women concerned with social problems and issues, including war; see Naomi Black, "The Mothers' International: The Women's Cooperative Guild and Feminist Pacifism," *Women's Studies International Forum* 7, no. 6 (1984): 467–76.

43. Elshtain, *Public Man, Private Woman*, 328. See also Jean Bethke Elshtain, "Feminist Discourse and Its Discontents: Language, Power, and Meaning," in Keohane, Rosaldo, and Gelpi, eds., *Feminist Theory*, 127–45.

44. Elshtain, "Antigone's Daughters," 55; and idem, "Antigone's Daughters Reconsidered," in White, ed., *Life-World and Politics*, 222–35, quotation on 229.

45. Ellen Ross, "New Thoughts on 'the Oldest Vocation': Mothers and Motherhood in Recent Feminist Scholarship," *Signs* 20, no. 2 (winter 1995): 397–413, quotation about love and care on 398; "oldest vocation" on 397.

46. Ibid., quotation on 398–99.

47. Judith Stacey, "Are Feminists Afraid to Leave Home? The Challenge of Conservative Pro-family Feminism," in Mitchell and Oakley, eds., *What Is Feminism?*, 219–48, quotations on 219, 232, 237, 241.

48. Deborah Rosenfelt and Judith Stacey, "Second Thoughts on the Second Wave," *Feminist Studies* 13, no. 2 (summer 1987): 341–61, quotations on 359–60. See also Ellen K. Feder and Eva Feder Kittay, "The Family and Feminist Theory," special issue of *Hypatia* 11, no. 1 (winter 1995).

49. Kathleen B. Jones, *Compassionate Authority: Democracy and the Representation of Women* (New York: Routledge, 1993), 151; Birte Siim, "Towards a Feminist Rethinking of the Welfare State," in Jones and Jónasdóttir, eds., *Political Interests of Gender*, 160–86, quotation on 165. See also Kathy Ferguson, *The Feminist Case against Bureaucracy* (Philadelphia: Temple University Press, 1984). On "both ways," see Alison M. Jaggar, "Sexual Difference and Sexual Equality," in Rhode, ed., *Theoretical Perspectives on Sexual Difference*, 239–54, quotations on 252–53.

50. On the reception of Elshtain, Carol Gilligan, and other "difference feminists," see Stephen K. White, "Difference Feminism and Responsibility to Otherness," chap. 6 of *Political Theory and Postmodernism* (Cambridge: Cambridge University Press, 1991).

51. Susan Stanford Friedman, "Authority in the Feminist Classroom: A Contradic-

tion in Terms?," in Culley and Portugues, eds., *Gendered Subjects,* 203–8, quotation on 208; and idem, "Making History," 11–53, quotation on 42; Elaine Marks, "The Poetical and the Political: The 'Feminist' Inquiry in French Studies," in Stanton and Stewart, eds., *Feminisms in the Academy,* 274–87, quotation on 275.

52. bell hooks, *Talking Back: Thinking Feminist, Thinking Black* (Boston: South End Press, 1989), 106, 108, 110–11.

53. Michele Wallace, "Art for Whose Sake?," *Women's Review of Books* 13, no. 1 (Oct. 1995): 8.

54. Virginia Sapiro, "Feminist Studies and Political Science—and Vice Versa," in Stanton and Stewart, eds., *Feminisms in the Academy,* 291–310, quotations on 300–301. For "competing explanations," see Virginia Sapiro, *Women in American Society: An Introduction to Women's Studies* (Palo Alto, Calif.: Mayfield, 1986), vii. In another instance, Karen Offen has called my attention to Jean Bethke Elshtain's repetition of the conventional error of locating the beginning of modern feminism in the work of Mary Wollstonecraft, despite pathbreaking historical scholarship about feminisms in many European countries which predate the late eighteenth century. See, e.g., Karen Offen, "Reclaiming the European Enlightenment for Feminism; or Prologomena to Any Future History of the Eighteenth Century," in Akkerman and Stuurman, eds., *Feminist Political Thought in European History.* The piece in question is Elshtain's "Exporting Feminism," in Simon, ed., *Neither Victim nor Enemy,* 173–89. The phrase *practicing conflict* is attributed to Mary Childers by Marianne Hirsch and Evelyn Fox Keller, "Conclusion: Practicing Conflict in Feminist Theory," in Hirsch and Keller, eds., *Conflicts in Feminism,* 370–85, quotation on 379.

55. Marianne Hirsch, in Jane Gallop, Marianne Hirsch, and Nancy K. Miller, "Criticizing Feminist Criticism," in Hirsch and Keller, eds., *Conflicts in Feminism,* 349–69, quotation on 361; Linda S. Kauffman, "The Long Goodbye: Against the Personal Testimony; or, An Infant Grifter Grows Up," in Greene and Kahn, eds., *Changing Subjects,* 129–46, quotations on 142–43, 349; Elshtain, *Public Man, Private Woman,* 335, 349; Karen Offen, "Feminism and Sexual Difference in Historical Perspective," in Rhode, ed., *Theoretical Perspectives on Sexual Difference,* 13–20, quotation on 20; Robyn Rowland, "Politics of Intimacy: Heterosexuality, Love and Power," in Bell and Klein, eds., *Radically Speaking,* 77–86, quotation on 81.

56. Sternhell, "Proper Study of Womankind," 1, 3, 4; Patai and Koertge, *Professing Feminism,* 176.

57. Sternhell, "Proper Study of Womankind," 3, 4.

58. Stimpson, "Women's Studies and Its Discontents," 70–71.

59. Ibid., 71, 75.

60. See, e.g., Barbara Scott Winkler, "Feminism and Generations," WMST-L, Oct. 3, 1996; thread on "thirtysumthin feminism," WMST-L, March 1996; Andrea

Dworkin, "Dworkin on Dworkin," in Bell and Klein, eds., *Radically Speaking,* 203–17, quotation on 205–6. On feminist generations and successions, see Jacqueline N. Zita, ed., "Third Wave Feminisms," special issue of *Hypatia* 12, no. 3 (summer 1997).

61. The reference to Ruth Perry is from a summary of a session she chaired on "Generations of Feminism," at "The Next Twenty-five Years," women's studies program administrators conference, Arizona State University, Tempe, Feb. 15, 1997.

62. See Maher and Tetreault, *Feminist Classroom,* 87.

63. Jean Fox O'Barr and Florence Howe have both pointed this out in personal communications.

64. Joyce Appleby, Lynn Hunt, and Margaret Jacob, *Telling the Truth about History* (New York: W. W. Norton, 1994), 33; William Issel, "Cultural Politics and Conservatism in Post–World War II America" (unpublished paper). Messer-Davidow finds the attack by cultural conservatives to be the product of "articulated systems—think tanks, training institutes, foundations, grass roots organizations, and legal centers," utilizing "vertical practices" through which to construct "institutional nodal points to leverage changes in national and local institutions." Messer-Davidow, "Manufacturing the Attack on Liberalized Higher Education," 43, 68.

65. Mary Louise Roberts, *Civilization without Sexes: Reconstructing Gender in Postwar France, 1917–1927* (Chicago: University of Chicago Press, 1994), 2–4; Louise Saumoneau, quoted in Marilyn J. Boxer, "Socialism Faces Feminism: The Failure of Synthesis in France, 1879–1913," in Boxer and Quataert, eds., *Socialist Women,* 75–111, quotation on 92; Karen Offen, *European Feminisms, 1700–1950* (forthcoming), chap. 8. On the conflict over the word *feminism* in the United States in the 1920s, see Nancy F. Cott, *The Grounding of Modern Feminism* (New Haven: Yale University Press, 1987), 96–97, 134–35.

66. Appleby, Hunt, and Jacob, *Telling the Truth,* 244, 272, 275.

Chapter 9: The "Feminist Enlightenment" and the University

1. Gerda Lerner, quoted in Karen J. Winkler, "Women's Studies after Two Decades: Debates over Politics, New Directions for Research," *Chronicle of Higher Education,* Sept. 28, 1988, A6. On the feminist enlightenment, see Jessie Bernard, "Re-Viewing the Impact of Women's Studies on Sociology," in Farnham, ed., *Impact of Feminist Research,* 193–216, quotation on 194.

2. Clark Kerr, *The Uses of the University,* 3d ed. (Cambridge: Harvard University Press, 1982), viii, 94, 95–96, 97, 108, 162.

3. "Feminism in the Academy," *Academe* 69, no. 5 (Sept.–Oct. 1983): 1.

4. The titles of the nine publications featured on the AACU brochure cover are "Changing the Major: Innovative Priorities in the Fields"; "Warming the Cli-

mate for Women in Academic Science"; "Strong Foundations: Twelve Principles for Effective General Education Programs"; "Assessing Higher Education"; "Diversity in Higher Education: A Work in Progress"; "Focus on Faculty" (illustrated by a photograph of a woman); "American Pluralism and College Curriculum: Higher Education in a Diverse Democracy"; "Liberal Learning and the Arts of Connection for the New Academy"; "The Drama of Diversity and Democracy: Higher Education and American Commitments."

5. Ernest L. Boyer, *College: The Undergraduate Experience in America* (New York: Harper and Row, 1987). On decline in cultural competence, see Boyer quoted by Malcolm G. Scully, "Study Finds Colleges Torn by Divisions, Confused over Roles," *Chronicle of Higher Education*, Nov. 5, 1986, 1, 16, quotation on 16; and "Prologue and Major Recommendations of Carnegie Foundation's Report on Colleges," ibid., Nov. 5, 1986, 16–22. See also Patrick G. Love and Anne Goodsell Love, *Enhancing Student Learning: Intellectual, Social, and Emotional Learning* (Washington, D.C.: ASHE/ERIC, 1996).

6. Alasdair MacIntyre, *Three Rival Versions of Moral Enquiry: Encyclopaedia, Genealogy, and Tradition* (Notre Dame: University of Notre Dame Press, 1990), 223–24. I thank Anita Silvers for introducing me to MacIntyre's work.

7. Ibid., 225–27, 230. MacIntyre excepts "applied ethics" from his conclusion (226–27).

8. Ibid., 228–29.

9. The three traditions are described by MacIntyre as follows: "The encyclopaedist's conception is a single framework within which knowledge is discriminated from mere belief, progress toward knowledge is mapped, and truth is understood as the relationship of *our* knowledge to *the* world, through the application of those methods whose rules are the rules of rationality as such. Nietzsche, as a genealogist, takes there to be a multiplicity of perspectives within each of which truth-from-a-point-of-view may be asserted, but no truth-as-such, an empty notion, about *the* world, an equally empty notion. There are no rules of rationality as such to be appealed to, there are rather strategies of insight and strategies of subversion. . . . The task of the genealogist . . . was to write the history of those social and psychological formations in which the will to power is distorted into and concealed by the will to truth." MacIntyre credits Foucault for "restoring Nietzsche's project to the professoriate" (53). The Thomistic tradition of Aquinas is based on Aristotelian and Augustinian conceptions of mind and inquiry (39, 42, 53, 109–10).

10. Ibid., 229, 230–31, 232.

11. Ibid., 235–36.

12. Kathryn Pyne Addelson, "Knower/Doers and Their Moral Problems," in Alcoff and Potter, eds., *Feminist Epistemologies*, 265–94, quotation on 283. On "ethical feminism" as an effort to redefine femininity and otherness, see Drucilla Cornell, "What Is Ethical Feminism," in Seyla Benhabib et al., *Feminist Con-*

tentions: A Philosophical Exchange (New York: Routledge, 1995), 75–106. See also Susan J. Hekman, *Moral Voices, Moral Selves: Carol Gilligan and Feminist Moral Theory* (University Park: Pennsylvania State University Press, 1995).

13. Olympe de Gouges, "Declaration of the Rights of Woman and Citizen," in Bell and Offen, eds., *Women, the Family, and Freedom*, vol. 1, 1750–1880, 104–9; Angelina Grimké, in ibid., 183–86, quotation on 183. For reports on the Beijing conference, see "Conference Reports," *Signs* 22, no. 1 (autumn 1996): 181–226.

14. See, e.g., Joan Wallach Scott, *Only Paradoxes to Offer: French Feminists and the Rights of Man* (Cambridge: Harvard University Press, 1996).

15. Jaroslav Pelikan, *The Idea of the University: A Reexamination* (New Haven: Yale University Press, 1992), 53–54, 60, 64.

16. Carl E. Schorske, "The New Rigorism in the Human Sciences, 1940–1960," *Daedalus* 126, no. 1 (winter 1997): 289–309, quotations on 295, 299, 304–5. The theme of this issue of *Daedalus* is "American Academic Culture in Transformation: Fifty Years, Four Disciplines."

17. Jane Roland Martin, *Changing the Educational Landscape: Philosophy, Women, and Curriculum* (New York: Routledge, 1994), 16. The anecdote about F. N. David's meeting with graduate students at the University of California, Riverside, is based on personal recollection. See also Carolyn Porter, "Getting Gendered," in Greene and Kahn, eds., *Changing Subjects*, 168–79.

18. Alison Bernstein and Jacklyn Cock, "A Troubling Picture of Gender Equity," *Chronicle of Higher Education*, June 15, 1994, B1–B3; California State University, *Statistical Abstract: To July 1995* (Long Beach, Calif.: CSU Institute for Teaching and Learning, n.d.), 239. For the 70 percent figure, see report by Linda Knopp for American Council on Education, "Facts in Brief," *Higher Education and National Affairs* 45, no. 16 (Sept. 16, 1996), 3. For further data, including doctorates by field and women faculty by rank, see Judith G. Touchton and Lynne Davis, comps., *Fact Book on Women in Higher Education*, (New York: ACE/Macmillan, 1991).

19. See, e.g., Leslie Rabine, "Stormy Weather: A Memoir of the Second Wave," in Green and Kahn, eds., *Changing Subjects*, 211–25.

20. bell hooks, *Teaching to Transgress: Education as the Practice of Freedom* (New York: Routledge, 1994), 136–37, 147, 193, 199; Carol Thomas Neely, "Loss and Recovery: Homes Away from Home," in Green and Kahn, eds., *Changing Subjects*, 180–94, quotation on 186; Madelon Sprengnether, "Generational Differences: Reliving Mother-Daughter Conflicts," in ibid., 201–8, quotation on 203; Martha A. Ackelsberg and Kathryn Pyne Addelson, "Anarchist Alternatives to Competition," in Miner and Longino, eds., *Competition*, 221–33; Dale M. Bauer, "Personal Criticism and the Academic Personality," in Roof and Wiegman, eds., *Who Can Speak?*, 56–69, quotation on 63; Nora Ephron, quoted in "Mélange," *Chronicle of Higher Education*, July 5, 1996, B2.

On welfare reform, in 1995 the historian Linda Gordon and the political scientist Frances Fox Piven drafted a statement and collected hundreds of signatures
opposing a congressional proposal; see "Women Academics Publish Petition
on Welfare Reform," *Women's Research Network News* 6, no. 3 (winter 1995):
1; at "The Next Twenty-five Years," women's studies program administrators
conference, Arizona State University, Tempe, Feb. 1997, the historian Sonya
Michel drew on a course she taught at Princeton University in 1995 on "Gender, Citizenship, and Social Policy" to lead a workshop opposing recent welfare reform. For an example of collaboration in teaching across racial and
seniority lines, see Donna Eder and Audrey Thomas McCloskey, "Teaching
across the Barriers: The Classroom as a Site of Transformation," *Transformations* 7, no. 1 (spring 1996): 37–49.

21. Andrew Lakritz, "Identification and Difference: Structures of Privilege in Cultural Criticism," in Roof and Wiegman, eds., *Who Can Speak?*, 3–29, quotation on 24.

22. Barbara Tomlinson, "The Politics of Textual Vehemence, or Go to Your Room
until You Learn How to Act," *Signs* 22, no. 1 (autumn 1996): 86–114, quotation on 112; Bernard, "Re-Viewing the Impact of Women's Studies on Sociology," 210. Bernard discusses Robert Merton's concepts of "social sadism" and
"sociological euphemisms" on 209.

23. See Arlie Russell Hochschild, "Inside the Clockwork of Male Careers," in
Howe, ed., *Women and the Power to Change*, 47–80; Marilyn J. Boxer,
"Designer Clocks for Academic Careers," *History Teacher* 29, no. 4 (Aug.
1996): 471–81, quotations on 472; Donna Shavlik, "Women Changing Work
within the Academy," *On Campus with Women* 25, no. 2 (winter 1996): 1;
Chamberlain, ed., *Women in Academe*, 291. An interesting footnote to a
changing university culture is that in 1997, student services at San Francisco
State University designated a special room for breastfeeding mothers.

24. Paula Kamen, *Feminist Fatale: Voices from the "Twentysomething" Generation Explore the Future of the "Women's Movement"* (New York: Donald I.
Fine, 1991), 263, 280–81. On the "chilly climate," see Bernice Resnik Sandler,
Lisa A. Silberberg, and Roberta M. Hall, *The Classroom Climate: A Chilly
One for Women* (Washington, D.C.: National Association for Women in Education, 1982); and idem, *The Chilly Classroom Climate: A Guide to Improve
the Education of Women* (Washington, D.C.: National Association for Women
in Education, 1996). For "Gilligan's Island," see Katha Pollitt, *Reasonable
Creatures: Essays on Women and Feminism* (New York: Alfred A. Knopf,
1995), 42–62.

25. Julius Getman, *In the Company of Scholars: The Struggle for the Soul of
Higher Education* (Austin: University of Texas Press, 1992), 161–62, 164.

26. Ibid., 171, 176.

27. David Damrosch, *We Scholars: Changing the Culture of the University* (Cambridge: Harvard University Press, 1995), 7, 29–31, 41, 77, 187.

28. Ibid., 86, 173, 185, 186.

29. Caryn McTighe Musil, "Relaxing Your Neck Muscles: The History of the Project," in Musil, ed., *Students at the Center*, 8; Banu Subramaniam, Rebecca Dunn, and Lynn E. Broaddus, "'Sir'Vey or 'Madam'Vey?," in O'Barr and Wyer, eds., *Engaging Feminism*, 127–38; O'Barr and Wyer discuss the survey on p. 124. See also Emily M. Bernstein, "Law School Women Question the Teaching," *New York Times*, June 5, 1996, B10.

30. Frank H. T. Rhodes, "The Place of Teaching in the Research University," in Cole, Barber, and Graubard, eds., *Research University in a Time of Discontent*, 179–89, quotation on 186. On teaching methods that resemble consciousness raising, see Jeannette Ludwig, "The One-Minute Paper," *Liberal Education* 81, no. 4 (fall 1995): 12–19. On the two cultures, see Marcia Westkott and Gay Victoria, "University of Colorado: Personalized Learning," in Musil, ed., *Courage to Question*, 22–24. On the attempt at San Francisco State to develop courses in the women's studies department and then move them to other departments, see Barbara Scott Winkler, "A Comparative History of Four Women's Studies Programs, 1970–1985" (Ph.D. diss., University of Michigan, 1992), 199–200.

31. For a generally positive view of the influence of women's studies, see Russell Jacoby, *Dogmatic Wisdom: How the Culture Wars Divert Education and Distract America* (New York: Doubleday, 1994), 189–90; and Andrew Lakritz, "The Equalizer and the Essentializers, or Man-Handling Feminism on the Academic Literary Left," *Arizona Quarterly* 46, no. 1 (spring 1990): 77–103. For a negative perspective, see Gertrude Himmelfarb, "Not What We Meant at All," review of *Telling the Truth*, by Joyce Appleby, Lynn Hunt, and Margaret Jacob, *Times Literary Supplement*, June 10, 1994, 8–9. On many truths, see Dale Spender and Cheris Kramarae, "Exploding Knowledge," in Kramarae and Spender, eds., *Knowledge Explosion*, 1–24, quotation on 6. For the quotation from Booth, see Wayne Booth, "Freedom of Interpretation: Bakhtin and the Challenge of Feminist Criticism," *Critical Inquiry* 9 (Sept. 1982): 45–76, quotation on 74; see also Liz McMillen, "A New Cadre at Chicago," *Chronicle of Higher Education*, Mar. 22, 1996, A11–12, A15.

32. Marilyn R. Schuster and Susan R. Van Dyne, "Curricular Change for the Twenty-first Century: Why Women?," in Schuster and Van Dyne, eds., *Women's Place in the Academy*, 3–12, quotation on 4. The figures from UCLA's Higher Education Research Institute are reported in *Chronicle of Higher Education*, Sept. 13, 1996, A13.

33. Ruth Perry, "I Brake for Feminists: Debates and Divisions within Women's Studies," *Transformations* 7, no. 1 (spring 1996): 10; Larry McLain, "Women's Studies, Cultural Studies: Teaching Literature in the Midwest," ibid., 7, no. 1

(spring 1996): 22. On "deinstitutionalized understanding," see Nicholas B. Dirks, Geoff Eley, and Sherry B. Ortner, "Introduction," in Dirks, Eley, and Ortner, eds., *Culture/Power/History*, 3–45, quotation on 4; on origins of cultural studies, see Stuart Hall, "Cultural Studies: Two Paradigms," in ibid., 520–38.

34. Virginia Smith, "New Dimensions for General Education," in Levine, ed., *Higher Learning in America*, 243–58, quotation on 255; Betty Powell, "WS a Fad," WMST-L, Oct. 3, 1996; Page Smith, *Killing the Spirit: Higher Education in America* (New York: Viking, 1990), 290. On the outsider-within perspective, see Patricia Hill Collins, "Learning from the Outsider Within: The Sociological Significance of Black Feminist Thought," *Social Problems* 33, no. 6 (1986): 14–32.

35. Carolyn G. Heilbrun, "Women, Men, Theories, and Literature," in Farnham, ed., *Impact of Feminist Research*, 217–25, quotation on 223; Judith Zinsser, *History and Feminism: A Glass Half Full* (New York: Twayne, 1993), 59, 90. Chairing the American Historical Association's Committee on International Historical Activities in 1985–90 was Karen M. Offen; in 1990–95, Jean H. Quataert; in 1995–2000, Renate Bridenthal. On the number of dissertations listed for July through December 1995, see UMI Dissertation Services, *Subject Catalog History: Selected Collection of Doctoral Dissertations and Masters Theses* (Ann Arbor, Mich.: University Microfilms International, n.d.) selected from *Dissertation Abstracts International* 56, nos. 1–6 (July–Dec. 1995) and *Masters Abstracts International* 33, nos. 4–6 (Aug.–Dec. 1995). For data for the period 1873–1960, see Linda Gordon et al., "Historical Phallacies: Sexism in American Historical Writing," in Carroll, ed., *Liberating Women's History*, 71 n. 1; the data given by Gordon et al. were taken from Arlie Hochschild, "The American Woman: Another Idol of Social Science," *Trans-action: Social Science and Modern Society* 8, no. 1–2 (Nov.–Dec. 1970): 13. On limited feminist influence in political science, see Helene Silverberg, "Gender Studies and Political Science: The History of the 'Behavioralist Compromise,'" in James Farr and Raymond Seidelman, eds., *Discipline and History: Political Science in the United States* (Ann Arbor: University of Michigan Press, 1993), 363–81.

36. For example, my 1975 dissertation on socialism and feminism in nineteenth-century France, which appeared in *Dissertation Abstracts International* in June 1976, would not be located by a search using the words "woman" or "women." It is listed under "feminism"; "women's studies" did not yet exist in the subject index.

37. The search was conducted at the Cecil H. Green Library, Stanford University, Mar. 21, Apr. 4, and Oct. 21 and 22, 1997. Information on indexing was obtained from Stephen Johgart, indexing editor with UMI, March 26 and April 21, 1997. From 1988 on, the totals include all theses reported in *Master's Abstracts International*. Of the total of 13,084 graduate degrees reported between 1978 and 1995 as women's studies, 10,786 (82.4%) were doctoral degrees.

38. Rose L. Glickman, *Daughters of Feminists* (New York: St. Martin's Press, 1993); and Kamen, *Feminist Fatale*. Cf. Garry Wills, "The 60's: Tornado of Wrath," *Newsweek*, Jan. 3, 1994, 41; Richard Rorty, "Fraternity Reigns," *New York Times Magazine*, Sept. 29, 1996, 156.

39. John R. Searle, "Rationality and Realism, What Is at Stake?," in Cole, Barber, and Graubard, eds., *Research University in a Time of Discontent*, 55–83, quotations on 56, 73.

40. Catharine R. Stimpson, "Women's Studies and Its Discontents," *dissent* 43, no. 1 (winter 1996): 69; Patrice McDermott, "On Cultural Authority: Women's Studies, Feminist Politics, and the Popular Press," *Signs* 20, no. 3 (spring 1995): 668–94; Kathleen B. Jones, *Compassionate Authority: Democracy and the Representation of Women* (New York: Routledge, 1993); Thomas Bender, *Intellect and Public Life: Essays on the Social History of Academic Intellectuals in the United States* (Baltimore: Johns Hopkins University Press, 1993), 32, 46, 141.

41. Bender, *Intellect and Public Life*, 143; Thomas Bender, "Politics, Intellect, and the American University, 1945–1995," *Daedalus* 106, no. 1 (winter 1997): 1–38, quotations on 24, 31.

42. Bender, *Intellect and Public Life*, 132, 139.

43. The following discussion draws on my paper "Women's Studies and Feminist Goals in a 'Post-Feminist' University," in Christoph Wulf, ed., *Education in Europe: An International Task* (New York: Waxmann Munster, 1995), 350–58; the paper was originally presented in Budapest in 1993. The problem of women's studies' image as the academic arm, not the brain, of feminism was posed by Judith Allen, director of women's studies at Indiana University, at "The Next Twenty-five Years," women's studies program administrators conference, Arizona State University, Tempe, Feb. 14, 1997. For an example of a feminist scholar as an expert witness in a legal case with high stakes, see the media coverage on Myra Strober, an economist at Stanford University and president of the International Association for Feminist Economics: Paul M. Barrett, "Wendt Divorce Dissects Job of 'Corporate Wife,'" *Wall Street Journal*, Dec. 6, 1996, B1, B8; Judith H. Dobrzynski, "Divorce Executive Style, Revisited," *New York Times*, Jan. 24, 1997, C1, C6; Margaret Carlson, "Divorce, Corporate Style," *Time*, Feb. 3, 1997, 38. (According to the last article, the wife in this case received an actual "Ph.T." ["Put Hubby Through"] degree from the dean of the Harvard Business School.)

44. Bender, "Politics, Intellect, and the American University," 17.

45. Marilyn R. Schuster and Susan R. Van Dyne, "Stages of Curriculum Transformation," in Schuster and Van Dyne, eds., *Women's Place in the Academy*, 13–29, quotation on 23; Jean Fox O'Barr, *Feminism in Action: Building Institutions and Community through Women's Studies* (Chapel Hill: University of North Carolina Press, 1994), 215–18; Jill K. Conway, "Coeducation and Women's Studies: Two Approaches to the Question of Woman's Place in the

Contemporary University," *Daedalus* 103, no. 4 (fall 1974): 239–49, quotation on 248.

46. Michael Awkward, "A Black Man's Place(s) in Black Feminist Criticism," in Roof and Wiegman, eds., *Who Can Speak?*, 70–91, quotation on 75–76.

47. Alice Kessler-Harris and Amy Swerdlow, "Pride and Paradox: Despite Success, Women's Studies Faces Uncertain Future," *Chronicle of Higher Education*, Apr. 26, 1996, A64–A65; Tania Modleski, *Feminism without Women: Culture and Criticism in a "Postfeminist" Age* (New York: Routledge, 1991), 3, 5; Annette Kolodny, "Paying the Price of Antifeminist Intellectual Harassment," in Clark et al., eds., *Antifeminism in the Academy*, 3–33.

48. Ellen Goodman, "A Hyped-Up Georgie-Porgie," *San Francisco Chronicle*, Oct. 15, 1996, A21.

49. O'Barr, *Feminism in Action*, 233.

50. *Institute for Research on Women and Gender Newsletter* 22, no. 1 (winter 1997): 11; Iris Litt, M.D., interview by author, Stanford, Calif., Apr. 30, 1997. The information on the University of Southern California is from Lois Banner, former director of its Program for the Study of Women and Men in Society, personal communication, Apr. 29, 1997. On South Carolina, see Sue V. Rosser and Katherine W. Mille, "A Grass-Roots Approach to Funding Women's Stud-ies," *NWSAction* 1, no. 4 (winter 1988): 1–3; see also Winkler, "Comparative History of Four Women's Studies Programs," 445. On Indiana University, see Judith Allen, "Fund Raising for Women's Studies" (paper presented at "The Next Twenty-five Years," women's studies program administrators conference, Arizona State University, Tempe, Feb. 13–15, 1997).

51. On Cincinnati, see Laura S. Struminger [Schor], "The Birth and Growth of 'Friends of Women's Studies' at the University of Cincinnati," *Frontiers* 8, no. 3 (1986): 83–86; also Robin Sheets, current director of women's studies at the University of Cincinnati, personal communication, May 12, 1997.

52. On the ethic of care, see Joan C. Tronto, "Beyond Gender Difference to an Ethic of Care," *Signs* 12, no. 4 (summer 1987): 644–63.

53. The phrase "constituted in conversation," alluding to Bakhtin, is taken from James F. Bohman, David R. Hiley, and Richard Shusterman, "Introduction: The Interpretive Turn," in Hiley, Bohman, and Shusterman, eds., *Interpretive Turn*, 1–14, quotation on 6.

54. Martin, *Changing the Educational Landscape*, 6, 8, 13. Martin's narrative of the impact on her thinking about educational theory when she added women provides a fine example of "the difference it makes" (1–32). On connecting women, family, and public life, see also Susan Miller Okin, *Justice, Gender, and the Family* (n.p.: BasicBooks, 1989).

55. Martin, *Changing the Educational Landscape*, 13, 228; see esp. chap. 13, "The Radical Future of Gender Enrichment," in ibid., 228–41.

Books

Aaron, Jane, and Sylvia Walby, eds. *Out of the Margins: Women's Studies in the Nineties.* London: Falmer Press, 1991.

Abel, Elizabeth, ed. *Writing and Sexual Difference.* Chicago: University of Chicago Press, 1982.

Adams, Elsie, and Mary Louise Briscoe, eds. *Up against the Wall, Mother: On Women's Liberation.* Beverly Hills, Calif.: Glencoe Press, 1971.

Adams, Parveen, and Elizabeth Cowie, eds. *The Woman in Question: m/f.* Cambridge: MIT Press, 1990.

Adelman, Clifford. *New College Course Map and Transcript Files: Changes in Course-Taking and Achievement, 1972–1993.* Washington, D.C.: U.S. Department of Education, Oct. 1995.

Akkerman, Tjitske, and Siep Stuurman, eds. *Perspectives on Feminist Political Thought in European History: From the Middle Ages to the Present.* London: Routledge, 1998.

Albrecht, Lisa, and Rose M. Brewer, eds. *Bridges of Power: Women's Multicultural Alliances.* Philadelphia: New Society, 1990.

Alcoff, Linda, and Elizabeth Potter, eds. *Feminist Epistemologies.* New York: Routledge, 1993.

Alexander, M. Jacqui, and Chandra Talpade Mohanty, eds. *Feminist Genealogies, Colonial Legacies, Democratic Futures.* New York: Routledge, 1997.

Andersen, Margaret L. *Thinking about Women: Sociological and Feminist Perspectives.* New York: Macmillan, 1983.

Andersen, Margaret L., and Patricia Hill Collins, eds. *Race, Class, and Gender.* 2d ed. Belmont, Calif.: Wadsworth, 1995.

Anzaldúa, Gloria, ed. *Making Face, Making Soul: Haciendo Caras.* San Francisco: Aunt Lute Books, 1990.

Appleby, Joyce, Lynn Hunt, and Margaret Jacob. *Telling the Truth about History.* New York: W. W. Norton, 1994.

Arendt, Hannah. *Essays in Understanding, 1930–1954.* Edited by Jerome Kohn. New York: Harcourt Brace, 1994.

Asian Women United of California. *Making Waves: An Anthology of Writings by and about Asian American Women.* Boston: Beacon Press, 1989.

Assiter, Alison. *Enlightened Women: Modernist Feminism in a Postmodern Age.* London: Routledge, 1996.

Banks, James, and Cherry A. McGee Banks, eds. *Handbook of Research on Multicultural Education.* 3d ed. New York: Macmillan, 1995.

Bannerji, Himani, Linda Carty, Kari Dehli, Susan Heald, and Kate McKenna. *Unsettling Relations: The University as a Site of Feminist Struggles.* Boston: South End Press, 1991.

Bebel, August. *Woman under Socialism.* New York: New York Labor News, 1904.

Belenky, Mary Field, Blythe McVicker Clinchy, Nancy Rule Goldberger, and Jill Mattuck Tarule. *Women's Ways of Knowing: The Development of Self, Voice, and Mind.* New York: BasicBooks, 1986.

Bell, Diane, and Renate Klein, eds. *Radically Speaking: Feminism Reclaimed.* N. Melbourne, Victoria, Australia: Spinifex, 1996.

Bell, Roseann P., Bettye J. Parker, and Beverly Guy-Sheftall, eds. *Sturdy Black Bridges: Visions of Black Women in Literature.* New York: Anchor Books, 1979.

Bell, Susan Groag, and Karen M. Offen, eds. *Women, the Family, and Freedom: The Debate in Documents.* 2 vols. Stanford: Stanford University Press, 1983.

Bender, Thomas. *Intellect and Public Life: Essays on the Social History of Academic Intellectuals in the United States.* Baltimore: Johns Hopkins University Press, 1993.

Benhabib, Seyla, Judith Butler, Drucilla Cornell, and Nancy Fraser. *Feminist Contentions: A Philosophical Exchange.* New York: Routledge, 1995.

Benhabib, Seyla, and Drucilla Cornell, eds. *Feminism as Critique: Essays on the Politics of Gender in Late-Capitalist Societies.* Cambridge, England: Polity Press, 1987.

Bloom, Allan. *The Closing of the American Mind: How Higher Education Has Failed Democracy and Impoverished the Souls of Today's Students.* New York: Simon and Schuster, 1987.

Bock, Gisela, and Susan James, eds. *Beyond Equality and Difference: Citizenship, Feminist Politics, and Female Subjectivity.* London: Routledge, 1992.

Bock, Gisela, and Pat Thane, eds. *Maternity and Gender Policies: Women and the Rise of the European Welfare States, 1880s–1950s.* London: Routledge, 1991.

Bowles, Gloria, ed. *Strategies for Women's Studies in the Eighties.* New York: Elsevier, 1984.

Bowles, Gloria, and Renate Duelli Klein, eds. *Theories of Women's Studies.* New York: Routledge and Kegan Paul, 1983.

Boxer, Marilyn J., and Jean H. Quataert, eds. *Connecting Spheres: Women in the Western World, 1500 to the Present.* New York: Oxford University Press, 1987.

———. *Socialist Women: European Socialist Feminism in the Nineteenth and Early Twentieth Centuries.* New York: Elsevier, 1978.

Boyer, Ernest L. *College: The Undergraduate Experience in America.* New York: Harper and Row, 1987.

Brand, Peggy Zeglin, and Carolyn Korsmeyer, eds. *Feminism and Tradition in Aesthetics.* University Park: Pennsylvania State University, 1995.

Bromwich, David. *Politics by Other Means: Higher Education and Group Thinking*. New Haven: Yale University Press, 1992.

Brown, Loulou, Helen Collins, Pat Green, Maggie Humm, and Mel Landells, eds. *W.I.S.H.: The International Handbook of Women's Studies*. New York: Harvester Wheatsheaf, 1993.

Brown, Wendy. *States of Injury: Power and Freedom in Late Modernity*. Princeton: Princeton University Press, 1995.

Bruffee, Kenneth A. *Collaborative Learning: Higher Education, Interdependence, and the Authority of Knowledge*. Baltimore: Johns Hopkins University Press, 1995.

Bulkin, Elly, Minnie Bruce Pratt, and Barbara Smith. *Yours in Struggle: Three Feminist Perspectives on Anti-Semitism and Racism*. Brooklyn, N.Y.: Long Haul Press, 1984.

Bunch, Charlotte. *Passionate Politics: Feminist Theory in Action. Essays, 1968–1986*. New York: St. Martin's Press, 1987.

Bunch, Charlotte, and Sandra Pollack, eds. *Learning Our Way: Essays in Feminist Education*. Trumansburg, N.Y.: Crossing Press, 1983.

Butler, Johnnella E., and John C. Walter, eds. *Transforming the Curriculum: Ethnic Studies and Women's Studies*. Albany: State University of New York Press, 1991.

Butler, Johnnella E., Sandra Coyner, Margaret Homans, Marlene Longenecker, and Caryn McTighe Musil. *Liberal Learning and the Women's Studies Major*. N.p.: National Women's Studies Association for the Association of American Colleges, 1991.

Butler, Judith. *Bodies That Matter: On the Discursive Limits of "Sex."* New York: Routledge, 1993.

———. *Gender Trouble: Feminism and the Subversion of Identity*. New York: Routledge, 1990.

Butler, Judith, and Joan W. Scott, eds. *Feminists Theorize the Political*. New York: Routledge, Chapman, and Hall, 1992.

Cade, Toni, ed. *The Black Woman: An Anthology*. New York: Signet, 1970.

Campus Life: In Search of Community. Princeton: Carnegie Foundation for the Advancement of Teaching, 1990.

Carroll, Berenice A., ed. *Liberating Women's History: Theoretical and Critical Essays*. Urbana: University of Illinois, 1976.

The Challenge of Connecting Learning. Washington, D.C.: Association of American Colleges, 1991.

Chamberlain, Mariam, ed. *Women in Academe: Progress and Prospects*. New York: Russell Sage Foundation, 1991.

Chaudhuri, Nupur, and Cheryl Johnson-Odim, eds. "Global Perspectives." Special issue of *NWSA Journal* 8, no. 1 (spring 1996).

Cheney, Lynne V. *Telling the Truth: Why Our Culture and Our Country Have*

Stopped Making Sense—and What We Can Do about It. New York: Simon and Schuster, 1995.

Chodorow, Nancy. *Feminism and Psychoanalytic Theory*. New Haven: Yale University Press, 1989.

———. *The Reproduction of Mothering: Psychoanalysis and the Sociology of Gender*. Berkeley: University of California Press, 1978.

Clark, Vèvè, Shirley Nelson Garner, Margaret Higonnet, and Ketu H. Katrak, eds. *Antifeminism in the Academy*. New York: Routledge, 1996.

Clough, Patricia Ticineto. *Feminist Thought: Desire, Power, and Academic Discourse*. Cambridge, Mass.: Blackwell, 1994.

Cole, Jonathan R., Elinor G. Barber, and Stephen R. Graubard. *The Research University in a Time of Discontent*. Baltimore: Johns Hopkins University Press, 1994.

Collins, Patricia Hill. *Black Feminist Thought: Knowledge, Consciousness, and the Politics of Empowerment*. New York: Routledge, 1990.

Conway, Jill Ker. *True North: A Memoir*. New York: Vintage Books, 1994.

Conway, Jill Ker, and Susan C. Bourque, eds. *The Politics of Women's Education: Perspectives from Asia, Africa, and Latin America*. Ann Arbor: University of Michigan Press, 1993.

Cott, Nancy F. *The Grounding of Modern Feminism*. New Haven: Yale University Press, 1987.

Coyner, Sandra. *Transforming the Knowledge Base: A Panel Discussion at the National Network of Women's Caucuses, First Biennial Meeting, 1989*. New York: National Council for Research on Women, 1990.

Cruikshank, Margaret, ed. *Lesbian Studies: Present and Future*. Old Westbury, N.Y.: Feminist Press, 1982.

Culley, Margo, and Catherine Portugues, eds. *Gendered Subjects: The Dynamics of Feminist Teaching*. Boston: Routledge and Kegan Paul, 1985.

Damrosch, David. *We Scholars: Changing the Culture of the University*. Cambridge: Harvard University Press, 1995.

Davis, Barbara Hillyer, ed. "Feminist Education." Special issue of *Journal of Thought* 20, no. 3 (fall 1985).

Davis, Natalie Zemon. *Society and Culture in Early Modern France: Eight Essays by Natalie Zemon Davis*. Stanford: Stanford University Press, 1975.

Dean, Jodi. *Solidarity of Strangers: Feminism after Identity Politics*. Berkeley: University of California Press, 1996.

Deats, Sara Munson, and Lagretta Tallent Lenker, eds. *Gender and Academe: Feminist Pedagogy and Politics*. Lanham, Md.: Rowman and Littlefield, 1994.

Deckard, Barbara. *The Women's Movement: Political, Socioeconomic, and Psychological Issues*. New York: Harper and Row, 1975.

de Groot, Joanna, and Mary Maynard, eds. *Women's Studies in the 1990s: Doing Things Differently?* New York: St. Martin's Press, 1993.

de la Torre, Adela, and Beatríz M. Pesquera, eds. *Building with Our Hands: New Directions in Chicana Studies.* Berkeley: University of California Press, 1993.

de Lauretis, Teresa, ed. *Feminist Studies/Critical Studies.* Bloomington: Indiana University Press, 1986.

Dewey, John. *Democracy and Education: An Introduction to the Philosophy of Education.* New York: Macmillan, 1930.

di Leonardo, Micaela, ed. *Gender at the Crossroads of Knowledge: Feminist Anthropology in the Postmodern Era.* Berkeley: University of California Press, 1991.

Dirks, Nicholas B., Geoff Eley, and Sherry B. Ortner, eds. *Culture/Power/History: A Reader in Contemporary Social Theory.* Princeton: Princeton University Press, 1994.

Disch, Estelle, ed. *Reconstructing Gender: A Multicultural Anthology.* Mountain View, Calif.: Mayfield, 1997.

DuBois, Ellen Carol, Gail Paradise Kelly, Elizabeth Lapovsky Kennedy, Carolyn W. Korsmeyer, and Lillian S. Robinson. *Feminist Scholarship: Kindling in the Groves of Academe.* Urbana: University of Illinois Press, 1987.

Echols, Alice. *Daring to Be Bad: Radical Feminism in America, 1967–1975.* Minneapolis: University of Minnesota Press, 1989.

Eisenstein, Zillah R. *The Radical Future of Liberal Feminism.* New York: Longman, 1981.

Eisenstein, Zillah R., ed. *Capitalist Patriarchy and the Case for Socialist Feminism.* New York: Monthly Review Press, 1979.

Elam, Diane, and Robyn Wiegman, eds. *Feminism beside Itself.* New York: Routledge, 1995.

Elshtain, Jean Bethke. *Public Man, Private Woman: Women in Social and Political Thought.* Princeton: Princeton University Press, 1981.

Engels, Frederick. *The Origin of the Family, Private Property, and the State.* Edited by Eleanor Burke Leacock. New York: International, 1972.

Evans, Sara. *Personal Politics: The Roots of Women's Liberation in the Civil Rights Movement and the New Left.* New York: Vintage, 1980.

Falco, Maria J., ed. *Feminism and Epistemology: Approaches to Research in Women and Politics.* New York: Haworth Press, 1987.

Faludi, Susan. *Backlash: The Undeclared War against American Women.* New York: Crown, 1991.

Faragher, John Mack, and Florence Howe, eds. *Women and Higher Education in American History: Essays from the Mount Holyoke College Sesquicentennial Symposia.* New York: W. W. Norton, 1988.

Farber, Jerry. *The Student as Nigger: Essays and Stories.* New York: Pocket Books, 1970.

Farnham, Christie, ed. *The Impact of Feminist Research in the Academy.* Bloomington: Indiana University Press, 1987.

"Feminist Pedagogy: An Update." Special issue of *Women's Studies Quarterly* 21, nos. 3 and 4 (fall–winter 1993).

Ferguson, Kathy. *The Feminist Case against Bureaucracy.* Philadelphia: Temple University Press, 1984.

Findlen, Barbara, ed. *Listen Up: Voices from the Next Feminist Generation.* Seattle: Seal Press, 1995.

Fiol-Matta, Liza, and Mariam K. Chamberlain, eds. *Women of Color and the Multicultural Curriculum: Transforming the College Classroom.* New York: Feminist Press, 1994.

Fischer, Gayle V., comp. *"Journal of Women's History," Guide to Periodical Literature.* Bloomington: Indiana University Press, 1992.

Fonow, Mary Margaret, and Judith A. Cook, eds. *Beyond Methodology: Feminist Scholarship as Lived Research.* Bloomington: Indiana University Press, 1991.

Fowles, Diana L., and Charlotte S. McClure. *Feminist Visions: Toward a Transformation of the Liberal Arts Curriculum.* Birmingham: University of Alabama Press, 1984.

Fox-Genovese, Elizabeth. *"Feminism Is Not the Story of My Life": How Today's Feminist Elite Has Lost Touch with the Real Concerns of Women.* New York: Doubleday, 1996.

———. *Feminism without Illusions: A Critique of Individualism.* Chapel Hill: University of North Carolina Press, 1991.

Fraser, Nancy, and Sandra Lee Bartky, eds. *Revaluing French Feminism: Critical Essays on Difference, Agency, and Culture.* Bloomington: Indiana University Press, 1992.

Freeman, Jo. *The Politics of Women's Liberation: A Case Study of an Emerging Social Movement and Its Relation to the Policy Process.* New York: David McKay, 1975.

Freeman, Jo, ed. *Women: A Feminist Perspective.* Palo Alto: Mayfield, 1975.

———. *Women: A Feminist Perspective.* 2d ed. Palo Alto: Mayfield, 1979.

———. *Women: A Feminist Perspective.* 3d ed. Palo Alto: Mayfield, 1984.

———. *Women: A Feminist Perspective.* 4th ed. Mountain View: Mayfield, 1989.

———. *Women: A Feminist Perspective.* 5th ed. Mountain View: Mayfield, 1995.

Freire, Paulo. *The Pedagogy of the Oppressed.* New York: Continuum, 1970.

Friedman, Ellen G., Wendy K. Kolmar, Charley B. Flint, and Paula Rothenberg, eds. *Creating an Inclusive College Curriculum: A Teaching Sourcebook from the New Jersey Project.* New York: Teachers College Press, 1996.

Frye, Marilyn. *The Politics of Reality: Essays in Feminist Theory.* Freedom, Calif.: Crossing Press, 1983.

Fuss, Diana. *Essentially Speaking: Feminism, Nature, and Difference.* New York: Routledge, 1989.

Gallop, Jane. *Reading Lacan.* Ithaca: Cornell University Press, 1985.

Gappa, Judith M., and David W. Leslie, eds. *The Invisible Faculty: Improving the Status of Part-Timers in Higher Education.* San Francisco: Jossey-Bass, 1993.

Garber, Linda, ed. *Tilting the Tower: Lesbians, Teaching, Queer Subjects.* New York: Routledge, 1994.

Garskof, Michelle Hoffnung, ed. *Roles Women Play: Readings toward Women's Liberation.* Belmont, Calif.: Brooks/Cole, 1971.

Getman, Julius. *In the Company of Scholars: The Struggle for the Soul of Higher Education.* Austin: University of Texas Press, 1992.

Giddings, Paula. *When and Where I Enter: The Impact of Black Women on Race and Sex in America.* New York: William Morrow, 1984.

Gilligan, Carol. *In a Different Voice: Psychological Theory and Women's Development.* Cambridge.: Harvard University Press, 1982.

Gilman, Charlotte Perkins. *The Man-Made World; or Our Androcentric Culture.* New York: Charlton, 1911.

Giroux, Henry. *Border Crossings: Cultural Workers and the Politics of Education.* New York: Routledge, 1992.

Glenn, Evelyn Nakano, Grace Chang, and Linda Rennie Forcey, eds. *Mothering: Ideology, Experience, and Agency.* New York: Routledge, 1994.

Glickman, Rose L. *Daughters of Feminists.* New York: St. Martin's Press, 1993.

Gluck, Sherna Berger, and Daphne Patai, eds. *Women's Words: The Feminist Practice of Oral History.* New York: Routledge, 1991.

Goldberger, Nancy Rule, Jill Mattuck Tarule, Blythe McVicker Clinchy, and Mary Field Belenky, eds. *Knowledge, Difference, and Power: Essays Inspired by Women's Ways of Knowing.* New York: BasicBooks, 1996.

Gordon, Avery F., and Christopher Newfield, eds. *Mapping Multiculturalism.* Minneapolis: University of Minnesota Press, 1996.

Gould, Carol C., and Marx W. Wartofsky, eds. *Women and Philosophy: Toward a Theory of Liberation.* New York: G. P. Putnam's Sons, 1976.

Grant, Judith. *Fundamental Feminism: Contesting the Core Concepts of Feminist Theory.* New York: Routledge, 1993.

Greene, Gayle, and Coppélia Kahn, eds. *Changing Subjects: The Making of Feminist Literary Criticism.* London: Routledge, 1993.

Grewal, Inderpal, and Caren Kaplan, eds. *Scattered Hegemonies: Postmodernity and Transnational Feminist Practices.* Minneapolis: University of Minnesota Press, 1994.

Grier, Barbara. *The Lesbian in Literature: A Bibliography.* 3d ed. Tallahassee, Fla.: Naiad Press, 1981.

Guy-Sheftall, Beverly, with Susan Heath. *Women's Studies: A Retrospective.* Report to the Ford Foundation. New York: Ford Foundation, 1995.

Hall, Peter Dobkin. *Inventing the Nonprofit Sector and Other Essays on Philanthropy, Voluntarism, and Nonprofit Organizations.* Baltimore: Johns Hopkins University Press, 1992.

Harding, Sandra. *The Science Question in Feminism*. Ithaca: Cornell University Press, 1986.

———. *Whose Science? Whose Knowledge? Thinking from Women's Lives*. Ithaca: Cornell University Press, 1991.

Harding, Sandra, ed. *Feminism and Methodology: Social Science Issues*. Bloomington: Indiana University Press, 1987.

Harley, Sharon, and Rosalyn Terborg-Penn, eds. *The Afro-American Woman: Struggles and Images*. Port Washington, N.Y.: Kennikat Press, 1978.

Hartman, Joan E., and Ellen Messer-Davidow, eds. *(En)Gendering Knowledge: Feminists in Academe*. Knoxville: University of Tennessee Press, 1991.

Hartman, Mary S., and Lois W. Banner, eds. *Clio's Consciousness Raised: New Perspectives on the History of Women*. New York: Harper Torchbooks, 1974.

Hedges, Elaine. *Getting Started: Planning Curriculum Transformation*. Towson, Md.: National Center for Curriculum Transformation Resources on Women, 1997.

Hekman, Susan J. *Moral Voices, Moral Selves: Carol Gilligan and Feminist Moral Theory*. University Park: Pennsylvania State University Press, 1995.

Hewitt, Nancy, Jean O'Barr, and Nancy Rosebaugh, eds. *Talking Gender: Public Images, Personal Journeys, and Political Critiques*. Chapel Hill: University of North Carolina Press, 1996.

Hewlett, Sylvia Ann. *A Lesser Life: The Myth of Women's Liberation in America*. New York: William Morrow, 1986.

Hiley, David R., James F. Bohman, and Richard Shusterman, eds. *The Interpretive Turn: Philosophy, Science, Culture*. Ithaca: Cornell University Press, 1991.

Hirsch, Marianne, and Evelyn Fox Keller, eds. *Conflicts in Feminism*. New York: Routledge, 1990.

hooks, bell. *Ain't I a Woman: Black Women and Feminism*. Boston: South End Press, 1981.

———. *Feminist Theory: From Margin to Center*. Boston: South End Press, 1984.

———. *Talking Back: Thinking Feminist, Thinking Black*. Boston: South End Press, 1989.

———. *Teaching to Transgress: Education as the Practice of Freedom*. New York: Routledge, 1994.

———. *Yearning: Race, Gender, and Cultural Politics*. Boston: South End Press, 1990.

Howe, Florence. *Myths of Coeducation: Selected Essays, 1964–1983*. Bloomington: Indiana University Press, 1984.

———. *Seven Years Later: Women's Studies Programs in 1976*. Report of the National Advisory Council on Women's Educational Programs. Washington, D.C.: U.S. Department of Education, June 1977.

Howe, Florence, ed. *Female Studies II*. Pittsburgh: KNOW, Inc., 1970.

———. *Women and the Power to Change*. New York: McGraw-Hill, 1975.

Howe, Florence, and Carol Ahlum, eds. *Female Studies III.* Pittsburgh: KNOW, Inc., 1971.

Hull, Gloria T., Patricia Bell Scott, and Barbara Smith, eds. *All the Women Are White, All the Blacks Are Men, but Some of Us Are Brave: Black Women's Studies.* Old Westbury, N.Y.: Feminist Press, 1982.

Hull, Suzanne W., ed. *The State of the Art in Women's Studies.* Reports presented at the Huntington Library Seminar in Women's Studies, 1984–1985. Apr. 1986. Mimeographed booklet.

Hunter College Women's Studies Collective. *Women's Realities, Women's Choices: An Introduction to Women's Studies.* New York: Oxford University Press, 1983.

Hunter College Women's Studies Collective. *Women's Realities, Women's Choices: An Introduction to Women's Studies.* 2d ed. New York: Oxford University Press, 1995.

Integrity in the College Curriculum. Washington, D.C.: Association of American Colleges, 1985.

Involvement in Learning: Realizing the Potential of American Higher Education. Washington, D.C.: United States Department of Education, 1984.

Irigaray, Luce. *This Sex Which Is Not One.* Translated by Catherine Porter with Carolyn Burke. Ithaca: Cornell University Press, 1985.

Jacoby, Russell. *Dogmatic Wisdom: How the Culture Wars Divert Education and Distract America.* New York: Doubleday, 1994.

Jaggar, Alison M. *Feminist Politics and Human Nature.* Totowa, N.J.: Rowman and Allanheld, 1983.

Jaggar, Alison M., and Paula Rothenberg, eds. *Feminist Frameworks: Alternative Theoretical Accounts of the Relations between Women and Men.* 2d ed. New York: McGraw-Hill, 1984.

Jaggar, Alison M., and Paula S. Rothenberg. *Feminist Frameworks: Alternative Theoretical Accounts of the Relations between Women and Men.* New York: McGraw-Hill, 1993.

Jaggar, Alison M., and Paula Rothenberg Struhl. *Feminist Frameworks: Alternative Theoretical Accounts of the Relations between Women and Men.* New York: McGraw-Hill, 1978.

James, Stanlie M., and Abena P. A. Busia, eds. *Theorizing Black Feminisms: The Visionary Pragmatism of Black Women.* London: Routledge, 1993.

Jaquette, Jane S., ed. *Women in Politics.* New York: John Wiley and Sons, 1974.

Johnson, Pauline. *Feminism as Radical Humanism.* Boulder, Colo.: Westview, 1994.

Jones, Kathleen B. *Compassionate Authority: Democracy and the Representation of Women.* New York: Routledge, 1993.

Jones, Kathleen B., and Anna G. Jónasdóttir, eds. *The Political Interests of Gender: Developing Theory with a Feminist Face.* London: Sage, 1988.

Kamen, Paula. *Feminist Fatale: Voices from the "Twentysomething" Generation Explore the Future of the "Women's Movement."* New York: Donald I. Fine, 1991.

Keller, Evelyn Fox, and Helen E. Longino, eds. *Feminism and Science.* Oxford: Oxford University Press, 1996.

Kelly, Joan. *Women, History, and Theory: The Essays of Joan Kelly.* Chicago: University of Chicago Press, 1984.

Keohane, Nannerl O., Michelle Z. Rosaldo, and Barbara C. Gelpi, eds. *Feminist Theory: A Critique of Ideology.* Chicago: University of Chicago Press, 1982.

Kerr, Clark. *The Uses of the University.* 3d ed. Cambridge: Harvard University Press, 1982.

Kesselman, Amy, Lily D. McNair, and Nancy Schniedewind, eds. *Women: Images and Realities. A Multicultural Anthology.* Mountain View, Calif.: Mayfield, 1995.

Kidd, Karen, and Ande Spencer, eds. *Guide to Graduate Work in Women's Studies.* 2d ed. College Park: University of Maryland and National Women's Studies Association, 1994.

Kimball, Roger. *Tenured Radicals: How Politics Has Corrupted Our Higher Education.* New York: HarperPerennial, 1991.

Klein, Julie Thompson. *Interdisciplinarity: History, Theory, and Practice.* Detroit: Wayne State University Press, 1990.

Klepfisz, Irena. *Dreams of an Insomniac: Jewish Feminist Essays, Speeches, and Diatribes.* Portland, Ore.: Eighth Mountain Press, 1990.

Kolmar, Wendy, and Patricia Vogt, eds. *Selected Syllabi for Women's Studies Courses.* College Park: University of Maryland and National Women's Studies Association, 1995.

Korenman, Joan. *Internet Resources on Women: Using Electronic Media in Curriculum Transformation.* Towson State University, Md.: National Center for Curriculum Transformation Resources on Women, 1997.

Kramarae, Cheris, and Dale Spender, eds. *The Knowledge Explosion: Generations of Feminist Scholarship.* New York: Teachers College Press, 1992.

Lakoff, Robin. *Talking Power: The Politics of Language in Our Lives.* New York: BasicBooks, 1990.

Langland, Elizabeth, and Walter Gove, eds. *A Feminist Perspective in the Academy: The Difference It Makes.* Chicago: University of Chicago Press, 1981.

Leo, John. *Two Steps Ahead of the Thought Police.* New York: Simon and Schuster, 1994.

Lerner, Gerda. *The Majority Finds Its Past: Placing Women in History.* New York: Oxford University Press, 1979.

———. *Why History Matters: Life and Thought.* New York: Oxford University Press, 1997.

Lerner, Gerda, ed. *Black Women in White America: A Documentary History.* New York: Random House, 1972.

Levin, Michael. *Feminism and Freedom.* New Brunswick, N.J.: Transaction Books, 1987.

Levine, Arthur, ed. *Higher Learning in America, 1980–2000.* Baltimore: Johns Hopkins University Press, 1993.

Levine, Lawrence W. *The Opening of the American Mind: Canons, Culture, and History.* Boston: Beacon Press, 1996.

Liberation Now! Writings from the Women's Liberation Movement. New York: Dell, 1971.

Lorber, Judith. *Paradoxes of Gender.* New Haven: Yale University Press, 1994.

Lorde, Audre. *Sister Outsider: Essays and Speeches.* Freedom, Calif.: Crossing Press, 1984.

Luebke, Barbara F., and Mary Ellen Reilly. *Women's Studies Graduates: The First Generation.* New York: Teachers College Press, 1995.

Luke, Carmen, and Jennifer Gore, eds. *Feminisms and Critical Pedagogy.* New York: Routledge, 1992.

Lynd, Robert S. *Knowledge for What? The Place of Social Science in American Culture.* Princeton: Princeton University Press, 1939.

MacIntyre, Alasdair. *Three Rival Versions of Moral Enquiry: Encyclopaedia, Genealogy, and Tradition.* Notre Dame: University of Notre Dame Press, 1990.

Maher, Frances A., and Mary Kay Thompson Tetreault. *The Feminist Classroom: An Inside Look at How Professors and Students Are Transforming Higher Education for a Diverse Society.* New York: BasicBooks, 1994.

Marks, Elaine, and Isabelle de Courtivron, eds. *New French Feminisms: An Anthology.* Amherst: University of Massachusetts Press, 1980.

Martin, Jane Roland. *Changing the Educational Landscape: Philosophy, Women, and Curriculum.* New York: Routledge, 1994.

McDermott, Patrice. *Politics and Scholarship: Feminist Academic Journals and the Production of Knowledge.* Urbana: University of Illinois Press, 1994.

Meehan, Johanna, ed. *Feminists Read Habermas: Gendering the Subject of Discourse.* New York: Routledge, 1995.

Millett, Kate. *Sexual Politics.* Garden City, N.Y.: Doubleday, 1970.

Miner, Valerie, and Helen E. Longino, eds. *Competition: A Feminist Taboo?* New York: Feminist Press, 1987.

Minh-ha, Trinh T. *Woman, Native, Other: Writing Postcoloniality and Feminism.* Bloomington: Indiana University Press, 1989.

Minnich, Elizabeth Kamarck. *Transforming Knowledge.* Philadelphia: Temple University Press, 1990.

Minnich, Elizabeth [Kamarck], Jean O'Barr, and Rachel Rosenfeld, eds. *Recon-*

structing the Academy: Women's Education and Women's Studies. Chicago: University of Chicago Press, 1988.

Mitchell, Juliet, and Ann Oakley, eds. *What Is Feminism?* Oxford: Basil Blackwell, 1986.

Modleski, Tania. *Feminism without Women: Culture and Criticism in a "Post-feminist" Age.* New York: Routledge, 1991.

Mohanty, Chandra Talpade, Ann Russo, and Lourdes Torres, eds. *Third World Women and the Politics of Feminism.* Bloomington: Indiana University Press, 1991.

Moi, Toril. *Sexual/Textual Politics: Feminist Literary Theory.* London: Methuen, 1985.

Moraga, Cherríe, and Gloria Anzaldúa, eds. *This Bridge Called My Back: Writings by Radical Women of Color.* Watertown, Mass.: Persephone Press, 1981.

Morgan, Frank B., and Susan G. Broyles. *Degrees and Other Awards Conferred by Institutions of Higher Education: 1992–93.* Washington, D.C.: U.S. Department of Education, Mar. 1995.

Morgan, Robin, ed. *Sisterhood Is Powerful: An Anthology of Writings from the Women's Liberation Movement.* New York: Vintage, 1970.

Moses, Claire Goldberg, and Leslie Wahl Rabine. *Feminism, Socialism, and French Romanticism.* Bloomington: Indiana University Press, 1993.

Musil, Caryn McTighe, ed. *The Courage to Question: Women's Studies and Student Learning.* Washington, D.C.: Association of American Colleges and National Women's Studies Association, 1992.

———. *Students at the Center: Feminist Assessment.* Washington, D.C.: Association of American Colleges and National Women's Studies Association, 1992.

Nelson, John S., Allan Megill, and Donald N. McCloskey, eds. *The Rhetoric of the Human Sciences: Language and Argumentation in Scholarship and Public Affairs.* Madison: University of Wisconsin Press, 1987.

Nicholson, Linda J., ed. *Feminism/Postmodernism.* New York: Routledge, 1990.

Nicholson, Linda, and Steven Seidman, eds. *Social Postmodernism: Beyond Identity Politics.* Cambridge: Cambridge University Press, 1995.

Nielsen, Joyce McCarl, ed. *Feminist Research Methods: Exemplary Readings in the Social Sciences.* Boulder, Colo.: Westview Press, 1990.

Novick, Peter. *That Noble Dream: The "Objectivity Question" and the American Historical Profession.* Cambridge: Cambridge University Press, 1988.

O'Barr, Jean Fox. *Feminism in Action: Building Institutions and Community through Women's Studies.* Chapel Hill: University of North Carolina Press, 1994.

O'Barr, Jean [Fox], and Mary Wyer, eds. *Engaging Feminism: Students Speak Up and Speak Out.* Charlottesville: University Press of Virginia, 1992.

Offen, Karen. *European Feminisms, 1700–1950.* Forthcoming.

Okin, Susan Moller. *Justice, Gender, and the Family.* BasicBooks, 1989.

———. *Women in Western Political Thought*. Princeton: Princeton University Press, 1979.

Oleson, Alexandra, and John Voss, eds. *The Organization of Knowledge in Modern America, 1860–1920*. Baltimore: Johns Hopkins University Press, 1979.

Paglia, Camille. *Sex, Art, and Culture: Essays*. New York: Vintage, 1992.

———. *Vamps and Tramps: New Essays*. New York: Vintage, 1994.

Paludi, Michele A., and Gertrude A. Steuernagel, eds. *Foundations for a Feminist Restructuring of the Academic Disciplines*. New York: Haworth Press, 1990.

Patai, Daphne, and Noretta Koertge. *Professing Feminism: Cautionary Tales from the Strange World of Women's Studies*. New York: BasicBooks, 1994.

Pateman, Carole. *The Disorder of Women: Democracy, Feminism, and Political Theory*. Stanford: Stanford University Press, 1989.

———. *The Sexual Contract*. Stanford: Stanford University Press, 1988.

Pearson, Carol R., Donna L. Shavlik, and Judith G. Touchton, eds. *Educating the Majority: Women Challenge Tradition in Higher Education*. New York: ACE/Macmillan, 1989.

Pelikan, Jaroslav. *The Idea of the University: A Reexamination*. New Haven: Yale University Press, 1992.

Pickering, Mary. *Auguste Comte: An Intellectual Biography*. Vol. 1. Cambridge: Cambridge University Press, 1993.

Pollitt, Katha. *Reasonable Creatures: Essays on Women and Feminism*. New York: Alfred A. Knopf, 1995.

Postman, Neil, and Charles Weingartner. *Teaching as a Subversive Activity*. New York: Delta, 1969.

Quest Staff. *Building Feminist Theory: Essays from "Quest."* New York: Longman, 1981.

Reiter, Rayna R., ed. *Toward an Anthropology of Women*. New York: Monthly Review Press, 1975.

Rhode, Deborah L., ed. *Theoretical Perspectives on Sexual Difference*. New Haven: Yale University Press, 1990.

Rich, Adrienne. *Blood, Bread, and Poetry: Selected Prose, 1979–1985*. New York: W. W. Norton, 1986.

———. *On Lies, Secrets, and Silence: Selected Prose, 1966–1978*. New York: W. W. Norton, 1979.

Richardson, Laurel, and Verta Taylor, eds. *Feminist Frontiers: Rethinking Sex, Gender, and Society*. Reading, Mass.: Addison-Wesley, 1983.

———. *Feminist Frontiers III*. New York: McGraw-Hill, 1993.

Riley, Denise. *"Am I That Name?" Feminism and the Category of "Women" in History*. Minneapolis: University of Minnesota Press, 1988.

Roberts, Mary Louise. *Civilization without Sexes: Reconstructing Gender in Postwar France, 1917–1927*. Chicago: University of Chicago Press, 1994.

Roof, Judith, and Robyn Wiegman, eds. *Who Can Speak? Authority and Critical Identity.* Urbana: University of Illinois Press, 1995.

Rosaldo, Michelle Zimbalist, and Louise Lamphere, eds. *Women, Culture, and Society.* Stanford: Stanford University Press, 1974.

Rosser, Sue V. *Biology and Feminism: A Dynamic Interaction.* New York: Twayne, 1992.

Rossi, Alice S., ed. *The Feminist Papers: From Adams to de Beauvoir.* New York: Columbia University Press, 1973.

Rowbotham, Sheila. *Women, Resistance, and Revolution: A History of Women and Revolution in the Modern World.* 1972; New York: Vintage, 1974.

Ruddick, Sara, and Pamela Daniels, eds. *Working It Out: 23 Women Writers, Artists, Scientists, and Scholars Talk about Their Lives and Work.* New York: Pantheon, 1977.

Ruth, Sheila. *Issues in Feminism: A First Course in Women's Studies.* Boston: Houghton Mifflin, 1980.

———. *Issues in Feminism: An Introduction to Women's Studies.* 2d ed. Mountain View, Calif.: Mayfield, 1990.

———. *Issues in Feminism: An Introduction to Women's Studies.* 3d ed. Mountain View, Calif.: Mayfield, 1995.

Sandler, Bernice Resnik, Lisa A. Silverberg, and Roberta M. Hall. *The Chilly Classroom Climate: A Guide to Improve the Education of Women.* Washington, D.C.: National Association for Women in Education, 1996.

———. *The Classroom Climate: A Chilly One for Women.* Washington, D.C.: National Association for Women in Education, 1982.

Sapiro, Virginia. *Women in American Society: An Introduction to Women's Studies.* Palo Alto, Calif.: Mayfield, 1986.

Schmitz, Betty. *Integrating Women's Studies into the Curriculum: A Guide and Bibliography.* Old Westbury, N.Y.: Feminist Press, 1985.

Schneir, Miriam, ed. *Feminism: The Essential Historical Writings.* New York: Vintage, 1972.

Schor, Naomi, and Elizabeth Weed, eds. *The Essential Difference.* Bloomington: Indiana University Press, 1994.

Schuster, Marilyn R., and Susan R. Van Dyne, eds. *Women's Place in the Academy: Transforming the Liberal Arts Curriculum.* Totowa, N.J.: Rowman and Allanheld, 1985.

Scott, Joan Wallach. *Gender and the Politics of History.* New York: Columbia University Press, 1988.

———. *Only Paradoxes to Offer: French Feminists and the Rights of Man.* Cambridge: Harvard University Press, 1996.

Scott, Joan Wallach, ed. *Feminism and History.* Oxford: Oxford University Press, 1996.

Shapiro, Ann-Louise, ed. *Feminists Revision History.* New Brunswick: Rutgers University Press, 1994.

Sherman, Julia A., and Evelyn Torton Beck, eds. *The Prism of Sex: Essays in the Sociology of Knowledge.* Madison: University of Wisconsin Press, 1979.

Showalter, Elaine, and Carol Ohmann, eds. *Female Studies IV: Teaching about Women.* Pittsburgh: KNOW, Inc., 1971.

Shteir, Ann B., ed. *Graduate Women's Studies: Visions and Realities.* North York, Ontario: Inanna Publications and Education, 1996.

Simon, Rita J., ed. *Neither Victim nor Enemy: Women's Freedom Network Looks at Gender in America.* Lanham, Md.: University Press of America, 1995.

Siporin, Rae Lee, ed. *Female Studies V.* Pittsburgh: KNOW, Inc., 1972.

Smith, Hilda L. *Reason's Disciples: Seventeenth-Century English Feminists.* Urbana: University of Illinois Press, 1982.

Smith, Mark C. *Social Science in the Crucible: The American Debate over Objectivity and Purpose, 1918–1941.* Durham, N.C.: Duke University Press, 1994.

Smith, Page. *Killing the Spirit: Higher Education in America.* New York: Viking, 1990.

Solomon, Barbara Miller. *In the Company of Educated Women: A History of Women and Higher Education in America.* New Haven: Yale University Press, 1985.

Sommers, Christina Hoff. *Who Stole Feminism? How Women Have Betrayed Women.* New York: Simon and Schuster, 1994.

Spacks, Patricia Meyer, ed. *Advocacy in the Classroom: Problems and Possibilities.* New York: St. Martin's Press, 1996.

Spelman, Elizabeth V. *Inessential Woman: Problems of Exclusion in Feminist Thought.* Boston: Beacon Press, 1988.

Spender, Dale, ed. *Men's Studies Modified: The Impact of Feminism on the Academic Disciplines.* Oxford: Pergamon Press, 1981.

Stanton, Domna C., and Abigail J. Stewart, eds. *Feminisms in the Academy.* Ann Arbor: University of Michigan Press, 1995.

Statham, Anne, Laurel Richardson, and Judith A. Cook. *Gender and University Teaching: A Negotiated Difference.* Albany: State University of New York Press, 1991.

Stimpson, Catharine R., with Nona Kressner Cobb. *Women's Studies in the United States.* Report to the Ford Foundation. New York: Ford Foundation, 1986.

Tanner, Leslie B., ed. *Voices from Women's Liberation.* New York: Mentor, New American Library, 1970.

Thorne, Barrie, with Marilyn Yalom, eds. *Rethinking the Family: Some Feminist Questions.* New York: Longman, 1982.

Tobias, Sheila. *Faces of Feminism: An Activist's Reflections on the Women's Movement.* Boulder, Colo.: Westview Press, 1997.

Tobias, Sheila, ed. *Female Studies I.* Pittsburgh: KNOW, Inc., 1970.

Touchton, Judith G., and Lynne Davis, comps. *Fact Book on Women in Higher Education.* New York: ACE/Macmillan, 1991.

Towns, Kathryn, with Caroline Cupo and Phyllis Hageman, comps. *Re-Membering: NWSA, 1977–1987.* 2d ed. College Park, Md.: National Women's Studies Association, 1994.

Vanderbilt, Kermit. *American Literature and the Academy.* Philadelphia: University of Pennsylvania Press, 1986.

Walkowitz, Judith R. *Prostitution and Victorian Society: Women, Class, and the State.* Cambridge: Cambridge University Press, 1980.

Ware, Cellestine. *Woman Power: The Movement for Women's Liberation.* New York: Tower, 1970.

White, Stephen K. *Political Theory and Postmodernism.* Cambridge: Cambridge University Press, 1991.

White, Stephen K., ed. *Life-World and Politics: Between Modernity and Postmodernity. Essays in Honor of Fred R. Dallmayr.* Notre Dame: University of Notre Dame Press, 1989.

Wilkinson, Sue, and Celia Kitzinger, eds. *Heterosexuality: A Feminism and Psychology Reader.* London: Sage, 1993.

Wilton, Tamsin. *Lesbian Studies: Setting an Agenda.* London: Routledge, 1995.

Wollstonecraft, Mary. *A Vindication of the Rights of Woman.* Edited by Carol H. Poston. New York: W. W. Norton, 1975.

"Women's Studies: A World View." Special issue of *Women's Studies Quarterly* 22, nos. 3 and 4 (fall–winter 1994).

"Women's Studies in Europe." Special issue of *Women's Studies Quarterly* 20, nos. 3 and 4 (fall–winter 1992).

Woolf, Virginia. *Three Guineas.* New York: Harcourt, Brace, 1938.

Yates, Gayle. *What Women Want: The Ideas of the Movement.* Cambridge: Harvard University Press, 1975.

Young, Iris Marion. *Justice and the Politics of Difference.* Princeton: Princeton University Press, 1990.

Zimmerman, Bonnie, and Toni A. H. McNaron, eds. *The New Lesbian Studies: Into the Twentieth-first Century.* New York: Feminist Press, 1996.

Zinsser, Judith P. *History and Feminism: A Glass Half Full.* New York: Twayne, 1993.

Essays and Articles

Abel, Emily, Deborah Rosenfelt, and Peg Strobel. "'Toto, I Think We're No Longer in Kansas': Reflections on the 1979 Conference." In Towns, Cupo, and Hageman, comps., *Re-Membering.*

Ackelsberg, Martha A., and Kathryn Pyne Addelson. "Anarchist Alternatives to Competition." In Miner and Longino, eds., *Competition*.

Addelson, Kathryn Pyne. "Knower/Doers and Their Moral Problems." In Alcoff and Potter, eds., *Feminist Epistemologies*.

Aiken, Susan Hardy, Karen Anderson, Myra Dinnerstein, Judy Lensink, and Patricia MacCorquodale. "Trying Transformations: Curriculum Integration and the Problem of Resistance." *Signs* 12, no. 2 (winter 1987).

Alarcón, Norma. "The Theoretical Subject(s) of *This Bridge Called My Back* and Anglo-American Feminism." In Anzaldúa, ed., *Making Face, Making Soul*.

Alcoff, Linda. "Cultural Feminism versus Poststructuralism: The Identity Crisis in Feminist Theory." *Signs* 13, no. 3 (spring 1988).

———. "The Problem of Speaking for Others." In Roof and Wiegman, eds., *Who Can Speak?*

Allen, Ann Taylor. "The March through the Institutions: Women's Studies in the United States and West and East Germany, 1980–1995." *Signs* 22, no. 1 (autumn 1996).

———. "Women's Studies as Cultural Movement and Academic Discipline in the United States and West Germany: The Early Phase." *Women in Germany Yearbook* 9 (1993).

Andersen, Margaret L. "Changing the Curriculum in Higher Education." *Signs* 12 no. 2 (winter 1987).

Aronowitz, Stanley. "Schooling, Culture, and Literacy in the Age of Broken Dreams: A Review of Bloom and Hirsch." *Harvard Educational Review* 58, no. 2 (May 1988).

Arpad, Susan S. "Burnout." *Women's Studies International Forum* 9, no. 2 (1986).

Awkward, Michael. "A Black Man's Place(s) in Black Feminist Criticism." In Roof and Wiegman, eds., *Who Can Speak?*

Baron, Ava. "On Looking at Men: Masculinity and the Making of a Gendered Working-Class History." In Shapiro, ed., *Feminists Revision History*.

Barrett, Michèle. "Psychoanalysis and Feminism: A British Sociologist's View." *Signs* 17, no. 2 (winter 1992).

Bauer, Dale M. "Personal Criticism and the Academic Personality." In Roof and Wiegman, eds., *Who Can Speak?*

Beck, Evelyn Torton. "Asking for the Future." *Women's Review of Books* 6, no. 5 (Feb. 1989).

———. "The Politics of Jewish Invisibility." *NWSA Journal* 1, no. 1 (1988).

Bell, Susan Groag, and Mollie Rosenhan. "A Problem in Naming: Women Studies—Women's Studies." *Signs* 6, no. 3 (spring 1981).

Bender, Thomas. "Politics, Intellect, and the American University, 1945–1995." *Daedalus* 126, no. 1 (winter 1997).

Bennett, Judith M. "Feminism and History." *Gender and History* 1, no. 3 (autumn 1989).

Berger, Birgitte. "Academic Feminism and the 'Left.'" *Academic Questions* 1, no. 2 (spring 1988).

Bernard, Jessie. "Impact of Women's Studies on Sociology." *Signs* 22, no. 1 (autumn 1996).

———. "Re-Viewing the Impact of Women's Studies on Sociology." In Farnham, ed., *Impact of Feminist Research.*

"Bibliography of Feminist Epistemologies." In Alcoff and Potter, eds., *Feminist Epistemologies.*

Bird, Elizabeth. "Women's Studies in European Higher Education: Sigma and Coimbra." *European Journal of Women's Studies* 3, no. 2 (May 1996).

Black, Naomi. "The Mothers' International: The Women's Cooperative Guild and Feminist Pacifism." *Women's Studies International Forum* 7, no. 6 (1984).

Booth, Wayne. "Freedom of Interpretation: Bakhtin and the Challenge of Feminist Criticism." *Critical Inquiry* 9 (Sept. 1982).

Bordo, Susan. "Feminism, Postmodernism, and Gender-Skepticism." in Nicholson, ed., *Feminism/Postmodernism.*

Bourne, Jenny. "Homelands of the Mind: Jewish Feminism and Identity Politics." *Race and Class* 29, no. 1 (summer 1987).

Bow, Leslie. "'For Every Gesture of Loyalty There Doesn't Have to Be a Betrayal': Asian American Criticism and the Politics of Locality." In Roof and Wiegman, eds., *Who Can Speak?*

Bowles, Gloria, and Renate Duelli Klein. "Introduction: Theories of Women's Studies and the Autonomy/Integration Debate." In Bowles and Klein, eds., *Theories of Women's Studies.*

Boxer, Marilyn J. "A Course in 'Feminology': Women's Studies in France circa 1902." *Women's Studies Quarterly*, international supplement no. 1 (Jan. 1982).

———. "Designer Clocks for Academic Careers." *History Teacher* 29, no. 4 (Aug. 1996).

———. "For and about Women: The Theory and Practice of Women's Studies in the United States." *Signs* 7, no. 3 (spring 1982).

———. "Socialism Faces Feminism: The Failure of Synthesis in France, 1879–1913." In Boxer and Quataert, eds., *Socialist Women.*

———. "Women: Historical and Cross-Cultural Perspectives." In vol. 5. of *Encyclopedia of Bioethics,* 5 vols., rev. ed., Warren T. Reich, editor-in-chief. New York: Simon and Schuster Macmillan, 1995.

———. "Women's Studies, Feminist Goals, and the Science of Women." In Pearson, Shavlik, and Touchton, eds., *Educating the Majority.*

Brewer, Rose M. "Theorizing Race, Class, and Gender: The New Scholarship of Black Feminist Intellectuals and Black Women's Labor." In James and Busia, eds., *Theorizing Black Feminisms.*

Brodribb, Somer. "Nothing Mat(t)ers." In Bell and Klein, eds., *Radically Speaking.*

Brush, Lorelei R., Alice Ross Gold, and Marni Goldstein White. "The Paradox of Intention and Effect: A Women's Studies Course." *Signs* 3, no. 4 (summer 1978).

Bunch, Charlotte. "Not by Degrees: Feminist Theory and Education." In Bunch and Pollack, eds., *Learning Our Way*.

Burke, Carolyn Greenstein. "Report from Paris: Women's Writing and the Women's Movement." *Signs* 3, no. 4 (summer 1978).

Burton, Antoinette. "'History' Is Now: Feminist Theory and the Production of Historical Feminisms." *Women's History Review* 1, no. 1 (1992).

Butler, Johnnella E. "Transforming the Curriculum: Teaching about Women of Color." In Butler and Walter, eds., *Transforming the Curriculum*.

Carfagna, Rosemarie. "Creating Gender Equity in the College Classroom." *College Board Review* 172 (summer 1994).

Carroll, Berenice A. "International Trends: Scholarship and Action. CCWHP and the Movement(s)." *Journal of Women's History* 6, no. 3 (fall 1994).

Carty, Linda. "Black Women in Academia: A Statement from the Periphery." In Himani Bannerji et al., *Unsettling Relations*.

Chamberlain, Mariam K., and Bernstein, Alison. "Philanthropy and the Emergence of Women's Studies." *Teachers College Record* 93, no. 3 (spring 1992).

Childers, Mary, and bell hooks. "A Conversation about Race and Class." In Hirsch and Keller, eds., *Conflicts in Feminism*.

Christ, Carol P. "Toward a Paradigm Shift in the Academy and in Religious Studies." In Farnham, ed., *Impact of Feminist Research*.

Christian, Barbara. "But Who Do You Really Belong to—Black Studies or Women's Studies?" *Women's Studies* 17 (1989).

———. "The Race for Theory." *Feminist Studies* 14, no. 1 (spring 1988).

Christopher, Susan. "Gendered Knowledge in the Core Curriculum." Paper presented at annual meeting of National Women's Studies Association, Skidmore College, June 1996. Based on Susan Christopher, "Required Knowledge: Incorporating Gender into a Core Curriculum." Ph.D. dissertation, Stanford University (1995).

Cixous, Hélène. "The Laugh of the Medusa." *Signs* 1, no. 4 (summer 1976).

Cole, Johnnetta. "Black Studies in Liberal Arts Education." In Butler and Walter, eds., *Transforming the Curriculum*.

Collins, Patricia Hill. "Learning from the Outsider Within: The Sociological Significance of Black Feminist Thought." In Fonow and Cook, eds., *Beyond Methodology*.

———. "Learning from the Outsider Within: The Sociological Significance of Black Feminist Thought." *Social Problems* 33, no. 6 (1986).

Conway, Jill K. "Coeducation and Women's Studies: Two Approaches to the Question of Woman's Place in the Contemporary University." *Daedalus* 103, no. 4 (fall 1974).

Coyner, Sandra. "The Ideas of Mainstreaming: Women's Studies and the Disciplines," *Frontiers* 8, no. 3 (1986).

———. "Women's Studies as an Academic Discipline: Why and How to Do It." In Bowles and Klein, eds., *Theories of Women's Studies.*

Crosby, Christina. "Dealing with Differences." In Butler and Scott, eds., *Feminists Theorize the Political.*

Davis, Barbara Hillyer. "Teaching the Feminist Minority." *Women's Studies Quarterly* 9 no. 4 (winter 1981).

———. "Teaching the Feminist Minority." In Bunch and Pollack, eds., *Learning Our Way.*

———. "Teaching the Feminist Minority." In Culley and Portugues, eds., *Gendered Subjects.*

Davis, Natalie Zemon. "City Women and Religious Change." In *Society and Culture in Early Modern France.*

———. "Women on Top." In *Society and Culture in Early Modern France.*

Davis, Natalie Zemon, Linda Gardiner, Cynthia Neverdon-Morton, Julia Penelope, and Margery Wolf. "Feminist Book Reviewing: A Symposium." *Feminist Studies* 14, no. 3 (fall 1988).

de Groot, Joanna, and Mary Maynard. "Facing the 1990s: Problems and Possibilities for Women's Studies." In de Groot and Maynard, eds. *Women's Studies in the 1990s.*

Delamont, Sara. "Old Fogies and Intellectual Women: An Episode in Academic History." *Women's History Review* 1, no. 1 (1992).

de Lauretis, Teresa. "The Essence of the Triangle or, Taking the Risk of Essentialism Seriously: Feminist Theory in Italy, the United States, and Britain." *differences* 1, no. 2 (summer 1989).

———. "Upping the Anti (sic) in Feminist Theory." In Hirsch and Keller, eds., *Conflicts in Feminism.*

Delphy, Christine. "French Feminism: An Imperialist Invention." In Bell and Klein, eds., *Radically Speaking.*

Dinnerstein, Myra. "Questions for the Nineties." *Women's Review of Books* 6, no. 5 (Feb. 1989).

Douglas, Carol Anne. "Radical Feminism, Past, Present, and Future." *off our backs* 26, no. 8 (Aug.–Sept. 1996).

duCille, Ann. "The Occult of True Black Womanhood: Critical Demeanor and Black Feminist Studies." *Signs* 19, no. 3 (spring 1994).

DuPlessis, Rachel Blau. "Reader, I Married Me: A Polygynous Memoir." In Greene and Kahn, eds., *Changing Subjects.*

Dworkin, Andrea. "Dworkin on Dworkin." In Bell and Klein, eds., *Radically Speaking.*

Eder, Donna, and Audrey Thomas McCloskey. "Teaching across the Barriers: The

Classroom as a Site of Transformation." *Transformations* 7, no. 1 (spring 1996).

Eisenmann, Linda. "Weathering 'A Climate of Unexpectation': Gender Equity and the Radcliffe Institute, 1960–1995." *Academe* 81, no. 4 (July–Aug. 1995).

Elshtain, Jean Bethke. "Antigone's Daughters," *Democracy* 2, no. 2, Apr. 1982.

———. "Antigone's Daughters Reconsidered." In White, ed., *Life-World and Politics.*

———. "Exporting Feminism." In Simon, ed., *Neither Victim nor Enemy.*

———. "Feminist Discourse and Its Discontents: Language, Power, and Meaning." In Keohane, Rosaldo, and Gelpi, eds., *Feminist Theory.*

———. "Feminist Political Rhetoric and Women's Studies." In Nelson, Megill, and McCloskey, eds., *Rhetoric of the Human Sciences.*

———. "The Power and Powerlessness of Women." In Bock and James, eds., *Beyond Equality and Difference.*

Faludi, Susan. "I'm Not a Feminist, but I Play One on TV." *Ms.* magazine, Mar.–Apr. 1995.

Fausto-Sterling, Anne. "Race, Gender, and Science." *Transformations* 2, no. 2 (fall 1992).

Finke, Laurie. "The Rhetoric of Marginality: Why I Do Feminist Theory." *Tulsa Studies In Women's Literature* 5, no. 2 (fall 1986).

Flanders, Laura. "The 'Stolen Feminism' Hoax: Anti-Feminist Attack Based on Error-Filled Anecdotes." *Extra!* Sept.–Oct. 1994.

Flax, Jane. "The End of Innocence." In Butler and Scott, eds., *Feminists Theorize the Political.*

Flieger, Jerry Anne. "Growing Up Theoretical: Across the Divide." In Greene and Kahn, eds., *Changing Subjects.*

Fonow, Mary Margaret, and Judith A. Cook. "Back to the Future: A Look at the Second Wave of Feminist Epistemology and Methodology." In Fonow and Cook, eds., *Beyond Methodology.*

———. "Knowledge and Women's Interests: Issues of Epistemology and Methodology in Feminist Sociological Research." In Nielsen, ed., *Feminist Research Methods.*

Fraser, Nancy. "Introduction: Revaluing French Feminism." In Fraser and Bartky, eds., *Revaluing French Feminism.*

Freedman, Estelle B. "Small-Group Pedagogy: Consciousness Raising in Conservative Times." In Garber, ed., *Tilting the Tower.*

———. "Theoretical Perspectives on Sexual Difference: An Overview." In Rhode, ed., *Theoretical Perspectives on Sexual Difference.*

Freeman, Jo. "The Tyranny of Structurelessness." *Berkeley Journal of Sociology* 17 (1972–73).

———. "The Tyranny of Structurelessness." In Jaquette, ed., *Women in Politics.*

Friedman, Susan Stanford. "Authority in the Feminist Classroom: A Contradiction in Terms?" In Culley and Portugues, eds., *Gendered Subjects.*

———. "Beyond White and Other: Relationality and Narratives of Race in Feminist Discourse." *Signs* 21, no. 1 (autumn 1995).

———. "Making History: Reflections on Feminism, Narrative, and Desire." In Elam and Wiegman, eds., *Feminism beside Itself.*

Frye, Marilyn. "Getting It Right." *Signs* 17, no. 4 (summer 1992).

———. "A Lesbian Perspective on Women's Studies." In Cruikshank, ed., *Lesbian Studies.*

Gallop, Jane, Marianne Hirsch, and Nancy K. Miller. "Criticizing Feminist Criticism." In Hirsch and Keller, eds., *Conflicts in Feminism.*

Gardiner, Judith Kegan. "Psychoanalysis and Feminism: An American Humanist's View." *Signs* 17, no. 2 (winter 1992).

Geiger, Susan, and Jacqueline N. Zita. "White Traders: The Caveat Emptor of Women's Studies." *Journal of Thought* 20, no. 3 (fall 1985).

George, Kathi. "On the Fringes of Academe: Creating the Pathway: Panel Conversation at the Tenth Anniversary Celebration of San Diego Independent Scholars, October 10, 1992." *Journal of Unconventional History* 4, no. 2 (winter 1993).

Ginsberg, Elaine, and Sara Lennox. "Antifeminism in Scholarship and Publishing." In Clark et al., eds., *Antifeminism in the Academy.*

Gluck, Sherna Berger. "Advocacy Oral History: Palestinian Women in Resistance." In Gluck and Patai, eds., *Women's Words.*

Goldberger, Nancy Rule. "Introduction: Looking Backward, Looking Forward." In Goldberger et al., eds., *Knowledge, Difference, and Power.*

Goodstein, Lynne. "The Failure of Curriculum Transformation at a Major Public University: When 'Diversity' Equals 'Variety.'" *NWSA Journal* 6, no. 1 (spring 1994).

Goodstein, Lynne, and LaVerne Gyant. "A Minor of Our Own: A Case for an Academic Program in Women of Color." *Women's Studies Quarterly* 18, nos. 1 and 2 (1990).

Gordon, Ann D., Mari Jo Buhle, and Nancy Schrom Dye. "The Problem of Women's History." In Carroll, ed., *Liberating Women's History.*

Gordon, Linda, Persis Hunt, Elizabeth Pleck, Rochelle Goldberg Ruthchild, and Marcia Scott. "Historical Phallacies: Sexism in American Historical Writing." In Carroll, ed., *Liberating Women's History.*

Gould, Carol C. "The Woman Question: Philosophy of Liberation and the Liberation of Philosophy." In Gould and Wartofsky, eds., *Women and Philosophy.*

Grant, Judith. "I Feel Therefore I Am: A Critique of Female Experience as the Basis for a Feminist Epistemology." In Falco, ed., *Feminism and Epistemology.*

Gubar, Susan. "Feminist Misogyny: Mary Wollstonecraft and the Paradox of 'It

Takes One to Know One.'" In Elam and Wiegman, eds., *Feminism beside Itself.*

Guerrero, Maria Anna Jaimes. "Civil Rights versus Sovereignty: Native American Women in Life and Land Struggles." In Alexander and Mohanty, eds., *Feminist Genealogies, Colonial Legacies, Democratic Futures.*

Hacker, Helen. "Women as a Minority Group." *Social Forces* 30 (1951).

Hall, Stuart. "Cultural Studies: Two Paradigms." In Dirks, Eley, and Ortner, eds., *Culture/Power/History.*

Haraway, Donna. "A Manifesto for Cyborgs: Science, Technology, and Socialist Feminism in the 1980s." In Nicholson, ed., *Feminism/Postmodernism.*

———. "Situated Knowledges: The Science Question in Feminism and the Privilege of Partial Perspective." *Feminist Studies* 14, no. 3 (1988).

Harding, Sandra. "Feminism, Science, and the Anti-Enlightenment Critiques." In Nicholson, ed., *Feminism/Postmodernism.*

———. "Introduction: Is There a Feminist Method?" In Harding, ed., *Feminism and Methodology.*

———. "Rethinking Standpoint Epistemology: What Is 'Strong Objectivity'?" In Alcoff and Potter, eds., *Feminist Epistemologies.*

Harrington, Lisa. "California Q&A: An Interview with Gloria Bowles." *California Monthly* 92, no. 3 (Jan.–Feb. 1983).

Hartman, Joan E. "Telling Stories: The Construction of Women's Agency." In Hartman and Messer-Davidow, eds., *(En)Gendering Knowledge.*

Hartmann, Heidi, Ellen Bravo, Charlotte Bunch, Nancy Hartsock, Roberta Spalter-Roth, Linda Williams, and Maria Blanco. "Bringing Together Feminist Theory and Practice: A Collective Interview." *Signs* 21, no. 4 (summer 1996).

Hartsock, Nancy C. M. "The Feminist Standpoint: Developing the Ground for a Specifically Feminist Historical Materialism." In Harding, ed., *Feminism and Methodology.*

———. "Feminist Theory and the Development of Revolutionary Strategy." In Eisenstein, ed., *Capitalist Patriarchy and the Case for Socialist Feminism.*

———. "Foucault on Power: A Theory For Women?" In Nicholson, ed., *Feminism/Postmodernism.*

———. "Political Change: Two Perspectives on Power." *Quest:* 1, no. 1 (summer 1974).

Hawkesworth, Mary. "Confounding Gender." *Signs* 22, no. 3 (spring 1997).

———. "Knowers, Knowing, Known: Feminist Theory and Claims of Truth." *Signs* 14, no. 3 (spring 1989).

Hedges, Elaine. "Resources for Curriculum Transformation." *NWSAction* 5, no. 2 (spring 1994).

Heilbrun, Carolyn G. "Women, Men, Theories, and Literature." In Farnham, ed., *Impact of Feminist Research.*

Hein, Hilde. "The Role of Feminist Aesthetics in Feminist Theory." In Brand and Korsmeyer, eds., *Feminism and Tradition in Aesthetics.*

Hekman, Susan. "The Feminization of Epistemology: Gender and the Social Sciences." *Women in Politics* 7, no. 3 (fall 1987).

———. "Truth and Method: Feminist Standpoint Theory Revisited." *Signs* 22, no. 2 (winter 1997).

Hickok, Kathy. "Lesbian Images in Women's Literature Anthologies." In Cruikshank, ed., *Lesbian Studies.*

Higginbotham, Elizabeth. "Designing an Inclusive Curriculum: Bringing All Women into the Core." *Women's Studies Quarterly* 18, nos. 1 and 2 (1990).

Higginbotham, Evelyn Brooks. "Beyond the Sound of Silence: Afro-American Women in History." *Gender and History* 1, no. 1 (spring 1989).

Hill, Leslie I. "The Ford Foundation Program on Mainstreaming Minority Women's Studies." *Women's Studies Quarterly* 18, nos. 1–2 (spring–summer 1990).

Himmelfarb, Gertrude. "The New Advocacy and the Old." In Spacks, ed., *Advocacy in the Classroom.*

———. "Not What We Meant at All," review of *Telling the Truth,* by Joyce Appleby, Lynn Hunt, and Margaret Jacob. *Times Literary Supplement,* June 10, 1994.

Hochschild, Arlie Russell. "Inside the Clockwork of Male Careers." In Howe, ed., *Women and the Power to Change.*

Hoff, Joan. "Gender as a Postmodern Category of Paralysis." *Women's History Review* 3 (1994).

———. "The Pernicious Effects of Poststructuralism on Women's History." In Bell and Klein, eds., *Radically Speaking.*

Hoffman, Nancy. "Black Studies, Ethnic Studies, and Women's Studies: Some Reflections on Collaborative Projects." In *Women's Studies Quarterly* 14, nos. 1 and 2 (spring–summer 1986).

Hogeland, Lisa Maria. "*Invisible Man* and Invisible Women: The Sex/Race Analogy of the 1970's." *Women's History Review* 5, no. 1 (1996).

hooks, bell. "Feminism: A Transformational Politic." In Rhode, ed., *Theoretical Perspectives on Sexual Difference.*

hooks, bell, with Tanya McKinnon. "Sisterhood: Beyond Public and Private." *Signs* 21, no. 4 (summer 1996).

Howe, Florence. "A Symbiotic Relationship." *Women's Review of Books* 6, no. 5 (Feb. 1989).

Hull, Gloria T., and Barbara Smith. "Introduction: The Politics of Black Women's Studies." In Hull, Scott, and Smith, *But Some of Us Are Brave.*

Iannone, Carol. Interview with Elizabeth Fox-Genovese. *Academic Questions* 5, no. 3 (summer 1992).

Issel, William. "Cultural Politics and Conservatism in Post–World War II

America." Unpublished paper, San Francisco State University, 1996.

Jacoby, Russell. "America's Professoriate: Politicized, Yet Apolitical." *Chronicle of Higher Education*, Apr. 12, 1996.

Jaggar, Alison M. "Sexual Differences and Sexual Equality." In Rhode, ed., *Theoretical Perspectives on Sexual Difference.*

Jeffreys, Sheila. "Return to Gender: Postmodernism and Lesbianandgay [sic] Theory." In Bell and Klein, eds., *Radically Speaking.*

Johnston, Susan. "Not for Queers Only: Pedagogy and Postmodernism." *NWSA Journal* 7, no. 1 (spring 1995).

Jones, Ann Rosalind. "Imaginary Gardens with Real Frogs in Them: Feminist Euphoria and the Franco-American Divide, 1976–88." In Greene and Kahn, eds., *Changing Subjects.*

Jones, Kathleen B. "Le Mal des Fleurs: A Feminist Response to *The Closing of the American Mind.*" *Women and Politics* 9, no. 4 (1989).

Jones, Nancy Baker. "'Confronting the PC 'Debate': The Politics of Identity and the American Image." *NWSA Journal* 6, no. 3 (fall 1994).

Kaplan, Caren. "The Politics of Location as Transnational Feminist Critical Practice." In Grewal and Kaplan, eds., *Scattered Hegemonies.*

Kauffman, Linda S. "The Long Goodbye: Against the Personal Testimony or, An Infant Grifter Grows Up." In Greene and Kahn, eds., *Changing Subjects.*

Keller, Evelyn Fox. "Feminism and Science." In Keller and Longino, eds., *Feminism and Science.*

Kelly-Gadol, Joan. "The Social Relations of the Sexes: Methodological Implications of Women's History." *Signs* 1, no. 4 (summer 1976).

Kent, Susan Kingsley. "Mistrials and Diatribulations: A Reply to Joan Hoff." *Women's History Review* 5, no. 1 (1996).

Keohane, Nannerl O. "Speaking from Silence: Women and the Science of Politics." In Langland and Gove, eds., *Feminist Perspective in the Academy.*

Kerber, Linda. "Diversity and the Transformation of American Studies." *American Quarterly* 41, no. 3 (1989).

———. "'Why Should Girls Be Learn'd and Wise?': Two Centuries of Higher Education of Women as Seen through the Unfinished Work of Alice Mary Baldwin." In Faragher and Howe, eds., *Women and Higher Education in American History.*

Kessler-Harris, Alice. "The View from Women's Studies." *Signs* 17, no. 4 (summer 1992).

Kimmel, Michael S. "Men and Women's Studies: Premises, Perils, and Promise." In Hewitt, O'Barr, and Rosebaugh, eds., *Talking Gender.*

King, Deborah K. "Multiple Jeopardy, Multiple Consciousness: The Context of a Black Feminist Ideology." *Signs* 14, no. 14 (autumn 1988).

King, Katie. "Producing Sex, Theory, and Culture: Gay/Straight Remapping in Contemporary Feminism." In Hirsch and Keller, eds., *Conflicts in Feminism.*

Kirschner, Susan, Jane Monnig Atkinson, and Elizabeth Arch. "Reassessing Coed-ucation." In Schuster and Van Dyne, eds., *Women's Place in the Academy.*

Klein, Renate. "(Dead) Bodies Floating in Cyberspace: Post-Modernism and the Dismemberment of Women." In Bell and Klein, eds., *Radically Speaking.*

———. "The Dynamics of the Women's Studies Classroom: A Review Essay on the Practice of Women's Studies in Higher Education." *Women's Studies International Forum* 10, no. 2 (1987).

———. "Passion and Politics in Women's Studies in the 1990's." *Women's Studies International Forum* 14, no. 3 (1991).

Kolodny, Annette. "Dancing between Left and Right: Feminism and the Academic Minefield in the 1980s." *Feminist Studies* 14, no. 3 (fall 1988).

———. "Dancing through the Minefield: Some Observations on the Theory, Prac-tice, and Politics of a Feminist Literary Criticism." *Feminist Studies* 6, no. 1 (spring 1980).

———. "Paying the Price of Antifeminist Intellectual Harassment." In Clark et al., eds., *Antifeminism in the Academy.*

Krieger, Susan. "Lesbian Identity and Community: Recent Social Science Litera-ture." *Signs* 8, no. 1 (autumn 1982).

LaCapra, Dominick. "History, Language, and Reading." *American Historical Review* 100, no. 3 (June 1995).

Lakritz, Andrew. "The Equalizer and the Essentializers, or Man-Handling Femi-nism on the Academic Literary Left." *Arizona Quarterly* 46, no. 1 (spring 1990).

———. "Identification and Difference: Structures of Privilege in Cultural Criti-cism." In Roof and Wiegman, eds., *Who Can Speak?*

Lee, JeeYeun. "Beyond Bean Counting." In Findlen, ed., *Listen Up.*

Lees, Susan. "Feminist Politics and Women's Studies: Struggle, Not Incorpora-tion." In Aaron and Walby, eds., *Out of the Margins.*

Lehrman, Karen. "Off Course," *Mother Jones*, Sept.–Oct. 1993.

Leidner, Robin. "Constituency, Accountability, and Deliberation: Reshaping Democracy in the National Women's Studies Association." *NWSA Journal* 5, no. 1 (spring 1993).

———. "Stretching the Boundaries of Liberalism: Democratic Innovation in a Feminist Organization." *Signs* 16, no. 2 (winter 1991).

Lerner, Gerda. "New Approaches to the Study of Women in American History." *Journal of Social History* 3, no. 1 (fall 1969).

———. "Placing Women in History: Definitions and Challenges." *Feminist Stud-ies* 3, no. 1–2 (fall 1975).

———. "Placing Women in History: Definitions and Challenges." In *The Majority Finds Its Past.*

Levin, Michael. "Women's Studies, Ersatz Scholarship." *New Perspectives* 17, no. 3 (summer 1985).

Liu, Tessie. "Teaching the Differences among Women from a Historical Perspective: Rethinking Race and Gender as Social Categories." *Women's Studies International Forum* 14, no. 4 (1991).

Longino, Helen E., and Evelynn Hammonds. "Conflicts and Tensions in the Feminist Study of Gender and Science." In Hirsch and Keller, eds., *Conflicts in Feminism.*

Lorde, Audre. "The Master's Tools Will Never Dismantle the Master's House." In *Sister Outsider.*

Ludwig, Jeannette. "The One-Minute Paper." *Liberal Education* 81, no. 4 (fall 1995).

Lunsford, Andrea A. "Afterthoughts on the Role of Advocacy in the Classroom." In Spacks, ed., *Advocacy in the Classroom.*

MacGregor, Jean, and Roberta S. Matthews. "The Challenge of Collaborative Learning: Creating Bridges between Communities." *Change* 26, no. 5 (Sept.–Oct. 1994).

Maher, Frances. "Pedagogies for the Gender-Balanced Classroom." *Journal of Thought* 20, no. 3 (fall 1985).

Maher, Frances A., with Mary Kay Tetreault. "*Women's Ways of Knowing* in Women's Studies, Feminist Pedagogies, and Feminist Theory." In Goldberger et al., eds., *Knowledge, Difference, and Power.*

Mahoney, Maureen A., and Barbara Yngvesson. "The Construction of Subjectivity and the Paradox of Resistance: Reintegrating Feminist Anthropology and Psychology." *Signs* 18, no. 1 (autumn 1992).

Makosky, Vivian P., and Michele A. Paludi. "Feminism and Women's Studies in the Academy." In Paludi and Steuernagel, eds., *Feminist Restructuring of the Academic Disciplines.*

Marks, Elaine. "The Poetical and the Political: The 'Feminist' Inquiry in French Studies." In Stanton and Stewart, eds., *Feminisms in the Academy.*

———. "Women and Literature in France." *Signs* 3, no. 4 (summer 1978).

Martin, Biddy, and Chandra Talpade Mohanty. "Feminist Politics: What's Home Got to Do with It?" In de Lauretis, ed., *Feminist Studies/Critical Studies.*

Martin, Jane Roland. "Methodological Essentialism, False Difference, and Other Dangerous Traps." *Signs* 19, no. 3 (spring 1994).

Mattingly, Carol. "Valuing the Personal: Feminist Concerns for the Writing Classroom." In Deats and Lenker, eds., *Gender and Academe.*

Maynard, Mary. "Beyond the 'Big Three': The Development of Feminist Theory in the 1990's." *Women's History Review* 4, no. 3 (1995).

McClure, Kirstie. "The Issue of Foundations: Scientized Politics, Politicized Science, and Feminist Critical Practices." In Butler and Scott, eds., *Feminists Theorize the Political.*

McDermott, Patrice. "On Cultural Authority: Women's Studies, Feminist Politics, and the Popular Press." *Signs* 20, no. 3 (spring 1995).

————. "The Risks and Responsibilities of Feminist Academic Journals." *NWSA Journal* 6, no. 3 (fall 1994).

McDowell, Deborah. "Transferences: Black Feminist Discourse: The 'Practice' of Theory." In Elam and Wiegman, eds., *Feminism beside Itself*.

McKay, Nellie Y. "Acknowledging Differences: Can Women Find Unity through Diversity?" In James and Busia, eds., *Theorizing Black Feminisms*.

McLain, Larry. "Women's Studies, Cultural Studies: Teaching Literature in the Midwest." *Transformations* 7, no. 1 (spring 1996).

McMartin, Flora Pearle. "The Institutionalization of Women's Centers and Women's Studies Programs at Three Research Universities." Ed.D. diss., University of California, Berkeley, 1993.

McNaron, Toni A. H., and Bonnie Zimmerman. "Introduction." In Zimmerman and McNaron, eds., *New Lesbian Studies*.

Messer-Davidow, Ellen. "Know-How." In Hartman and Messer-Davidow, eds., *(En)Gendering Knowledge*.

————. "Manufacturing the Attack on Liberalized Higher Education." *Social Text* 36 (fall 1993).

Mies, Maria. "Toward a Methodology for Feminist Research." In Bowles and Klein, eds., *Theories of Women's Studies*.

Miles, Tiya. "Lessons from a Young Feminist Collective." In Findlen, ed., *Listen Up*.

Milkman, Ruth. "Women's History and the Sears Case." *Feminist Studies* 12, no. 2 (summer 1986).

Minnich, Elizabeth Kamarck. "Friends and Critics: The Feminist Academy." In Beth Reed, ed., *Toward a Feminist Transformation of the Academy: Proceedings of the Fifth Annual Great Lakes Colleges Association Women's Studies Conference*. Ann Arbor, Mich.: Great Lakes College Association Women Studies Program, 1979.

Moi, Toril. "Representation of Patriarchy: Sexuality and Epistemology in Freud's Dora." *Feminist Review* 9 (Oct. 1981).

Monk, Janice. "Integrating Women into the Geography Curriculum." *Journal of Geography* 82, no. 6 (1983).

Moraga, Cherríe. "From a Long Line of Vendidas: Chicanas and Feminism." In de Lauretis, ed., *Feminist Studies / Critical Studies*.

Moraga, Cherríe, and Barbara Smith. "Lesbian Literature: A Third World Feminist Perspective." In Cruikshank, ed., *Lesbian Studies*.

Mouffe, Chantal. "The Legacy of *m/f*." In Adams and Cowie, eds., *Woman in Question*.

Neely, Carol Thomas. "Loss and Recovery: Homes Away from Home." In Greene and Kahn, eds., *Changing Subjects*.

Offen, Karen. "Defining Feminism: A Comparative Historical Approach." *Signs* 14, no. 1 (autumn 1988).

———. "Feminism and Sexual Difference in Historical Perspective." In Rhode, ed., *Theoretical Perspectives on Sexual Difference.*

———. "Reclaiming the European Enlightenment for Feminism; or, Prologomena to Any Future History of the Eighteenth Century." In Akkerman and Stuurman, eds., *Feminist Political Thought in European History.*

———. "'What! Such Things Have Happened and No Women Were Taught about Them': A Nineteenth-Century French Woman's View of the Importance of Women's History." *Journal of Women's History* 9, no. 2 (summer 1997).

Omolade, Barbara. "A Black Feminist Pedagogy." *Women's Studies Quarterly* 21, nos. 3 and 4 (fall-winter 1993).

Ong, Aihwa. "Teaching the Differences among Women from a Historical Perspective: Rethinking Race and Gender as Social Categories." *Women's Studies International Forum* 14, no. 4 (1991).

Perry, Ruth. "I Brake for Feminists: Debates and Divisions within Women's Studies." *Transformations* 7, no. 1 (spring 1996).

Perry, Ruth, Joyce Antler, Renee Fall, Laura Levine Frader, Carol Hurd Green, Barbara Haber, Alice Jardine, and Christiane Zehl Romero. "Inventing a Feminist Institution in Boston: An Informal History of the Graduate Consortium in Women's Studies at Radcliffe College." *NWSA Journal* 8, no. 2 (summer 1996).

Phelan, Shane. "(Be)Coming Out: Lesbian Identity and Politics." *Signs* 18, no. 4 (summer 1993).

Pheterson, Gail. "Alliances between Women: Overcoming Internalized Oppression and Internalized Domination." *Signs* 12, no. 1 (autumn 1986).

Poovey, Mary. "The Differences of Women's Studies: The Example of Literary Criticism." In Stanton and Stewart, eds., *Feminisms in the Academy.*

———. "Feminism and Deconstruction." *Feminist Studies* 14, no. 1 (spring 1988).

Porter, Carolyn. "Getting Gendered." In Greene and Kahn, eds., *Changing Subjects.*

Rabine, Leslie. "Stormy Weather: A Memoir of the Second Wave." In Greene and Kahn, eds., *Changing Subjects.*

Rapping, Elayne. "Politics and Polemics." *Women's Review of Books* 14, no. 1 (Oct. 1996).

Register, Cheri. "Brief, A-Mazing Movements: Dealing with Despair in the Women's Studies Classroom." *Women's Studies Newsletter* 7, no. 4 (fall 1979).

Rhodes, Frank H. T. "The Place of Teaching in the Research University." In Cole, Barber, and Graubard, eds., *Research University in a Time of Discontent.*

Rich, Adrienne. "Claiming an Education." In *On Lies, Secrets, and Silence: Selected Prose, 1966–1978.*

———. "Compulsory Heterosexuality and Lesbian Existence." *Signs* 5, no. 4 (summer 1980).

———. "Conditions for Work: The Common World of Women." Foreword to Ruddick and Daniels, eds., *Working It Out.*

———. "Toward a More Feminist Criticism" [1981]. In *Blood, Bread, and Poetry.*

Richardson, Diane, and Victoria Robinson. "Theorizing Women's Studies, Gender Studies, and Masculinity: The Politics of Naming." *European Journal of Women's Studies* 1, no. 1 (spring 1994).

Riger, Stephanie, Carrie Brecke, and Eve Wiederhold. "Dynamics of the Pluralistic Classroom: A Selected Bibliography." *NWSA Journal* 7, no. 2 (summer 1995).

Robinson, Victoria, and Diane Richardson. "Repackaging Women and Feminism: Taking the Heat Off Patriarchy." In Bell and Klein, eds., *Radically Speaking.*

Rodgers, Carolyn. "It Is Deep." In Bell, Parker, and Guy-Sheftall, eds., *Sturdy Black Bridges.*

Rorty, Richard. "A Leg-Up for Oliver North," review of *Dictatorship of Virtue: Multiculturalism and the Battle for America's Future*, by Richard Bernstein. *London Review of Books*, Oct. 20, 1994.

Rose, Sonya O. "Gender History / Women's History: Is Feminist Scholarship Losing Its Critical Edge?" *Journal of Women's History* 5, no. 21 (spring 1993).

Rosenfelt, Deborah S. "'Definitive' Issues: Women's Studies, Multicultural Education, and Curriculum Transformation in Policy and Practice in the United States." *Women's Studies Quarterly* 22, nos. 3 and 4 (fall–winter 1994).

———. "Ethnic Studies and Women's Studies at UC Berkeley: A Collective Interview." *Radical Teacher* 14 (Dec. 1979).

———. "A Time for Confrontation." *Women's Studies Quarterly* 9, no. 3 (fall 1981).

———. "What Women's Studies Professors Do That Mainstreaming Can't." *Women's Studies International Forum* 7 no. 3 (1984).

Rosenfelt, Deborah, and Judith Stacey. "Second Thoughts on the Second Wave." *Feminist Studies* 13, no. 2 (summer 1987).

Ross, Dorothy. "The Development of the Social Sciences." In Oleson and Voss, eds., *Organization of Knowledge in Modern America.*

Ross, Ellen. "New Thoughts on 'the Oldest Vocation': Mothers and Motherhood in Recent Feminist Scholarship." *Signs* 20, no. 2 (winter 1995).

Rosser, Sue V., and Katherine W. Mille. "A Grass-Roots Approach to Funding Women's Studies." *NWSAction* 1, no. 4 (winter 1988).

Rowland, Robyn. "Politics of Intimacy: Heterosexuality, Love, and Power." In Bell and Klein, eds., *Radically Speaking.*

Rubin, Gayle. "The Traffic in Women: Notes on the 'Political Economy of Sex.'" In Scott, ed., *Feminism and History.*

Ruby, Jennie, Farar Elliott, and Carol Anne Douglas. "NWSA: Troubles Surface at Conference." *off our backs* 20, no. 8 (Aug.–Sept. 1990).

Ruddick, Sara. "Maternal Thinking." *Feminist Studies* 6, no. 2 (summer 1980).

Salper, Roberta. "Women's Studies." *Ramparts* 10, no. 6 (Dec. 1971).

Sapiro, Virginia. "Feminist Studies and Political Science—and Vice-Versa." In Stanton and Stewart, eds., *Feminisms in the Academy.*

Scanlon, Jennifer. "Keeping Our Activist Selves Alive in the Classroom: Pedagogy and Political Activism." *Feminist Teacher* 7, no. 2 (1993).

Schmitz, Betty, Johnnella E. Butler, Deborah Rosenfelt, and Beverly Guy-Sheftall. "Women's Studies and Curriculum Transformation." In Banks and Banks, eds., *Handbook of Research on Multicultural Education.*

Schniedewind, Nancy. "Cooperatively Structured Learning: Implications for Feminist Pedagogy." In Davis, ed., "Feminist Education."

———. "Teaching Feminist Process in the 1990s." *Women's Studies Quarterly* 21, nos. 3 and 4 (fall–winter 1993).

Schorske, Carl E. "The New Rigorism in the Human Sciences, 1940–1960." *Daedalus* 126, no. 1 (winter 1997).

Schuster, Marilyn R., and Susan R. Van Dyne. "Curricular Change for the Twenty-first Century: Why Women?" In Schuster and Van Dyne, eds., *Women's Place in the Academy.*

———. "Placing Women in the Liberal Arts Curriculum." *Harvard Educational Review,* 54, no. 4 (Nov. 1984).

Scott, Joan Wallach. "Deconstructing Equality-Versus-Difference: Or the Uses of Poststructuralist Theory in Feminism." *Feminist Studies* 14, no. 1 (1988).

———. "The Evidence of Experience." *Critical Inquiry* 17 (1991).

———. "Gender: A Useful Category of Historical Analysis." *American Historical Review* 91, no. 5 (Dec. 1986).

Scully, Diana. "Overview of Women's Studies: Organization and Institutional Status in U. S. Higher Education." *NWSA Journal* 8, no. 3 (fall 1996).

Searle, John R. "Rationality and Realism, What Is at Stake?" In Cole, Barber, and Graubard, eds., *Research University in a Time of Discontent.*

Sedgwick, Eve Kosofsky. "Against Epistemology." In James Chandler, Arnold I. Davidson, and Harry Harootunian, eds., *Questions of Evidence: Proof, Practice, and Persuasion across the Disciplines.* Chicago: University of Chicago Press, 1994.

———. "Jane Austen and the Masturbating Girl." In Chandler, Davidson, and Harootunian, eds., *Questions of Evidence.*

Shapiro, Judith. "Anthropology and the Study of Gender." In Langland and Gove, eds., *Feminist Perspective in the Academy.*

Shavlik, Donna. "Women Changing Work within the Academy." *On Campus with Women* 25, no. 2 (winter 1996).

Short, Thomas. "'Diversity' and 'Breaking the Disciplines': Two New Assaults on the Curriculum." *Academic Questions* 1, no. 3 (summer 1988).

Showalter, Elaine. "Feminist Criticism in the Wilderness." In Abel, ed., *Writing and Sexual Difference.*

———. "Introduction: Teaching about Women, 1971." In Showalter and Ohmann, eds., *Female Studies IV.*

Shrewsbury, Carolyn M. "What Is Feminist Pedagogy?" *Women's Studies Quarterly* 21, nos. 3 and 4 (fall–winter 1993).

Sievers, Sharon. "Six (or More) Feminists in Search of a Historian." *Journal of Women's History* 1, no. 2 (fall 1989).

Siim, Birte. "Towards a Feminist Rethinking of the Welfare State." In Jones and Jónasdóttir, eds., *Political Interests of Gender.*

Silverberg, Helene. "Gender Studies and Political Science: The History of the 'Behavioralist Compromise.'" In James Farr and Raymond Seidelman, eds., *Discipline and History: Political Science in the United States.* Ann Arbor: University of Michigan Press, 1993.

Silvers, Anita. "'Defective' Agents: Equality, Difference, and the Tyranny of the Normal." *Journal of Social Philosophy,* 25th-anniversary special issue, 1994.

Slocum, Sally. "Woman the Gatherer: Male Bias in Anthropology." In Reiter, ed., *Toward an Anthropology of Women.*

Smiley, Marion. "Feminist Theory and the Question of Identity." *Women and Politics* 13, no. 2 (1993).

Smith, Virginia. "New Dimensions for General Education." In Levine, ed., *Higher Learning in America.*

Smyth, Ailbhe. "A (Political) Postcard From a Peripheral Pre-Postmodern State (of Mind), or How Alliteration and Parentheses Can Knock You Down Dead in Women's Studies." *Women's Studies International Forum* 15, no. 3 (1992).

Snitow, Ann. "A Gender Diary." In Scott, ed., *Feminism and History.*

Spacks, Patricia Meyer. "The Difference It Makes." In Langland and Gove, eds., *Feminist Perspective in the Academy.*

Spender, Dale, and Cheris Kramarae. "Exploding Knowledge." In Spender and Kramarae, eds., *Knowledge Explosion.*

Sprengnether, Madelon. "Generational Differences: Reliving Mother-Daughter Conflicts." In Greene and Kahn, eds., *Changing Subjects.*

Stacey, Judith. "Are Feminists Afraid to Leave Home? The Challenge of Conservative Pro-Family Feminism." In Mitchell and Oakley, eds., *What Is Feminism?*

———. "Disloyal to the Disciplines: A Feminist Trajectory in the Borderlands." In Stanton and Stewart, eds., *Feminisms in the Academy.*

Stanton, Domna C., and Abigail J. Stewart. "Remodeling Relations: Women's Studies and the Disciplines." In Stanton and Stewart, eds., *Feminisms and the Academy.*

Steinitz, Victoria, and Sandra Kanter. "Becoming Outspoken: Beyond Connected Learning." *Women's Studies Quarterly* 19, nos. 1 and 2 (1991).

Sternhell, Carol. "The Proper Study of Womankind." *Women's Review of Books* 12, no. 3 (Dec. 1994).

Stimpson, Catharine R. "Women as Knowers." In Fowles and McClure, *Feminist Visions.*

———. "Women's Studies and Its Discontents." *dissent* 43, no. 1 (winter 1996).

———. "Women's Studies: An Overview." In *University of Michigan Papers in Women's Studies.* Special issue. (Ann Arbor: Ann Arbor Women's Studies Program, May 1978).

Stimpson, Catharine R., Joan N. Burstyn, Domna C. Stanton, and Sandra M. Whisler. "Editorial," *Signs* 1, no. 1 (autumn 1975).

Strathern, Marilyn. "An Awkward Relationship: The Case of Feminism and Anthropology." *Signs* 12, no. 2 (winter 1987).

Strumingher [Schor], Laura S. "The Birth and Growth of 'Friends of Women's Studies' at the University of Cincinnati." *Frontiers* 8, no. 3 (1986).

Terborg-Penn, Rosalyn. "Discrimination against Afro-American Women in the Woman's Movement, 1830–1920." In Harley and Terborg-Penn, eds., *Afro-American Woman.*

———. "The Historical Treatment of the Afro-American in the Woman's Suffrage Movement, 1900–1920: A Bibliographical Essay." *Current Bibliography on African Affairs* 7 (summer 1974).

———. "Nineteenth-Century Black Women and Woman Suffrage." *Potomac Review* 7, no. 3 (spring–summer 1977).

Tesfagiorgis, Freida High W. "In Search of a Discourse and Critique/s That Center the Art of Black Women Artists." In James and Busia, eds., *Theorizing Black Feminisms.*

Tetreault, Mary Kay Thompson. "Feminist Phase Theory." *Journal of Higher Education* 56 (July–Aug. 1985).

Thorne, Barrie. "Contradictions, and a Glimpse of Utopia: Daily Life in a University Women's Studies Program." *Women's Studies International Quarterly* 1 (1978).

Tomlinson, Barbara. "The Politics of Textual Vehemence, or Go to Your Room Until You Learn How to Act." *Signs* 22, no. 1 (autumn 1996).

Trecker, Janice Law. "Women's Place Is in the Curriculum." *Saturday Review*, Oct. 16, 1971.

Tronto, Joan C. "Beyond Gender Difference to an Ethic of Care." *Signs* 12, no. 4 (summer 1987).

Umansky, Lauri. "'The Sisters Reply': Black Nationalist Pronatalism, Black Feminism, and the Quest for a Multiracial Women's Movement, 1965–1974." *Critical Matrix* 8, no. 2 (1994).

Wagner, Valeria. "In the Name of Feminism." In Elam and Wiegman, eds., *Feminism beside Itself.*

Wallace, Michele. "Art for Whose Sake?" *Women's Review of Books* 12, no. 1 (Oct. 1995).

Walters, Suzanna Danuta. "From Here to Queer: Radical Feminism, Postmodernism, and the Lesbian Menace (or, Why Can't a Woman Be More Like a Fag?)." *Signs* 21, no. 4 (summer 1996).

Warnke, Georgia. "Discourse Ethics and Feminist Dilemmas of Difference." In Meehan, ed., *Feminists Read Habermas.*

Watts, Steven. "The Idiocy of American Studies: Poststructuralism, Language, and Politics in the Age of Self-Fulfillment." *American Quarterly* 43, no. 4 (Dec. 1991).

Weiler, Kathleen. "Revisioning Feminist Pedagogy." *NWSA Journal* 7, no. 2 (summer 1995).

Weisstein, Naomi. "Woman as Nigger." *Psychology Today* (Oct. 1969).

———. "Woman as Nigger." In Tanner, ed., *Voices from Women's Liberation.*

Westkott, Marcia, and Gay Victoria. "A Survey of the Women's Studies Major." *NWSA Journal* 3, no. 3 (autumn 1991).

White, Luise. "'They Could Make Their Victims Dull': Genders and Genres, Fantasies and Cures in Colonial Southern Uganda." *American Historical Review* 100, no. 5 (Dec. 1995).

Winkler, Barbara Scott. "A Comparative History of Four Women's Studies Programs, 1970–1985." Ph.D. diss., University of Michigan, 1992.

"Women's Studies Programs—1994." *Women's Studies Quarterly* 22, nos. 1 and 2 (spring–summer 1994).

"Women's Studies Programs—1997." *Women's Studies Quarterly* 25, nos. 1 and 2 (spring–summer 1997).

Woodbridge, Linda. "The Centrifugal Classroom." In Deats and Lenker, eds., *Gender and Academe.*

Young, Iris Marion. "Gender as Seriality: Thinking about Women as a Social Collective." In Nicholson and Seidman, eds., *Social Postmodernism.*

———. "The Ideal of Community and the Politics of Difference." In Nicholson, ed., *Feminism/Postmodernism.*

Young-Bruehl, Elisabeth. "The Education of Women as Philosophers." In Minnich, O'Barr, and Rosenfeld, eds., *Reconstructing the Academy.*

Zimmerman, Bonnie. "In Academia and Out: The Experience of a Lesbian Feminist Literary Critic." In Greene and Kahn, eds., *Changing Subjects.*

———. "One Out of Thirty: Lesbianism in Women's Studies Textbooks." In Cruikshank, ed., *Lesbian Studies.*

———. "The Politics of Transliteration: Lesbian Personal Narratives." *Signs* 9, no. 4 (summer 1984).

———. "Seeing, Reading, Knowing: The Lesbian Appropriation of Literature." In Hartman and Messer-Davidow, eds., *(En)Gendering Knowledge*.

Zinn, Maxine Baca, Lynn Weber Cannon, Elizabeth Higginbotham, and Bonnie Thornton Dill. "The Costs of Exclusionary Practices in Women's Studies." *Signs* 11, no. 2 (winter 1986).

Signs: A Journal of Women in Culture and Society, 15–16, 48–49, 176–79
Siim, Birte, 216
Silvers, Anita, 111–12
SIROW. *See* Southwest Institute for Research on Women
Situated knowledge, 75
Slocum, Sally, 131
Smith, Barbara, 19, 107; on lesbians of color, 108–9; on oppression, 113; on racism, 120
Smith, Page, 57, 240
Smith, Virginia, 240
Smith-Rosenberg, Carroll, 18
Snitow, Ann, 143, 189–90
Social change, 77, 162–66
Social concerns, 234; scholarship and, 244
Socialist feminism, 128, 164–66
Social science, 74, 162–63
Solidarity, reflective, 124–25
Sommers, Christina Hoff: criticism of, 219; loyalty oath and, 197; *Who Stole Feminism?* 203–8
Sommers, Tish, 19
Southwest Institute for Research on Women (SIROW) (University of Arizona), 47–48, 59–60
Spacks, Patricia Meyer, 53
Spelman, Elizabeth: on disembodiment of women, 150–51; on diversity, 148; on meaning of "woman," 138
Spelman College Women's Center, 48
Sprengnether, Madelon, 233
Stacey, Judith, 73, 215
Standpoint theory, 129, 135
Stanford University, 47, 250; curricular change at, 200
Steinitz, Victoria, 89
Sternhell, Carol, 219
Stimpson, Catharine R., 220; on critics of women's studies, 191; on feminist criticism, 174; on future of women's studies, 243; on postmodernism, 141; on *Signs,* 15; on women's studies' impact on traditional disciplines, 49

Strumingher Schor, Laura, 250
Student-centered education, 5–6
Students, 39; assessing learning of, 91–99; empowerment of, 80–82, 188–89; faculty and, 98; motivations of, 96–97
Subjectivist knowers, 85
Swerdlow, Amy, 247

Talking Back, 111
Tarule, Jill Mattuck, 84–86
Taylor, Verta, 110
Technology, activism aided by, 185–86
Tenure lines, 39–40
Terminology, 67, 77, 244; "ethical," 230; "female," 13; "feminist," 13, 223; "gender," 140, 145; identity politics and, 117; "multidisciplinarity," 42; in publishers' brochures, 154; "woman," 145; "womanist," 137; "women," 13; "women's studies," 3, 13–14, 33
Tetreault, Mary Kay Thompson: on feminist classrooms, 97, 118; on *Women's Ways of Knowing,* 87–88; positional pedagogy and, 219
Textbooks, 28–31, 110; diversity and, 122
Theories of Women's Studies, 136
Third World women, 109–10
This Bridge Called My Back, 106, 148
Thorne, Barrie, 19
Tobias, Sheila, 4, 37
Tomlinson, Barbara, 234
Transformations, 66–67
Transnational feminism, 117
Treisman, Uri, 98
Truth, new definitions of, 76, 144
Twayne Publishers, 54

Umansky, Lauri, 121
University of Arizona, 47–48, 59–60, 63, 66
University of California, Berkeley, 167
University of Cincinnati, 250
University of Colorado, 92–93

University of Missouri-Columbia, 95
University of North Carolina, 240

Van Dyne, Susan R., 53, 239, 246;
stages of change in curriculum and
classroom (chart), 64–65

Wagner, Valeria, 173
Walker, Alice, 19; course on black
women writers, 107, 169; on female
relationships, 121
Walkowitz, Judith, 131
Wallace, Michele, 217
Weisstein, Naomi, 19, 104, 127
Wellesley College, 46, 62, 93–94
WFN (Women's Freedom Network),
207–9
Wills, Garry, 242–43
WMST-L electronic list, 35–36, 185–86
Wollstonecraft, Mary, 104, 144
Woman, as a concept, 19, 138
Womanist, as a term, 137
Women: A Feminist Perspective, 28–
29, 110
Women: Images and Realities, 111
Women of color, 101; feminist theory
and, 137; identity politics and, 121–
22; postmodern feminism and,
147–48
Women's centers, 173
Women's culture, 137
Women's Freedom Network, 207–9
Women's Freedom Network Newslet-
ter, 208–9

Women's liberation movement, 10,
170–71
Women's Realities, Women's Choices:
An Introduction to Women's Studies,
29, 110
Women's studies: community involvement and, 170; criticism of, 3, 172,
193; debates within, 201–20; definitions of, 30; as a discipline, 37–43,
68–78; future of, 247–52; impact on
the academy, 231–38; impact on culture, 242–47; impact on the disciplines, 238–42; origins of, 7–14, 25–
26; parameters for, 34–37; as a political act, 161–67; as a term, 3, 33; as a
title, 13–14; typical undergraduate
degree program, 27
Women's Studies and Socialist Feminism, 164–66
Women's Ways of Knowing, 21, 84–87
Woolf, Virginia, 18, 52, 223
Wyer, Mary, 89–90

Yamada, Mitsuye, 151
Yanagisako, Sylvia, 102, 115
Young, Iris Marion, 156–57
Young-Bruehl, Elisabeth, 52, 143

Zimmerman, Bonnie: on influence of
women's movement, 170–77; on
multidisciplinarity, 70; on personal
experience, 118, 133; on visibility of
lesbians in women's studies, 107, 111
Zinsser, Judith, 240